THE MEDICAL
IMAGINATION

EARLY AMERICAN STUDIES

Series editors:

Daniel K. Richter, Kathleen M. Brown,
Max Cavitch, and David Waldstreicher

Exploring neglected aspects of our colonial,
revolutionary, and early national history and culture,
Early American Studies reinterprets familiar themes
and events in fresh ways. Interdisciplinary in character,
and with a special emphasis on the period from about
1600 to 1850, the series is published in partnership with
the McNeil Center for Early American Studies.

A complete list of books in the series
is available from the publisher.

THE MEDICAL IMAGINATION

LITERATURE AND HEALTH
IN THE EARLY UNITED STATES

SARI ALTSCHULER

PENN

UNIVERSITY OF PENNSYLVANIA PRESS

PHILADELPHIA

Publication of this volume was aided by the
C. Dallett Hemphill Publication Fund.

Published by
University of Pennsylvania Press
Philadelphia, Pennsylvania 19104-4112
www.upenn.edu/pennpress

Printed in the United States of America on acid-free paper
1 3 5 7 9 10 8 6 4 2

Library of Congress Cataloging-in-Publication Data

Names: Altschuler, Sari, author.
Title: The medical imagination: literature and health in the
   early United States / Sari Altschuler.
Other titles: Early American studies.
Description: 1st edition. | Philadelphia: University of
   Pennsylvania Press, [2018] | Series: Early American studies |
   Includes bibliographical references and index.
Identifiers: LCCN 2017028650 | ISBN 9780812249866
   (hardcover: alk. paper)
Subjects: LCSH: Literature and medicine—United States—
   History—18th century. | Literature and medicine—United
   States—History—19th century. | Medicine—United States—
   History—18th century. | Medicine—United States—
   History—18th century. | Medicine—Philosophy—History—
   18th century. | Medicine—Philosophy—History—
   19th century. | Medical literature—United States—
   History—18th century. | Medical literature—United
   States—History—19th century. | American literature—
   1783–1850—History and criticism. | Diseases in literature.
Classification: LCC PS217.M44 A45 2018 |
   DDC 810.9/356109033—dc23
LC record available at https://lccn.loc.gov/2017028650

For my family, Donna, Alan, Daniel, and Chris, with love

You are at sea about poetry and science—neither is the other, but in science there are times when, starting from facts, imagination is on the wing. It casts its treasure at the feet of reason.

—S. Weir Mitchell to Amelia Gere Mason (March 24, 1912)

I imagined poetry might, if given the chance, even heal medicine itself.

—Rafael Campo, *The Art of Healing: A Doctor's Black Bag of Poetry* (2003)

CONTENTS

INTRODUCTION

EXPER'IMENT, *Experimen'tum*; same etymon. (F.) *Expérience.*
A trial, made on the bodies of men or animals, for the purpose of
detecting the effect of a remedy, or of becoming better acquainted
with their structure, functions, or peculiarities. In a more general
sense, it means any trial instituted with the intent of becoming
better acquainted with any thing.
　　　　—Robley Dunglison ("The Father of American Physiology"),
　　　　　　　　　　　　　　　　　　　　　Medical Lexicon (1839)

In the fall of 1841, physician and novelist Dr. Robert Montgomery Bird (1806–
1854) stood before a group of new medical students and delivered what must
have been a dispiriting talk. In *The Difficulties of Medical Science*, Bird explained that medicine faced many challenges. Every science, he told his students, was, "and of a necessity must be, imperfect," but the difficulties of
medicine were "greater and more numerous."[1] It was hard to reproduce results,
for example. It was impossible to observe healthy, functioning organs. The
senses were imperfect, and human bodies were incommensurably unique. "It
is *physically* impossible," Bird stressed, to "know many things it would delight
Medicine to know."[2] Bird was committed to medicine, whose "whole object"
was to benefit humanity and to reduce suffering, but he worried about the
immense physical and ethical impediments to medical research. "How shall
we detect the workings of the invisible and intangible enemies around us?" he
asked. "How shall we trace the mechanism of a disease? how shall we follow
even the operation of a remedy, through the darkness of a microcosm of which
we are so ignorant?"[3] "We have no window of Momus," Bird lamented, "to
give us vistas of *living* pathology."[4]

Invoking Momus, the classical figure who teased Hephaestus for making
the body without a window through which to see the human heart, Bird

offered a humanist's alternative to the insufficiencies of medical observation and physical experimentation.[5] Doctors and surgeons had difficulty safely or ethically opening up the living human body—especially before the development of anesthesia and germ theory.[6] Unable to see physiology or "living pathology," doctors could observe little about how the body worked. Momus was the god of satire, whom Laurence Sterne called the "arch-critick."[7] In conjuring Momus, Bird not only invited his students to integrate classical learning into their understanding of medicine (not unusual in a time when classical education was necessary for the serious study of medicine) but also asked his students to think critically and creatively about the tools at their disposal for medical inquiry.[8]

Throughout his life as in his lecture, Bird's literary and medical interests intersected. He used the classics, quoted verse, and invoked Shakespeare in his medical writings.[9] He wrote poetry while he studied medicine, and his extant medical notes can be found on the backs and in the margins of history, drama, and fiction manuscripts.[10] Bird likely found pleasure scribbling his lecture on "artificial stimulants" on the back of a diatribe against American business practices from one of his novels and medication notes on the back of a page about race and immigration.[11] The repeated proximity of these projects—fiction and medicine, often on the same pages—suggests Bird was working on them simultaneously and that they informed each other (Figure 1).

It may have been *physically* impossible to know certain aspects of health, but, like many doctors of his era, Bird also used imagination and literary form to explore challenging questions in medicine. Bird was a physician who understood that genres were strategies; their different forms allowed writers to examine different facets of health. This was especially true in his novels. He used fiction to investigate aspects of health that were difficult—if not "impossible"—to test physically, as well as those that were better pursued through humanistic methods. Like the eponymous narrator of his 1836 novel *Sheppard Lee: Written by Himself*, Bird hoped readers would "have a more liberal understanding of the subjects of knowledge."[12]

Robert Montgomery Bird offers a particularly illuminating, but by no means unique, window onto the medical work of literature; in fact, medicine and literature had a long, entangled history in the Atlantic world. Richard Blackmore (1655–1729), Samuel Garth (1661–1719), John Armstrong (1709–1779), Mark Akenside (1721–1770), and John Keats (1795–1821) were just some of Britain's notable physician-poets during the eighteenth and early nineteenth centuries, and doctors like Tobias Smollett (1721–1771) and Oliver Goldsmith

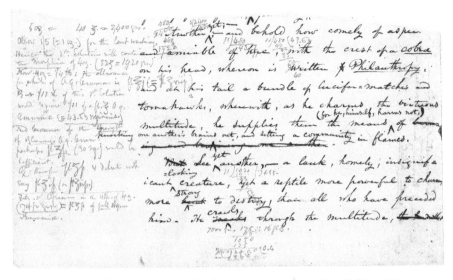

Figure 1. Robert Montgomery Bird works on materia medica (left) and his novel *The Infidel* (1835) (right). The back of this page is blank. Courtesy of the University of Pennsylvania Rare Book and Manuscript Library.

(1730–1774) composed in other literary genres.[13] In the Caribbean, men like James Grainger (1721–1766) wrote medical poems and sent them back to the metropole, hoping to make their fame.[14] Even prominent physicians who were not well-known for their poetic aspirations, like vaccine inventor Edward Jenner (1749–1823), penned verse that circulated in both literary and medical contexts.[15] In this period of classical revival, doctors fashioned themselves after Apollo, god of both medicine and poetry.[16] Physician-writers were not anomalies but rather actors engaging in a long and robust tradition of literature and medicine.[17]

Founding Father and famed physician Benjamin Rush (1746–1813), the most famous American doctor for nearly a century, explained why: "Exactly the same thing takes place in the act of judgment in selecting and combining related ideas and rejecting such as are not related, as takes place in selecting and combining words, in writing poetry and rhyme. The ear combines related words, or such as—to use a common phrase—do not jangle with each other; and rejects such as are not related."[18] With practice, this cognitive process came to seem natural rather than nurtured, but Rush pressed his students not to be deceived: good medical thinking was the product of a well-trained mind, and poetry was an excellent tool for developing one. Poetry also helped train the perceptions that made judgment possible. Given the value Rush placed on poetry, it is not surprising that he also made "frequent recurrences to the poets" in his medical writing because they viewed phenomena, "whether natural or morbid, with a *microscopic eye*, and hence many things arrest their attention, which escape the notice of physicians."[19] In describing poetic vision as a "microscopic eye," Rush radically repurposed a phrase that had a long European genealogy to describe the valuable role poetry ought to play in producing medical knowledge. Whereas eighteenth-century writers like Alexander Pope (1688–1744) claimed no one had a microscopic eye (it would be painful and dangerous, he argued), Rush celebrated this faculty. In Rush's view, poetry was creative and exacting—essential for mastering the kind of thought and perception that lay at the heart of good medical practice and discovery.[20]

From the earliest days of health care in the United States doctors turned heroic couplets toward the ends of heroic medicine. Samuel Latham Mitchill (1764–1831) used poetry in 1797 to make his case about the geography of human health, as did Joseph Young when he quoted Alexander Pope's verse in the pages of the New York journal the *Medical Repository* to defend the use of analogy in place of observation in science.[21] A North Carolinian student of Rush, Charles Caldwell (1772–1853), urged doctors to be poetic and imaginative in their medicine in 1797, hoping they would follow the example of British physician-poet Erasmus Darwin and combine "the researches and decisions of the *understanding*, with the sportings [*sic*] and flights of *imagination*."[22] A physician-poet himself, Caldwell believed it would not be long before an American Darwin emerged: "From the rapid and general diffusion of physical science throughout our country, and from the growing taste for the beauties of literature acquiring such depth of root in the American mind," he wrote, "we are . . . encouraged to flatter ourselves, that [the arrival of such a figure] is not deeply buried in the ever-teeming matrix of time."[23] Emphasizing Darwin's history as a country doctor, Caldwell pushed his counterparts in the United States to consider the physician-poet path for themselves.

In the late eighteenth and early nineteenth centuries, doctors wrote poetry that was formally strict; constrained meter and rhyme organized their theories and observations. Ordered poetic form kept a tight rein on doctors' imaginations. Although doctors' poetry filled the pages of American journals and magazines well into the nineteenth century, their work has gone largely unnoticed because much of the verse—highly structured and widely practiced as it was—has seemed uninteresting to a more modern eye.[24] Its form was, however, largely the point, and the practice of writing this kind of poetry was valuable training for the medical mind.

Writers outside the medical establishment also found literary forms valuable for producing medical knowledge. In the 1790s Charles Brockden Brown experimented with the potentially fatal "force of imagination" in his novel *Ormond*, just as he understood his fictional story *Arthur Mervyn* "methodize[d] reflections" that contributed to "medical and political discussions . . . now afloat in the community."[25] Likewise, Bird's contemporary Edgar Allan Poe penned "prescient descriptions" in short stories that were celebrated in elite medical journals from *JAMA* to the *Lancet*.[26] The prevalence of nineteenth-century doctor-writers—not only Bird but also Martin Robison Delany, William Arthur Caruthers, Oliver Wendell Holmes, and Silas Weir Mitchell, to name a few—should not surprise us. Nor should the prevalence of other doctors like Thomas Chivers, John Kearsley Mitchell, and Samuel George Morton, who wrote literature.[27] Cultural critics and medical researchers have repeatedly marveled at the serendipitous instances in which "fiction anticipates science" rather than understanding fiction could produce it.[28] Recognizing how much medical work literature did in the early United States reframes our understanding of both medical and literary history.

Humanistic Inquiry and the History of Medicine

Why has this tradition been so difficult to see? The first answer lies in the history of American medicine as a field of inquiry. Originally it was a remarkably presentist field, invested in the past only insofar as it revealed important figures, milestones, and breakthroughs for medical science from a contemporary perspective. This meant that historians of medicine were not so much interested in understanding how medicine worked in earlier periods as they were in how the past contributed to medical success measured in contemporary terms. Beginning with the turn toward a social history of medicine around 1980, historians of medicine adopted a more capacious understanding of health to great effect, opening the door to fields including demography, anthropology, sociology, linguistics, and historical epidemiology but, notably, not to literature.[29] Historians of American medicine are still working to move beyond a version of the field that principally uses empirical methods to study the rise of empiricism.[30]

One problem with an over-investment in empiricism-oriented history is that medicine was not an exclusively empirical enterprise in the early United States—far from it. In fact, although this period is often described as marking the shift from rationalism to empiricism, the epistemological conflicts in medicine that took place in these years tell a more complicated story.[31] A simple narrative of the period might suggest that traditional medicine through the early 1820s depended on *rationalism*, a high-minded, philosophical approach to medicine. In its preference for simplicity, rationalism supported "heroic" treatments that led doctors like Rush to irresponsibly blister and bleed patients sometimes to death. In the first decades of the nineteenth century, the story continues, the ineffectiveness of these methods gave rise to a pluralistic medical culture in which alternative practices rivaled traditional medicine. Even traditional physicians grew sick of rationalism by the 1830s and turned to French and German medicine to become *empiricists*—doctors trained in clinical observation and scientific experimentation—a move that began the path toward modern medicine.[32] Insofar as this history highlights the degree to which ineffectual physicians in the United States relied on European intellectual work and innovation, it depicts the first century of American medicine as derivative, an indictment American literature scholars of the period will recognize from their own past.[33]

When we adopt a dismissive tone in describing early U.S. medicine, we uncritically accept medical histories that originated with fin-de-siècle physicians who were hoping to bolster their own precarious authority by denigrating the profession's recent past. Abraham Flexner epitomized this attitude in his *Medical Education in the United States and Canada* (1910), a report that revolutionized medical schooling in the early twentieth century by insisting on empiricism. The promise of early medical schools, he writes, "was not long maintained. Their scholarly ideals were soon compromised and then forgotten" in corrupt institutions, replaced by "exaggeration, misstatement, and half-truths."[34] Occasionally, "of course, the voice of protest was heard, but it was for years a voice crying in the wilderness."[35]

However, the medical history of the early United States is far more complicated and interesting than an empiricism-oriented history can reveal. A first step toward seeing this history is to remember that the transition from rationalism to empiricism took decades and that the terms of these epistemologies remained unstable throughout the period. The medical word "rational" could mean anything from "common sense" to a deductive philosophical approach or a practice that partook of a professional exclusivity and was overly concerned with rules.[36] Likewise, "empirical" could be used to name objective experimental practices, "mechanical, indiscriminate practice," or professional ignorance, as the related and derogatory term "empiric" implied.[37]

More important, focusing exclusively on rationalism and empiricism cannot account for a crucial third term nineteenth-century doctors and writers used to understand human health: imagination. Rationalism may have declined uncertainly over the first half of the nineteenth century, but both rationalists and empiricists continued to insist on the epistemological value of the imagination. Nevertheless, it is because early American doctors spoke of tears and horror that they have been seen, retrospectively, as amateurs, and it is because they wrote in diverse genres that they have not been seen as committed professionals. This formal flexibility, however, defined American medical thought, and it is precisely because doctors and writers were able to speak in multiple registers and occupy multiple roles that their original thoughts about human life and health circulated freely and effectively. Rather than be surprised by the number of American doctor-writers, we ought to understand that the prevalence of such individuals reveals the epistemological and discursive structure of American medicine in which philosophy, literature, and physical experimentation were not incompatible approaches but rather a diverse, adaptive, and adaptable tool kit for medical knowing. We have had trouble doing so because these ways of knowing from the recent past are so different from our own.

In fact, humanistic training was a part of the ideal medical education in the long nineteenth century. The first medical school in the United States, the University of Pennsylvania, began offering training only to those who already demonstrated competencies in math, Latin, and natural and experimental philosophy.[38] Since most medical literature, including theses, was written in Latin, proficiency in the classics was considered essential to a successful career. Medical leaders in New England reaffirmed this commitment when they met in Northampton, Massachusetts, in 1827 to discuss the future of medical education. They recommended that, beginning in 1829, every student should have "in addition to a good English education, a sufficient knowledge of the Latin language to read the Aeneid of Virgil and the select orations of Cicero, [and] to have a good acquaintance with geometry and natural philosophy."[39] Ten years later, Joseph Eve, a South Carolina–born physician, agreed, seconding the recommendations of the Medical College of Georgia that the "most varied and extensive learning is required in a physician. . . . Next to the vernacular tongue, the Latin and Greek languages are most important as preliminary to the study of medicine" and that "a knowledge of these languages is of incalculable value to the student, and can not be dispensed with but at the expense of one or two additional years of hard study."[40] While it was not always possible to enforce such prerequisites, Americans remained committed to a vision of medical training with this humanistic standard at its core, and medical schools would not fully break with it until early in the twentieth century.[41]

Imaginative Experimentation

In this pluralistic world of medical epistemology, doctors and writers used their imagination and literary tools to produce medical knowledge, a practice I am calling *imaginative experimentation*.[42] The term "imaginative experimentation" describes both the various ways in which doctors and writers used their imaginations to craft, test, and implement their theories of health and the role literary forms played in developing that work. My use of the word "experiment" here retains Robley Dunglison's "more general sense" of "any trial instituted with the intent of becoming better acquainted with any thing."[43] This sense is particularly useful in moments where imaginative experiments provided new avenues for medical knowledge. While some imaginative experiments influenced a number of doctors and writers to come, others had only a single instantiation. I have worried less about whether certain imaginative experiments were repeated or repeatable and instead worked to demonstrate the creativity and ingenuity of particular attempts—experiments in the broader sense of the word.

Rationalists and empiricists alike privileged this role for the imagination throughout the long nineteenth century.[44] As Dunglison wrote in his 1832 textbook *Human Physiology*, "It is to the capability of indulging to the necessary extent in [a] kind of mental abstraction, that we are indebted for the solution of every abstruse problem, relating to science or art."[45] Later in the century, avowed empiricist S. Weir Mitchell also privileged imaginative experimentation. A champion of vivisection and microscopy *and* a doctor-novelist, Mitchell explained that "there are times when, starting from facts, imagination is on the wing. It casts its treasure at the feet of reason."[46] He pictured his "poetic imagination" as "a wild-winged thing" that formed an important part of medical and scientific discovery: "the wild flight after the [empirical] proving . . . may be hopeless," he wrote, "but seen with the eye of imagination the page reads clear."[47] Mitchell called this use of the imagination "science on the wing."[48] When a friend wrote to ask whether science and the imagination were at odds, Mitchell replied: "'Science and imagination at war'? Why? The latter is the very soul of the former."[49]

For doctors like Rush, Bird, and Mitchell the imagination was fundamental to medical and scientific work. The medical imagination was not for them a tool of last resort only to be used when other methods of discovery had failed, although it was certainly useful then, too; rather, imaginative experimentation formed part of a more flexible and dynamic complex of knowing. Imagination worked with other epistemological tools including observation, physical experimentation, philosophy, and history toward the ends of discovery.[50] In this less disciplinarily regimented time, epistemological flexibility allowed doctors and writers to work through thorny medical complexities, and the imagination assisted practices like observation and physical experimentation that alone could only partly explain health.

Using the imagination in medicine was a less foreign concept for eighteenth- and nineteenth-century Americans than it is for us today, since, until at least the mid-nineteenth century, medical knowledge was understood to be formed in the mind of the brilliant observer—not through depersonalized, objective observation.[51] In 1798, Johann Wolfgang von Goethe expressed the perspective thus: "to depict [pure phenomena], the human mind must fix the empirically variable, exclude the accidental, eliminate the impure, unravel the tangled, discover the unknown."[52] For doctors, "experiment" was related to the French word *expérience*, which capaciously suggests both "experiment" and "experience," and, through at least the 1830s, the medical definition for "experience" came from "'to *practise*.' A knowledge of things, acquired by *practice*."[53] The meaning of the word would continue to develop over the course of the nineteenth century, but as early as 1848, Dunglison marked the shift toward objectivity in a revised definition: "expe'rience, [from the Greek for] 'a *trial*.' A knowledge of things acquired by *observation*."[54] Here Dunglison moves the site of knowledge production from the more intimate involvement with the knower (suggested by "practice") to the detached position (suggested by "observation"). Nonetheless, through at least 1860, the definition retained the primacy of the mind as a site of knowledge production: "To profit by experience," Dunglison writes, "requires a mind capable of appreciating the proper relations between cause and effect."[55] Before the mid-nineteenth century, knowledge came from an intelligent knower who used trained mental faculties to construct truth from imperfect perceptions. "Only in the mid-nineteenth century," Lorraine Daston and Peter Galison write, "did scientists begin to yearn for this blind sight, the 'objective view,'" that is, "seeing without interference, interpretation, or intelligence."[56] Even this emerging perspective continued to be contested throughout the early twentieth century.[57]

Especially before the mid-nineteenth century, an important strain of medical research depended more on the mind and body of the individual investigator than on an objective detachment. Of physicians' nonobjective practice of experimenting on their own bodies, for example, Bird wrote that doctors daily "peril life and health in the performance of such experiments" because the "moral code of medicine calls upon [physicians] to encounter the first danger *themselves*."[58] Methods that used doctors' bodies and minds made sense to writers like Bird both because they freed medical research from a number of ethical quandaries and because they brought experiments closer to the physician's observation and judgment. For thinkers like Bird and Rush, doctors and writers possessed "epistemologically weighty" bodies and minds that offered more valuable information than that provided by other experimental subjects because their trained perceptions were deemed more reliable.[59]

This emphasis on privileged minds, along with the privileged role of the imagination in the period, granted authority to the imaginative experiments.[60] The imagination was a particularly fertile site for this kind of experimentation not only because of the centrality of the imagination to the highest orders of thought but also because the imagination was linked directly to somatic health in the eighteenth century. In the 1720s, for instance, England was captivated by the story of Mary Toft, who claimed, after a memorable dream, to fall ill and some months later to give birth to a "monstrous" creature and a series of rabbits.[61] Erasmus Darwin countered this idea by declaring "that the world has been long mistaken in ascribing great power to the imagination of the female," whereas it was really the father's imagination that shaped the fetus.[62] Scottish medical philosopher William Cullen believed that "a number of people can . . . by the power of their own imagination, throw themselves into a real epileptic fit" and told the story of a woman who developed such troubling associations with a gown that seeing one brought on "sickness and vomiting."[63] Edinburgh's Robert Whytt and London's William Rowley firmly avowed the mental causes of fainting and convulsions.[64] On the American side, Benjamin Rush connected the imagination to fever in *Medical Inquiries and Observations Upon the Diseases of the Mind* by recalling a story told by Lucian in which a tragedy performed midsummer in Abdera greatly exacerbated a fever outbreak, "produc[ing], very naturally, a repetition of the ideas and sounds that excited their disease."[65] Throughout the nineteenth century Americans continued to believe that imaginative enterprises like literature produced somatic effects.[66] Since the imagination and the health of the human body were intimately linked, experimenting imaginatively provided an avenue through which Americans could both theorize and promote health.[67]

Genre was the grammar of this experimentation. Literary genres were excellent forms for exploring theories of the body. Poetry helped doctors experiment at scales—from the minute to the global—that they could not observe directly or test physically, and formally rigorous poetry allowed physicians to explore medical questions imaginatively using creative and ordered intellectual thought. Fiction allowed thinkers to test medical phenomena that would have been unethical to explore physically and also to work through complex problems without committing to a particular solution. Novelistic forays into the lives of others permitted doctors to examine experiences beyond what their individual embodiment would have otherwise allowed. And the picaresque allowed doctors and writers to investigate a variety of loosely connected situations and embodiments to understand problems in health from a broader variety of perspectives. Imaginative literary forms, in turn, also promoted health insofar as genres like satire, sentimentalism, and the gothic shaped the moral, emotional, intellectual, and physiological constitutions of readers. These were only some of the reasons why doctors and writers used literary form to experiment with health in the early United States, but they suggest the array of advantages imaginative experiments offered for pursuing medical questions.

Physiology and the Problems of Medical Knowing

Imaginative experimentation was a widespread practice that was especially useful in health fields like physiology where empirical knowing could be quite difficult. Physiology, which referred broadly to the functioning of living organisms, has long been harder to capture than its sometime twin, anatomy. The history of anatomy fits well within narratives of rising empiricism. Our accounts of the nineteenth century are full of dissections in which the secrets of the human body were laid bare to the naked eyes of curious physicians.[68] And yet, in the nineteenth century, anatomy was mostly important for what it could reveal about physiology—people were less interested in dead bodies

in and of themselves than in what they might reveal about the dynamic workings of the live human body. As a popular early nineteenth-century textbook
explained, physiology was "the science of life" while anatomy was merely "the
science of organization."[69] These definitions remained relatively stable throughout the period. In 1861, Oliver Wendell Holmes rephrased them thus: "Anatomy studies the organism in space. Physiology studies it also in time."[70] In
1856, Robley Dunglison wrote of the importance of physiology in his textbook
on the subject, "There is no department, perhaps, of medicine, to which the
attention of so many investigators has been, and is, directed as to that of physiology."[71] (Dunglison opened the first volume of that textbook with nine lines
from Milton.)[72]

Physiology was vitally important for understanding human health, but
learning about it was notoriously tricky business. At a practical level, understanding how the healthy, living body worked through direct observation and
physical experimentation was all but impossible. Even though doctors were
surrounded by healthy bodies all day every day, they had very little experience with their workings either on the outside or on the inside. Medical con-
sultations rarely came with the kind of physical examination we consider
routine today. Such exams were highly unorthodox and potentially offensive.[73]
Patients came to doctors to describe their medical *complaints*, not to disrobe.[74]
Whereas the prohibitions around knowing the healthy body from the outside
were most often ethical, the limitations to knowing the healthy body from
the inside were both ethical and practical: the vivisection of living humans
was largely considered horrifying, and in any case, the first cut into healthy
flesh rendered it unhealthy.

Physiology was also hard to know because it depended on an idea of a
body in constant motion. The body was always moving, adapting, reacting,
and changing. While Benjamin Rush's now well-worn sentence aligning men
with "Republican machines" has come to stand in for how many scholars explain understandings of the body in the early United States, doctors like Rush
did not hold a mechanistic view of the human body.[75] Instead, they worked
to know the body as an ever shifting, pushing, pulsing thing that was deeply
and dynamically engaged in the work of living.

Circulation provides a useful example of this dynamism and of the difficulties involved in trying to understand healthy physiology through physical investigation. Posthumous anatomical dissection could only offer so much
to the researcher interested in the dynamic work of healthy circulation. Nor
could the highly fraught practice of vivisection, which gained momentum in

the mid-nineteenth century, offer a complete picture of circulation in the healthy body—even if cutting open a living human body to see how the heart worked could somehow be ethically performed.[76] The limitations of ocular knowledge were also registered in the use of the pulse to determine health (tactile knowledge) and the development of the stethoscope (auditory knowledge).[77] This proliferation of approaches to knowledge production suggests that none of them was completely satisfying.

Physiology posed further challenges to medical knowing because its keywords were also social and political concepts. This was no accident: the period's rationalist physicians prized unitary systems that explained how the world worked at a variety of levels. Healthy American bodies comprised the healthy body politic, and, as such, the body served as a metonym (rather than a metaphor) for social and political life. Nevertheless, the various entanglements of terms like "circulation" and "sympathy" made theories of the body much weightier and more difficult, especially for empiricism. Circulation was a concept that extended from blood vessels to global networks of exchange, and sympathy cohered both bodies and nations.

Imaginative experimentation was, thus, especially useful for fields like physiology when physical means of knowing were limited, but it was also an invaluable mode of inquiry in its own right. Observation and physical experimentation could tell medicine only so much about the human body. Even if a window of Momus were able to reveal its healthy inner workings, many eighteenth- and nineteenth-century doctors and writers believed their imaginations would still be needed to convert that observation into discovery. Imaginative experimentation was an important tool of inquiry that helped doctors and writers explore what could not be seen, draw novel conclusions from observation and experiments, and understand aspects of health that exceeded mechanistic paradigms.

Epistemic Crises

I have organized the book around a series of moments I am calling *epistemic crises*. During these crises, a central precipitating event, such as an untreatable epidemic disease, a significant discovery, or a political crisis, unseats central ideas about the health of the human body. In these moments, problems of knowledge and epistemology come into relief. The epistemic crises of the period between the revolution and the Civil War—from yellow fever and cholera to the American Revolution and the discovery of anesthesia—are particularly rich for opening up the tools of knowledge production and viewing the nineteenth-century complex of knowing: they reveal both the limitations of epistemologies such as objectivity and empiricism alone and the work of imaginative experimentation. Especially at these moments when core understandings of human health were fundamentally destabilized, doctors and writers used their imaginations to experiment with new strategies for knowing and to investigate new solutions. This book is thus organized by a series of epistemic crises that upended commonly held beliefs about human health and demanded new ways of thinking.

My thinking about epistemic crisis is indebted to a long history of conversations in science studies about the history and shape of scientific knowledge.[78] Central to the work of key figures in this field, from Ludwik Fleck to Bruno Latour, is the idea that scientific thought is collectively produced and that particular ways of thinking—variously called thought styles, paradigms, or epistemes—dominate particular periods.[79] While theorists like Fleck and Michel Foucault spend more analytical energy on the modes of thinking themselves, scholars like Latour and Thomas Kuhn are more attentive to the processes through which certain ways of thinking come to dominate scientific thought. For Kuhn, these moments of "paradigm shift" are prompted by "crises," in which major discoveries unsettle foundational premises of scientific thinking or anomalies appear that last "so long and penetrate so deep that one can appropriately describe the fields affected by [them] as in a state of growing crisis."[80] Such crises are, according to Kuhn, "a necessary precondition for the emergence of novel theories."[81] They attend both recognized scientific revolutions and "many other episodes that [are] not so obviously revolutionary."[82] Following Kuhn, philosopher Alasdair MacIntyre clarifies that such episodes are "epistemological crises" but takes issue with Kuhn's notion of crisis as a complete break with the past. Instead, MacIntyre emphasizes that moments of crisis are necessarily linked to the worldviews that dominate before and after, and that the resolution of a crisis thus always involves a new perspective that better explains both the crisis and the paradigm that preceded it.

My term "epistemic crisis" draws on this intellectual lineage, but it also departs by focusing on medical rather than scientific knowledge.[83] For Kuhn and other theorists of physical science, crises are either the result of discovery or the building up of anomalies. These processes of epistemic change in fields like Kuhn's home discipline, physics, are necessarily different from those in medicine in which external forces like epidemics prompt crises with more force and immediacy. The social, cultural, religious, and political imminence of crises in medicine is distinct from crises in the physical sciences. Laypeople are well aware when a pandemic arrives; nonhuman agents like microbes demand immediate explanation and action.[84] In the cases of crisis-causing diseases like yellow fever and cholera, physicians' epistemological failures register quickly in the broader community. Competing accounts emerge not only from within medicine but also from a variety of other sources from lay practitioners to the clergy that shape and contest physician authority. More generally, because medicine is structurally interpersonal (centered around encounters between doctors and patients), because medical issues like pain and disease affect all human bodies, and because medical knowledge is intimately bound up with fundamental issues of ethics, medicine's ways of knowing are necessarily more public and subject to a wider variety of forces than paradigms in fields like physics and chemistry. Epistemic crises in medicine are both more pressing and more complex.[85]

I have also adopted this language of "crisis" throughout for historical reasons. Crisis was a key concept in nineteenth-century medicine. According to Noah Webster, the primary definition of crisis was medical: "1. In medical science, the change of a disease which indicates its event; that change which indicates recovery or death."[86] The second definition preserved the sense of an eventful alteration that either heals or destroys but framed it more broadly as "2. The decisive state of things, or the point of time when an affair is arrived to its highth [sic] and must soon terminate or suffer material change."[87] Crisis writ more broadly names a period after which a system—in this case a system of ideas—would adapt or end. Medical definitions of the period explicitly privilege the role of the mind in crisis. As with "experiment" and "experience," Dunglison's original definition of medical "crisis" privileges the knower, coming from "*Diacrisis*, Judgment; from κρίνω, 'I judge,'" whereas by 1848, he limits the word to a more objective sense, "*Diac'risis, Dijudica'tio*, 'decision'" and "κρίνω, 'I decide.'"[88]

Epistemic crises are imaginatively rich. Kuhn describes crises in science as necessarily creative: "Like artists, creative scientists must occasionally be able to live in a world out of joint—elsewhere I have described that necessity as 'the essential tension' implicit in scientific research."[89] MacIntyre likewise turns toward creativity in crisis, using literary examples—Shakespeare's *Hamlet* and Jane Austen's *Emma*—to explain epistemological crises as fundamentally narrative.[90] During the more prolonged epistemic crises of this book we can more clearly see this experimental and imaginative work.

The chronological moments of crisis in the chapters that follow do not cumulatively narrate an unwavering forward march of medical progress. Instead, they demonstrate that, while breakthroughs undoubtedly occurred during the period, new ways of medical knowing were always also the product of their historical context, specific to times and places in which such inquiry took place. What accretes over the course of the book, then, is not a story of medical heroism and advancement but an account of the varied epistemological uses of imagination and literary form to produce medical knowledge, especially but not exclusively in moments where physical experimentation proved insufficient for medical knowing. Although they were not the only moments in which doctors and writers turned to their imaginations to investigate medicine's mysteries, epistemic crises are valuable flashpoints that illuminate a broader practice; they are useful for framing the work of imaginative experimentation.

The crises that organize this book fall into three categories: political crises, crises of disease, and crises of discovery. Chapters 1 and 4 treat crises in which medical and political events conspired to challenge the fundamental premises of human health. Chapter 1 tells the story of how, in the wake of the revolution, Americans were forced to seek out new republican models of health to replace the monarchical ones they had brought from Europe. Chapter 4 explores how emergent ideas about issues including race, sex, region, and species fractured those unitary republican models, necessitating new investigations into the nature of human difference. Chapters 2 and 3 treat disease crises in which the arrival of epidemic diseases revealed the ineffectiveness of particular medical paradigms through spectacular failures in treatment (Figure 2). Chapter 2 tracks how, when yellow fever returned to the eastern seaboard in the 1790s after decades of reprieve, it forced doctors to reimagine fundamental ways of understanding medical communication. Chapter 3 argues that when in 1832 cholera appeared for the first time ever in the Americas, it fundamentally reframed notions of medical geography. The last chapter of the book explores the crisis of discovery set in motion by the development of anesthesia, in which the sudden availability of a state without feeling forced Americans to reevaluate the nature and value of pain.

Just as these crises were distinct in their nature, effects, and temporalities, each also had its own geographic scope. The 1790s yellow fever pandemic, for example, was an Atlantic event, but in the United States it registered as a series of locally shocking outbreaks in Philadelphia and New York that told a national story.[91] The "Asiatic" cholera outbreak in 1832, on the other hand, was

Figure 2. Robert Cruikshank, "A Cholera Patient" (c. 1832). A representation
of the epistemic crisis caused by the arrival of cholera in Britain. Courtesy of
the Wellcome Library, London.

understood by many as a truly global crisis that had traveled from India
through Russia into and across Europe and finally through Canada and into
the United States. Conversations about American health crises were intimately
bound up in the ideas and events occurring around the Atlantic, but, during
the first century of U.S. medicine, Americans most often understood health
in national terms because of close connections they imagined between corporeal

and political systems. In this book about ways of knowing, I have relied largely on the actors' own understandings of their work, which were usually, although not always, national—even if today we understand events like the yellow fever epidemics and cholera pandemics as irreducibly transnational. This transnational perspective does surface at times—especially in the 1850s work of figures like Martin Robison Delany and Baron Ludwig von Reizenstein—but it is largely the exception not the rule. And even as the national scale emerges as the most commonly used for the project of American health, I have worked to situate the discussions of each chapter in their local and transnational contexts as well.

Finally, neither the epistemic crises I describe nor the imaginative practices used to understand them were limited to the period explored here. Just as this book offers a U.S. history in an Atlantic (and at times global) context, it understands medicine and literature in the context of a broader history of humanistic work in medicine. The period covered by this book extends from the American Revolution to the Civil War, and yet this history of imaginative experimentation grew out of eighteenth-century Atlantic practices and continued for decades after the Civil War. I focus on the period roughly between 1775 and 1866, however, because it was a particularly vibrant moment for using the imagination and literary form to understand crises in medicine. This introduction and the conclusion suggest the longer history of imaginative experimentation, especially as it grew more difficult to practice in the late nineteenth century. Perhaps unexpectedly, it was precisely because the professionalizing forces of the Progressive Era were making humanistic inquiry in medicine more difficult that doctors and writers were much more vocal and explicit about its value for medicine during those decades. It was not until the early twentieth century that medical education was systematically reorganized to exclude humanistic thinking from medical work—and even then, prominent medical researchers continued to insist on the importance of a medical imagination.

Past, Present, Future

At its most ambitious, this book aims to reframe our understanding of the relationship between literature, medicine, and the imagination in the first century of the United States and the relationship between health and the humanities today. Moving beyond the idea that literature simply reflected medical ideas of the period, *The Medical Imagination* argues that the imagination and literary form robustly contributed to medical knowledge, offering important epistemological tools for knowing health in the early United States. I argue that literature allowed eighteenth- and nineteenth-century doctors to assay medical hypotheses that were difficult to test otherwise for physical or ethical reasons, to augment knowledge acquired through observation and experience, to investigate that knowledge, and to transform data into discovery. This work builds on that of Rita Charon, Cristobal Silva, and Priscilla Wald, who powerfully demonstrate medicine's narrative structure, as well as that of Russ Castronovo, Justine Murison, Jane Thrailkill, and Bryan Waterman, who compellingly show how medical models shaped the period's literature, to analyze a discursively permeable past in which doctors and writers used poetry, fiction, and other literary forms to produce original medical knowledge, especially when medical philosophy and physical experimentation failed to produce satisfying results. *The Medical Imagination* fuses these strands of inquiry to describe a world in which doctors wrote medicine in literary genres and literature proposed medical theory. In other words, this book aims to expand our understanding of literature's cultural work beyond the social and the political to the medical. In so doing, *The Medical Imagination*'s recovered history not only demonstrates literature's central role in knowing health in the eighteenth and nineteenth centuries but also illuminates promising new avenues for medical and scientific education, research, and practice today.

It is my hope that the argument this book makes about the past will help us reimagine the role of the humanities in medicine and the health professions in the present and future by sharpening our articulations and expanding our vision. In recent years the medical humanities have provided an important set of responses to pressing issues in contemporary medicine. Concerned about a field of health care driven more by routinized procedure and the bottom line than a more complete sense of patient care, medical humanists have founded physician reading groups and added courses to medical curricula countrywide. Medical humanities programs insist that "the humanities and arts [can] provide insight into the human condition, suffering, personhood, our responsibility to each other, and offer a historical perspective on medical practice."[92] These programs largely look to the material examined by humanities disciplines—stories, poetry, painting, and history—to cultivate a productive empathy that can improve doctor-patient relations.

As such, the term "medical humanities" is largely a misnomer. The word "medical" in such programs refers not to the field of medicine broadly but almost exclusively to the clinical encounter. While it is crucial to improve medical communication and empathy, we should also be thinking capaciously about what the humanities can offer medical epistemology.[93] Any given form of knowing, after all, imposes standards and rhetorical structures that necessarily constrain what can be known, and, given the myriad ethical concerns involved in the practice of medical experimentation and the limitations of current medical research to address widespread conditions, it is worth considering additional ways of investigating health.[94] To undertake this work, we need to revisit not only what "medical" means for the medical humanities but also what the word "humanities" means in this context. On closer inspection, most programs that understand themselves as medical or health humanities do not make much use of the broad and powerful array of humanistic modes of inquiry; rather, they examine the same materials as humanities fields toward the ends of a well-meaning but vaguely conceived sense of empathy. The term "humanities" thus refers not to a set of rigorous intellectual and epistemological tools but to something more like an interest in humanity.[95] In the conclusion, I argue that we must move past these articulations—often too loose and too limited—and insist on the intellectual potential of humanities tools, methods, and insights to shape and improve the health professions.

As the figures of this study demonstrate, this step is, in important ways, not a new one. As recently as a century ago—and long before that—doctors and writers used literature and the imagination to investigate, to know, and to practice medicine in the United States. Their disciplinary structures differed from ours, but we would do well to draw insights for our own times from their more precise and capacious understandings of the epistemological contributions of humanistic inquiry.[96] There is not only a long prehistory to but a usable past for the medical and health humanities. *The Medical Imagination* thus concludes by calling for a sharper and more expansive articulation of what the humanities are and what they can do for the study of health and the practices of health care. Demanding such rigor will pave the way for more robust and useful iterations of the medical and health humanities in the future—moving the field more definitively from matters of feeling to methods of knowing.

CHAPTER I

REVOLUTION

IMAGINA'TION, *Imagina'tio, Figura'tio, Phanta'sia, Dianoë'ma,* from *imago, imaginis,* "image." The faculty of forming in the mind an assemblage of images and combinations of ideas which are not always in connexion with external objects.
                                    —Robley Dunglison, *Medical Lexicon* (1839)

When Benjamin Rush spoke to his students about the imagination he used the language of exploration. The imagination, he explained in his medical lectures at the University of Pennsylvania, was "the pioneer of all the other faculties."[1] Developing the metaphor, Rush described the wide-ranging powers of the imagination that "ascend above the heavens, and explore the worlds that revolve around the earth, [the imagination] descends into the regions of darkness. . . . This faculty is as various in its objects, as it is active in its excursions."[2] It was, he insisted, "a Christopher Columbus with respect to invention and discoveries. It traverses mountains near and remote, it concentrates past, present and future ages, it penetrates into the secrets of nature and art, it surveys kingdoms and countries on every part of the globe."[3]

Exploration and Columbus in particular were useful ways of understanding the imagination for Rush: they allowed him both to suggest the wholly novel, world-altering nature of the discoveries that imagination made possible and to ground those revolutionary discoveries in the American land itself. Exploration suited Rush's understanding that the imagination was virtually boundless in its scope—"as various in its objects, as it is active in its excursions." The imagination literally opened up new landscapes of possibility. He clarified this work for his students in contradistinction to the closely related faculties, memory and fancy. Memory was powerful but could only reproduce facts in order, organized by space and time, while imagination was more creative in its activities, artfully rearranging memory, observation, and experience to make new knowledge possible.[4] If memory produced no new vistas or ideas, fancy produced the wrong kind. Fancy was responsible for the decorative and fantastical "nonentities such as fairies and monsters."[5] Whereas fancy trafficked in the trivial and the outlandish, imagination—even in forms like painting, poetry, novels, and dreams—drew its capacious new knowledge only from observation and experience.[6] Concerned "exclusively about realities," imagination was a grounded-yet-creative faculty that mapped the way for all kinds of useful knowledge.[7] For Newton it revealed the material world's secrets; for Locke and Hartley it unraveled the mysteries of the mind; and for Shakespeare it unlocked "every work of nature and art."[8] Medical students across the United States would likewise benefit from using their imaginative faculties. As Rush stressed, imagination was "essential to genius" and "the source of all those discoveries in the arts and sciences, which are not the results of accident."[9]

The figure of Columbus was also well suited to the imaginative project in which Rush saw himself engaged: just as the Age of Exploration had opened up new geographic vistas, Rush believed the Age of Revolution created new medical and scientific opportunities for discovery. He pressed his students to understand that, in the eighteenth century, as in the fifteenth, the Americas were the geographic locus of that new knowledge. The American Revolution had unfettered thought, laying nature bare for imaginative Americans to know, and the American landscape provided the ideal environment for pursuing that inquiry. "All the doors and windows of the temple of nature have been thrown open by the convulsions of the late American revolution," Rush declared less than a month before the Constitution took effect: "This is the time, therefore, to press upon her altars."[10] The postrevolutionary United States had "already drawn from [the new land] discoveries in morals, philosophy, and government"; it was time to draw new medical knowledge "from the same source."[11] Two years later, Rush pressed further. "We live, gentlemen, in a revolutionary age," he explained to his students: "our science has caught the spirit of the times, and more improvements have been made in all its branches, within the last twenty years, than had been made in a century before. From these events, so auspicious to medicine, may we not cherish a hope, that our globe is about to undergo those happy changes, which shall render it a more safe and agreeable abode to man, and thereby prepare it to receive the blessing of universal health and longevity."[12] For Rush, the "revolutionary age" had coevolved with the nation itself; the intellectual potential released by the revolution in combination with America's unique geography placed the nascent republic and its citizens in a position to realize the promise of "universal health." Americans had only to make use of the new modes of thought the revolution and the landscape made possible to attain this medical ideal. Rush reminded his students of their exceptional position again two years later when, in penning a preface to a volume of his magnum opus, *Medical Inquiries and Observations*, on July 4, he connected his own "freedom in thinking" to the day itself.[13]

The American Revolution certainly opened up exciting new ways of thinking about medicine, but it also made new ways of thinking necessary. At an immediate level, such thinking was required because doctors believed the revolution had directly impacted the bodies of Americans, as Rush explained in writings like "Influence of the Military and Political Events of the American Revolution Upon the Human Body."[14] That impact was wide-ranging, resulting in increased fertility and "insensibility to cold hunger and danger" as well as medical conditions like hypochondria, fevers, convulsions, and sudden death.[15] In a systemic way, however, the revolution presented a more serious and fundamental conceptual problem: European medicine theorized health on the model of monarchy (a central organ—either brain or heart—that ruled the body like a king), and Americans needed new, republican models of health. In other words, the revolution prompted an epistemic crisis that demanded members of the fledgling nation reconceive their basic ideas about human health in response to their new circumstances. In conversation with thinkers around the Atlantic, doctors and writers in the new United States experimented imaginatively with the pressing question of how to understand health after the revolution, and, like Rush, they often drew insight from a geographic imaginary that connected republican intellectual models to the land itself. These 1790s experiments in republican health ranged in scale from the molecule to the state.

Imagining the Republican Body

As a Founding Father, educator, prolific writer, and physician, Benjamin Rush had played a central role in the American Revolution, a revolution whose intellectual core was republicanism.[16] Rush played official roles in the founding of the republic—signing the Declaration of Independence, becoming the surgeon general of the Continental Army, and serving as treasurer of the U.S. Mint—and was also a close friend and advisor to key political figures like John Adams and Thomas Jefferson.[17] The republicanism that spurred the revolution was more a new way of seeing the world than a specific structure of government.[18] Usefully vague in the 1770s, it was a system based in virtue and equality whose end was, as the original Latin *res publica* suggested, public good. For the late eighteenth-century colonists who would become Americans, republicanism was an ideal derived from its classical origins in ancient Greece and Rome and fundamentally opposed to monarchy. The creation of the U.S. government pragmatically resolved some of this ambiguity in politics, but, inevitably, some of the philosophy's principle proponents like Rush remained somewhat dissatisfied with this compromised articulation. They continued to work toward more perfect republican forms.[19]

Medicine provided an ideal venue for this imaginative republicanism. Understanding perfect forms to be both divinely ordained and replicated at all levels of life, many thinkers like Rush believed the model for corporeal and governmental health to be the same. The American body was not simply a metaphor for the state; rather, citizen bodies metonymically comprised the republic. Thus, not only was the body an ideal locus for understanding republican structures in their purest forms (unhampered by political compromise), but republican visions of health were also imperative for maintaining the health of the republic. In this way, thinkers like Rush hoped that republican health would provide a more solid and salubrious basis for the republican polity.

For Rush, the challenge of republican health manifested itself in the difficulty of understanding the human body. Sharing this difficulty with his students, he opened his lectures on the Institutes of Medicine by discussing the insufficient approaches of the great European professors Albrecht von Haller, William Cullen, James Gregory, and Andrew Duncan to teaching physiology, which he found "in many instances to be wholly artificial."[20] Modeling his own use of imagination toward the ends of new discovery, he invited his students on a mental journey—to outer space. Although Rush's particular strategy for approaching human physiology may seem odd to a contemporary reader, it was less so for his students, who would have recognized Rush's use of a long respected genre in scientific inquiry. Since ancient Greece, such stories had been used for medical and scientific discovery, and natural philosophers, doctors, and social commentators—including Galileo, Kepler, Copernicus,

Voltaire, and Swift—had all engaged in such imagined voyages to understand more about life on earth.[21] This particular form allowed Rush to distance himself as much as possible from the European physiology lessons he found lacking and allowed him to present physiology in a way that he proudly declared was "different from any that is to be met with [in] books."[22]

Rush narrates his process of imaginative discovery thus: traveling to outer space, he happens upon a local alien and "perceived that it possessed certain avenues of knowledge, called senses. I found, upon inquiry, that he possessed intelligence and speech, which distinguished him in an eminent degree from the animals that surrounded him."[23] Striking up a conversation, Rush asks the alien about the history of his body, how he sustains it, "and the secret causes upon which his life and actions, both of body and mind depended."[24] The alien politely replies to Rush's questions, giving him a complete account of the origins of human life and the nature of physiology.[25] Satisfied with these answers, Rush then turns from this living alien to another (hopefully different) alien: "After having obtained as much information from the living subject of our physiological inquiries as was possible, I proceeded in my imagination to examine the internal structure of a dead body, by means of dissection, maceration, and microscopical observations."[26] He compares the results of this imagined dissection with what he can remember about having vivisected "brute animals in their living state."[27] Finally, feeling his "curiosity excited to know what was the nature of that matter which composed the human body," he conducts a chemical analysis on the dissected parts.[28]

The new theory of human physiology Rush developed was premised on the notion of an engaged body that operated according to republican principles. Following his Scottish mentor, medical professor William Cullen (1710–1790), Rush believed "a living system is a tremendous oscillatory mass of matter," a structure in constant motion; he cared less, in other words, for anatomy than for physiology.[29] This actively participatory body absorbed, parried, and engaged a barrage of internal and external stimuli: "motion,—sensation—and thought. . . . These three, when united, compose perfect life. It may exist without thought, or sensation, but neither sensation, nor thought, can exist without motion."[30] Thus the body's motion—its response to and participation in mechanisms of internal and external circulation—served as the key element of life that made all other features possible. Not a static vessel through which life passes, the body was always busy with the business of living—a shifting, pushing, pulsing mass of material, each part of which dynamically contributes to the whole. Unlike the animist's body-as-passive-receptacle or the mechanist's body-as-machine, this living matter raised the stakes for understanding how the body works. Rush would eventually tell his students: "Simple anatomy is a mass of dead matter. It is physiology which infuses life into it. . . . It is physiology, like a skilful [*sic*] architect, which connects them together, so as to form from them an elegant, and useful building."[31] The body was a moving agent whose health depended on a vigorous but carefully balanced set of encounters. Certainly, for Rush, the body was still a "masterpiece of divine workmanship," but, as he adopted from William Cullen, "the human body is not an automaton or self-moving machine, but is kept alive and in motion by the constant action of stimuli upon it."[32] Rush's model was dynamic, not mechanistic.[33]

Cullen was Rush's mentor in Edinburgh; nevertheless, after the revolution, Cullen and Rush could no longer agree on how that active body worked.[34] Cullen abandoned his initial belief in the body as a "tremendous oscillatory mass of matter," teaching that all disease began in the nervous system and that the circulatory system was stimulated only afterward through spasms.[35] Cullen's nervous system was a well-ordered apparatus receiving stimuli through the nerve endings, communicating those messages to the brain and feeding information back through the nerves' distinct pathways.[36] Modifying Cullen's work, Rush returned to the vision of William Harvey (1578–1657), the English physician who had discovered the circulation of the blood. Harvey held that both healthy regulation and malignant corporeal disturbances began with the circulatory system and affected the nervous system only secondarily if at all.[37]

But Rush also modified Harvey's work toward republican ends. According to Rush, the blood vessels—not the heart—kept the body alive, delivering life-supporting stimuli through internal networks of circulation. Harvey had celebrated the free flow of circulation but also an omnipotent heart; he claimed the heart as "the foundation of [animal] life, the sovereign of everything within them . . . upon which all growth depends, from which all power proceeds."[38] Dedicating his book to England's king Charles I, Harvey had imagined the circulatory system as a monarchy where the heart was king of the body.[39] Revising Harvey, Rush proposed the heart as a relatively weak organ—a mere muscle controlled by blood vessels and nerves. Drawing his inspiration from geography, Rush pictured the heart as an empty "ocean" to which the blood "returns . . . in triumph" after the real work had been done in its tributaries, the vessels.[40] Evacuating centralized power from the heart, Rush told his students that stomach, lungs, nerves, and lymph nodes work "All! all! for the

benefit of the arteries. The blood vessels are certainly of the greatest consequence to the Animal; all other parts are subservient to them."[41]

Moving away from the step-by-step pathway of the nervous system and
the top-down control of the heart, Rush radically altered earlier corporeal
models. The body sustained life only through the general diffusion of stimuli—
salutary or harmful—around the whole body and back through the point of
origin. Whereas the introduction of a stimulus into the nervous system might
conceivably be limited only to the pathways that channel it and a powerful
heart might fully regulate its effects, an element entering Rush's circulatory
system necessarily spread relatively unhindered throughout the whole body.
Rush's system depended on this healthy blood flow, which dispersed, collected,
and redistributed stimuli in and around the body. Movement in the blood
vessels was part of a balancing act that made possible the health of inextricably interconnected body parts: "the whole human body is so formed and
connected, that impressions made in the healthy state upon one part, excite
sensation, or motion, or both, in every other part of the body."[42]

For Rush, the system of internal circulation was necessarily complemented
by an external one. The circulation of the body through the world in turn excited the blood vessels of the internal system. "Life," Rush writes, "depends
upon the action of certain stimuli upon the sensibility and contractility, which
are thus extended in different degrees, over every external and internal part
of the body. These stimuli are as necessary to its existence and preservation, as
air is to flame."[43] Animal life required both internal and external stimulation,
and all body parts could live only through the constant flow of stimuli. Nevertheless, in disease, this stimulation affected the whole body through the blood
vessels—as the people did the state in a direct democracy—and, uncontrolled,
it could be terrifying.[44]

Thus, despite serving as the basis for all life and health, Rush believed
that circulation required vigilance and care. "The cause of all diseases," he explained, "consists in the excessive, or preternatural excitement . . . the cure of
all diseases depends simply upon the abstraction of stimuli from the whole,
or from part of the body, when the motions excited by them are in excess;
and in the increase of their number and force, when motions are of moderate
nature."[45] Rush's therapeutics follow suit: Rush proposed either more or less
exposure to external stimuli—fresh air and cold water or purging, bleeding,
sequestration, and rest—depending on whether he considered the ailing body
under- or overstimulated.[46] In other words, individual bodies needed to

encounter stimuli in balanced amounts that circulation by itself could not ensure.

It was here that revolution, which had made this thinking possible, resurfaced as a problem for republican health. Even though Rush found himself indebted to the "revolutionary age" for his medicine, he worried about the circulation of revolutionary energy back into American bodies. At a bodily level, revolution threatened health; it caused thirst, convulsions, and consumption. He also identified the effects of unwanted revolutionary energy as the cause of various mental illnesses, when revolutionary stimuli irritated blood vessels in the brain and disturbed its functioning. The mental disturbances resulting from revolution ranged from hypochondria and melancholia to a more specialized disease, *revolutiana*.[47] Even after the war was over, the revolution had continued to affect the minds of Americans, as the "excess of passion for liberty, inflamed by the successful issue of the war," caused "a species of insanity," which Rush called *anarchia*.[48] Rush's difficult negotiation with the thorny issue of revolution, which both gave birth to his ideas and imperiled them, was registered in shifting medical proclamations: whereas Rush had once enthusiastically proclaimed "the human species" nowhere "in a more perfect state, than in France, Britain, Ireland, and the United States," by 1799, Rush had deleted France and Ireland from the lecture.[49]

Sympathy and the Republican Mind

"Sympathy" was Rush's term for the body's system of regulation that checked and balanced the democratic work of circulation.[50] It served as a secondary but no less vital mechanism of health. At a corporeal level, sympathy was the mechanism by which the body responded to circulating stimuli, managing the vagaries of circulation by communicating information between different organs and systems.[51] Sympathy primarily conveyed information about stimuli and disease between organs, diffused illness around the body so that it was less deadly, and transferred salubrious elements like medication back to diseased parts.[52] If circulation's free-flow imperative brought the body into contact with an almost limitless number of heterogeneous stimuli, sympathy offered a conservative response to this ideal of free flow. Organs, bodies, and nations needed to be open to stimuli, come what may, but health depended on that flow being channeled only in between certain parts, through specific routes, and in particular directions.

This corporeal model of sympathy was structured by republican political philosophy and grounded in the American geography. Dispensing with the idea that states cohered their people through obedience to a monarch, many philosophers in the eighteenth century believed that both the body and the body politic were held together through emotional and intellectual sympathy.[53] Since sympathies that connected bodies and states were metonymically linked, Rush's nervous system was a kind of republican government for the body that he also believed would help secure U.S. political forms. Revising hierarchical visions proposed by his Scottish mentors, Rush's nervous system worked from the bottom up: "The nerves . . . arise, as we before said, from the Brain and c [sic] and ramify all over the body, or I would rather say, they commence in all parts of the body, and terminate in the Brain," as representative officials derived power from constituents.[54] For a man who found a "simple democracy" to be "one of the greatest evils," Rush viewed the healthy brain as an organ that negotiated stimuli salubriously and judiciously on behalf of its corporeal constituents.[55]

The nervous system was a key component of corporeal sympathy, but it was not the only sympathetic check on circulation's democracy. Sympathy was a special case of sensibility, "a certain connection of feeling in the nerves."[56] Rush clarifies more generally "that stimuli applied to one part of the body may extend over and affect every other part."[57] Sympathy was the mechanism by which one part of the body communicated with others and helped promote the health of the whole: vomiting might signal a kidney stone, and the diffusion of illness around the body might ameliorate a particular disease's impact. In addition to these more general properties of sympathy, Rush detailed specific directions of sympathy and types of sympathetic response.[58] It was terrifying that illness could circulate all over the body, but sympathy's specific pathways allowed physicians to intervene. Knowing the liver sympathized with the stomach— and vice versa—made purging a logical treatment for liver dysfunction. It also meant the liver would not cause respiratory problems. Specifying pathways and directions, Rushian sympathy made corporeal responses comprehensible, predictable, and increasingly manageable.

Like Rush's republican medicine more generally, this model of sympathy, and the brain in particular, was both inspired by and grounded in the geography of the United States. As the nexus of the senses and the organs, of the body and the mind, and of the body and the body politic, Rush understood the brain to be the most important part of the body. It was best conceived as "a large city accessible by many different ways—By canals under ground—by passing through the air, or by sailing into the Harbour."[59] In other words, the healthy brain was best understood as a kind of city like his own—Philadelphia—the center of the republic. If circulation was best compared to the network of rivers, streams, and tributaries that fed into the ocean, the brain was most like the city that regulated the networks through which stimuli circulated. "Every sensation must go back to the brain before it can excite a sympathetic action," Rush explained.[60] As Philadelphia did for the republic in its years as the capital, the brain controlled the networks of circulation but was also sustained only by its relation to them.[61] Rush knew he did not fully understand corporeal sympathy, but he looked forward to a time when doctors knew as much about its mechanisms as they did about the circulatory system. "Discovery will not cease in Anatomy and Physiology, any more than in Navigation, while there is any 'Terra Incognita' in the animal body," Rush told his students.[62] Lamenting the areas of brain that were still "a wilderness, where I am sorry to say, I see many footsteps returning but none advancing," he looked forward to "the time, when we shall be as intimately acquainted with the mysteries of the brain and mind, as we now are with the circulation of the Blood."[63]

Rush recommended the study of the mind to his students as "the most important branch of all the sciences."[64] The materiality of the brain was intimately connected to its function, and its physiology could be studied through the workings of the mind. In cases where criminals "suddenly reformed," for example, Rush believed "that the organization of those parts of the body, in which the faculties of the mind are seated, undergoes a physical change; and hence the expression of a 'new creature,' which is made use of in the Scriptures to denote this change, is proper in a literal, as well as a figurative sense."[65] As both a republic-minded physician and an Enlightenment revolutionary, Rush understood the site of reason to be a crucial space for the maintenance of human health.[66]

Sympathy was, thus, not simply a constellation of physiological functions but a core aspect of Rush's ideas about the maintenance of health. It was simultaneously a category of bodily relationships and a group of cognitive responses through which the outside world registered in the body. For Rush, rhetoric was central to the salubrious work of shaping the sympathies and thus the health of American bodies and minds, a process historian Jason Frank has called Rush's "art of sympathy."[67] This art of sympathy made use of the innate reaction of bodies to circulating stimuli that could be rhetorically molded for social and political good. Rush's ideas about sympathy explain how all parts of "the people"—organs, bodies, states—could, together, produce a healthier whole.

Nowhere is this work clearer than in Rush's instrumental role in producing one of the single most important documents of the American Revolution: Thomas Paine's pamphlet "Common Sense." In his autobiography, Rush claims that he had already "put some thoughts upon paper" on the subject of American independence by 1775 but worried about its reception.[68] Not wishing to risk his own position in Philadelphia, Rush encouraged newly emigrated British revolutionary Thomas Paine (1737–1809) to write "Common Sense." Unlike Rush, Paine had little to lose, and John Adams would later recall that Rush "furnished him with the arguments . . . and gave him his title."[69] While it remains unclear exactly how much Rush contributed to the writing of "Common Sense," he certainly played an important role in getting it published.[70] This suggests Rush began the work of shaping republican sympathies through rhetoric as early as 1775.

Governing the mind through the art of sympathy was key both to Rush's political work and to his republican medical vision. Harmful stimuli upset blood vessels, blood vessels disturbed the brain, and the brain stimulated adjacent blood vessels to diffuse illness throughout the body. Because these stimuli could be physical, perceptual, emotional, or intellectual, they posed a multivalent threat. Rush believed any disease risked madness or death if the blood vessels' irregular action spread "to the nerves, and to that part of the brain which is the seat of the mind, both of which . . . communicate more promptly, deranged action to the blood-vessels of the brain" through "diffused morbid irritability."[71] As a meeting place of the nervous system and the other body parts, the mind and the body, and the body and the body politic, the mind ensured the health of citizen bodies and the republic.

Regulating Health Through Genre

This focus on the mind meant imaginative experimentation was not just a means of theorizing republican health but also a method of practicing it. In addition to identifying the imagination as the source of all discovery, Rush understood it to be a powerful tool in his art of sympathy and to play a direct role in human health. Happy dreams, for example, "always stimulate and strengthen the body," while negative outlets for the imagination like stressful dreams and nightmares "debilitate and fatigue it."[72] The positive effects of imagining ranged from helping patients convalesce to rescuing them from the brink of death.[73] Rush told his students that "the influence of the imagination, and will, upon diseases" had been "clearly proved."[74] And, although the "extent of the influence" of these powers had "not yet been fully ascertained," he was sure that positively fueling patients' imaginations promoted health.[75] "The success of this measure," Rush concluded, "has much oftener answered than disappointed my expectations."[76] Through the imagination, the brain could sympathetically stimulate all other parts of the body.

Literary genres—like sentimentality, satire, and the gothic—were forms Rush used to accomplish this work. They stimulated salubrious corporeal sympathies. When contemplating circulating dangers to the mind, for example, Rush peppers his writing with sentimentality. He asks: "Can any thing be anticipated more dreadful than universal madness?" and exclaims, "How undescribable, and even incomprehensible, must be that state of mind, which thus extinguishes the deep seated principles of life!"[77] After a particularly harrowing description, Rush writes that he would like to "lay down my pen, and bedew my paper with tears."[78] Cases of madness cause him to "contemplate, with painful and melancholy wonder, the immense changes in the human mind that are induced by a little alteration in the circulation of the blood in the brain."[79] Laying bare his own emotions in sentimental prose, Rush scripts reader sympathies for the mentally ill while also modeling how to feel. Readers would ideally be physically affected by the sentimental prose, which would, in turn, form sympathetic bonds that would both make them more likely to care for others and encourage them to be smarter about their own health.

Rush uses satire to similar ends. In his essays "On Different Species of Mania" and "On Different Species of Phobia," for example, Rush diagnoses satirical conditions, such as "The Dress Mania," "The Church Phobia," and "The National Mania," the latter of which afflicted British Lord Chatham until he grew ill at the "very name of Bourbon" and "fainted at the idea of American independence."[80] In many cases, Rush's categories of mania and phobia were humorous renderings of more serious afflictions that threatened the bodies of American citizens.[81] Even as he warned of "The National Mania" in the British context, Rush stressed the need for a "more intense and peculiar affection" of Americans for their country.[82] The "Doctor Phobia" was similarly a "distemper . . . often complicated with other diseases" in which sick people avoided medical assistance because they feared bleeding, blistering, drugs, or "a long bill."[83] Nevertheless, Rush suggests more seriously that this phobia emerges in part out of an "ignorance of the danger of their disorders."[84]

His playful ribbing in the "Doctor Phobia" encourages readers to see the wisdom of seeking a consultation. Likewise, in "The Love Mania," Rush asserts that "all marriages, without a visible or probable means of subsistence, are founded in madness," as are "all premature attachments between the sexes which obstruct the pursuit of business"—and yet, Rush believed that love could kill.[85] "The symptoms of love, when it creates disease," Rush explains earnestly elsewhere, "are sighing, wakefulness, perpetual talking, or silence."[86] Friends and family need to keep watch, since "the effects of unsuccessful love are dyspepsia, hysteria, hypochondriasis, fever, and madness. The last has sometimes induced suicide, while all others have now and then ended in death."[87] (Ovid, he suggests, has some excellent thoughts on the subject.) In the case of love and other manias Rush's satire trained reader sympathy, as his sentimentality had, toward the ends of health.

Rush even used the gothic in his practice of republican health. In one physiology lecture, Rush strove to shape students' compassion through terrifying stories in which people appeared to die but were actually alive. One woman was placed in a coffin for days and her funeral procession had already begun when, "just as the people were about to nail on the lid of the coffin, a kind of perspiration was observed on the surface of her body."[88] The woman later recounted that she was aware at every moment of the ordeal but could not move or speak. "She was perfectly conscious of all that happened around her. She distinctly heard her friends speaking and lamenting her death at the side of her coffin," Rush explained, dwelling in the details to maximal effect: "She felt them pull on the dead clothes, and lay her in it. The feeling produced a mental anxiety which she could not describe. She tried to cry out, but her mind was without power, and she could not act on her body. . . . It was equally impossible for her to stretch out her arm or open her eyes, as to cry, although she continually endeavoured to do so. The internal anguish of her mind was at its utmost height when the funeral hymns began to be sung, and when the lid of the coffin was about to be nailed on."[89] Illustrating the terrifying failures of observation, Rush encourages his students' sympathetic imaginations. Inviting them to imagine each step of her traumatizing experience, he shapes their reactions to deceased patients as well as their respect for the limits of their own knowledge. Rush heightens his students' own sensations through a gothic conjuring of the experience of the undead, molding the responses of these future doctors to the bodies of the dead as well as the living.

As America's first advocate of bibliotherapy (healing through reading), Rush invested explicitly in the therapeutic power of literary form for his republican vision of health.[90] Any proper hospital, he counseled his students, needed a library.[91] In 1802, he wrote that these libraries should include informative books "upon philosophical, moral, and religious subjects," as well as "amusing books," particularly those featuring travel.[92] Stimulating patients' geographic imaginations thus was "extremely exhilarating to convalescents, and to persons confined by chronic disease."[93] By 1812, Rush expanded his prescriptions to include novel reading.[94] Here he trusted the word of poet William Cowper, who had been institutionalized for mental illness and "often relieved his melancholy by reading novels."[95] Culling advice from *Hamlet* and relying on the "microscopic eye[s]" of poets like Samuel Rogers, William Cowper, and Alexander Pope, Rush was a health humanist, after a fashion; his republican medicine depended on humanistic tools both for discovery and for the promotion of corporeal health.

By the early nineteenth century, Rush's republican medicine had gained widespread acceptance across the United States, and when he died in 1813 he was memorialized as a revolutionary. In South Carolina, physician David Ramsay (1749–1815) eulogized Rush by connecting his medicine with the revolution itself: "The same hand which subscribed the declaration of the political independence of these States accomplished their emancipation from medical systems formed in foreign countries."[96] It was only to be lamented, Ramsay continued, "that the great reformer who introduced the innovations, commonly called the American system of medicine, did not live a few years longer to discover more of the laws of animal economy, more principles in medicine, and at the same time, to perfect those he had already discovered and promulgated."[97] Philadelphia educator William Staughton (1770–1829) likewise pictured Rush in revolutionary terms for his grieving students: "When the melancholy intelligence arrived, that the hero and father of our country was no more, I remember to have heard an officer, as he dropt the honest tear, exclaim, 'Well, I rejoice I have been a soldier under Washington.' With a like sensibility, methinks I hear each of you utter, what you will often repeat, 'I rejoice I have been a pupil under Rush.' "[98]

Rush trained a generation of medical students, and the profound influence he exerted over U.S. medicine could be observed long after his death. He was the most visible and influential theorist of republican health, and he established a tradition of imaginative experimentation in the United States. Nevertheless, as an Enlightenment rationalist and a medical revolutionary, Rush hoped his pupils would learn from his teachings while also developing their own ideas about medicine. Connecticut-born literary physician Elihu

Hubbard Smith (1771–1798) was one such pupil. As a member of the Friendly Club, he spent the 1790s in the company of a coterie of New York intellectuals including literary men like Charles Brockden Brown and physicians like Edward Miller (1760–1812) and Samuel Latham Mitchill.[99] Thus, while he deeply respected Rush's work—employing many of the same tools as Rush and also pursuing the question of republican health—Smith developed his own vision, which fundamentally differed from Rush's in scale; whereas Rush examined republican health at the level of the body, Smith did so at the level of the state.[100]

Elihu Hubbard Smith's Healthy Republic

Like Rush, Elihu Hubbard Smith believed in the power of literature, and poetry in particular, to sharpen observation, to order the imagination, and to expand the scope of medical and scientific inquiry and discovery. In addition to writing poetry while studying and practicing medicine, Smith brought forth the first anthology of poetry in the United States—a work he imagined as a literary "repository" (complemented a few years later by his *Medical Repository*) that would expand access to and craft "a more scientific and refined" audience for American poetry.[101] Smith drew this medical and literary inspiration from Rush and British physician-poet Erasmus Darwin, whose lengthy scientific poem *The Botanic Garden* (1791) sought "to inlist Imagination under the banner of Science."[102] In 1798, Smith shepherded an American edition of *The Botanic Garden* into print. From Darwin, Smith learned how to use literature not only for fanciful descriptions but also for imaginative investigation into scientific phenomena. Darwin's poetry, as its paratext explained, allowed "Fancy, seated in her rock-roof'd dell," to listen in on "the secrets of the vernal grove."[103] The nymphs of Darwin's poem observe the natural phenomena—"watch[ing] the billowy Lavas as they boil" and "in widening waves expand"—and inspire scientific discovery—they "disjoin, unite, condense, expand, / And give new wonders to the Chemist's hand."[104] The poem likewise credits these agents of imagination with insight and invention.[105]

Like his fellow literary physician Charles Caldwell, who published his own American edition of *The Botanic Garden* in Philadelphia that same year, Smith considered Darwin's poem essential reading for America's budding doctors.[106] In a six-page poetic "Epistle," Smith announced that the history of scientific discovery would never be the same after Darwin. Darwin's work would "charm the taste" and "thought excite" of young and old who would alike find "Their minds illumined . . . By all of fancy, all of reason."[107] And, while Smith and his coeditors cautioned against the use of fancy in their medical journal the *Medical Repository*, Darwin's verse controlled these imaginative sallies. Smith was certain Darwin's nymphs would provide "keen inticement" to his American readers, "prompt[ing] the prying mind, / By treacherous fears nor palsied nor confined, / Its curious search embrace the sea, and shore, / And mine and ocean, earth and air explore" until "growing time / Unfold the treasures of each differing clime."[108]

The environmental focus of Darwin's scientific poetry made it especially useful for Smith's experimentation with republican health. Whereas Rush certainly thought seriously about the environmental causes of disease, he did so in the more general context of his concern with stimuli that might harm the body. Smith, however, believed that to solve the problem of republican health, one needed to understand the complete picture. It was not enough to examine the individual body; one needed to focus on the environment in which it lived—"each differing clime." Like Rush, Smith believed the American landscape and intellectual shifts after the revolution provided ideal conditions to imagine a republican health, and, like Rush, he believed those lessons might inspire "universal health and longevity" around the world. In Smith's republican model the environment was the key to corporeal health, but it was the cultivation and spread of useful medical information that maintained the health of the republic.[109]

Smith's most involved imaginative experimentation with republican health took the form of utopian fiction. "The Utopia" begins geographically.[110] Smith describes Utopia as a western republic, insulated "in the interior of the United States, nearly equi-distant from the Atlantic & the Mississippi."[111] It is dotted with small hills but contains "no great waters" or marshes that might breed or bring disease. Streams crosshatch the fecund land, but the state is cut off from commerce, since its rivers come from the mountains rather than neighboring states. Smith augments his yeoman fantasy with the "pure & healthful" air and its temperate climate.[112] The perfect climate is maintained by the "equal cultivation of the soil, & distribution of water & woods, & the absence from the ocean & the great Rivers & Lakes."[113]

Far from commercial ports, this republic's carefully cultivated environment produces its health. The central activity of this farmer's republic is working the land. This attention to the land simultaneously yields sustenance, society, virtue, and physical well-being. "The people can never engage extensively in commerce or manufactures," Smith explains: "obliged to cultivate the earth, they must, of consequence become a hardy, temperate, frugal, laborious, & enterprising race of men."[114] Contact with the land renews their health daily, and Utopia's remoteness keeps harmful stimuli from entering the republic. What manufactures exist are exclusively local, "the produce of [the citizens'] own labour."[115] In this ideal state, the healthy land makes the citizens healthy, and their labor ensures the health of their bodies, the land, and the republic—a salubrious closed system. Connecting Smith's 1790s literary treatise and political vision to his medical hopes, Catherine O'Donnell Kaplan calls "The Utopia" "a kind of prescription, a recipe for health written in the face of disease."[116] Calling particular attention to Utopia's geography, she notes that "Utopia's wide, straight boulevards are the precise opposite of the 'streets narrow, crooked, & unpaved' that Smith believed collected water and filth and so contributed to New York's deadly epidemics."[117] "The Utopia" is certainly a prescription for wellness "in the face of disease"—but, more than that, it is an imaginative experiment with a unique republican vision of health. Smith likely hoped his environmental model of health would serve not only for the newly acquired territories but for the United States as a whole.

This yeoman idea secured virtue and equality, but, like all republics, Utopia still needed a mediating body to ensure its health. For Smith, the regulating bodies of Utopia were its institutions—above all, its medical institutions. Smith's Utopia is a republic, quite literally, overrun by doctors. Whereas by 1800 there were only four medical schools in the United States, the most prominent of which graduated about ten students a year, Smith's sixty-square-mile agrarian Utopia contains at least 1,283 medical men—a low estimate that does not include the greater number of doctors Smith estimated in Utopia's towns.[118] (New Jersey, by comparison, is 8,723 square miles, almost 150 times the size of Utopia.) This doctor's republic organized these men into county Medical Societies that would have quarterly one- or two-day meetings in which the members present papers they have written and other members can offer any "Hint, Doubt, & Inquiry [they] please."[119] The papers are then debated and vetted. Facts are recorded in a separate, vetted register. Both registers are under strict control of a representative figure called the Censor, who publishes the papers and facts he "may deem proper to lay before the public" in a quarterly periodical.[120] The society also maintains a museum and a library, collects taxes, and licenses all physicians. The College of Medicine has an equally elaborate set of duties: it centralizes medical information and governs all medical practice and information.

The carefully controlled circulation of medical information maintains
Utopia's health. An extraordinary number of papers are written, and the institutions of medicine centralize, control, and authorize what information about
the environment and health circulates through the republic. Licensing requires
doctors to submit papers, each society member produces four papers a year,
each medical society keeps two sets of registers and produces a periodical,
and the College of Medicine collects papers from throughout the republic.
All writing is vetted through reasoned discussion and wise selection, and the
best papers are reproduced semiannually through volumes published by the
College of Medicine. Rational information, not sympathy, secures health.[121]

Teeming with medical bodies, minds, and information, Utopia was clearly
supposed to serve as a model far beyond its bounds. Smith represents the
republic's environment, for example, as ideal but by no means unique; rather,
the basic geographical features of the "neighboring states"—topography, air,
and soil—are "no wise distinguished."[122] Utopia's medical institutions are
likewise not isolated. Smith imagines not only that his medical Utopia will
remain in deep and continued dialogue with doctors and scientists around the
world but also that aspiring doctors will "frequently appear from every part
of the Continent" to study at Utopia's "celebrated University."[123] When they
finish their study, these students turn emissaries for Utopia's ideal medical system, spreading its vision far and wide. And, while Smith did not finish "The
Utopia," his hopes for this model of republican health appear to have mir-
rored that which he imagined for Erasmus Darwin's work: that it would "one
vast brotherhood mankind unite / In equal bands of knowledge and of right."[124]

If Smith articulated his theory of republican health in "The Utopia," he
practiced it in the *Medical Repository*, the first U.S. medical journal, which
Smith coedited with his friends and fellow physicians Edward Miller and Samuel Latham Mitchill in New York.[125] In the journal's first published sentence,
Smith articulated its environmental focus: "The design of the Papers which
will be presented to the Public under this title is to illustrate the connection
subsisting between Climate, Soil, Temperature, Diet, &c. and Health," Smith
wrote.[126] If Americans understood more about the nature of the republic in
which they lived, they could be healthier, and that, in turn, would make for
a healthier republic. This was also the kind of information the editors asked
from their contributors, who they hoped would send observations not only about
disease but about the environmental determinants of disease, the "condition
of *Vegetation*—with regard to growth, vigour, and disease . . . marking the influence of manures, and the local situation, both as to elevation and soil, air

and water," and the "state of the *Atmosphere*."[127] The "more minute and precise, the more useful will it be," the editors explained.[128]

It was a republican vision: thoughtful citizens from across the United
States would write in with their observations about health and the environment in the United States, and the editors would sift through, edit, and compile the best and most useful of those accounts, circulating them to promote
health across the republic. Toward these ends, the editors compiled a subscrip-
tion list in advance of publication of 266 individuals across fourteen of the
sixteen states.[129] Like the periodicals Smith imagined each county in Utopia
would produce, the *Repository*'s editors also planned their journal as a serial
compendium of medical writing from physicians that would also include "all
new papers from abroad, as well as in other parts of the United States, & . . . all
articles of Medical Intelligence. Beside, they contain Meteorological tables of
every town in the county."[130] This information, when managed responsibly,
could secure the health of the republic.

Once more, the land and the revolution made this ambitious and innovative project possible. While such a compendium would be useful in any
country, the editors wrote, the United States was uniquely suited to such a
project, containing advantages of "new and peculiar importance. These exist
in our extensive territory; in the variety of its soil, climate, elevation, and
aspect; in the varied descent, population, intermixture, institutions, manners, and consequent diseases of its inhabitants," as well as in myriad other
features.[131] Moreover, a general facility with language and "general diffusion
of knowledge, and turn for observation, among all classes of citizens" were
uniquely American and proved "powerful incentives to medical industry;
which should inspirit the exertions of physicians to give that importance, in a
professional view, to their country, which, fertile as she is in occasions, she
loudly calls for at their hands."[132] Furthermore, "it will be obvious to every
one," the editors of the *Repository* concluded their circular address, that "as
the benefits which may result from its success are limited to no description of
men, we are the more encouraged to solicit assistance from all whose situations enable them to afford it. We address ourselves, therefore, not to physicians only, but to men of observation, and to the learned, throughout the
United States."[133] In fact, the editors imagined that one day, "when thus completed, the volume of every year will form the history of health of the United
States . . . a single glance of the eye will be equal to perceive what diseases
prevailed at the same time, in all the intermediate situations, from St. Mary's
to St. Croix, and from the Missisippi [*sic*] to the Atlantic; and individual

experience, as well as new discoveries, will be propagated with unexampled benefit and celerity, to every part of the United States."[134] This vision of the *Medical Repository*'s circulation and early American reading practices far exceeds the possibilities of any textual circulation in the Atlantic basin with the exception of the Bible.[135]

The *Repository*'s vision was so staunchly republican that it might seem a perfect pair with Rush's ideas about the body—but it was not. While Rush also valued carefully culling, evaluating, and circulating healthy information, in practice, he maintained tight control over those networks, depending mostly on his own ability to produce information and to orchestrate U.S. health. He circulated medical knowledge largely through letters, lectures, books, and other single-author fora, incorporating observations from others as evidence but maintaining his own firm control. When Smith sought Rush's blessing for the journal, he encountered resistance.[136] His coeditor Edward Miller tried again, approaching Rush in person to attempt to persuade him. Both editors were unsuccessful in garnering Rush's support, and, on Christmas Day 1797, Smith concluded "there is good reason to believe Dr. Rush cool, at least, if not hostile to the Repository."[137] Ultimately, the *Medical Repository* was quite successful— enjoying an early demand and a long run—but Smith initially feared Rush's snub would mean, at least in Philadelphia, the *Repository* would "come to nothing."[138]

Imagining Health Through the Chemical Revolution

On September 22, 1797, just after the first installment of the *Medical Repository* appeared in print, Samuel Latham Mitchill sent Smith, his friend and coeditor, a medical poem he planned to publish in the journal's next installment. Like Smith, Mitchill was a literary physician, and he had drafted a poetic vision of republican health that he called "The Doctrine of Septon."[139] He wanted Smith's opinion. Smith likely felt a bit uncomfortable publishing a somewhat fantastical poem in the *Repository*—committed as the journal was meant to be to banning "creative fancy"—but he respected Mitchill's intellect and likely believed in the project, which was, after all, "attempted after the Manner of Dr. Darwin."[140] The problem, Smith wrote, was with Mitchill's verse. After reading "The Doctrine of Septon," Smith felt compelled to "suggest corrections—for some of the verses are very bad."[141] Nevertheless, Mitchill's poem was another iteration of the project Smith and Rush were also undertaking in the 1790s: in it, Mitchill imaginatively experimented with his own ideas of septon, a chemical he cast as life's universal antagonist responsible for all death and decay, which formed the cornerstone of his molecular vision of republican health.[142]

Mitchill opens "The Doctrine of Septon" with a geographically imaginative scene of exploration. "GNOMES!" he arrestingly addresses the agents of his project: "You beheld with pity and with pain, / Organic relics strew the fertile plain."[143] Echoing Rush's descriptions of the imagination as an explorer that "ascends above the heavens," "explores the worlds that revolve around the earth," and "descends into the regions of darkness," Mitchill moves quickly beyond this singular environment, imagining a gnomic exploration of life across a variety of landscapes, investigating life in forms that span land-based plants and animals—"Lords of the earth"—to aquatic ones—"tenants of the flood"—and in regions both above the ground and below.[144] From this expansive global perspective, "The Doctrine of Septon" contracts to the microscopic. Manifesting the vast scope of his own medical imagination, Mitchill shrinks his creatures to the size of particles in the second stanza where they bear witness to the origins of life—"where embryo germs to being start / The brain almost coeval with the heart"—as well as the embryo's development as "nice organs, ere the natal hour / Acquire a portion of *sensorial power*."[145] If Rush imagined republican health at the level of the body and Smith figured it at the level of the state, Mitchill's poem theorizes republican health at the level of molecules that nonetheless operated on a global stage. Mitchill needed a poem to do so—the global and the microscopic were scales of inquiry that had to be imagined to be pursued.

Mitchill based his medical ideas about septon on the new chemistry of the late eighteenth century. Recently discovered oxygen was the key element promoting the "life and vigour" of the human body, and septon was its opposite.[146] For Mitchill, septon was a more specific chemical name for a substance "arm'd with power to intervene / And disconnect the animal machine"; previously it had been only vaguely theorized as miasma or bad airs that arose from any number of sources in the environment—from still waters, from decaying animal and plant matter, from the land itself.[147] Septon allowed Mitchill to be more specific than previous doctors about how health worked at the molecular level and to offer a more general and complete account of health, sickness, aging, and death while also providing a new, firmer basis for medical intervention.

While a chemistry-based medicine, firmly located in what we now call the hard sciences, might seem like the last place for the imagination, as should already be clear, thinkers like Mitchill used imaginative experimentation to surmount fundamental barriers to knowing body chemistry in the late eighteenth century. Like Rush in his imaginative dissection and chemical analysis of his alien, Mitchill conjures gnomes that view health as medical observation cannot: "Man's constitution thus full well YE knew, / From OXYGEN its life and vigour drew."[148] They see disease take root in the body, "infus[ing]" it with "the peccant principle of death."[149] The poem's heroic couplets and iambic pentameter rationally order this medical experiment. Nevertheless, Mitchell's repeated staccato address to his "GNOMES!" breaks the poem's meter, arresting the reader and repeatedly calling the agents of his inquiry to attention. The jarring spondees ("GNOMES! you descry, with keen, lyncean eyes, / The foul *mephitic vapours* as they rise") both ground his investigation and highlight his own imaginative sallies; gnomes allow Mitchill to probe the depths of problems that were otherwise unknowable. They bring Mitchill's inquiry inside the live workings of the human body even more than Rush's imagined dissection or chemical assays could, opening its "dark recesses to the day."[150]

Mitchill emphasizes the poem as a site of medical knowledge through its form. In addition to the poem's rigid meter and technical language, Mitchill added scientific glosses using key medical terms in the margins of each stanza (Figure 3). This feature distinguished Mitchill's work from the poems of other physician-writers like Erasmus Darwin after whom Mitchill styled his poem.[151] The technical glosses in the margins were, ordinarily, a common feature of scientific writing rather than poetry, and they conveyed the medical and scientific information contained within each accompanying stanza. These summaries list key medical concepts such as *"Excitability, stimulus, excitement, & exhaustion"* or descriptions such as *"Effects of* Septon *and its* compounds, *on the* mind *and* body, *in* producing diseases."[152] While the marginal notes assist with the basic concepts conveyed and authorize the verse as medicine, the terms by themselves fall far short of the vision Mitchill's imaginative voyage constructs of life and health.[153]

If Mitchill's theory emerged from the same philosophical crucible that inspired his American contemporaries, it was also indebted to another intellectual movement of late eighteenth century: the chemical revolution.[154] The phrase "chemical revolution" refers to a scientific movement that fundamentally reframed both chemistry and politics around the Atlantic world. It is often credited to French scientist Antoine-Laurent Lavoisier, who desired in 1773 to perform experiments that would bring about "une révolution en physique et en chimie."[155] Its signal event was the discovery of oxygen. Lavoisier's

And felt, sad recompence of duty broke,
Vengeful *Remorse,* thy deep and deadly stroke:—
Hence *Pain,* hence *Sin,* their wasteful course began;
Thro' all her offspring vile corruption ran;
And Man, deprav'd, to *vice* and *error* hurl'd,
Still proves the *Septon* of the *moral world.*

GNOMES! you descry, with keen, lyncean eyes,   *Production*
The foul *mephitic vapours* as they rise;   *of* peftilen-
Stand by while captivating SEPTON draws   tial fluids, *by*
Unwary OXYGEN to aid his cause;—   *the union of*
                                                       fepton *with*
—Thus JUNO's charms, entranc'd, the thunderer held,   oxygene.
While her lov'd Grecians claim'd the bloody field;—
—Their *silent* union gives the MONSTER birth,
Who wastes with *septic fury* half the earth;—
—Embrac'd by TITAN, thus, in days of yore,
The fifty-handed giant TERRA bore;
With like destruction, on the ARGIVE TRAINS,
The DELIAN PAIR aveng'd their priestess' chains.—
GNOMES! your quick steps HIS subtle flight pursue,
And hold the many-changing FIEND in view;
YOUR guardian cares his secret arts betray;
YOU ope his dark recesses to the day;
YOU mark his conquests o'er the leafy race;
'Mid haunts of men his treacherous foot-steps trace;
In varying shapes, as best he loves to pass,
Of *heavier acid* or of *lighter gas;*

Figure 3. A stanza of Samuel Latham Mitchill's poem "The Doctrine of
Septon" published in the second number of the *Medical Repository* (1791).
Courtesy of the American Antiquarian Society.

discovery of oxygen revolutionized the medical understanding of respiration,
combustion, oxidation, and the composition of water; it also paved the road
for a new scientific nomenclature. Nevertheless, like all revolutions, the chemical revolution was a site of bitter contestation. Karl Wilhelm Scheele (1742–
1786), Joseph Priestley (1733–1804), and Lavoisier (1743–1794) all claimed to
have discovered oxygen. The Swedish Scheele first isolated the gas in 1772 but
did not share his findings widely, the British Priestley discovered it in 1775
but called it "dephlogisticated air," and, after learning of Priestley's work, the
French Lavoisier published his own findings, naming the chemical "oxygen."

It is in relation to the very public politics of the chemical revolution that
we can see more precisely how Mitchill's poem was not only highly imaginative

but also deeply republican. The revolutionary contestations of the chemical revolution were certainly epistemological and ontological, but they were also political and ideological. Priestley and Lavoisier, the most prominent figures of the debate, held opposing political views and those differences overtly structured their scientific understanding. Priestley used his chemical discoveries to undergird arguments for the democratic expansion of civil rights in England. In chemical terms, Priestley understood dephlogisticated air to be a gas free of corrosive material that made life and health possible, and he connected this discovery directly to his politics. In 1781, Priestley argued that his inquiries into dephlogisticated air were "not now a business of *air* only, as it was at the first; but appears to be of much greater magnitude and extent, so as to diffuse light upon the most general principles of natural knowledge," a realm he understood to be the "only foundation of all those *arts* of life, whether relating to peace or war, which distinguish *civilized* nations from those which we term *barbarous*."[156] Dephlogisticated air was everywhere, and its discovery proved that democracy was the world's natural order. Grounding his politics in an argument about the chemical basis of all life, Priestley vociferously argued for expanded civil rights in England. These politics eventually forced him into hiding, and, after he was burned in effigy alongside Thomas Paine, Priestley left for the United States.[157] When he arrived, Priestley was warmly greeted by America's famous scientifically minded politicians Benjamin Franklin and Thomas Jefferson as a "specimen" of scientific achievement and revolutionary thinking, but Priestley quickly wore out his welcome as his democratic politics proved too radical for the republican revolutionaries in the United States.[158]

Lavoisier, in contrast, was a French aristocrat who believed chemistry held the key to political stability. Working for the French government in the years leading up to the French Revolution, Lavoisier promoted a much more conservative vision of institutional change. He hoped that systematizing French science and government would stimulate more orderly change that would render further political upheaval unnecessary. Both Priestley and Lavoisier were Enlightenment figures broadly interested in the idea of revolution, but while Priestley hoped his chemistry would topple the prevailing political order, Lavoisier worked toward stabilizing hierarchy. In other words, when Lavoisier renamed dephlogisticated air "oxygen," he was not just reconceiving the gas as a stand-alone element but rejecting the logic that grounded Priestley's political theory. While Priestley's dephlogisticated air was a ubiquitous and exceptional gas defined by its independence from corrosive material, Lavoisier defined oxygen as only one element in a broader chemical order whose structure illuminated a model of orderly hierarchy in nature. Rejecting Priestley's more radical ontology and believing he could secure the French system from within, Lavoisier remained in Paris as the French Revolution began—and was beheaded by Robespierre as a traitorous agent of the old guard.[159]

Mitchill took a middle road: he adopted Lavoisier's language but rendered it in terms that were nonetheless legibly indebted to Priestley's phlogiston theory. In the end, Mitchill could not definitively side with either. His chemical theory owed Priestley a debt for his early air-quality experiments with nitrous oxide. Septon, which was nitrous oxide, grew out of those experiments insofar as, for Priestley, the goodness of the air depended inversely on the amount of nitrous oxide present. Following Priestley, Mitchill sought a unitary, egalitarian model of health in which health was based on a single, ubiquitous entity. But the rational, systematized thinking of Lavoisier was also appealing to Mitchill, especially in the context of 1790s U.S. politics. By the time Priestley arrived in America, those who had supported the revolution against abuses of power in the 1770s and 1780s had also seen egalitarian claims like Priestley's spill much blood abroad during the French Revolution and threaten security at home during the Whiskey Rebellion. In this context, Lavoisier's belief in the salubrious power of natural—if hierarchical—order made more sense. By the late 1790s, doctors and scientists in the Atlantic had also largely sided with Lavoisier, deciding that oxygen was a better way of conceiving the gas that made all life and health.

In navigating between the two, Mitchill crafted a republican health alternative. Emphasizing oxygen's negative counterpart septon—rather than the healthy gas itself—Mitchill illustrated the need for representative forces that would act on oxygen's behalf. Although the ubiquitous, democratic basis of health, oxygen alone could not by itself preserve it. "Unwary Oxygen," Mitchill warned, was sometimes unwittingly lured by "captivating septon," breeding disease.[160] The *"silent* union" of the two "gives the MONSTER birth, / Who wastes with *septic fury* half the earth."[161] Here Mitchill's gnomes transform from witnesses into agents of health, as Mitchill explains that the gnomes' "guardian cares [Septon's] secret arts betry" and "ope his dark recesses to the day."[162] In other words, as the poem continues, the gnomes become not merely spectators but educators. With "duteous zeal" they not only inform but "With wise dispatch their various stations gain, / And guard the Mine, the Mountain, and the plain."[163] This dissemination of useful information makes it possible for salubrious agents to rally behind the cause of health. "POTASSA seize a *Septic* foe, / His brawny arms around fast-griping throw; / Then plung'd in flames, as shuddering hosts admire, / Himself unhurt, consumed the wretch by fire."[164] Likewise, "CALX a *nitric* miscreant found, / And grip'd, and pull'd, and dragg'd him to the ground."[165]

What is clear from the verse Mitchill did complete is that oxygen by itself could not guarantee health but needed a representative force to keep septon in check. Thus Mitchill creates a space for a regulatory force, even if the poem breaks off before he can complete his republican model. Extending the analogy in Priestley's political terms, the people themselves (dephlogisticated air/oxygen) were certainly all equal but often "unwary" and required a cannier regulatory force. Mitchill signals his republicanism through language and imagery familiar to Americans from the revolutionary war: septon is a *"Tyrant"* that leads a war against the human body. It "[musters] thick his fierce *azotic bands*," threatening "the citadel of life commands."[166] After setting up near the brain, septon deploys a number of "unsuspected wounds" to its "unconscious prey."[167] It "shews greedy CANCER how he best may thrive, / and gorge and feast on human flesh" and "Tells FEVER, as in ambuscade he lies, / An hundred ways to take us by surprize."[168] Developing a neoclassical frame for the battle between septon and oxygen—featuring Grecians, Juno, and Hercules—Mitchill emphasizes both its epic and its republican nature. Inviting his readers to see health as a battle best articulated in Greek and Roman terms, Mitchill aligns his medical project with the republican philosophy that inspired the American Revolution, but his verse remains stuck in the epic battle itself rather than its resolution. He sets the stage for republican health but stops short of fully picturing it.

Mitchill's republican commitment distinguished his work from that of his fellow chemical revolutionaries Priestley and Lavoisier—a democrat and ambivalent monarchist—but he trod lightly in articulating these differences, perhaps recognizing that such delicacy might translate into a broader audience for his theories.[169] Priestley's theory of phlogiston had largely lost favor by the time he arrived in the United States, but he was still a towering scientific figure in the Atlantic world. New to the American medical scene, Priestley was still committed to phlogiston and looking for allies. When he published a 1796 defense of phlogiston in Philadelphia, he sent Mitchill a copy.[170] Explicit about the political ends of this chemical argument for an audience he hoped would be sympathetic, Priestley wished men like Mitchill would not "surrender [their] own judgment to any mere *authority* [like Lavoisier], however respectable."[171] Priestley continued, making the connection yet clearer:

"As you would not, I am persuaded, have your reign to resemble that of *Robespierre*, few as we are who remain disaffected, we hope you had rather gain us by persuasion, than silence us by power."[172] Linking Lavoisier to Robespierre was a bold and reasonably crass move in the wake of the scientist's recent execution at the latter's hands—perhaps signaling Priestley's growing desperation. Still, Priestley's message about thoughtful revolution would have resonated with revolutionaries on both sides of the Atlantic, even if his unwavering commitment to democracy did not. Mitchill disagreed with Priestley but engaged him in the respectful dialogue he sought: Mitchill dedicated forty-three separate entries over the first six volumes of the *Medical Repository* to the phlogiston debate.[173] Mitchill's principal tactic in his exchanges with Priestley was to downplay the chemical and ideological differences between himself and Priestley, reducing their disagreements to a quibble over terms.[174] After all, Lavoisier was dead, while Priestley was a feted scientist living in the United States.[175]

Mitchill's tact paid off. Despite their intellectual and political differences, Priestley promoted Mitchill's work, likely spurring septon's short-lived international acceptance in medical communities on both sides of the Atlantic during the late eighteenth and early nineteenth centuries. "I have no doubt of your having made a most important discovery," Priestley wrote Mitchill in a letter the latter published in 1799, "which ranks with the most brilliant that this age, fertile in discoveries, can boast, that the cause of contagious fever is of an *acid* nature, and some modification of the *nitrous*, which may, properly enough, be called *septon*."[176] Mitchill had convinced Priestley that septon was a "brilliant" expansion of his own work.[177] Mitchill's friend Charles Brockden Brown reported the next year: "*septon* appears to be gaining ground very rapidly in Europe and America . . . [Mitchill's] nomenclature has been adopted in Italy, and favourably mentioned in France."[178] Septon's medical moment was bright but brief: in the 1802 American edition of Quincy's medical dictionary it garnered a lengthy entry, but it was gone by the 1811 edition.

This medical success far outstripped Mitchill's poetic legacy. In writing "The Doctrine of Septon," Mitchill aspired to the medical and literary fame of other doctor-poets like Darwin. Likely hoping to secure a place in a pantheon of famous physician-poets, he paid homage to Darwin in his title, shared the poem with Smith, and sent his work across the ocean to literature and medicine enthusiast and physician Thomas Beddoes in Bristol.[179] Nevertheless, the poem was a poetic failure, and Mitchill knew it. Elihu Hubbard Smith likely did not mince words when he returned Mitchill's draft; the poem's artistic failures were readily apparent. Flaunting his expansive imagination at first, Mitchill could not sustain the energy of his early stanzas throughout. Allowing his imagination to spread capaciously over the molecules and landscapes of republican health at the outset, by the last stanza, Mitchill's imagination flags, his verse barely offering more than its medical glosses. The poem concludes with the scientific description "Combustion of oil by septon, acid, and *their mutual decomposition*," which is barely enhanced by Mitchill's portrayal in the verse, which pictures the event as a "terrific anger" that "boil[ed], / When AQUA-FORTIS met with HEATED OIL;—/ Both vanquish'd, falling underneath the shock, / Expire'd in the blaze and suffocating smoke."[180] Imaginative only insofar as violent verse anthropomorphizes the liquids, this account displays none of the creativity—rich analogy, unexpected scale, and unusual perspective—that animated Mitchill's first lines. Barely expanded beyond the technical language in its margins, Mitchill's poem becomes truly workmanlike, as if exhausted by early energies too great to sustain. Mitchill seems to have felt so, too: ending the poem abruptly and without conclusion, Mitchill chastises himself for burning his imagination too bright and quickly flaming out—violating a "poetical precept" but not a medical one.[181]

The Legacies of Revolutionary Medicine

The American Revolution initiated an epistemic crisis, but the quest for republican models did not end with its first generation of thinkers. Rather, Americans repeatedly returned to the project of experimenting imaginatively with comprehensive systems of health, especially at moments of political crisis. The metonymic link between the well-being of the body and that of the state, which served as a robust strain of medical thinking through the nineteenth century, put pressure on doctors and writers to continue articulating new models, especially at moments when the republic itself was in danger.

Benjamin Rush's niece Rebecca Rush offers a useful literary example of this continued work. On the eve of the War of 1812—a moment in which it looked like the American experiment might fail—Rush penned *Kelroy* (1812), a novel that refigured the nation's health as a project for and by women. Turning her uncle's ideas about the medical value of the imagination and literary form to her own ends, Rush used *Kelroy* to argue that women's bodies and women's care should be at the center of republican visions. Imaginatively assaulting Benjamin Rush's medicine, which modeled itself on an imperiled political system, Rebecca Rush presents the novel's "respectable" Philadelphia physician as ridiculous. Though he thinks quite well of himself, doctor Blake dresses "in the fashion of twenty years back, and his shoe-buckles of the same pattern. His hair was plaistered back from his forehead, and powdered as white as snow; his face was round, and red, and his features remarkably small, particularly his eyes, which resembled a pig's, both in size and expression."[182] Clumsy, ill spoken, anachronistic, and dense, Blake is, worst of all, medically impotent. Rush's characters first laugh at Blake, calling him "the most ridiculous man alive," "a fool," and "a perfect idiot," but Blake's incompetence endangers the health of Philadelphia, the nation's medical and one-time political capital.[183]

While her uncle's vision of the nation's health largely dismissed the bodies and care of women, at the moment of his system's possible collapse, Rebecca Rush focuses her medical vision on women. Creatively reimagining the therapeutic landscape, Rush's novel refashions her uncle's ideas about the centrality of sympathy to health care in a largely female environment. Opening and closing with the deaths of white men, the picture of health that occupies the pages between is concerned almost exclusively with the sympathetic and care-oriented networks of women.[184] The novel foregrounds the female body and its sympathies largely in the absence of men's bodily concerns. Relentlessly under attack from suitors, fire, strokes, and grief, these female bodies are cared for by a network of sympathetic women who prove better able to maintain the republic's health.[185] Rebecca Rush's model serves as a rejoinder to professional medicine, which was increasingly sidelining women's bodies, women's health care, and women's health work through the medical differentiation of the sexes, the medicalization of women's health, and the patriarchal appropriation of women's health care through the rise of fields like obstetrics.[186]

Half a century later, physician-writer Oliver Wendell Holmes (1809–1894) also undertook the project of imagining a new republican model of health. With the United States on the verge of civil war, he drew from the pathbreaking cell theory of German physiologist-cum-political-revolutionary Rudolf Virchow (1821–1902) to craft a theory of the body as a "cell-republic."[187] This vision was, like the republican medicine before it, particularly American and indebted to the U.S. particularity, which emerged from the land itself. "The American climate remoulds the European [constitution], and casts a new die of humanity," Holmes explained to the American Medical Association at the end of its inaugural year (1848): "why should it not differ in the susceptibilities which, awakened, become disease?"[188] American doctors, he continued, ought "not to set English portraits of disease in American frames"; rather, a medicine based in U.S. distinctiveness offered "a true field for the American medical intellect."[189] Using cell theory to revise Rush's republican medicine explicitly, Holmes writes that "the increased and diminished action of the vessels, out of which medical theories and methods of treatment have grown up, have yielded to the doctrine of local cell-communities."[190] The notion of a cell-republic demonstrated that cells, "belonging to this or that vascular district . . . help themselves, as contractors are wont to do from the national treasury."[191] These "local cell-communities" were not irreconcilably separate, brought together merely by some sense of the statistical average; rather, they shared a common purpose and drew alike from the body's "national treasury."[192] Making the political frame of his medical vision yet clearer, Holmes explains, "The more you examine the structure of the organs and laws of life, the more you will find how resolutely each of the cell-republics which make up the *E pluribus unum* of the body maintains its independence."[193] Seeking a system of unity on the verge of civil war, Holmes declared the body, like the United States itself, "a sum of vital unities."[194]

The crisis prompted by the American Revolution was by no means concluded by the close of the eighteenth century—nor was it the only such crisis U.S. doctors and writers confronted during the period. In the 1790s, a series of quick and deadly yellow fever epidemics thrust American medicine into a more concrete, disease-driven epistemic crisis. This return of yellow fever after a decades-long hiatus certainly intersected with and at times amplified the revolutionary crisis, but the disease's unknown etiology and mechanism of transmission also presented pressing issues of their own. At the root of those issues was the problem of communicating health.

CHAPTER 2

YELLOW FEVER

COMMUNICATE, *v. i.* To partake of the Lord's supper. *Taylor.*
Instead of this, in America, at least in New England, *commune* is
generally or always used.

2. To have a communication or passage from one to another; to
have the means of passing from one to another; as, two houses
communicate with each other; a fortress *communicates* with the
country; the canals of the body *communicate* with each other.
Arbuthnot.

3. To have intercourse; *applied to persons.*

4. To have, enjoy or suffer reciprocally; to have a share with
another.

> Ye have done well that ye did *communicate* with my
> affliction. Phil. iv.
> —Noah Webster, *An American Dictionary* (1828)

CONTAGION. (From *contingo,* to meet or touch each other.)
Effluvia. Miasma. Virus. Lues. Infection. The very subtile [*sic*]
particles arising from putrid or other substances, or from persons
labouring under contagious diseases, *which communicate the disease
to others*; thus the contagion of putrid fever, the effluvia of dead
animal or vegetable substances, the miasma of bogs and fens, the
virus of small-pox, lues venereal, &c. &c.
> —Philadelphia edition of *Quincy's Lexicon-Medicum*
> (1817, emphasis added)

As the leaves began to turn in the fall of 1793, all eyes were on Philadelphia. Yellow fever had returned for the first time in almost thirty years and this time with dramatic intensity. Talk of the fever was incessant, and no one knew what to do. Yellow fever would claim almost 5,000 lives in the city that year, but numbers were hard to come by in a city from which so many had fled—and newspapers were reporting up to 15,000 deaths.[1] Yellow fever would strike Philadelphia eight times in the next twelve years, and while the array of 1790s outbreaks around the Atlantic were by no means isolated events, they caused an epistemic crisis in the United States because of their spectacular devastation, because of the impotence of American medicine in the face of that devastation, and because of the amplifying coincidence of the epidemics with the social and political conditions of the postrevolutionary moment.[2]

The lack of effective medical knowledge about yellow fever produced chaos and terror across the United States as well as lengthy and contentious debates among physicians about the nature and etiology of the disease. While today we recognize that the fever was likely brought by mosquitoes aboard one of the many ships traveling up the coast from the Caribbean (where yellow fever appeared regularly), no one understood the situation in this way.[3] In the 1790s Americans were split between those who understood the epidemic as transmitted through the local environment (climatists) and those who believed the disease transmittable via goods, animals, and people (contagionists).[4] As the questions raised by yellow fever echoed loudly across the landscape, some Americans worried that the outbreak might be a kind of divine retribution for their recent revolutionary actions or for their political, social, and economic behavior thereafter.[5] It did not help that the disease emptied the capital, disrupting the major activities of the U.S. government.[6]

Newspaper editor and poet Philip Freneau succinctly captured the climate of Philadelphia that year in a set of stanzas on the "Pestilence":

> HOT, dry winds forever blowing,
> Dead men to the grave-yards going:
>   Constant hearses,
>   Funeral Verses;
> Oh! what plagues—there is no knowing! . . .
>
> Doctors raving and disputing,
> Death's pale army still recruiting—

What a pother
One with t'other!
Some a-writing, some a-shooting.

Nature's poisons here collected,
Water, earth, and air infected—
O, what pity,
SUCH A CITY
Was in such a place erected![7]

Freneau takes the chaos of the city in the face of the failures of medical practice and epistemology—"there is no knowing!"—as the subject of his poem. At the very time that the clamor of "constant hearses" and "funeral verses" fill the streets, doctors displayed their ineffectual knowledge in the face of fever through their meaningless words and actions. While Freneau bends toward climatist theories in his poem, he does not spare the theory's advocates his biting critique. They too spill ink and exchange heated words while "Death's pale army [is] still recruiting."[8] It would be wrong, however, to take Freneau's poem too seriously. Choosing the limerick as the form for his poem about the fever, Freneau insists on dark humor in the moment of crisis. Limericks had long been used to respond to human impotence in the face of death and dying, and the feverish activity in fever-ridden Philadelphia captures the chaos of this disease-based epistemic crisis.

Still, the limerick was a bold choice for a moment in which yellow fever *communication* in all forms—of information, of narrative, of emotion, and of disease—resided at the heart of the nation's epistemic crisis.[9] Most immediately, Americans wanted to know how disease passed from the environment to the individual or between the sick individual and the healthy one—in their language, how it was *communicated*. The focus on communication made sense because it was a term that all could agree was at the core of the issue, even if they could not agree on what it meant. Contagionists and climatists alike worried about the communication of yellow fever. Other terms were more fraught. "Contagion," for example, usually referred to infection transmitted interpersonally but at times was so confused that in the 1817 Philadelphia edition of Quincy's *Lexicon-Medicum* its definition included words like "effluvia" and "miasma"—climatological explanations.[10] "Communication," then, was a term capacious enough to capture the whole of the debate without being itself too specific or quibbling.

More than a battle over terminology, the language of etiology and the origins of disease were intimately bound up in one another. Americans understood narratives could play a role in stemming and in promoting yellow fever. One Philadelphian described the effects of fever stories on himself thus: "Considering the general terror, I have more than once felt my pulse, to discover whether I was really alive or not. . . . Of all things, this yellow fever is the most insidious—its approaches are generally gradual—a person imagines himself well when he is dying—others lose the use of reason entirely, and die in that situation."[11] Fever narrative could deeply affect both the mind and the body.

This concern about narrative stemmed largely from the eighteenth-century belief that the imagination was intimately connected to health—in fact, the imagination could kill.[12] Americans in the period understood this mechanism thus: a harmful element might "be taken into the body and pass out of it, without producing the fever, unless it be rendered active by some occasional cause."[13] That cause could be environmental or physiological, but it could also be the dangerous imaginings ill-considered narratives could communicate and the emotions they stimulated, like grief and fear. This inflamed imagination produced a "fatigue of the body and mind" that left individuals highly susceptible to disease.[14] Benjamin Rush agreed with the College of Physicians that mental and physical overexertion often determined who fell ill from yellow fever and who did not: "In many people," Rush wrote, "the disease was excited by a sudden paroxism of fear."[15] It did not help that words like "terror" and "havoc" punctuated grim accounts of the epidemic. Hoping to prevent deaths from yellow fever *and* the unhealthy imagination and fear aroused by the disease, the College of Physicians recommended that Philadelphians stay away from the afflicted, that the bodies be disposed of as quietly as possible, and that the city stop the death knells from tolling.[16] Printer Mathew Carey explained that "the expedience of this measure was obvious, as they had before been constantly ringing almost the whole day, so as to terrify those in health, and drive the sick, as far as the influence of imagination could produce that effect, to their graves."[17] Perhaps, then, Freneau wrote his quick-paced light verse to conjure new imaginaries, offering a communicable antidote to the heavy and incessant communication of disease and death.

The yellow fever outbreaks of the 1790s occurred during a moment when the imagination and narrative were understood to be intimately connected to corporeal well-being, and, thus, imaginative experimentation was a crucial tool for communicating health, if one that needed to be used carefully. As narrative, rumor, and the imagination were at the center of the issue of communication, Americans struggled to strike a balance between communicating information about the disease and communicating the disease itself. Literary form was understood to be simultaneously a means of investigating the communication of yellow fever, of stemming its progress, and of promoting it. Thus doctors and writers approached imaginative experimentation during the yellow fever crisis in a variety of ways. Two episodes in particular—the debate between Mathew Carey, Absalom Jones, and Richard Allen and the one between the editors of the *Medical Repository* and Charles Brockden Brown—show how Americans experimented with narrative form and a controlled imagination as a risky but crucial means to understand yellow fever communication and to communicate health.

Printing Disease Narratives

The voluminous narratives of the fever varied widely—especially in terms of style and form. These varieties were prompted by differential beliefs about the relationship between disease narratives and the production of the disease itself. Some accounts were purposefully even in their tone. In September a paper in Worcester, Massachusetts, published an "account of the malignant fever which at present rages in Philadelphia."[18] Not wishing to further alarm anyone, the writer opined that communication was "confined to contact, or to the reach of the breath of the infected person"—but encouraged "all who can" to "leave town."[19] In their mildest form, accounts used clinical description. Rather than investing in florid narratives, this writer chose only to list symptoms dispassionately, unwilling to risk exciting the emotions or the imagination. A fever set in with a few days of mild symptoms, he explained, followed by granular black vomit, and "after a little time a comatoze delirium takes place, vibices appear, the skin becomes yellow, as do the adnata of the eyes; and finally, the patient dies . . . on or about the seventh or eighth day."[20]

Other reports were less measured. In October 1793, a Greenfield, Massachusetts, paper printed a firsthand account from Philadelphia: "The papers must have amply informed you of the melancholy situation of this city, for five or six weeks past," the correspondent explained. "Grave digging has been the only business carrying on; and indeed I may say of late Pit digging, where people are interred indiscriminately in three tiers of coffins."[21] He continues, "People have been hitherto so pannic [*sic*] struck, that little has been attended to but the means of self preservation; gloom and melancholy is on every person's countenance; *nothing but yellow fever is talked of.*"[22]

These formal and stylistic concerns signaled Americans' understanding of literary form as an integral part of yellow fever communication during and immediately following the 1793 epidemic. The writings of three individuals who remained in Philadelphia during the 1793 epidemic—Irish-immigrated printer Mathew Carey (1760–1839) and prominent black preachers Richard Allen (1760–1831) and Absalom Jones (1746–1818)—dramatize how individuals experimented with healthy disease communication during the epistemic crisis brought on by yellow fever. In particular, the debates between the three highlight the centrality of narrative form to the production of knowledge about the disease.

Mathew Carey was one of the most vocal Philadelphians during the first epidemic and in the years that followed. Carey made his way first in Dublin and was then apprenticed to Benjamin Franklin in Paris in the early 1780s. A radical figure, he left Ireland for political reasons and emigrated to Philadelphia in 1784 where he founded an eventually prominent printing and publishing business. Carey stayed in the city through at least the beginning of the 1793 epidemic and assisted the newly formed Committee of Health that sought to quell general panic and assist ailing citizens. On November 14, Carey published *A Short Account of the Malignant Fever*, which went through four editions by mid-January 1794. In the following year, more editions followed, including translations into French and German.[23]

Carey wanted to set the story straight and to free print networks from the diseased communication pulsing through them. He understood the temptation to tell terrifying tall tales about the outbreak but urged writers to resist. "It would be extraordinary if so very favourable an opportunity of inventing marvellous stories, should have been suffered to pass over without some prodigies being recorded," he explains. "Mankind are ever prone to the extravagant, especially when their passions are warmed. And pity and terror, two passions particularly calculated to foster this disposition, being roused into action to the highest degree, the marvellous stories, which were every where current, and which even stole into print, can be easily accounted for."[24] But this "extravagant" narration was dangerous. Not only did these dangerous stories augment the "pity and terror" that had prompted them, but, as Carey understood well, this diseased communication imperiled the lives of ever more citizens.

Carey refused to fan the flames of panic and the imagination. He clarified, "I have not attempted any embellishment or ornament of stile; but have alone aimed at telling plain truths in plain language."[25] Emphasizing form and style as key to his message, Carey argues that the disorganized style of his prose is evidence of its veracity. "I have to offer the following apology," he wrote. "Many of the circumstances and reflexions towards the conclusion, which would have come with more propriety in the beginning, did not occur, until some of the first half of the sheets were not only written, but printed. I had no choice, therefore, but either to omit them, or place them somewhat out of order. I preferred the latter."[26] Carey unfolds *A Short Account* in the order the events and observations occurred, offering chronological fidelity as proof of its truth, unrefined by the artistry of argument. (Benjamin Rush would make a similar claim in his own 1794 treatise of the fever.)[27] Furthermore, Carey claims to have protected himself from sallies of emotion that might sully his text. "I have suppressed many a harsh, unkind comment, which was forcing itself on me," he explains, working to remain stoic even while describing the lamentable behavior of U.S. citizens during "a period of horror and affright."[28]

Since Carey believed that adding to but not deleting prose made for the healthiest communication of the knowledge, he committed to this habit in subsequent editions. The improved fourth edition published on January 16, 1794, included the prefaces to all the previous editions. In that edition, furthermore, he hired people to "go thro' the city and liberties, and make enquiry at every house, without exception, for the names and occupations of the dead" to provide a reliable account of the fever in the form of a factual tabulation.[29] Citizen fear, among other things, made it impossible to complete his task, but, "imperfect as the list still remains," he hoped it would "be found useful in removing anxious doubts, and conveying to persons in different countries, the melancholy information of the decease of relatives, which, but for such a channel of communication, would in many cases, be difficult if not impossible."[30]

Still, on rare occasion Carey invited the reader's imagination and emotion. In a description of the charitable acts of particular individuals of the city, Carey laments, "I feel myself affected at this part of my subject, with emotions, which I fear my unanimated stile is ill calculated to transfuse into the breast of my reader. I wish him to dwell on this part of the picture, with a degree of exquisite pleasure equal to what I feel in the description."[31] Here Carey wants it both ways. On one hand, he insists on his "unanimated stile," which cannot and will not stir feelings in his reader. On the other hand, he invites his reader to rouse her own imagination by "dwell[ing]" on portraits of self-sacrifice. Carey resolves the contradiction by working to shape the reader's emotion through naming it.

What Carey did not want to communicate was the excessive emotion—particularly fear—that was inspired by so many narrative accounts of the fever. Fear was the most dangerous reaction to fever stories. "It is to be observed," he wrote, "that the fear of the contagion was so prevalent, that as soon as any one was taken ill, an alarm was spread among the neighbours, and every effort was used to have the sick person hurried off to Bushhill, to avoid spreading the disorder. The cases of poor people forced in this way to that hospital, though labouring under only common colds, and common fall fevers, were numerous and afflicting. There were not wanting instances of persons, only slightly ill being sent to Bushhill, by their panic-struck neighbour."[32] Fear and flight were the wrong reactions. Fear could prompt not only yellow fever but divine retribution. Carey tells the story of an urban man who abandoned his wife to the fever and slept outside to avoid catching it from her. Presuming her dead the next morning, he bought a coffin, "but on entering the house, was surprised to see her much recovered. He fell sick shortly after, died, and was buried in the very coffin, which he had so precipitately bought for his wife, who is still living."[33] These fears of person-to-person transmission were unfounded, Carey furthered, telling the story of Thomas Boyles's family, residents of Bushhill when it was converted into a hospital. Carey explains that neither he nor his family ever fell sick: "Let these instances suffice at all future times to prevent fear from totally overpowering the understanding, and producing scenes of cruelty that make a feeling being blush for his species."[34]

Carey worked hard to communicate healthy information to a diseased citizenry, but he also transmitted information that endangered a number of Philadelphia inhabitants; most notably, following Benjamin Rush, Carey propagated the idea that African Americans were immune to yellow fever. African Americans' relationship to communication about the fever had been quite different than that of the white citizens of Philadelphia. While white residents of the city engaged in panicked fever talk spurred by a general terror, African Americans were assured that they were not susceptible to the fever and that they could assist with impunity.

Thus, in 1794, Absalom Jones and Richard Allen took Carey up on his invitation to correct the account, addressing three kinds of diseased communication propagated by Carey's narrative: the entwined lies that African Americans had mercenarily profited from the fever, that they were immune to the disease, and that they were immune to fears of the disease. Implicitly arguing, then, that Carey had not dispassionately "suppressed many a harsh, unkind comment" when it came to African Americans, Jones and Allen revised the narrative form of truthful communication. Seeking to set the story straight, Jones and Allen wrote that in September "a solicitation appeared in the public papers, to the people of colour to come forward and assist the distressed, perishing, and neglected sick; with a kind of assurance, that people of our colour were not liable to take the infection."[35] In response these black men felt it their duty to help the sick who had been left to die by a frightened white population. They encountered "scenes of woe indeed!" but "The Lord was pleased to strengthen us, and remove all fear from us, and disposed our hearts to be as useful as possible."[36] Here Jones and Allen lean on the right-feeling sympathies and religious faith Carey praised, while accusing Carey of biased narration. Taking their sense of duty further, Jones and Allen publicly advertised their assistance during the epidemic, inspired by "real sensibility" rather than "fee or reward."[37]

By way of example, Jones and Allen relate the moving account of a poor black man who refused a generous reward for bringing water to a stricken man after a number of white men had refused. "Master," Sampson explained, "I will supply the gentleman with water, but surely I will not take your money for it."[38] That same man "went constantly from house to house where distress was, and no assistance without fee or reward" until "he was smote with the disorder, and died," and "after his death his family were neglected by those he had served."[39] Their *Narrative* goes on to catalogue a number of stories in which black men and women refused generous compensation and exposed themselves to yellow fever, many of them falling ill or dying in spite of what Rush and Carey claimed about black immunity. Jones and Allen are uninterested in Carey's suppression of "harsh" truths; rather, they favor harsh truths and moving stories over stoic but dangerous mischaracterizations.

Finally, Jones and Allen insist that African American members of the community had the same fears about disease but listened nonetheless to the rational discourse of Philadelphia's medical men and behaved benevolently. According to Jones and Allen, "even [white] friends when they met in the streets were afraid of each other, much less would they admit into their houses the distressed orphan that had been where the sickness was; this extreme seemed in some instances to have the appearance of barbarity."[40] The "terror of the times" did not stop African American men and women from helping.[41] While "many of the white people, that ought to be patterns for us to follow after, have acted in a manner that would make humanity shudder," black men and women had routinely promoted social and somatic health during the crisis.[42] One black man, for example, after witnessing another man shove a woman into a gutter, saved her from suffocating and brought her to the hospital for care.[43] While Jones and Allen shared notable narrative similarities with Carey—for example, the moral logic in which individuals who flee the sick pay with their lives—their formal style differed markedly. Rather than pursuing a stoic, "unanimated stile," Jones and Allen preferred emotional communication, committing to carefully chosen flourishes over dispassionate accounts. They concluded both their *Narrative* and the letter to the mayor of Philadelphia that followed it with poems.[44]

Healthy Communication in the *Medical Repository*

Carey, Jones, and Allen were just three vocal participants in the heated debates about yellow fever communication; such disputes also animated many levels of discourse in those tense years from private correspondence to public medical debates involving the most respected medical names in the new United States.[45] In 1794, Benjamin Rush published his own *Account of the Bilious Remitting Yellow Fever, as it Appeared in the City of Philadelphia, in the Year 1793*. In it Rush explained that in August 1793 he had believed yellow fever had arrived "from some damaged coffee," though he could not tell whether it was "propagated by contagion, or by the original exhalation."[46] But in the weeks that followed, Rush retreated from this opinion, unsure of the fever's cause. By November, he was at odds with the College of Physicians, and especially with its president, prominent physician John Redman (1722–1808), who had once been his own mentor. The college believed the fever to be spread through infected individuals and imported from abroad, while Rush now "believed it to have been generated in our city."[47] Still connecting it to "marshy ground" and "putrid masses of matter," this conclusion did not contradict Rush's initial assessment about the decaying coffee, even as he argued that the disease itself had not been imported from abroad.[48]

Ninety miles to the north, physicians Edward Miller, Samuel Latham Mitchill, and Elihu Hubbard Smith were also working to solve the problem of disease communication. They witnessed New York's yellow fever epidemics in 1795, 1797, and 1798 with the knowledge they accumulated from reading about Philadelphia in 1793. The New York doctors were young, but they were men of their own opinions and the epistemic crisis caused by medicine's inability to know what caused yellow fever encouraged them to experiment with new forms of medical communication that diverged from the work of prominent older physicians like Rush. Like Rush, these three believed that medical health was metonymically connected to political health and largely agreed with Rush's climatist theory of fever.[49] Supporting Rush's theories against a contagionist stance while also advocating for his own vision of republican medicine, for example, Smith writes, "Yellow Fever always first appears or appears only in Sea Ports. The reason is obvious. . . . In the country, vegetation & ventilation unite to dissipate or neutralize the pestiferous miasma [. . . but] It would be, perhaps, impossible to create such diseases, by any importation, in well built, & ventilated towns, the inhabitants of which were temperate & cleanly."[50]

Nevertheless, Smith's position on the communication of yellow fever differed subtly from Rush's as did the work of the New York coterie more generally. Whereas Rush forcefully promoted the climatist theory of disease, he also proclaimed that the 1793 epidemic was caused by rotting coffee on the docks—the refuse of Atlantic trade.[51] Smith admitted no such possibility: "Every fact recorded, when rightly considered, tends to prove, not only that Fevers are of local birth, but that they are rarely exported."[52] Though this statement reads like a promotion of Rush's later climatist claims, Smith's position is more extreme. Rush depicts yellow fever stomach degeneration "resembling coffee impregnated with its grounds," an analogy that reveals the vestiges of his initial claims and aesthetically links the fever to foreign imports.[53] Smith, however, adamantly rejects the image; insisting on language that links the fever to its local origins, he describes a vomit "of a blackish appearance, commonly described as resembling coffee-grounds; but bearing a nearer resemblance to blood partly burnt+diluted with muddy water."[54] This aesthetic refusal is not accidental. "I never saw an instance of that tar-like vomit," Smith continues, "which has been noticed by some writers. But, of all others, that which struck me as evidential of the greatest derangement of the Stomach, was the vomiting up of, what appeared to be a thin blood, in which floated a flaky, filmy substance, which I supposed to have been the villous coat of the stomach."[55]

Smith rejects even hackneyed similes that linked the fever to transnational trade.[56] In opting for descriptive precision over dangerous analogy, Smith clarifies his commitment to the communication of accurate information. But, as a doctor with literary aspirations, Smith also demonstrates in his refusal a resistance to the tendency of medical metaphors to collapse the various etiological theories of fevers, the distinctions between American bodies and goods of trade, and physiological fact with imaginative fancy. Smith planned to develop his own physiological theories of circulation after conducting further research, but he never got the chance to begin.[57]

Smith, Miller, and Mitchill sought to transmit their ideas about what constituted healthy communication through their own prose form: the *Medical Repository*. This form differed from Carey's in that it culled true stories and reasoned opinions from around the Atlantic in an effort to stem the circulation of dangerous stories by communicating healthy information. Like Freneau, the editors of the *Medical Repository* were troubled by the contentious disputes that developed over yellow fever communication and understood how perilously it could divide the medical community. Rather than fall prey to the sallies of "a-writing" and "a-shooting" Freneau had so succinctly critiqued, these doctors strove for a republican model to order health communication.

The *Medical Repository* offered a collaboratively produced alternative to Rush's top-down medical communication. Whereas Rush gave lectures, wrote books, and took on apprentices to circulate his medical opinions, the *Medical Repository* aimed to circulate healthy communication without relying on a single, authoritative account. The journal collected medical information from around the globe for the "general diffusion of knowledge, and . . . for observation, among all classes of [the country's] citizens."[58] The first three volumes contained everything from histories to meteorological charts and from poems to reviews and natural histories. Furthermore, it culled and circulated accounts from Georgia to New Hampshire and from numerous physicians around the Atlantic world.

The goal was to circulate a compendium of useful information from an array of trustworthy sources that would secure yellow fever information from the dangerous and unpredictable sallies in communication. This aim was exemplified by an early letter in the *Repository* from Massachusetts physician Joseph Warren, who wrote to the corresponding secretary of the American Academy of Arts and Sciences, Eliphalet Pearson, "In the month of December last, I communicated to the public a number of facts relative to the fever which prevailed the last autumn in the town of Boston, calculated to counteract the effects of a publication in the city of Philadelphia, in which the opinions of the Physicians on the nature of the disease, and the method of practice, were grossly misrepresented."[59] The *Repository* prized this kind of correspondence and correction. Warren's letter offered true facts from a reliable source to counter the proliferation of narratives that imperiled the citizenry through misinformation that could dangerously inflame the imaginations and emotions of U.S. citizens.

The editors of the *Medical Repository* understood the "communication" for which they were responsible broadly. It was a journal produced for the health of all citizens. While the yellow fever epidemics were a profound problem for American medicine, they also offered an opportunity for the new, healthy, and diverse kind of communication Smith, Miller, and Mitchill envisioned for their journal. "The present time seems particularly favourable to such attempts," they wrote, referring to the *Repository*. "The distressing [yellow fever] events which have been so recently witnessed, in various parts of our country, have awakened the curiosity of others, as well as of physicians; and while they have quickened the zeal and observations of the latter, [they] have excited the eager apprehensions of all. This has created an uncommon interest, in respect to medical opinions, among the people at large."[60] From this view, epidemics made the people better observers, and their distinct and varied perspectives should be drawn upon and communicated to facilitate the health of all.

This appeal for communication from a wide swath of educated and observant men throughout the United States encouraged the three doctors to gather accounts in diverse genres—from the results of scientific experimentation and medical reviews to historical accounts and first-person testimonials, as the first volume makes clear—that together would work to ensure the health of U.S. citizens. The compilers of the *Medical Repository* hoped that by accumulating histories, theories, and accounts from around the world they could promote universal health. The many uses of the word "communication" within the *Repository* illustrate this abundantly: the term in the journal variously referred to the transmission of disease ("communication with the sick"), oral discussion ("communication with her"/"Mr. Scott's communication"), formal correspondence ("communication on a professional subject"), a letter ("a communication made the 11th of the 9th month"), the relationship between two organs ("communication between the bladder and cyst of the abscess"), the relationship between two geographical spaces ("communication between Hawkins's-Point and the city"/"communication between two cities"), and news

("If any other case of this disease should have occurred to any other of our readers . . . the communication of them is requested").[61]

The editors, then, sought to compile a kind of repository of communication that, cumulatively, could offer a kind of narrative cure. By 1802, the *Repository* bore a new epigraph by Francis Bacon that made this vision explicit: "Our great quantity of books looks like superfluity," the epigraph begins, "which, however, is not to be remedied by destroying those we have already, but by publishing more good ones, that, like the serpent of Moses, might devour the serpents of the enchanters."[62] To this end, they collected information from physicians and citizens from all over the United States, from Europe, and from the Caribbean on topics as diverse as history, geology, medical treatment, medical observation, and medical theory. This information also took a variety of forms, as the *Repository* regularly featured an array of different articles, reviews of new and influential medical works, letters from abroad, particular case studies, tables of proto-statistics, domestic and foreign news, and an appendix with items of further interest. Far from a mouthpiece for their own beliefs or even local and national opinion, the *Repository* sought to collect information from all over the world, encourage debate over various topics, and offer a variety of forms and styles of proof of contemporary and historical medical occurrences. Through this patchwork of forms, Smith, Miller, and Mitchill worked to expose their readers to reasoned narrative (rendered in the *Repository* as "fact"), which they believed could inoculate citizens against dangerous stories.[63]

Thus, in spite of the *Repository*'s generic variety, the editors envisioned clear limits to the forms that would appear in the journal. Most notably, the "laborious process of reasoning" exemplified by the journal left "little flattering" to any "creative fancy."[64] But, as Mitchill's poem "The Doctrine of Septon" makes clear, these proclamations of reasoned and unbiased communication in contrast to "creative fancy" did not offer a simple philosophical declaration against the uses of the imagination in medicine. Rather, their proclamation was rooted in broader concerns about the power of narrative and the imagination to create disease—in particular the role of the unchecked imagination in propagating the series of yellow fever epidemics that had struck the coastal United States.[65] In the 1796 preface to *Zoonomia*, a text read avidly by the Friendly Club, Erasmus Darwin had written, polemically, "All diseases originate in the exuberance, deficiency, or retrograde action, of the faculties of the sensorium [the brain], as their proximate cause; and consist in the disordered motions of the fibres of the body, as the proximate effect of the exertions of those disordered faculties."[66] In this lengthy treatise on "the Laws of Organic Life," Darwin repeatedly returned to the imagination as a central feature of life and health.[67] The belief that the "faculties of the sensorium" might be a key space for controlling health and disease prompted physicians like Rush and Smith to put their faith in well-ordered artistic forms for healing, such as music and poetry, to heal the ailing "sensorium."[68] Rush recommended reading as a cure and his hospital had a library for that purpose, while Smith republished Darwin's long scientific poem, *The Botanic Garden*, believing it would promote health.[69] In his diary, Smith worried about the imaginative effects of stories told about the 1795 outbreak. He wrote, "Wherever you go, the Fever is the invariable & unceasing topic of conversation. . . . People collect in groups to talk it over and to frighten each other into fever, or flight. . . . In one shape, or the other, the fever is constantly brought into view; and the soul sickens with the ghastly and abhorred repetition."[70] Seeing "creative fancy" as a motivating force behind these distorted fever narratives, Smith invested in the *Medical Repository* to spread reasoned narrative that would inoculate U.S. citizens against the harmful effects of fever fictions and the dangerous sympathies they spurred—at least until he died in the 1798 New York epidemic.[71]

And while Smith and his coeditors may have wished to draw a firm line between the "fancy" of rigorously ordered poetry like that of Erasmus Darwin and Samuel Latham Mitchill and the "creative fancy" of popular fictions like that of Charles Brockden Brown, Smith must have known that this distinction was, to some degree, a fantasy. In fact, the *Medical Repository* was more formally connected to troubling "creative" genres than its circular's pronouncements would suggest. Following the practices of generations of physicians, each volume centrally featured collections of letters linking the discussions of the New York coterie to medical men around the Atlantic.[72] These letters (like Warren's) may have announced their distance from nonfactual accounts, but their formal features blurred the very lines they sought to draw. Letters in medical texts such as the *Repository* resembled the epistolary origins of the period's novels in which different perspectives were offered without a dominant voice to guide the reader and control his/her reactions. (Susanna Rowson had worried about precisely this feature of epistolary novels when she introduced a heavy-handed narrator in *Charlotte Temple*.) This formal similarity was not merely circumstantial; Atlantic world doctors were already using fictional epistles as a form for medical work. Jean-Jacques Menuret de Chambaud, for example, created the character Mme de *** in 1770 to write letters detailing the virtues of inoculation for smallpox that he hoped would make the medical practice popular.[73] Consistent with the form of many early novels, Menuret uses a veil of fiction to write letters that would improve the lives of his readers. Addressing the Société Royale des Sciences de Montpellier in his title, Menuret directly linked the work of his epistolary fiction to one of the most prestigious scientific institutions in France. Thus the form of the *Medical Repository* was closer to that of Charles Brockden Brown's fictional nightmares than its editors might have hoped.

Communicating Yellow Fever in *Arthur Mervyn*

Newspaperman, poet, and gothic novelist Brown befriended Smith in Philadelphia, and it was through Smith that he became involved with Miller, Mitchill, and the other members of the Friendly Club. To some the friendship between Brown and Smith seemed odd. Friend and fellow Friendly Club member William Dunlap would write, "No two men were ever more sincerely attached to each other . . . yet in many particulars no two men were ever more different."[74] Despite their temperamental and intellectual differences, their relationship flourished within a network of bright and talented young men working in fields that included medicine, literature, politics, law, and theater. Both Brown and Smith were writers, and neither considered literature a hobby. Often referred to as America's first professional novelist, Brown edited magazines and wrote novels, stories, poems, and political pamphlets while Smith published poetry, wrote drama, and produced the first anthology of American poetry. The two coauthored a thirty-five-poem dialogue in the pages of the *Gazette of the United States* and hashed out literary questions together. Interested in the "literary character" of the *Medical Repository*, Smith asked Brown for his feedback as he strove for "medical eloquence."[75] Brown asked the same of Smith. Just two months before his death, Smith wrote in his diary, "Finished what Brown has written of 'Wieland.' Corrected a proof of Repository & one of Wieland."[76] Smith was Brown's roommate at the time of his death.

Though the two were quite close, they took very different positions on the communication of yellow fever. While Smith believed that disseminating reasoned, factual narratives would communicate health, Brown used fever fictions to inoculate his readers from the more dangerous stories circulating in the late 1790s. These models of communication illustrate divergent beliefs about the potential of imagination and literary form for the ends of American health.

Charles Brockden Brown was concerned about the health of the republic, but he did not harbor Smith's fears about the imagination. In fact, Brown believed the possibilities offered by the new republic expanded the strategies available to writers. As Edward Cahill observes, for Brown, fiction trumps more fact-based genres like history "because it portrays not only certainties but also probabilities. Fiction does not disavow the truth but aims to extend its scope."[77] In the preface to his gothic novel *Edgar Huntly*, Brown illustrates this perspective thus: "The flattering reception that has been given, by the public, to Arthur Mervyn, has prompted the writer to solicit a continuance of the same favor."[78] That favor involves indulging him yet again in an exploration of the "new springs of action" and "new motives to curiosity" opened up by the new country. "That the field of investigation, opened to us by our own country, should differ essentially from those which exist in Europe, may be readily conceived," he continues. "It is the purpose of this [imaginative] work to profit by some of these sources; to exhibit a series of adventures, growing out of the condition of our country, and connected with one of the most common and most wonderful diseases or affections of the human frame. One merit the writer may at least claim; that of calling forth the passions and engaging the sympathy of the reader, by means hitherto unemployed by preceding authors."[79] In other words, Brown saw his novel exploring new "field[s] of investigation" opened up by the American landscape that "differ[ed] essentially" from European ones, and understood imaginative works to be intimately involved in that project.

While Smith wrote "The Utopia" and edited the *Medical Repository*, Brown penned some of the most disturbingly dystopian epistolary fiction of the era. Relying on Smith for medical information but lacking his faith in systems, Brown reshaped Smith's ideas about communication and engaged the fraught concept of sympathy that Smith had avoided in "The Utopia"; in so doing, he recast the physiological discussion in gothic terms. Brown watched Smith's climatist system fail him as Smith contracted yellow fever while attempting to nurse an infected fellow physician, Giambattista Scandella—a recent immigrant newly arrived in New York—back to health.[80] After both men died, Brown committed himself to finding alternate means of communicating health.

Not far into Charles Brockden Brown's *Arthur Mervyn, or, Memoirs of the Year 1793* (1799–1800), Brown's eponymous protagonist hears a "rumor" of the 1793 yellow fever epidemic overtaking Philadelphia. "This rumor," Mervyn muses, "was of a nature to absorb and suspend the whole soul." Living in the countryside, at a safe distance from the nation's capital, Mervyn continues, "A certain sublimity is connected with enormous dangers, that imparts to our consternation or our pity, a tincture of the pleasing. This, at least, may be experienced by those who are beyond the verge of peril. My own person was exposed to no hazard. I had leisure to conjure up terrific images, and to personate the witnesses and sufferers of this calamity. This employment was not enjoined upon me by necessity, but was ardently pursued, and must therefore have been recommended by some nameless charm."[81] Perversely, Mervyn enjoys these stories of illness and death. He associates the fever, which would claim nearly 5,000 lives and temporarily dismantle the U.S. government, with the sublime; he unabashedly admits he received the stories with "a tincture of the pleasing" and "some nameless charm."[82] He lets his imagination roam, vicariously inhabiting the bodies of the ill—both visually and emotionally—not out of concern but out of pleasure. Mervyn "conjure[s] up terrific images" and "personate[s] the witnesses and sufferers of this calamity." This morbid role-playing is motivated by his feeling of security; as a citizen removed from the site of danger, Mervyn is perversely delighted.

Mervyn quickly offers another listener. "Others were very differently affected," he explains. "As often as the tale was embellished with new incidents, or enforced by new testimony, the hearer grew pale, his breath was stifled by inquietudes, his blood was chilled and his stomach was bereaved of its usual energies. A temporary indisposition was produced in many. Some were haunted by a melancholy bordering upon madness, and some, in consequence of sleepless panics, for which no cause could be assigned, and for which no opiates could be found, were attacked by lingering or mortal diseases."[83] Drawing on Smith's belief that too much imaginative sympathy could sicken the listener, Mervyn describes narratives that infect. For more sensitive souls, the spreading stories of disease are inextricably entwined with the disease itself. They cause "chilled" blood, stomach sickness, "a temporary indisposition . . . in many," and, for some, madness and death.[84] Brown offered this second scenario repeatedly in his fiction.[85]

Nevertheless, Brown's protagonist identifies with the first scenario and not with Smith's vision of narrative contagion embodied in the second hearer. In *Arthur Mervyn*, sympathy has gone awry; information meant to inform and instruct Mervyn instead prompts a gruesome pantomime of the sick for the enjoyment of the well. In so doing, the novel dramatizes the extremes of what Susan Sontag has described as the split between the "kingdom of the well" and the "kingdom of the sick."[86] It is a gothic vision of communication, but one Brown readily identified in himself after Smith's passing. Chastising himself retrospectively for his own levity in the face of fever, Brown wrote his brother, "My sensations, in this state of things are so different from my sensations last summer . . . I do not wonder that I then remained in the city, but that . . . I could muse and write cheerfully in spite of the groans of the dying and the rumbling of hearses, and in spite of a thousand tokens of indisposition in my own frame."[87]

The split between the two responses to illness narratives is more broadly useful for rethinking the relationship between illness and the imagination. Smith was the optimist. His vision of health figured a United States perfectible through the communication of healthy information around the body politic. He worried about sympathy and the imagination but ultimately imagined them tamable through reason. Brown, who watched Smith die following this philosophy while he was writing the first volume of *Arthur Mervyn*, could not blithely champion a vision of salubrious circulation or the triumph of reason over sympathy.[88] Contrary to what others have suggested, the friends were not perfectly aligned in their views. Especially in the wake of Smith's death, Brown broke with Smith's model and used gothic modes to promote sympathy and a healthy imagination among citizens. The gothic turmoil and narrative uncertainty of *Arthur Mervyn* force readers into a situation of discomfort or, quite literally, *dis*ease in order to foster a new kind of engagement—a mechanism I am calling *narrative inoculation*.[89]

I want to be clear here that in using the term "narrative inoculation" I am not effacing the differences between physical inoculation and the prophylactic work of narrative.[90] Nor am I flattening the differences between, for example, smallpox, a disease that could be combated through inoculation, and yellow fever, a disease that, at the time, could not. By "narrative inoculation" I am naming exposure to a disease through narrative for the purpose of building up the body's immunity to narratives of the disease that Americans believed could sicken readers. As Smith's beliefs suggest and the introduction to this book details, the imagination was understood to bear a much closer relationship to health in the eighteenth century; imaginative acts were thought to be capable of fortifying or imperiling the body of the thinker. Brown's practice was possibly an experiment with Rush's speculation that a little bit of fear might counter the early effects of fever. "Perhaps a moderate degree of fear served to balance the tendency of the system to indirect debility from the excessive stimulus of the contagion, and," Rush had written in 1794, "thereby to preserve it in a state of healthy equilibrium."[91] Fiction offered a perfect vehicle for controlled exposure to illness narratives.

Narrative inoculation was Brown's own imaginative response to the problems of public health, but it was one that partook of a broader cultural engagement in the late eighteenth century with what Katherine Gaudet has called "inoculation logic."[92] The concept of inoculation had, by the late eighteenth century, permeated Atlantic world culture, signifying more than just the practice of introducing a small amount of a particular disease (in the eighteenth century, smallpox) into the body of a healthy person to encourage the body to build up an immunity. The word had its origins in horticultural practice, and, beginning in the fifteenth century, it meant "to set or insert (an 'eye,' bud or scion) in a plant for propagation."[93] By the seventeenth century it meant more generally "to engraft" or "to join or unite by insertion."[94] And in the eighteenth century it had gained its dual medical definitions—meaning both to transmit a small amount of disease to stimulate immunity and to transmit disease more generally.[95] Social progressives also adopted the term in the eighteenth and nineteenth centuries, employing "inoculation logic" to inspire healthier behavior.[96]

Inoculation logic bore a special relationship to the novel in this period. While anti-novelists decried the contagious nature of fiction, more progressive thinkers proposed fiction's value—particularly for inoculating women against bad marriages. Erasmus Darwin promoted fiction's usefulness in helping women choose husbands wisely, citing "a lady of fortune" who believed that had she read novels, she would have "chosen better."[97] Continental European novels in the mid- to late eighteenth century also took part in contemporary inoculation discourse, drawing connections between inoculation and moral training that could be quite literal. Genevan Jean-Jacques Rousseau featured a prominent illustration labeled "L'inoculation de l'amour" in his novel *Julie, ou, La nouvelle Héloïse* (Figure 4).[98] Though wary of the scandalous phrasing, Théodore Tronchin, Paris's most prominent inoculating physician, insisted Rousseau use the language of inoculation to refer both to their love and to the disease that scars the paramours after Julie's lover lies about being inoculated and risks his life to kiss her hand.[99] In another French cautionary tale of the period, *Les Contemporaines*, Rétif de La Bretonne morally instructs his readers through a suitor who secretly inoculates his love interest with the smallpox vaccine to temporarily affect her appearance and cure her of her flirtatious habits.[100] In the United States, Massachusetts-born Judith Sargent Murray (1751–1820) employed this logic in *The Gleaner*, writing her novel to introduce young girls to the ways of the world without exposing them to the fantasies promoted by more dangerous novels.[101]

Brown was quite familiar with this discourse. He referenced Darwin repeatedly and modeled his heroine in *Ormond* on *The Gleaner*'s Constantia,

Figure 4. "L'inoculation de l'amour." Designer Gravelot, Engraver N. Le Mire. Jean-Jacques Rousseau, *Julie, ou, La nouvelle Héloïse, ou, Lettres de deux amans, habitans d'une petite ville au pied des Alpes/recueillies et publieés par J.-J. Rousseau*. Vol. 2. Neufchatel, Paris: Duchesne, 1764. Courtesy of the Special Collections Department, Bryn Mawr College Library.

but he took inoculation logic a step further. Brown used novels as not only a social but also a somatic prophylactic. Through narrative inoculation, Brown exposed healthy readers to narratives of disease and to the emotional and psychological position of the ill. Brown's fiction might make them temporarily sick, but it ultimately inured them to more potent exposure. Because Smith and Brown believed in the physiological effects of communication, narrative inoculation was not only a psychological but also a physiological prophylactic. Narrative inoculation provides a powerful example of the work imaginative writing could perform at the turn of the nineteenth century and expands our understanding of the medical work of fiction.

The Healthy Imagination in *Arthur Mervyn*

When Smith died, Brown wrote despairingly to his brother James, "The die is cast. E.H.S. is dead. O the folly of prediction and the vanity of systems!"[102] Brown was distraught by his loss, but he was also articulating an important distinction between the friends' philosophies. Friend to both, William Dunlap would later quip, "Brown was without system in every thing; Smith did nothing but by rule."[103] Elihu Hubbard Smith built prophylactic projects around the predictable nature of systems; conversely, Brown's dystopian *Arthur Mervyn* communicates health beyond the "vanity of system."

Arthur Mervyn resists easy summary. The novel follows the young Mervyn as he transforms himself from naïve country bumpkin into sophisticated urbanite. After his mother and siblings die and his father remarries, Mervyn leaves home to try his fortunes in Philadelphia. Upon arriving, he finds himself destitute and is forced to work for a nefarious forger, Welbeck. When the criminal reveals himself for what he is, Mervyn leaves the city and discovers a pastoral retreat with the Hadwins, who offer Mervyn a possible surrogate for his lost yeoman inheritance. Nevertheless, the fever compels Mervyn to return to the city during the height of the epidemic in search of his sweetheart's sister's lover. Mervyn appears to contract yellow fever and finds himself on the doorstep of Stevens, the empathetic doctor who records his story. This event prompts the novel's narration. The second volume tests the fine points of Mervyn's story. Upon recovering, Mervyn circulates through the city, apparently trying to right the wrongs of Welbeck, in whose deeds he (unwittingly?) took part. Mervyn also begins his medical training to try to remedy the social and physical ills of yellow fever. He abandons rural life for a career as a physician and the love of Ascha Fielding, the intellectual, cosmopolitan, wealthy partner he now deserves. The novel is divided between the first half (1799), which Stevens narrates, with frequent breaks and embedded narratives, and the second half (1800), in which Mervyn tells his own story. Brown began the first volume before Smith fell ill and completed the second half in the two years after Smith's death.

The preface to *Arthur Mervyn* confidently details the novel's medical potential:

> Amidst the medical and political discussions which are now afloat in the community relative to [the epidemic], the author of these remarks has ventured to methodize his own reflections, and to weave into an humble narrative, such incidents as appeared to him most instructive and remarkable among those which came within the sphere of his own observation. It is every one's duty to profit by all opportunities of inculcating on mankind the lessons of justice and humanity. . . . Men only require to be made acquainted with distress for their compassion and their charity to be awakened. He that depicts, in lively colours, the evils of disease and poverty, performs an eminent service to the sufferers, by calling forth the benevolence in those who are able to afford relief, and he who pourtrays examples of disinterestedness and intrepidity . . . rouses in the spectators, the spirit of salutary emulation.[104]

In this passage Brown articulates a belief about the medical value of his novel, echoing Smith's sentiments in the *Medical Repository* and "The Utopia" about the salubrious value of circulating information. He offers *Arthur Mervyn* as "methodize[d]" reflections that will add to the "medical and political discussions" circulating about the epidemic. Nevertheless, the preface makes claims about the medical work of narrative that (it should be apparent from my opening vignette) stand at odds with the medical work of the novel as a whole. Brown avers that "men only require to be made acquainted with distress for their compassion and their charity to be awakened," but, as Brown admitted in his letter to James, he did not even believe that to be true about himself. Brown ought not, then, to be taken at the preface's word.

In fact, any sure-handed reading that heralds Mervyn's triumphant rise in a world he learns to manage neglects a fundamental, unresolved problem in

Arthur Mervyn: Can Mervyn be trusted? Some readers find Mervyn honest, variously claiming Mervyn as "Brown's American hero," a character imbued with "the indefatigability and creativity with which he attempts to make himself useful to others," and "a new kind of hero: the successful and moral American."[105] Others insist on Mervyn's duplicity, regarding Mervyn sometimes tamely as a "meddlesome, self-righteous bungler who comes close to destroying himself and everyone in his path" and sometimes more dangerously as a "chameleon of convenient virtue" or a "chameleon of convenient vice."[106] Teresa Goddu productively argues for Mervyn's uncertain honesty in terms of well-being: "the critical debate," she writes, "depends on a dichotomy that the novel proposes and then subverts . . . *Arthur Mervyn* collapses the difference between confidence and contagion, making the Enlightenment narrative of good health indistinguishable from the gothic narrative of disease."[107] If we understand this uncertainty in the context of Cathy Davidson's argument that the early U.S. novel "carved out its literary territory in the here-and-now of the contemporary American social and political scene and commented upon and criticized that scene, but left the solution of these problems up to the individual reader," then we can see that the "indeterminacy of the solution" was, as Davidson suggests, "as basic to the form as the incisiveness of its critique."[108] In other words, by refusing to settle the question of the eventual physician Mervyn's veracity, *Arthur Mervyn* forces his readers to assume responsibility for those who suffer.

The novel's inconclusive judgments go beyond the narrative reliability of the novel; they extend to its medical debates. Overtly, *Arthur Mervyn* champions Smith's theory of fever.[109] Mervyn mentally chastises an acquaintance who abandons his sick friend, calling his behavior "as absurd as it was wicked. To imagine this disease to be contagious was the height of folly; to suppose himself secure, merely by not permitting a sick man to remain under his roof, was no less stupid."[110] Furthermore, Mervyn repeatedly describes the physical sensation of the locally derived miasma, "a vapour, infectious and deadly, [that] assailed my senses. It resembled nothing of which I had ever before been sensible . . . I felt as if I had inhaled a poisonous and subtle fluid . . . some fatal influence appeared to seize upon my vitals; and the work of corrosion and decomposition to be busily begun."[111] Mervyn briefly wonders "whether imagination had not some share in producing my sensation" but dismisses the thought: "That I had imbibed this disease was not to be questioned."[112] Nonetheless, we cannot know for sure whether Mervyn has been infected with yellow fever.

Indeed, *Arthur Mervyn* goes further than a merely grammatical troubling of the medical certainty; it also reproduces the problem of knowing that Americans faced during the crisis. Mervyn's tale of how he contracted the fever returns us to the opening description in which Dr. Stevens spies Mervyn's ailing body. To Stevens, "the posture in which he sat, the hour, and the place immediately suggested the idea of one disabled by sickness," which leads Stevens to the "obvious" conclusion "that his disease was pestilential"—even though Stevens admits that his "sight was imperfectly assisted by a far-off lamp."[113] Such imperfections structure the three sentences of Stevens's diagnosis that follow as well; the diagnosis hinges on the verbs "indicate" and "seem."[114] If we fail to believe fully in Mervyn, come to understand that we cannot know him fully, or judge him a consummate liar, then the novel upends proclamations of medical authority. On one hand, then, the novel critiques the theories of Dr. Edward Stevens—the contagionist for whom the narrator is presumably named—insofar as the flawed perceptions of the character Stevens reveal the limitations of empirical epistemologies and undermine medical certainty.[115] On the other hand, Mervyn's observations about the miasmatic airs that surround him cannot be trusted either.

While Mervyn frequently describes pestilential airs, the movement of the narrative traces a model of contagion.[116] (I use the term "contagion" advisedly in this section to refer to the interpersonal transmission of disease. Like my use of the term "contagionist," this use is closer to the contemporary meaning than to the still unsettled word in the late eighteenth century.) While most Philadelphians fled the yellow fever epidemic, Mervyn moves relentlessly toward it. He enters the city at the height of the fever and seeks out the dens of disease. Teresa Goddu identifies Mervyn, "despite his motives," serving as "the agent of disruption and the carrier of diseased discourse" in the second part, if not, I would add, the agent of disease itself.[117] Mervyn repeatedly enters without knocking; he moves uninvited through spaces, trespassing and generally arriving unwelcome and unknown. Doors are never locked when he enters, but Mervyn often has trouble leaving. To excuse the fact that doors often "yielded to [his] hand," Mervyn describes such events as "involuntary" or offers thin explanations such as "it was evident that, at present, it was without inhabitants," "I forgot to knock at the door," "no evil was intended by my negligence," and "this intrusion, when I have explained the reason of it will, I hope, be forgiven."[118] This cycle of trespassing and confinement repeatedly traps Mervyn and the reader in sites of moral corruption implicating Mervyn in scenes of kidnaping, rape, prostitution, and murder.[119] Mervyn may fervently decry the interpersonal transmission of yellow fever, but his body betrays him. The novel experiments with moving its protagonist and reader imaginatively along the course of the disease, and, as if infected themselves with this paradigm, Brown scholars, too, cannot help but use the language of contagion in describing the novel.

Not only does Mervyn replicate the progress of contagious disease, he also consumes the narratives of others much like such diseases consume the bodies of their victims. Others have argued that *Arthur Mervyn* parallels the medical efforts of Smith and other Friendly Club members, reining in pernicious "rumor" through Mervyn's methodical ascendency toward scientific knowledge and narrative authority: "the idea of narrative control as both prophylactic and treatment for disease is most extensively illustrated by Mervyn, who cures himself by gradually becoming the sole narrative voice."[120] It is not, however, clear that this control is healthy; Mervyn may simply be an unhealthy consumer of narrative. He is repeatedly mistaken for characters (Clavering, Lodi, Wallace) whose stories are subsumed by Mervyn and then discarded. Mervyn follows the same pattern in his romantic affairs, falling for and leaving woman after woman (Betty, Clemenza, Eliza). Mervyn feeds on the life stories of others. Like the fever, the narrative progresses not through logical, sequential steps but rather by a series of scenes that become familiar through their repetition and become significant through their similarity and accumulation. Any vision of stability in Mervyn's final narrative control is further undermined by the conclusion's feverish pitch.[121] The movement toward narrative control cannot be unequivocally celebrated as the triumph of Mervyn's medical voice. As Mervyn's voice grows prominent, he also draws the reader ever closer to the kind of infectious excess doctors had identified as a predisposing cause of illness.[122]

Thus *Arthur Mervyn* resists aligning itself with either side of the medical debate. While those who connect Brown with Rush's and Smith's medical theories see his work supporting climatist conclusions, scholars who highlight Brown's transnational concerns emphasize models of contagion.[123] In fact, *Arthur Mervyn* espouses one philosophy and enacts another. As Cristobal Silva similarly observes of Brown's treatment of yellow fever in *Ormond*, Brown's novel "plays both theories off of each other in order to dramatize the interconnectedness of illness and narrative."[124] Instead of deciding that *Arthur Mervyn* is in fact climatist or contagionist, I would like instead to recognize once again the novel's refusal to settle important questions. This refusal is important not only in its insistence on the relationship between illness and narrative but because dwelling in uncertainty produces the feelings of disease in Brown's reader.

The theme, structure, and somatic effect of the narrative on the reader heighten this sense. The reader experiences an augmented awareness of illness through Brown's relentless litany of ailing bodies. While apparently ill in Stevens's house, Mervyn recounts his mother's passing, meditates on his siblings' early consumptive deaths, and reminisces about the dying Clavering. Susan Hadwin, Edward Hadwin, Amos Watson, and Welbeck die, too, though Brown will not reduce this rash of deaths to the epidemic. Mervyn muses on his own imminent mortality to justify his return to fever-stricken Philadelphia: "The seeds of an early and lingering death are sown in my constitution," he decides. "We are a race . . . exposed, in common with the rest of mankind, to innumerable casualties; but if these be shunned, we are unalterably fated to perish by *consumption*."[125] Mervyn stakes out his exceptional susceptibility to illness but also reminds his readers of their own constitutional frailty. Though the novel resists settling on one cause for illness and mortality, ten chapters in the middle find Mervyn in an environment replete with the sense of sickness; "effluvia of a pestilential nature [assail]" both Mervyn and the reader "from every corner."[126] *Arthur Mervyn* locates the reader in the "kingdom of the sick."

That *Arthur Mervyn* augments this sense of disease in the reader through its lack of resolution makes the novel radically distinct from other illness and disease narratives. As a genre, such narratives move us "out of the familiar everyday world" into one in which our comfortable, familiar spaces have been radically altered by the presence of illness, Anne Hunsaker Hawkins argues.[127] These *pathographies*, as she calls them, offer "us cautionary parables of what it would be like if our ordinary life-in-the-world suddenly collapsed. And indeed most of us, at some time or another, have recognized that the apparent orderliness and coherence of our lives is something of an accident, or a gift, or a miracle that renews itself day after day."[128] And yet, paradoxically, she explains, "most of us behave as though this miracle were quite natural—a constant around which we can organize our lives. Thus we plan for the next day, and we go to sleep at night in confidence that the world (and we ourselves) will be the same the following morning. Pathographical narratives offer us a disquieting glimpse of what it is like to live in the absence of order and coherence."[129] Significantly, Hawkins identifies the fictional quality of our perceptions of the world's coherence. We recognize in flashes that our operating assumptions about life are only temporary realities—crafted fictions we have fooled ourselves into believing. Illness and disease enact the inevitable disruption of the "meaning and purpose" we attribute to our lives and fracture the unified narratives we have woven about

ourselves in the world.[130] These stories offer more than chaos and rupture, however, and Hawkins insists on the healing work of narrative. "The task of the
author," Hawkins announces, "is not only to describe this disordering process
but also to restore to reality its lost coherence and to discover, or create, a meaning that can bind it together again."[131] If disease necessarily enacts a rupturing of
reality, its stories collect the pieces. Accounts of illness, then, perform a repara-
tive function, patching or recrafting the jolted individual's perception of the
world such that she and the reader have a paradigm through which to reengage.
Our fantasies of perpetual able-bodiedness are, disease and illness remind us,
fictions, but stories suture the pieces and provide productive fantasies from
which we heal our fractured lives.[132]

Arthur Mervyn performs none of this suturing. The novel's loose ends proliferate and its lack of comfortable resolution demands the reader retain the
perspective of the ill. An unexplained changeling, the improbable intrusion of
the voice of Mervyn's dead sister's seducer, the novel's abrupt change of narrator,
and the repeated but unresolved and unintegrated story of Clavering index just
a few of these moments.[133] In other words, Arthur Mervyn provides what
Hawkins would call "a disquieting glimpse of what it is like to live in the absence
of order and coherence" but declines the pathographical "task of the author" not
only to convey the experience of illness "but also to restore to reality its lost coherence and to discover, or create, a meaning that can bind it together again."

Brown's gothic fiction not only gave readers the sense of what it was like
to live with disease but, Brown believed, could make readers a little sick as
well. James Dawes writes persuasively of the corporeal reactions to Brown's
narrative techniques: "our pupils dilate slightly, we feel a sudden chill as the
down on our arms and legs bristles."[134] Here we might recall Brown's Baxter
of Ormond whose imagination causes more serious somatic effects. Creeping
along a fence at night, Baxter imagines he has been exposed to yellow fever,
falls ill, and dies. Brown writes that Baxter "may be quoted as an example of
the force of imagination."[135] Reading Brown, Dawes concludes, "is not only a
question of how fiction makes us care, but how it makes us sick."[136] In arguing for the capacity of Brown's fiction to enfeeble the reader physically, Dawes
takes seriously an early nineteenth-century reviewer who noted Brown's stories affect "the liveliest sense of danger. . . . If we do not return to [his nov-
els], it is to avoid suffering."[137] Dawes interprets this sickening as an aesthetic
strategy, hoping to understand why we read gothic fiction, but his observation can and should be extended to Brown's medical and political ends. If, as
another contemporary reviewer contends, readers find themselves "sometimes

oppressed and sickened" by Brown's fever tales, we should understand these reactions in the context of Smith and Brown's belief that stories could kill.[138]

Narrative Inoculation

If stories could kill, it seems strange if not perverse that Brown would pursue novel writing in the wake of Smith's tragic death. This pantomime of the sick appears at odds with Brown's insistence in the preface and elsewhere that he writes for moral, medical, and political good.[139] Readings that seek to parse Brown's positive medical message from dangerous stories lean on Brown's aversion to "rumor." It is easy to dismiss some of Brown's more disturbing representations if the reader places interpretive emphasis on this word. While Mervyn is in the countryside, "rumor" of the fever arrives from Philadelphia that prompts him and the rural locals to perform distasteful mockery or fall ill from inappropriate empathy. Readings that privilege the distinction between rumor and fact easily dispense with Mervyn's musings as a Smith-inspired illustration of the need for true stories. But these readings forget that *Arthur Mervyn* is a novel, not a medical repository, that Brown felt himself compelled by such stories, and that a rumor is simply a compelling fiction. As *Arthur Mervyn* repeatedly illustrates, the line between fact and fiction was very difficult to draw.

Brown's despair about the "vanity of systems" suggests that he was not convinced that a traditional model could provide a recipe for health. Smith's unfinished and unpublished "The Utopia" provided a stark reminder of the fallacy of such idealistic thinking. As a medical project, *Arthur Mervyn* diverges from the *Medical Repository* and "The Utopia." Brown's novel does more than circulate information about the fever; it uses fiction to explore the more complicated nuances of the relationship between the imagination and medicine. Brown did not merely expose the pernicious effects of illness narratives but experimented with using those imaginative acts to inoculate his readers, directing fever fictions toward the ends of public health. Though publishing in a culture that inherently distrusted novels, Brown understood that he could not blithely privilege fact.[140] Acknowledging the fine, often indiscernible, line between fact and fiction, *Arthur Mervyn* uses narrative uncertainty to place the reader in the insecure position of not knowing, throwing the ordinary assumptions of able-bodied readers into question and placing his readers in the epistemic position of the ill.

Arthur Mervyn promotes health not by disseminating medical truths, as Smith would have liked, but by engaging in a different kind of imaginative experiment. He circulates fever fictions to promote empathy (a form of sympathy, as Brown would have understood it), exposing readers to tales of disease and connecting Brown's readers to those who suffer; Brown stimulates readers' imaginations in a controlled setting to fortify them against subsequent, less regulated encounters. Brown engages the sympathies Smith feared. He depicts illness as the norm, crafts an account in which illness is both pervasive and diffuse, uses Mervyn's movement in the novel to replicate contagion theories of disease drawing the reader who elects to follow him into the path of infection, and, finally, never resolves the complexities he weaves into the novel's plot, leaving his readers cognitively, emotionally, and mildly physically ill through the final page. *Arthur Mervyn* demands that readers spend five hundred pages inhabiting the "kingdom of the sick" so that they might emerge better caretakers and, thus, better republican citizens. In this manner, the novel enacts a kind of narrative inoculation: it intimately exposes readers to diseased states, better fortifying them for subsequent yellow fever outbreaks and impelling them to take social action to ease the discomfort they feel when finishing the novel.

Brown explained this prophylactic work to his friend the politician and writer Margaret Bayard (1778–1844). Reading *Wieland*, Bayard had found herself "sick from [the] effects" of Brown's fiction, which "almost metamoph[ize]s the reader into the actor, & fills him with the same terrors, infects his understanding." *Arthur Mervyn* likewise gave her nightmares, filling her dreams "with nothing else but scenes of death," and she refused to read more of his affecting fiction. In a letter to her then fiancé Samuel Harrison Smith in the spring of 1800, she relayed Brown's reaction to her refusal: he "condemned the weakness of my mind, & advised me to strengthen it by immuring it to such scenes and & images."[141]

Brown would have been quite familiar with the prophylactic value of inoculation. Not only had the technique been used for almost a century to prevent smallpox in the West, but the very first medical essay in the *Medical Repository* was by Smith on inoculation.[142] While Smith remained wary of the practice's potential to bring on stiffness, inflammation, and fever, he nonetheless understood the practical compromises physicians needed to make to ensure health and administered the prophylactic himself. Imperfect, inoculation was still a crucial measure for a diseased environment.

Significantly, Brown's narrative inoculation manages to avoid reproducing in its readers either of the problematic reactions to illness narratives mapped by

Mervyn. *Arthur Mervyn* neither allows for a perverse pleasure nor imperils its readers through contagious and pestilential exposure. In fact, the novel provides a venue to harness dangerous rumor. The gothic novel compels reading through mystery, suspense, and the desire for restored order, but, unlike rumor, it contains these elements in the pages of a book the reader can always put down. *Arthur Mervyn* might make a reader feel or even fall a little ill, but it does so to strengthen. The novel's fever fictions provide the necessary dose of exposure to acquaint people with the circumstances of the disease and allow them to feel its discomfort. Fortified by experience and some measure of exposure, Brown's inoculated readers may go forth better socially, morally, and medically equipped to handle the repeated outbreaks Brown and his readers had come to expect.[143]

When William Dunlap insisted on the differences between Smith and Brown, he suggested that their divergences were necessary complements. Smith was the doctor, Brown the writer; Smith was systematic, Brown without system. "They were both," Dunlap writes, "recorders of the passing events of their lives, their studies, their thoughts, and their actions; but in this as in other things Brown was fitful and irregular, while Smith was uniform, diligent and orderly."[144] But these differences unravel at the slightest pull. Brown and Smith were opposites whose compatible projects relied on each other. Smith grappled with the vagaries of sympathy, circulation, communication, and cosmopolitan life, though he fantasized about escaping them. And Brown could delve deeper into gothic horrors to inure citizens because Smith (and Mitchill and Miller after him) salubriously circulated corrective medical information. They were opposite but complementary thinkers who, through various imaginative acts, took different tacks toward the same end. Thus when Smith addressed the *Medical Repository* "not to physicians only, but to men of observation, and to the learned, throughout the United States," he meant men like Brown. And when Brown's faith in straightforward medical solutions was shaken in the wake of Smith's death, he did not abandon the project but experimented with innovative imaginative techniques to circulate material about health and to promote it as Smith had so often urged "men of observation" to do.

The Legacies of the Yellow Fever Crisis

The disease-based epistemic crisis initiated by yellow fever's return in the 1790s did not quickly subside. Rather, like the structural crisis initiated by the revolution, its aftershocks were felt well into the nineteenth century. A notable

feature of yellow fever's crisis is the long legacy of self- and imaginative experimentation as ways of knowing yellow fever and, more pressingly, its methods of communication. Doctors and writers continued to use their own minds
and bodies to know yellow fever at least until 1900, when a self-experiment
proved the disease was carried and transmitted by mosquitoes.[145]

Doctors like Stubbins Ffirth, who wrote his 1804 medical thesis on the
question of yellow fever communication, did not think it ethical to infect
others with the disease in their own pursuit of knowledge, nor did Ffirth wish
to leave the discovery to the untrained mind or senses. For this reason, he experimented on himself to determine whether the infamous "black vomit"
communicated the fever. Ffirth sought to prove yellow fever's endemic nature,
to advance treatment, and to prevent fear, since "an imagined exposure to contagion producing a fright, acts as an exciting cause, by which means hundreds
have taken the disease and died."[146] Seeking rigor in his self-experimentation,
Ffirth inhaled vomit, put it in his eye, ate it, drank it, and repeatedly placed
the vomit of infected individuals into open incisions around his body.[147]
"Having satisfied myself that the black vomit could not communicate the
disease," he writes, "I thought of desisting from any further experiments,"
but he continued to self-experiment with the black vomit through multiple
outbreaks for the sake of certainty.[148] He then repeated the experiments with
blood, sweat, saliva, bile, and urine from infected individuals to confirm
that yellow fever could not be caught directly from another person. Thus
Ffirth proved to his own mind that yellow fever was not contagious and
thanked his professors at the conclusion of his medical dissertation for "not
forc[ing him] to believe, or quietly to acquiesce," but for leaving him "at liberty to examine for himself and direct his judgment, according as facts are
presented to him . . . allow[ing him] to reason for himself, and to publish the
results of his observations and reflections, to form a theory therefrom, and to
give it to the world."[149]

Doctors and writers continued to privilege their minds and imaginations
as tools for knowing yellow fever throughout the nineteenth century. In the
immediate aftermath of the devastating 1853 yellow fever epidemic in New
Orleans, for example, Baron Ludwig von Reizenstein published *The Mysteries
of New Orleans*, a novel that offered a new theory of yellow fever. In the
imaginary of this health care worker, amateur entomologist, and writer, the
source of the epidemic is a plant named *Mantis religiosa* (after the Latin name
for an insect, the praying mantis).[150] Over hundreds of pages, Reizenstein weaves
a complicated plot in which yellow fever flows from the seeds of *Mantis reli-*

giosa down the Red River into New Orleans as penance for the city's participation in racial slavery. "On the day of liberation," the novel's self-proclaimed
messiah, Hiram, prophesies, "when the chains fall to the ground everywhere
with a great jangling, the *Mantis religiosa* will disappear forever, and New Orleans will be free from that plague of fever that now falls on the town with
an intensity never known before."[151] At the hidden site of *Mantis religiosa*'s
production, Hiram brings a German immigrant, Emil, and a black prosti-
tute, Lucy, to give birth to a child named Toussaint L'Ouverture, and the final
scene finds them leaving for the West Indies on a ship also named *Toussaint
L'Ouverture* with the suggestion that Toussaint will return in eighteen years
to wreak bloody vengeance for New Orleans's participation in slavery. Here
the narrative connects its epidemiology to beliefs originating in the 1790s that
yellow fever had returned on vessels carrying the goods and bodies of the Atlantic market and to antislavery understandings of yellow fever offered by
Reizenstein's contemporaries like William Wells Brown in *Clotel* (1853).[152]

Reizenstein's imaginative experimentation with *Mantis religiosa* is less fantastical than it may seem. First, the yellow fever outbreaks in the United
States *were* a result of the Atlantic slave trade, the fever having made its way
on tightly packed slavers from Africa and traveling to the United States via
the Caribbean.[153] Second, Reizenstein published his *Mantis religiosa* theory
just a decade after men like Edgar Allan Poe and John Kearsley Mitchell first
theorized the fungal origins of fevers, speculating that the more general category of fever was caused by fungus, another not quite plant, not quite animal entity. Like the work of other antebellum theorists, Reizenstein undertakes
an imaginative experiment to explore medical mechanisms largely hidden from
empirical observation.[154]

Yellow fever's mosquito etiology was proved at long last through the self-
experiments of Walter Reed's collaborators in Cuba in 1900. Cuban doctor
Carlos Finlay had hypothesized the etiology of yellow fever in 1881 but could
not prove it. Nineteen years later, eleven individuals in the Reed Commission,
as it was called, agreed to let yellow fever–carrying mosquitoes bite them to
prove that the insects were the long-sought communicators of the disease.
Once more, experimenters performed trials on themselves as an ethical and
reliable way to discern the cause of yellow fever, even though it meant risking
their lives—and even dying—in the pursuit of scientific knowledge.[155]

Perhaps counterintuitively, it was shortly after this moment, after Louis
Pasteur's advancement of germ theory and after a constellation of experiments

that demonstrated diseases like yellow fever were in fact transmitted by human carriers (if sometimes indirectly), that doctors largely abandoned the word "contagion" in favor of the language of communication. While the language of "contagion" continues to be popular for describing the transmission of disease and culture today, rising medical professionals as early as 1920 codified "communicable disease" as the term of choice for diseases that could be interpersonally transmitted.[156] Current medical dictionaries disparage "contagion" as a "term originated long before [the] development of modern ideas . . . and has since lost much of its significance, being included under the more inclusive term *communicable disease.*"[157] Perhaps such a shift makes sense insofar as the move away from "contagion" distances post-Pasteurian physicians from the messy and contested history of medical epistemology ("some a-writing, some a-shooting") and moves them toward more technical professional language. And yet the professional turn to "communicable disease" brings to the fore a concept that had long resided at the center of those same disputes. Ironically, then, the attempt to discard a historically fraught term by labeling it antiquated only professionally cemented the very sedimented history of disease communication proponents of the new terminology were working to disavow, invoking the very long legacy of debates about disease communication.

The question of yellow fever's communication in particular remained a pressing one over the century following the 1790s epidemics, even if it became a more southern one as the decades passed. The disease continued to serve as a lightning rod for physiological, social, and political health concerns at least through the time of the Reed Commission. Nor was it the only communicable disease to do so. Certainly the terrors of diseases like typhus, typhoid fever, and tuberculosis continued to loom large in the American consciousness, but no disease more spectacularly troubled prevailing medical epistemologies than cholera; as with yellow fever, the disease-based epistemic crisis initiated by the arrival of cholera prompted questions that profoundly shaped the way Americans knew health for decades to come.

CHAPTER 3

CHOLERA

CHOL'ERA and CHOL'ERA-MOR'BUS (*Path.*) *Chohrrha'gia, Fellif'lua pas'-sio, Hol'era,* χολερα, from χολή' bile, and ῥέω, "I flow." According to others, from χολαδες, "intestines." . . . In India the *spasmod'ic chol'era.* (F.) *Mort de Chien,* is frightful in the rapidity of its progress. . . . In temperate climates, it is not usually a disease of much consequence.
　　—Robley Dunglison and John Green, *New Dictionary* (1833)

CHOLERA and CHOL'ERA-MORBUS, *Chol'era-morbus, Cholera nostras* seu *vulga'ris, Sporad'ic Chol'era, Cholerrha'gia, Pas'sio choler'ica, Fellif'lue passio, Hol'era, Bilis flux'io,* (F.), *Choladrée lymphatique, Hydrocholadrée, Choléra-morbus sporadique, Ch. Européen, Trousse-galant,* from χολή "bile," and ῥέω, "I flow." According to others, from χολαδες, "intestines," or from χολερα "the gutter of a house to carry off the rain." . . . The disease is most common in hot climates,—and in temperate climates, during summer. *Spasmod'ic, Asiati'ic, Malig'nant, In'dian, Epidem'ic, Pestilen'tial, Convulsive Nervous, Eastern,* or *Orient'al Cholera, Asphyx'ia pestilen'ta, Pestilen'tial asphyx'ia, Chol'eric Pest'ilence, Cholera orienta'lis* seu *In'dica* seu *Epidem'ica* seu *Asphyx'ia, Typhus Bengalen'sis, Chol'ero-typhus, Ganglioni'tis peripher'glii'tis, Cholerrhoe'a lymphat'ica, Psorenter'ia, Achol'ia, Typhoid Fever of India, Hyperanthrx'is, Enterop'yra Asiat'ica, Trisplanch'nia, Trisplanchni'tis, Hoemataporrho'sis, Hoematorrho'sis, Morbous ory'zeus, Rice disease* . . . *Mort de Chien,* is frightful in the rapidity

of its progress, the patient sometimes dying in a few hours from
first onset. In temperate climates, common cholera is not usually a
disease of most consequence.

> —Robley Dunglison, *Medical Lexicon* (1860)

"During the dread reign of the Cholera in New York," Edgar Allan Poe begins his short story "The Sphinx," "I had accepted the invitation of a relative
to spend a fortnight with him in the retirement of his *cottage orné* on the banks
of the Hudson . . . we should have passed the time pleasantly enough, but for
the fearful intelligence which reached us every morning from the populous
city."[1] Set during the 1832 cholera outbreak, the terror Poe's narrator describes
would have been both familiar and visceral for his readers. Cholera had appeared in North America for the first time ever on June 6, 1832. It came from
Ireland on a boat called *The Carrick* and quickly moved through Quebec and
Montreal down the East Coast. Even though Americans had been steadily receiving reports of cholera's movement since 1830, its appearance surprised
many who were convinced that cholera would never arrive because they believed it was naturally endemic to India and could not cross the Atlantic. In
this period before John Snow discovered cholera was waterborne and before
germ theory, how cholera arrived and how it claimed its victims was anyone's—
and everyone's—guess. But when it did, the consequences were devastating.
An otherwise healthy individual might have stomach pains in the morning,
suffer vomit and diarrhea by noon, turn blue at three, and be dead by
nightfall.[2]

This spectacular scourge killed half the people it infected, and doctors'
almost complete inability to do anything about cholera dealt a profound blow
to the rapid professionalization of American medicine in the 1820s. The medical community's inability to manage, treat, or even agree upon the nature of
the horrifying disease they had been tracking for almost two years wreaked
havoc on the medical profession in the United States. In the twelve years following cholera's 1832 arrival, twelve of thirteen states repealed their medical
licensing laws.[3] Not only did this global cholera pandemic, which spanned
twenty years (1829–49) worldwide, spur a number of changes to systems of
knowledge production in American medicine, but it ushered in a new era in
which alternative practices—Thomsonian herbalism, domestic medicine, and
an array of medical quackery—vied for respectability alongside traditional
medicine. The ineffectiveness of traditional physicians encouraged many an-

tebellum Americans to advocate for putatively democratized systems of medicine.[4] (In spite of all this, the truly radical or democratic spirit of these very visible shifts is debatable, as many alternative practices still relied on traditional physicians to gird their claims.)[5] With the limitations of a narrowly understood medicine made manifest, ways of medical knowing proliferated.

Poe's story investigates the central epistemological crisis prompted by cholera—namely the problem of how to understand medical geography in the wake of the deadly pandemic. Having fled the city, Poe's protagonist nonetheless registers the effect of stories that reach him: "we learned to expect daily the loss of some friend. At length we *trembled* at the approach of every messenger. The very air . . . seemed to us redolent with death. That *palsying thought*, indeed, took entire possession of my soul. I could neither speak, think, nor dream of any thing else."[6] The very threat of cholera's *communication*—in all senses of the word—imperils Poe's protagonist.

Uncertain of his own safety in the Hudson Valley and agitated by cholera stories, the narrator grows certain he will soon die. Lost in "the gloom and desolation of the neighboring city," the narrator suddenly spies a harbinger of his own death. This "living monster of hideous conformation . . . [was] far larger than any ship of the line in existence. . . . The mouth of the animal was situated at the extremity of a proboscis some sixty or seventy feet in length."[7] Poe's narrator takes this enormous creature with a skull on its back to be a sure sign of his impending death. That is until his more rational friend calmly demonstrates the narrator's sensory misperception. It so happens the protagonist has mistaken a death's-head moth for a seventy-foot monster. In revealing the protagonist's error to be one of ocular perception Poe unsettles the notion that empirical inquiry produces useful and healthy knowledge about cholera. The friend cannot see the moth and turns to a "school boy account" to quell the narrator's fears.[8] The friend thus appeals to the narrator's mind, not to his faulty observation, to dispel the dangerous illusions of the senses—just as Poe turns to a short story, and away from objective observation, to teach his readers how best to know proximal threats to their health through fiction.[9]

The problem at the center of "The Sphinx" is one of geography. The narrator cannot discern if he is vulnerable to the cholera pandemic or if he has escaped. Is the countryside safer than the city? How can he know? The moth, too, presents a more proximate geographical problem: misperceiving the creature at a distance, he is certain of its destructive power, but one-sixteenth of an inch from his eye, the narrator can be assured of his safety. More ominously for the reader, however, the death's-head's natural habitats are in Europe and western Asia—precisely the spaces across which cholera had traveled—and, thus, in some sense, its correct identification renders the threat more real.

"The Sphinx" provides a window onto the disease-based epistemic crisis prompted by cholera's arrival in the United States. Though earlier epidemics had disrupted corporeal and political ideologies, the cholera pandemic revealed just how much the transnational movement of microbes (though Jacksonian Americans would not have understood it as such) could disrupt epistemic structures. As medical theories failed spectacularly in the face of cholera, the resulting crisis pushed geography into the center of discussions about medical theory.[10] In response to the new geographies cholera traced, physicians and writers around the globe crafted maps and texts that imagined the porousness, boundedness, and circulation—or lack thereof—of particular neighborhoods, national seaboards, continents, and the globe itself. It was these terrors of cholera's unpredictable movement that work like Poe's examined.

In the wake of massive and spectacular deaths, disruptions to medical theory, and the dismantling of medical authority, antebellum Americans experimented with new and radical imaginings of U.S. and global geography. These new visions responded to current events—the movement of ideas, print, bodies, and microbes—as Americans worked to understand the unexpected movement of a quick and merciless pandemic. Mapping was one important tool for knowing and imagining cholera, but it could not answer some of the most basic and pressing questions cholera posed. Doctors and writers including Edgar Allan Poe, John Kearsley Mitchell, Harriet Beecher Stowe, and Martin Robison Delany turned to literary forms to make sense of cholera's new radical geography. In the cases of Poe and Mitchell, this imaginative experimentation produced a new theory of medical geography, while in the cases of Stowe and Delany, cholera's new landscapes were used to radically reimagine the American body politic.

Mapping Cholera

A dramatic reframing of the landscape was a central effect of cholera, and mapping offered an early strategy for knowing this new medical geography. Physicians and laypeople alike turned to maps to trace cholera's movement. In Paris and England, reports circulated of people tracing cholera's path on maps at home.[11] Thanks to the cutting-edge technology of lithography, maps could now be produced much more cheaply and in far greater quantities and so the practice of medical mapping proliferated.[12] These maps responded aggressively to an issue at the heart of the epistemic crisis caused by cholera: how to understand the geography of health. The burgeoning practice of medical cartography promised new answers to pressing questions such as what made one place healthy and another diseased, whether some regions were healthier than others, how contagion traveled, and whether diseases were contagious at all. These geographical renderings were not objective accounts of cholera's history but, rather, they offered arguments for cholera's climatist or contagionist etiology.[13]

Medical cartography emerged around the Atlantic as a way of knowing and containing the threat. While the prehistory of epidemiology has a longer and more storied past, the practice of mapping disease was not very old in 1832, having begun only in the 1790s.[14] The oldest extant example of medical cartography is Valentine Seaman's map of yellow fever in New York, which he published in the 1798 volume of the *Medical Repository*, but this method of knowing disease did not gain popularity until the 1832 cholera outbreak, largely thanks to the advent of lithography in the intervening years.[15]

One of the first American maps to make use of this new technology to track cholera appeared in Boston in March 1832.[16] A. Sidney Doane, a Boston-born physician, had just returned from Paris, where the disease raged, and was eager to publish a volume to quell what he regarded as newspaper-spawned fears about cholera's imminent arrival. In January of that year, for example, the *National Daily Intelligencer* ran multiple columns on "Pestilential Cholera in Asia and Europe" that tabulated the tens of thousands killed by recent cholera outbreaks in eastern European and Asian cities and "*two and a half millions of people*" yearly in India—numbers the article urged readers to "consider . . . a minimum far below the reality."[17] Despite the numerous calculations in the article, its author confesses a very incomplete knowledge of "this sweeping destroyer" as he traces it traveling with great ease over vast and diverse landmasses, leaving readers with the poignant questions, "Will it reach America? Or will the Atlantic ocean place a bound to its Western invasion?"[18] Doane was impatient to produce his translation of the exciting work on cholera by French doctor Henri Scoutteten (1799–1871) to allay such fears. Instead, Doane offers a "consoling reflection" that the "facts constantly accumulating only confirm, that the Cholera Morbus will not extend to us."[19] The central feature of the volume was a cholera map the Boston firm Carter and Hendee published of "Chart of the Progress of the Cholera-Morbus, 1831" (Figure 5).

The comprehensive map appears to have been drawn at the direction of Doane.[20] This unorthodox map focuses on the Indian subcontinent with

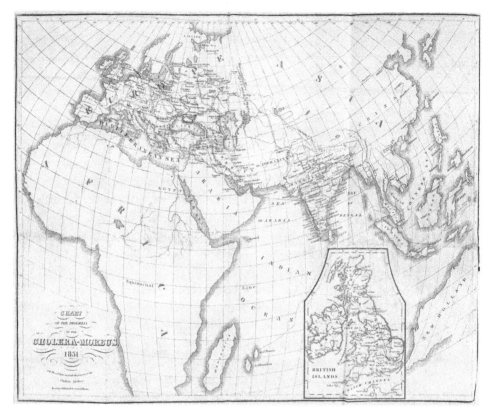

Figure 5. A. Sidney Doane's cholera map, which appeared before the title page
of his translation of Scouttenten's *A Medical and Topographical History of the
Cholera Morbus* (Boston, 1832). Courtesy of the American Antiquarian Society.

borders stretching from Timor and Borneo to the west coast of Africa. Still,
Asia and Europe press up against the frame, suggesting cholera will not traverse either ocean. Boston's notable absence visually argues that cholera could
not breach the ocean. Advocating for cholera's generally endemic nature to
the Indian subcontinent and weakness outside of it, Doane emphasized that it
could not reach the United States. He hoped Americans would, thus, read his
book "with pleasure."[21]

Not three months later, cholera crossed the Atlantic. Two weeks after its
arrival in Canada, Bostonians read that "the dreadful scourge of India" had
"made a tremendous leap across the widest ocean" and was entering "the heart

of our continent."[22] Taking its report from a Quebec lodger who had brought news of the scourge to the United States, the article continues, "He witnessed its first symptoms upon *five* emigrants standing upon the wharf, and before they could be conveyed to the hospital, *two* of them died. A servant woman living in the house where he boarded, was seized with the disease, and died within *three hours*; and a crockery merchant of his acquaintance living in the upper town, was carried off within *six hours!* Three persons were attacked on board the steamboat in which he came passenger to Montreal, and before they reached the next landing, one of them . . . was a corpse—the other two could not have survived."[23] Over and over, reports provided excruciating details not only about the course of the disease but about its rapidly changing geography as Americans watched cholera come to them and hoped until the last moment that it would not.

In the wake of such reports, Americans needed new geographic imaginaries. Amariah Brigham (1798–1849), then a physician practicing in western Massachusetts, was one of the first to take up the challenge, crafting a map in August of that year that reflected the geographical changes in recent months (Figure 6). Brigham's map resembles Doane's, with the familiar hand-drawn red lines tracing cholera's route and also eliminating the Atlantic, but to very different effect. Whereas the tight frame of Doane's map reassures readers, suggesting cholera's containment, Brigham's map presses North America against Europe, eliminating the Atlantic as a barrier. Brigham's defamiliarizing geography effectively renders longitude and latitude moot. Dublin, for example, appears equidistant between Paris and Boston and southern Florida aligns roughly with the Cape of Good Hope. Brigham marks the distortions of his map with a dividing line, but the red-hued course of the disease crosses easily from lower New Brunswick through the Arctic Circle down the St. Lawrence, highlighting Brigham's spectacular geography.

In light of the ever-accumulating reports detailing cholera's steady march across North America, it is difficult to imagine that anyone denied that cholera was new and very contagious. Nevertheless, many laypeople and physicians strongly opposed such talk.[24] An Albany doctor, for example, proclaimed this epidemic merely a more extreme version of the broad category of "cholera morbus," which named a variety of diseases including diarrhea and dysentery. The Asiatic cholera, he wrote, was to "cholera morbus" as "influenza to a common cold."[25] Likewise, the southern doctor-novelist William Arthur Caruthers, who treated New Yorkers in 1832, offered a similar theory in his novel *The Kentuckian in New-York* (1834). While Caruthers's protagonist Victor Chevillere

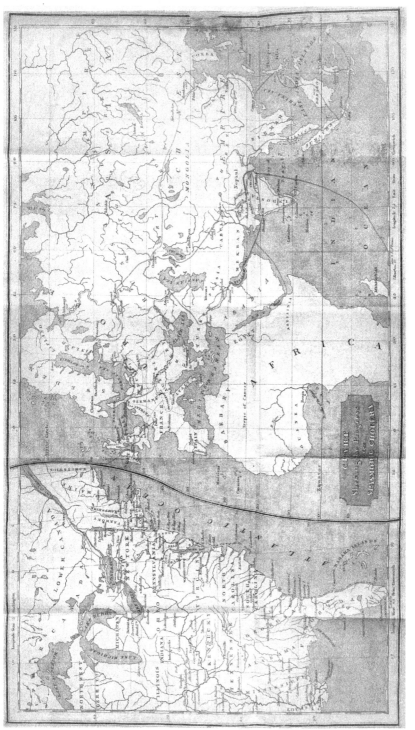

Figure 6. Amariah Brigham's "Chart Showing the Progress of the Spasmodic Cholera," which appeared before the title page of his *Treatise on Epidemic Cholera* (Hartford, 1832). Courtesy of the New York Academy of Medicine.

recognizes the pandemic as "the pestilence of the East," Caruthers's frequent comparisons of its appearance in New York with the "ague" and "fever" suffered by Victor's confidante Beverly Randolph in South Carolina suggest the cholera in New York was simply a fiercer iteration of known fevers exacerbated by the "far more filthy, degraded, and wretched" conditions of northern city life.[26] These physicians remained committed to a climatist model that had long linked epidemics to miasma—or "bad air"—exhaled from the ground.

Like the contagionists, climatists also used cartography to argue for their perspective—in this case, that the 1832 outbreaks were endemic, miasmatic exhalations exacerbated by the filth accumulating largely in urban areas. Leading Philadelphia cartographer Henry Schneck Tanner (1786–1858), for example, adamantly decried arguments for the circulation of the disease suggested by Doane's and Brigham's maps and printed his own in protest. In the October 1832 advertisement for his *Geographical and Statistical Account of the Epidemic Cholera* (1832), Tanner accused prior medical cartography of shoddy work. "Among the almost infinite variety of publications on the Epidemic Cholera," Tanner wrote from Philadelphia, "there is none, I believe, which gives any satisfactory account of the geographical progress, and statistical details, of the subject."[27] Above all, Tanner wished to "[avoid] that common and absurd mode of delineating, by definite lines, *the exact route of the pestilence, from place to place!!*"[28] Tanner almost certainly meant maps like Doane's and Brigham's, and used thirty-five pages of statistical charts to ground cholera in specific locales.[29]

Tanner had committed his livelihood to celebrating circulation through the nation; a cartographer of regional and national transit, Tanner published a cholera map that refused the argument that these very routes were the same ones that transported cholera. His cholera map argued for the disease's local origins through shaded areas that suggested its geographically restricted nature (Figure 7). Though an "explanation" in miniscule print indicates that the colored blocks actually mark cholera's temporal progression—where green shows "Cholera, previous to 1830," yellow "those in 1830," blue "1831," and red "1832"—the visual effect of Tanner's colored regions supports a reading of the four colors as discrete events. Tanner diminished the size of the epidemic using the conventional Mercator projection, which also gave his vision authority through a cartographical standard used to map the globe since the seventeenth century. Furthermore, Tanner countered the clamorous daily news about the pandemic's progress by minimizing the affected regions. He extended the

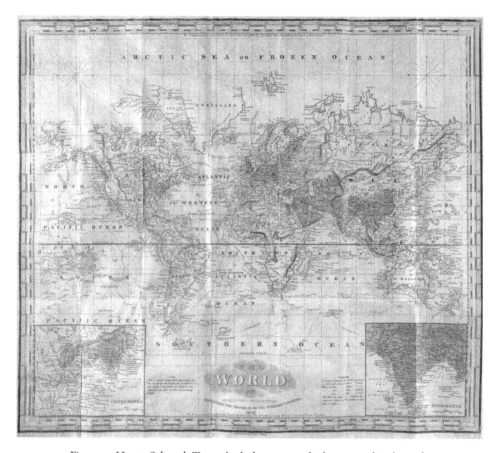

Figure 7. Henry Schneck Tanner's cholera map, which appeared in his volume *A Geographical and Statistical Account of the Epidemic Cholera* (Philadelphia, 1832). Courtesy of the New York Academy of Medicine.

oceanic space on the map by about a third with the map title and geographical designations. Likely already at work on the book he would title *The American Traveller* (1834), Tanner used his skill and fame to argue against the movement of America's newest traveler, the Asiatic cholera.

This climatist argument was also visible on a local scale, through city maps that detailed cholera outbreaks. Physician David Meredith Reese, who a few years later would be responsible for quarantining cholera in New York, nonetheless drew a map of the 1832 New York epidemic that argued for cholera's local origins (Figure 8). (Reese's city map was just one such map. In the 1830s,

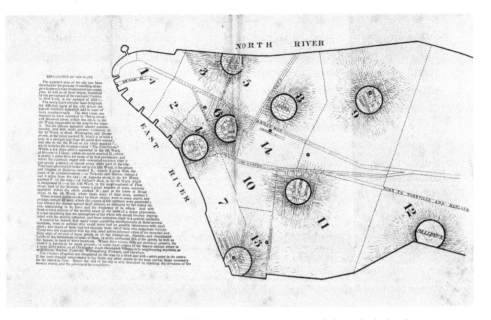

Figure 8. A political map of lower Manhattan reimagined through cholera by
David Meredith Reese in *A Plain and Practical Treatise on the Epidemic Cholera*
(New York, 1833). Courtesy of the American Antiquarian Society.

maps of urban outbreaks would also be produced in cities like Exeter, Leeds,
and Hamburg.) Reese's urban imaginary fascinatingly refigures the geography of lower Manhattan in terms of the outbreak. It argues for cholera's local
containment to the dirty and poor parts of the city, visually bound by heavy
black circles. Picturing only the streets of Manhattan Reese understands to
be affected, his map argues that residents of other streets ought not worry.
Most originally, Reese emphasizes the distinction between healthy and unhealthy regions with a visual depiction of the miasmatic airs emanating from
their points of origin. Miasma close to the water travels further, according to
this logic, than that contained by land. With the epidemic thus delimited,
Reese suggests that smart New Yorkers have nothing to fear. That Reese layered
his visual argument onto a district map invited New Yorkers also to understand
the disease in political terms.

A decade and a half later, popular novelist Charles E. Averill would develop the logic of maps like Reese's in *The Cholera-Fiend, or, The Plague Spreaders of New York* (1850). Fictionalizing the 1849 New York epidemic, the novel
depicts characters plotting to manufacture a cholera outbreak for their own

gain. Averill's central figures use a city map to chart the graveyards whose
coffins they will disinter to spread fever around the city. In a nightmarish
inversion of the cartographical impulse to contain the pandemic in New York,
Averill's antagonists open the graves of New Yorkers who fell prey to the disease to allow miasmatic air to infect the population, lining the pockets and
solving the problems of a corrupt physician and minister. For the reader, their
plot is a terrifying partial success, and though the misanthropes ultimately suc-
cumb to their own greed, losing their lives at the site of infection, the novel
refigures mapping technology not to contain cholera's geographic course but
to propagate it.

Maps were a powerful way of knowing medical geography, but the problem of medical geography prompted by the movement of cholera's microbes
nonetheless defied cartography. The maps themselves suggest their own epistemological limitations. They were simultaneously current, comprehensive, and
necessarily obsolete. Doane's title, "Chart of the Progress of Cholera-Morbus,
1831," exemplifies this, covering the chronology of Scoutteten's text but not that
of cholera's movement as depicted in the map. The map's vast perspective,
encompassing both Europe and Asia, likewise suggests a comprehensiveness
and finality that was belied continuously by emerging information up to and
beyond the moment of its printing. Doane also featured an inset of the British
Isles he thought would be particularly interesting to his Boston readers. It
featured four outbreaks beyond the scope of Scoutteten's text—Sunderland
(November 1831), Edinburgh (January 1832), London (February 12, 1832), and
Dublin (March 1832). Yet more information became available between the
time that the map was printed and the time it was circulated. As extant copies
show, the map's hand-colored lines systematically exceed the spaces indicated
for them with more current information than was available at the time of the
map's printing. These red lines traverse the British Isles, though no dotted lines
precede them, and red lines from London and Edinburgh converge on an undated Glasgow outbreak (Figure 9).[30] Brigham encountered a similar trouble.
By the time Brigham drew his map he knew cholera had reached as far west
as Detroit and as far south as Edenton, North Carolina, but his uncertainty is
registered by the series of dateless locations in the United States. In August
1832 it seems the disease was moving too quickly to know.[31]

The epistemological failures of these maps stemmed from both their pre-
tense of comprehensiveness and the seemingly irreconcilable contradictions
of the disease itself. Even in Europe, information would have taken days if
not months to travel, and U.S. mapmakers received information about the dis-

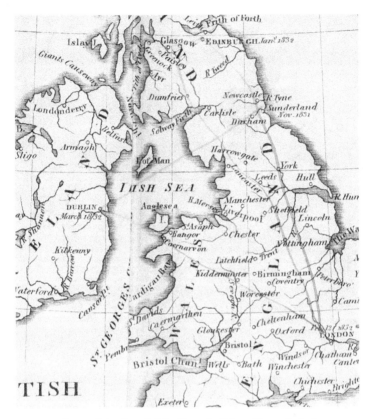

Figure 9. Inset of the British Isles from A. Sidney Doane's cholera map.

ease's movement always weeks to months later. In a striking example of the necessary belatedness of news, a paper in Northampton, Massachusetts, finally published a horrifying account of cholera's April atrocities in Paris on the very day in June when the pandemic arrived in North America.[32] The tremendous degree of uncertainty in maps that sought to present the authoritative truth about the disease was inevitable, especially because available medical paradigms could not settle whether it was local or imported and whether it was portable or contagious. There were no ready answers. While an avid climatist, Tanner registers these conundra in his map. Resisting arguments about cholera's movement in the text, Tanner nonetheless includes "a faint line" that "exhibits the supposed course of the Epidemic from place to place" (Figure 10).

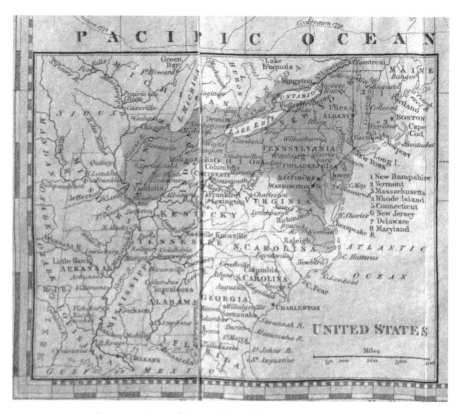

Figure 10. Inset of Henry Schneck Tanner's cholera map.

In short, the disease's arrival revived older debates between climatists and contagionists. The fever epidemics that had swept the American landscape every few years since the nation's founding were understood to have one cause, if disparate effects, and Americans had spent decades arguing whether that cause was environmental or contagious. Doctors could not agree about what caused cholera, but the movement of cholera meant medical theorists needed increasingly to contort their ideas to fit cholera into theories about local environmental causes or "miasma." John Kearsley Mitchell described the apparent paradox thus: "Many cases are cited where the cholera came with bodies of men, caravans, and ships, and seemed to be propagated by personal communication," and yet "we must for the present suppose that *it is portable* and yet *is not contagious*."[33] "Perhaps no disease has so much puzzled the etiologist as cholera," Mitchell continued:

Its singular local origin [the Indian subcontinent], its yet more singular progress, its apparent inconsistencies, its diffusion from a tropical point over the habitable globe, and especially its invasion, in winter, of the frozen steppes of Tartary and Russia, all tend to confuse the observer of epidemics. At one time, slowly, against the monsoon, it advances on a long geographical line, at the rate of from one to two miles a day, whilst at another, it flies on the wings of commerce, almost as fast as there are means of conveyance from men and merchandize. At one time, it ascends or descends along the valley of an innavigable stream, slowly and regularly, as if progressive by its own locomotion; at another, it flies with the ship or the locomotive, across seas and continents.[34]

Going to great lengths to deny the disease's contagiousness while charting its tremendous mobility, Mitchell grapples with the apparent contradictions of cholera's communication patterns. Whereas climatist theories had once conceptually protected the body politic from unchecked flow, cholera flaunted its circulatory nature whether a mile at a time across the landscape or "fl[ying] on the wings of commerce." Cholera easily traversed porous political, geographical, and corporeal boundaries. And while somatic concerns had long been linked with social and political ones, this was particularly true for cholera. In literal terms, the social, economic, and political features of antebellum America—the growth of cities, rise in population density, development in transportation technologies, and increasingly global market— *did* create the conditions through which fever arrived, and the movement of cholera affected these conditions in turn, in reciprocal but unpredictable ways.

Thinkers like John Kearsley Mitchell thus recognized cartography's limited ability to answer these fundamental questions about cholera. In the form they selected to set down definitive facts about the epidemic, they announced their failure to record the geography of this fast-moving, dynamic, and ontologically uncertain disease. Cartography registered the way in which cholera insisted on new geographies, even as the maps themselves revealed the failure of emerging epistemologies to know those issues. The problem with medical cartography was, in many ways, the same problem physicians had identified with anatomy. This new visual epistemology provided a "science of organization," but it could not convey the dynamism of living systems—it fell short, in other words, of providing a "science of life."[35]

Mapping was a compelling addition to the tool kit of medical epistemology, but it was still inadequate to the ontological and etiological challenges
cholera presented. Americans once more turned to their literary imaginations
during an epistemic crisis to theorize medicine and refigure U.S. health. The
imagination was a fertile space for cholera inquiry not only because of the epistemological possibilities of literary form for knowing cholera but because
narrative and the imagination were understood to be connected to the
communication of cholera. One way of disavowing cholera's novelty, for example, was to rely on the intimate relationship between disease and narrative. Cholera could be a new version of an old disease if in fact it were the
stories of cholera that exacerbated the disease's effects on the body through
the receiver's imagination.[36] Narrative was thus responsible, in one vision of
cholera, for spurring the imagination in such a way as to reproduce the effects
of the spectacular cholera on the body of the recipient. In another vision,
literary form provided a venue for doctors and writers to experiment imaginatively with cholera during the epistemic crisis.

Poe's 1839 story "The Fall of the House of Usher" offers an illuminating
illustration of the uses of the imagination and literary form to understand cholera and the disease's reframing of medical geography. While Poe's articulation of the imagination's relationship to discovery would grow more overt in
his subsequent stories, "The Fall of the House of Usher" provides an example
of a medical theory that began in a fictional short story and made its way into
the medical literature of the antebellum era. Emerging out of the 1830s cholera climate, Poe's story imaginatively experiments with fungus as the cause of
fevers, creatively reimagining U.S. geography to solve the central conundrum
of cholera discourse.[37] In the decade that followed, Poe's friend John Kearsley
Mitchell rewrote the fungal theory as a medical treatise, disseminating his
work through the medical community as a powerful new theory of cholera.[38]

Poe's Gothic Experiment

Though Poe addressed the 1830s cholera pandemic directly only a decade after,
his medical work began much earlier. Poe avidly followed developments in
science and medicine and the inspiration for at least one story, "The Case of
M. Valdemar" (1845) (a story many read as a real scientific account), has been
credited to Poe's familiarity with the medical work of A. Sidney Doane.[39] Furthermore, stories like "The Masque of the Red Death" (1842) reveal Poe's

continued interest in the geography of health and the permeability of medical boundaries. "The Fall of the House of Usher" offers perhaps the best example of Poe's own medical theorizing—thinking about disease that would make its way into medical lectures by the 1840s. Rather than using maps, however, Poe turned to the gothic—with its terrifying suspense, hidden passages, decaying walls, and unstable geography—to represent the affective experience of cholera and its narratives, to remap cholera's geography, and to explore how cholera might be simultaneously not contagious and portable.[40]

As "The Sphinx" amply demonstrates, Poe put stock in narrative and the imagination as ways of knowing—rather than objectivity. In the opening of "The Murders in the Rue Morgue" (1841), Poe explains that "the *truly* imaginative [is] never otherwise than profoundly analytic."[41] The form of the gothic, too, better fit Poe's and Mitchell's understanding of the world in the wake of cholera, and their imaginative experiments provided a venue in which they could investigate minute fungal cells as a solution to the conundrum about cholera's medical etiology, which was confounding medical thinkers around the globe.

Poe's gothic medicine was also a strategy that countered other rising paradigms, especially the twinned corporeal models of anatomy and factory labor that rose to prominence. These models challenged the dynamism of physiology that Poe's and Mitchell's work sought to know. Mechanistic models set firm somatic boundaries—boundaries that were, in fact, too clean and too defined, and threatened the very principles of life itself. For Poe and Mitchell, as for Benjamin Rush and other physiological thinkers, the human body was not "an automaton" or "a self-moving machine." But as the century progressed, physiology, the body's vital materialism, increasingly needed to be defended against the rising tide of industrial and anatomical paradigms. The international obsession with Johann Maelzel's automaton—known as "the Turk" because of its costume—exemplified this tension. Appearing to be a moving, thinking competitor that was also a machine, the chess player captivated the attention of thousands around the Atlantic including Benjamin Franklin, Napoleon Bonaparte, and Andrew Jackson. Poe was not impressed. He rightly suspected that human life could not be mechanistically replicated and that the machine could only simulate human thought and behavior because it contained a human player. He published a widely read exposé titled "Maelzel's Chess-Player" (1836) debunking the Turk. Bodies and minds were not machines, and, in detecting the dupe, Poe reasserted vital boundaries. "Maelzel's Chess-Player" made its way from Philadelphia to Charleston, inspiring Mitchell to purchase, restore, and exhibit the Turk at the Chinese Museum in Philadelphia, exposing the trick.[42] At the heart of these actions was a shared understanding that life and health were dynamic processes whose mysteries were best approached thoughtfully through practices like imaginative experimentation and not through reductive, mechanistic paradigms.[43] In using the gothic to understand a medical crisis, as Poe did in "The Sphinx" and "The Fall of the House of Usher," he employed a genre that foregrounded perceptual problems and troubled epistemologies that relied too much on uncritical observation.

"The Fall of the House of Usher" is the story of a man who answers the request of an old friend dying in his ancestral mansion. The unnamed narrator arrives in time for the death of Usher's sister Madeline, whom they bury in the walls of the house. The narrator tries to use reason to resist what he perceives to be Usher's increasingly frantic, illness-wrought delusions, only to be proven wrong and drawn into Usher's world when a bloody Madeline re-emerges from the grave to collapse on the body of her brother. The narrator flees the scene as the house collapses into the pond below.

The story opens with a lone rider passing into a decaying landscape. The space should evoke a sense of familiarity in Poe's protagonist; he travels the route to his sick childhood friend's ancestral home. But the atmosphere is moist with clouds that hang "oppressively low," "rank sedges," and "decayed trees."[44] Defamiliarized, the space produces an "an iciness, a sinking, a sickening of the heart" that the narrator connects to melancholia and "gloom" but also with the symptoms of approaching illness.[45] The narrator insists that he cannot understand the "mystery" that produces his feelings, but they begin with moisture, decomposing plant matter, and "a black and lurid tarn"—still water—that hideously mirrors the decaying foliage—"the gray sedge, and the ghastly tree-stems"—that surrounds the House of Usher.[46] More than a simple use of the pathetic fallacy, Poe writes a landscape-made-strange that recalls descriptions of miasma so linked by some theorists to the 1830s cholera pandemic. "The Fall of the House of Usher" provides an original theory of the fungal origins of fevers.

Poe sets the story in an environment fully overrun by fungus. Though the story "seems a thesaurus of Gothic clichés: the lonely wanderer; the dreary landscape; the decaying castle; the reflecting tarn," as 1960s critic J. O. Bailey noted, the fungus signals a striking difference: "the typical Gothic castle is hung with moss or ivy; Poe's fungus seems a unique and more deadly parasite, invented for a purpose to be examined."[47] Poe sets the story "in the autumn of the year," the peak season for fungal growth.[48] The narrator approaches the decaying house and peers into the tarn, envisioning "about the whole mansion and domain . . . an atmosphere peculiar to themselves and their immediate vicinity—an atmosphere which had no affinity with the air of heaven, but which had reeked up from the decayed trees, and the grey wall, and the silent tarn—a pestilential and mystic vapour, dull, sluggish, faintly discernible, and leaden-hued."[49] But the narrator insists this diseased atmosphere "must have been a dream."[50] "Shaking [it] off from [his] spirit," the rider, like a good physician, turns to scrutiny: "I scanned more narrowly the real aspect of the building," discovering an old, discolored edifice with "minute fungi overspread the whole exterior, hanging in a fine tangled web-work from the eaves."[51] He is surprised to note that no other aspect of the house displays "excessive decay" except the "barely perceptible fissure," but "in this there was much that reminded me of the specious totality of old woodwork which has rotted for long years in some neglected vault with no disturbance from the breath of the external air."[52]

Fungus spreads, almost imperceptibly at first, through the story as well. When Usher attempts to retreat from illness into narrative the story he selects offers no respite: the "suggestions arising from this ballad" lead Usher to contemplate the perverse "sentience of all vegetable things."[53] This thought leads Usher to dwell on this sentience as "fulfilled in the method of collocation of [the house's] stones—in the order of their arrangement, as well as in that of the many *fungi* which overspread them, and of the decayed trees which stood around—above all, in the long, undisturbed endurance of this arrangement, and in its reduplication in the still waters of the tarn."[54] Inspired by the power of narrative to convey scientific information, Usher is haunted by the so particularly ordered stones of his own home that, like the trees without, decay from the inside by the fungi that surround them. Only the word "fungi" is italicized in the passage.

Fungus was especially ripe for gothic articulation. It grew at night in untended spaces and multiplied at a seemingly unnatural rate. It worked stealthily—the spread of fungus and its rotting of plant and animal matter occurred almost imperceptibly. In the 1830s, exciting developments in microscopy promised new insights into taxonomy, but scientists could not decide if fungus was plant or animal. Fungus appeared to be, rather, an unnatural plant that needed no sun and flourished in darkness—and new developments in microscopy revealed that these unnatural fungal cells were dangerously indistinguishable from animal cells. Fungus surreptitiously spawned from "an almost invisible single cell" to a cloud with ten million sporules, "so minute as to look like smoke."[55]

Refusing to rest lightly on the "sentient" stones of the House of Usher, the fungus infiltrates their core and becomes an explanatory paradigm for the story. Usher's decaying body metonymically corresponds to the fungus-rotted house and ancestral line. His hair, with its "more than web-like softness and tenuity," stands in for the "minute fungi" that "overspread the whole exterior, hanging in a fine, tangled web-work from the eaves."[56] Furthermore, the collapse of seemingly disparate identities—Usher, Madeline, the narrator—reproduces fungal cells' ability to mimic and invade plant and animal cells. The effect of the corrupted stones, Usher explains, "was discoverable . . . in that silent yet importunate and terrible influence which for centuries had moulded the destinies of his family, and which made *him* what I now saw him."[57] Usher's dark pun on the family's "moulded" destinies reveals the dangerous permeability of the fungi.

At first glance, it appears Poe did not substantially revise "The Fall of the House of Usher." Nevertheless, some subtle but significant changes were made to the story between its 1839 publication in *Burton's Gentleman's Magazine* and its inclusion in the commonly reproduced 1845 collection *Tales* that highlight Poe's increasing scientific interest in fungus.[58] Poe's friendship with Mitchell likely influenced the changes to the story, and those changes work to foreground Poe's medical theorizing. Between the editions, Poe adds credence to Usher's belief in "the sentience of all vegetables" in the later edition by adding a scientific footnote that makes use of two authors whom Mitchell also cites.[59] Additionally, the later edition breaks a long paragraph that originally introduced the fungi into the story. In the earlier editions of the introduction, Poe buries the "minute fungi" that "overspread the whole exterior" nine sentences into the paragraph, whereas in the 1845 edition "the real aspect of the building" becomes its own paragraph, more clearly foregrounding the responsibility of "minute fungi" for the perfectly preserved but fully rotten condition of the house. Finally, the 1845 edition shifts its italics from the phrase "*the gradual yet certain condensation of an atmosphere of their own about the waters and the walls*"—which reads more like contemporary descriptions of "miasma"—to a single italicized word: "*fungi.*"[60]

Fungal theory took cholera's defamiliarized geographies and rendered the problem local, even minute. A well-known town, street, home, or tree stump might maintain its appearance from afar but be entirely decayed within. Within these hollowed-out landscapes, cholera's causative agent incubated and reproduced, corrupting everything around almost invisibly. Poe's cholera story thus offered a deeply paranoid vision of the landscape that reflected not only the dramatic experience of cholera but also the quick and unpredictable reorientation toward familiar geography that the disease necessitated.

Mitchell's Fungus

Poe revised his story to highlight the fungal theory it contained while he and Mitchell were living and working in Philadelphia, and Mitchell's medical theorizing owes a profound debt to his friendship with Poe.[61] Like Poe, Mitchell was raised in Virginia and identified with his southern roots despite living his entire adult life in Philadelphia. He was a professor of medicine at the Philadelphia Medical Institute and Jefferson Medical College and a teacher of chemistry at the Franklin Institute. Mitchell was, as Philadelphia novelist George Lippard wrote in 1844, "celebrated no less for his medical attainments than his poetical genius."[62] Poe and Mitchell's friendship dates at least to the first issue of *Burton's Gentleman's Magazine* (1839) in which Poe published a long, laudatory, and generous review of a book of poetry Mitchell had written, but they had likely been friends at least since the mid-1830s. Poe was such an admirer of Mitchell's poetry that he came to Mitchell's literary defense. Railing against Rufus Griswold's representation of Mitchell in *Poets and Poetry of America*, Poe criticized, "How came [Griswold] to alter Dr. J. K. Mitchell's song in such a manner that the author scarcely knows his own production? Just think of the impudence of the thing—Rufus Wilmot Griswold altering a production of Dr. J. K. Mitchell!"[63] In turn, Mitchell treated Poe's wife, Virginia, for the tuberculosis of which she would eventually die, and Mitchell's son Silas Weir Mitchell would later recall both Poe's visits and his father's loans to the often broke writer.[64] An early daguerreotype of the two captured the scientific nature of their friendship.[65]

Mitchell was a particularly good collaborator for Poe not only because he was a physician-poet but also because he believed the organizing principle of health was *permeability*. In the early 1830s he published two essays on the topic: "On the Penetrativeness of Fluids" and "On the Penetration of Gases."[66] In these essays he examined the ability of fluids and gases to travel through membranes both inside and outside of the body. Mitchell tested the penetrativeness of animal membranes, examining the "organic molecular infiltration," the circulation of particles through and around the body, and considered "the most striking generality" of his findings to be "the *high power* of penetrativeness of *gases* for *organic molecular tissue*."[67] He believed permeability was "*the master-spirit of animal and vegetable motion*, the ruling power of chemical science, the governing influence of atmospheric composition, the presiding genius of respiration, circulation, and nutrition, the cause of disease, and the restorer of health."[68] Permeability was the key to the health of both human bodies and the environment. Mitchell's commitment to permeability was likely cemented by his own experience with cholera, which almost killed him in 1832, but he did not connect it to cholera until after Poe wrote "The Fall of the House of Usher."

After Poe published the story, Mitchell began his own gothic investigation of the disease. (Before that time, his poetry had been sentimental and adventurous and his medical writing stoic and technical.) Newly appointed as professor of medicine in the early 1840s, Mitchell began delivering a lecture called "On the Cryptogamous Origins of Malarious and Epidemic Fevers," eventually publishing his work as a pamphlet in 1849. (The word "malarious" in the title is a categorical description of fevers usually blamed on *mal aria*, or "bad airs.") The essay offers a gothically inflected argument that fevers—particularly yellow fever and cholera—arise from minute fungi that proliferate *unseen*, permeating the environment. The reader is prepared for Mitchell's gothic medicine by his evocative title. He might have used the more neutral term "fungal" but chose its synonym "cryptogamous" to indicate the fevers' origins in spaces wedded ("gamous") to the "hidden, concealed, secret" ("crypto").[69]

For Mitchell, these permeating "Goths of phytology" bore the spirit of Poe's dark tales.[70] The "fungi are distinguished for their *diffusion and number*," Mitchell explained, "*for their poisonous properties, and their peculiar seasons of growth, for the minuteness of their spores and for their love of darkness and tainted soils, and heavy atmospheres*."[71] In this terrifying geographical refiguring that could not be visually contained, the fungi's affinity to darkness and corruption is affirmed by Mitchell's observation that the "most common malarious diseases are not producible by exposure in sickly places *during the daytime*. Whatever may be their cause, it seems to have activity almost solely at night."[72] Furthermore, "*darkness* appears to be essential to either [their] existence or [their] power."[73] The dangers of these "dubious beings" arise from their invisibility, enchantment, unnatural inversion of the vegetable order ("love of darkness"), and the fact that "they could scarcely be microscopically distinguished from the primordial formative cells of our own tissues."[74] Fungi produced additional fright because their "bloodlike" appearance filled observers with "disgust and horror."[75]

Mitchell knew that readers might doubt the terrifying power he attributed to fungi. He acknowledges, "It may be thought that the cause assigned is not adequate to the rapid production of the effect. Can a minute vegetable, however distributed, contaminate the air of a large marsh or field, in the course of a few minutes or hours?"[76] Mitchell reminds readers who doubt "how minute a quantity of a reproductive organic virus is, in other cases, necessary to the infection of a proper subject."[77] Additionally, Mitchell points out, "a mushroom growth is proverbial in every language. In a single night, under favorable circumstances, leather, or moist vegetable matter, may be completely covered with mould. Of the more minute fungi, some species pass through their whole existence in a few minutes, from the invisible spore to the perfect plant."[78]

Certainly, these descriptions of uncanny doubling (the lack of ability to distinguish between self cells and other), rapid reproduction, invisible forces, soundless destruction, semblance to blood, enchantment, and horror bear a striking resemblance to Poe's gothic. Likewise, Mitchell's emphasis, particularly his use of haunting description, strategic repetition, and italics, are reminiscent of Poe's narrative strategies. And, though Mitchell was a well-known writer, before he met Poe his published medical writing and verse bore no traces of the gothic.

What makes thinking about fever—particularly cholera—so terrifying, Mitchell explains, is the difficulty in discerning what makes one place healthy and another disease ridden: "Nay, two places, in all observable respects alike in elevation, local relations, atmospheric phenomena and geological structure, may differ totally in their degree of healthfulness. Even in the same place, the line of limitation of disease-producing power may be a common road, a narrow street, a stone wall, or a belt of woods."[79] Mitchell's reflections recall Poe's narrator, who cannot understand "what was it that so unnerved [him]" about the House of Usher. He reflects that possibly "a mere different arrangement of the particulars of the scene, of the details of the picture, would be sufficient to modify, or perhaps to annihilate" the effect.[80] Nevertheless, both accounts link fungal invasion to a lack of productivity. Poe's Usher is an effete aristocrat whose "unramified" lineage, sequestered in an ancestral home, is doomed to rot from lack of healthy activity and circulation. Mitchell links his fungal experience to the site of a formerly productive milldam, which was a healthy space during its 117 years of activity but not three years later hosts stumps "entirely disintegrated by the dry rot, and that they crumbled in the handling." There, Mitchell finds "innumerable spores" of the aptly named "Polyporus Destructor and Merulius Vastator, cryptogamous plants."[81]

While both Mitchell and Poe paint a gothic horror scene in the absence of honest labor and healthy circulation, Mitchell's fungal politics are explicitly global and xenophobic. Poe's story signals the nation's dangerous porousness with its lack of geographical specificity—the House of Usher could be, terrifyingly, *anywhere*. Mitchell chooses, instead, to articulate this dangerous permeability by linking fungal growths explicitly to sites of transnational trade: Rio, Canton, Jamaica. Even Mitchell's descriptions of the fungi are themselves xenophobic. Mitchell envisions these "tribe[s]" of "anomalous vegetables" invading while all the other vegetables sleep.[82] This deviant "race of vegetables" waits until "more perfect forms have completed their annual task" and then healthy plants "submit to the inroads of these Goths of phytology."[83] Mitchell's politics display an anxiety about both the rapidly changing demographics of the American landscape and the arrival of America's least welcome newcomer: the Asiatic cholera.

While this fungal theory may seem outlandish to contemporary readers, it was actually a remarkably powerful way of understanding cholera, one that briefly gained acceptance on both sides of the Atlantic.[84] Fungal theory provided an innovative solution to the climatist/contagionist debates about the origins of diseases like yellow fever and cholera that had long occupied American medical theorists. Explicitly rejecting popular but vague miasmatic explanations, fungal theory identified a specific substance that was transportable and locally propagated. If the major divide between climatist and contagionist theories was that climatists believed fevers came from decaying or unhealthy matter in the environment and contagionists understood them to be caused by mobile animals or sick people, Poe and Mitchell's fungal theory found a middle way by cleverly locating cholera in a mobile, living creature that caused decay. Drawing from the climatist understanding, this theory figured fungus as an agent of decay that emerged from the local environment but that also resembled the microscopic animals (animalcules) others understood to propagate disease through their movement. In fact, Poe and Mitchell were remarkably close to identifying cholera's etiology: just a few years later, doctors would discover that cholera *was* transmitted through tiny creatures that permeated both bodies and the environment—although the barely perceptible, not quite animal, not quite plant agents of transmission did not turn out to be fungi.

The epistemic crisis caused by the arrival of cholera continued for decades. Its flames were fanned repeatedly by the serious and terrifying series of cholera outbreaks that punctuated the American landscape from 1832 to 1834 and returned with a vengeance in 1849, following the familiar path from India across Europe and the Atlantic. Public health efforts worked to stem the movement of the disease through quarantines, but even after John Snow isolated cholera's mechanism of transmission in 1854, it would take decades for cities to be able to manage the disease effectively. Poe was personally haunted by the specter of cholera up until his death. During the outbreak in the summer of 1849, Poe wrote his mother-in-law, Maria Clemm, to say that he believed he had contracted cholera and begged her to come die with him.[85] John R. Thompson later reported that Poe suffered a terrifying vision in which "a thousand pictures of suffering and death danc[ed] hideously before me," culminating in a nightmare featuring an ominous black bird.[86] In this dark twist on the story Poe had imagined in "The Sphinx," the portentous creature turns to Poe at the dream's end and declares, "I am the Cholera and you are the cause of me!"[87] Whether or not the story of Poe's nightmare is apocryphal, it suggests cholera's deep imprinting on both the writer and the period. (Poe died two months later.)

In other words, cholera left its mark on a generation. Radical geographic reframing prompted by the epistemic crisis was turned to radical political ends by abolitionist writers like Harriet Beecher Stowe, Frederick Douglass, and Martin Delany in the 1850s. Numerous factors—the generalized fear of immigrants, the infamous infected Irish travelers aboard *The Carrick*, and Mitchell's xenophobic renderings—that circulated in the wake of cholera's first outbreaks would have led writers like Stowe and Delany to understand cholera's geographic refiguring as not only political but racial. Nevertheless, there was also a longer history of linking the cholera pandemic directly to slavery, one that returned with particular force during cholera's recurrence in the 1850s. This is particularly evident in Stowe's experimentation in *Dred: A Tale of the Great Dismal Swamp* (1856) and Martin Delany's response to that novel, *Blake, or, The Huts of America* (1859, 1861–62). These novels seek not only to understand cholera's medical geography but also to use cholera's reorienting effects to imagine new possibilities for antislavery revolution.

Race, Cholera, and the Radical Geography of the 1850s

From the time of the very first outbreaks, preachers and laypeople alike had identified cholera as a divine retribution for the moral failings of Americans. Pressure for a national moral accounting was particularly powerful, leading to a strong lobby for a nationwide day of fasting. Andrew Jackson rejected this suggestion as unconstitutional, which gave ammunition to his opponent in that year's presidential race, Henry Clay, who fervently advocated for one (although Clay was no model of religion or temperance himself).[88] Seventeen years later when cholera returned, Zachary Taylor would fully endorse a national fast to prevent the further spread of cholera.[89] Christian interpretations of both the 1832–34 and 1849–54 series of U.S. outbreaks largely supported a worldview that held cholera was a worse iteration of known diseases, exacerbated by a wide range of sins that ranged from drinking to adultery and religious declension.[90]

Among African Americans and abolitionists, this divine etiology of cholera explained the U.S. iterations of the pandemic as retribution for the moral failings of all involved in the slave trade. This understanding of cholera was particularly potent in the South where outbreaks followed quickly on the heels of legislation enacted in the summer of 1832 in response to Nat Turner's rebellion.[91] James Williams recorded in his slave narrative that his brother "preached a sermon" that year "in which he compared the pestilence to the plagues which afflict the Egyptian slave-holders, because they would not let the people go."[92] Frederick Douglass also recalled the connection between the largest slave rebellion in the South and the arrival of cholera in his autobiography *My Bondage and My Freedom* (1855). Of that time, Douglass remembers, "The insurrection of Nathaniel Turner had been quelled, but the alarm and terror had not subsided. The cholera was on its way, and the thought was present, that God was angry with the white people because of their slaveholding wickedness, and, therefore, his judgments were abroad in the land. It was impossible for me not to hope much from the abolition movement, when I saw it supported by the Almighty, and armed with DEATH!"[93] Thus, at least among African American and abolitionist communities, a narrative of cholera as retribution for participation in slavery circulated throughout the outbreaks. Harriet Beecher Stowe (1811–1896) undertook a particularly extensive experiment with this understanding of cholera and its ramifications for U.S. medical geography in her 1856 novel *Dred: A Tale of the Great Dismal Swamp*.

Stowe's radical fiction emerged out of her intimate experience with cholera. Left alone to care for her children during the 1849 Cincinnati outbreak, Stowe maintained her courage even as local deaths mounted to more than one hundred a day. "On Tuesday one hundred and sixteen deaths from cholera were reported, and that night the air was of that peculiarly oppressive, deathly kind that seems to lie like lead on the brain and soul," she reported in a letter to her husband on June 29, but she urged him not to return: "none of us are sick, and it is very uncertain whether we shall be."[94] Nevertheless, by mid-July her then youngest son Charley had contracted cholera and died just a few weeks later. "I write as though there were no sorrow like my sorrow," the grieving Stowe wrote her husband, "yet there has been in this city, as in the land of Egypt, scarce a house without its dead. This heart-break, this anguish, has been everywhere, and when it will end God alone knows."[95]

It is not surprising that Stowe, the daughter of a preacher and wife of a theologian, would understand her experience typologically; nevertheless, in yoking cholera to the Egyptian plagues—the biblical account whose antislavery uses were long familiar to her—she cast cholera, after accounts like Williams's and Douglass's, as divine retribution for the sins of American slavery.[96] Her son Charles Edward Stowe (1850–1934) reinforced this connection when he later linked young Charley's death to Stowe's deep empathy with slave mothers. "'Uncle Tom's Cabin' was a cry of anguish from a mother's heart," Charles explained, "and uttered in sad sincerity. It was the bursting forth of deep feeling with all the intense anguish of wounded love."[97] Charley's passing certainly hovers over the early fictional scenes of mothers losing their children at the slave auction in *Uncle Tom's Cabin*. Nevertheless, this writing did not relieve Stowe of the moral imperative spurred by her loss. Rather, Stowe treated the fundamentally reorienting experience of the disease and its deep ties to the sins of slavery more fully in *Dred*.

Dred is an antislavery novel focused at first on the sentimental courtship of two young Southern plantation owners, Nina Gordon and Edward Clayton. Despite the good intentions of these slave owners, nefarious forces—Nina's despicable brother Tom, pro-slavery mobs, the immoral law, and cholera—hijack the mostly moral efforts of the novels' main characters. Nina and Clayton's story structures the first half of *Dred*, but the protagonists of the second half are two black figures of resistance: Nina's unrecognized black brother Harry and the novel's titular character Dred, son of historical revolutionary Denmark Vesey (1767–1822). The fulcrum around which the novel pivots is a camp-meeting-cum-slave-market in which the threat of cholera is made real. The climax occurs when a seemingly possessed Dred pronounces the coming scourge as retribution for slavery. Clayton's early wish for social good at all costs is then literalized when Nina dies tending to cholera-stricken enslaved men and women on her plantation. Her death marks the foreclosure of benevolent slave owning as a possible solution to slavery's ills, and the event radicalizes both Clayton and Harry, the latter of whom now finds himself property of his cruel brother Tom thanks to a legal technicality. The victims of Southern woes—not just cholera but cruel masters and an unjust law—all escape to the Great Dismal Swamp. Upon Dred's unexpected death at Tom's hands, the characters flee northward to New York, New England, and Canada.

The novel's treatment of cholera reproduces familiar experiences and narratives of the disease. Nina's aunt receives a letter "describing the march through some Northern cities of the cholera, which was then making fearful havoc on our American shore."[98] The letter continues, detailing how the disease has baffled the medical establishment: "Nobody seems to know how to manage it . . . physicians are all at a loss. It seems to spurn all laws. It bursts upon cities like a thunderbolt, scatters desolation and death, and is gone with equal rapidity. People rise in the morning well, and are buried before evening. In one day houses are swept of a whole family."[99] Although the letter is full of fearful portents, only Harry imagines the disease might reach them. These fictional accounts echo the nonfictional cholera accounts with which Stowe herself was so familiar and the disjunctive temporalities she had experienced in 1849 between the travel of cholera and the always belated movement of the news about the disease. As cholera draws nearer, Nina speaks with an incompetent physician, "quite *au fait* on the subject," who "entertain[s] Nina nearly half an hour with different theories as to the cause of the disease, and with the experiments which had been made in foreign hospitals."[100] This philosophizing and physical experimentation, however, prove not just useless but dangerous as they lead the physician to a "particular pet" theory that causes him almost to welcome the disease.[101] Nina's very first encounter with cholera reveals the "difference between written directions for a supposed case, and the actual awful realities of the disease."[102]

Nina's death is likewise drawn from familiar accounts and Stowe's own experience. When the epidemic does arrive, Nina swears to protect the plantation and its people, eventually sacrificing her own life to the duty she owes Canema's enslaved men and women. In a tragic replication of Stowe's own experience, Nina writes Clayton telling him not to worry or to return to the plantation, intent on caring for the sick on her own. When Clayton finally does arrive, it is too late: Nina has already contracted cholera. As in Stowe's own experience, proximity to the disease brings out Nina's best qualities; unlike Stowe's experience, the shift toward social responsibility that begins for Nina with the arrival of cholera is realized by other characters like Clayton and Harry who are inspired by Nina's passing to take up a more radical antislavery position. Nina, like Stowe's son Charley, is a necessary sacrifice for the greater good.

Heavy allusions to the Exodus story prepare readers to hypothesize along with Stowe that cholera is divine retribution for slavery. Her chapters lay bare the story's typological frame, with titles such as "The Warning," "The Voice in the Wilderness," "The Flight into Egypt," and "The Desert." Dred also voices this biblical frame at a climactic moment when he disrupts a camp-meeting-turned-slave-sale with a booming, prophetic paraphrase of Exodus: "Behold, it cometh! Behold, the slain of the Lord shall be many! . . . There shall be a cry in the land of Egypt, for there shall not be a house where there is not one dead!"[103] The reader soon understands that Dred is prophesying that cholera will descend like the plagues on the Egyptians. Finally, when cholera arrives, Stowe peppers her descriptions of the disease with the adjective "peculiar," reminding her readers once more of its intimate connection to the "peculiar institution."[104]

Stowe's moral etiology for cholera reframes hemispheric geography in unexpected ways. At the novel's start, North Carolina seems a reasonably healthy, ordered place. Nina and Clayton seem like they might find happiness as slave owners; Nina's cruel brother Tom has been banished; and even smart, educated enslaved individuals like Harry can be content with their lot, since Harry sees himself fulfilling a temporary filial duty in watching over Nina, from whom he expects eventual freedom. Canema is a stable, healthy, and mostly contained little world. Cholera changes all this. When the disease nears, Stowe emphasizes cholera's uncanny ability to reframe familiar spaces, presaging the dramatic geographical reorientation in *Dred*:

None has been more irregular, and apparently more perfectly capricious, in its movements. During the successive seasons that it has been epidemic in this country, it has seemed to have set at defiance the skill of the physicians. . . . Certain sanitary laws and conditions would seem to be indispensible, yet those who are familiar with it have had fearful experience how like a wolf it will sometimes leap the boundaries of the best and most carefully-guarded fold, and, spite of every caution and protection, sweep all before it.

Its course through towns and villages has been equally singular. Sometimes, descending like a cloud on a neighborhood, it will leave a single village or town untouched amidst the surrounding desolations, and long after, when health is restored to the whole neighborhood, come down suddenly on the omitted towns, as a

ravaging army sends back a party for prey to some place which has
been overlooked or forgotten. . . . Sometimes it will ravage all the
city except some one street or locality, and then come upon that,
while all else is spared. Its course, upon Southern plantations, was
marked by similar capriciousness, and was made still more fatal by
that peculiar nature of plantation life.[105]

The capriciousness of cholera's course flouts characters' misguided sense of
safety. While characters like the poor, old Tiff seek shelter on Nina's seemingly safe plantation, Canema's inhabitants soon fall prey to the scourge. In
an inversion of William Arthur Caruthers's depiction of cholera as a disease
disproportionately affecting the North, Stowe asserts the disproportionate vul-
nerability of Southern plantations. At Canema, previously a bucolic ideal,
cholera indiscriminately punishes the bodies of even benevolent participants
in American slavery.

However, in spite of the seeming haphazardness of cholera's movements
across the landscape of the United States, the Great Dismal Swamp remains decidedly healthy. Given prevailing theories of disease, it is striking that a swamp
becomes the safest space in the novel; this overgrown and untended space,
which is home to peripatetic and lower-class bodies, should have been a prime
site for cholera according to miasmatic, fungal, and contagionist theories alike.
That the darkest, wettest, and most fungus-ridden space is the only one spared
would have been striking for any reader of the time. The language with which
Stowe describes the area evokes miasmatic and fungal theories of fever, highlighting the extraordinariness of the swamp's exclusion. "The singularly unnatural and wildly stimulating properties of the slimy depths from which they
spring," she details, almost parroting the language of doctors like Mitchell, "assume a goblin growth, entirely different from their normal habit. All sorts of
vegetable monsters stretch their weird, fantastic forms among its shadows. There
is no principle so awful through all nature as the principle of *growth*."[106] Furthermore, as a home to fugitives, this unkempt environment should be most pestilential, since both contagionists and anti-contagionists believed cholera to
disproportionately affect poor and mobile populations. What appears to make
the Dismal Swamp the perfect locale for health in *Dred* is that the geography's
dense resistance to human cultivation allows it to shelter fugitives. Since Stowe
believed cholera to be caused not by miasma or fungus but by slavery, she emphasizes the unexpected healthiness of the area in contradistinction to the
well-tended but cholera-ridden spaces.

Given the way in which participation in slavery structures the cholera outbreak, it is perhaps unsurprising that Stowe links Dred's revolutionary power
directly to the swamp. "It is difficult to fathom the dark recesses of a mind so
powerful and active as his," she explains, but to try we must understand "those
desolate regions which he made his habitation."[107] She invites her readers to
imagine Dred's being as one "of the largest and keenest vitality, to grow up so
completely under the nursing influences of nature, that it may seem to be as
perfectly *en rapport* with them as a tree; so that the rain, the wind, and the
thunder . . . seem to hold with it a kind of fellowship, and to be familiar com-
panions of existence. . . . So completely had [Dred] come into sympathy and
communion with nature, and with those forms of it which more particularly
surrounded him in the swamps, that he moved about among them with as
much ease as a lady treads her Turkey carpet."[108] Stowe furthermore hints that
this connection may be not only natural but supernatural: "Dred was under
the inspiring belief that he was the subject of visions and supernatural communications."[109] The novel lends credibility to this "inspiring belief" through
Dred's prophecy of the cholera outbreak.

Dred is, in other words, a prophetic transcendental figure that Stowe encourages readers to both celebrate and fear. After all, Dred serves as a figure
of the healthy, if ambiguous, scourge born of the swamp. "The Great Dismal
Swamp was, by midcentury, a particularly well-established symbol for the noc-
turnal and the unexplained in the long transatlantic half-life of high romanticism," literary critic Martha Schoolman explains.[110] But because Dred comes
from the Great Dismal Swamp and not the woods of Massachusetts, he com-
munes with dark transcendental forces whose epistemological and ontological
uncertainty makes the swamp a perfect site for Stowe's gothic medicine. Likewise, Dred, who emerges from twinned forces of the "darkly struggling, wildly
vegetating swamp of human souls" that inhabit the swamp and the "delirious
exuberance of vegetation," is the agent of "the wrath of an avenging God,"
not a merciful one.[111] Stowe does not explicitly condone this unwieldy force.
Dred's affinities with the pandemic force itself render his revolutionary power
both visionary and terrifying. In this way, Dred resembles the fungal cells that
captured Poe's and Mitchell's imaginations. Like the fungus that was not exactly plant or animal but a seemingly unnatural plant, Dred is simultaneously
the novel's agent of revolutionary change and the harbinger of mass destruction; Dred may ultimately be healthy, but it is not clear he is *good*. Perhaps as
a result of this ambiguity, Stowe kills off the character before his truly revolutionary work can begin.

The ambiguous nature of both Dred and the Great Dismal Swamp means they can provide a temporary haven from which revolution may grow, but neither can provide a final solution to slavery. Whereas Harry was initially wary of both Dred and the swamp, following Nina's death, he eventually seeks shelter with Dred in the swamp's community. Likewise Tiff flees to Dred and the swamp to protect his adopted children, and the swamp shelters Clayton when his own community turns on him for his abolitionist beliefs. Still, this swamp is a "wilderness" and not the Promised Land; salvation is not located there, but the possibility for revolutionary action and deliverance emerges from within it.

The figure of the revolutionary prophet in *Dred* represents a major development in Stowe's thinking about antislavery narratives. Whereas in *Uncle Tom's Cabin* Stowe figured colonization as the solution to slavery, just one year later she regretted this. The proceedings of the American and Foreign Anti-Slavery Society reported that Stowe had written in a letter saying "that if she were to write 'Uncle Tom' again, she would not send George Harris to Liberia."[112] Robert Levine argues this statement was a response to a fervent debate about the novel featuring major African American intellectuals of the period who criticized Stowe's narrative choices in *Uncle Tom's Cabin* (1852).[113] Stowe's ambivalent portrayal of Dred was a step closer to imagining a sweeping reformulation of race relations in America, but the ultimate impossibility of revolution within the pages of the novel remains troubling.

One of the most prominent African American thinkers to respond to Stowe was Martin Robison Delany (1812–1885). He wrote a novel reframing her work on abolitionism, contagious disease, and radical geography not three years after *Dred*. In *Blake, or, The Huts of America* (1859, 1861–62) Delany invites readers to view his novel in dialogue with Stowe's work through a pair of epigraphs from her recent poem "Caste and Christ" (1853) that introduce the two volumes of *Blake*. Given the invocation of Nat Turner, the scenes set in the Great Dismal Swamp, and the focus of both novels on an almost supernaturally powerful black revolutionary figure whose power is modeled on the work of contagious disease, it seems clear that Delany had *Dred* in mind when he penned *Blake*.[114]

Stowe's cholera novel likely interested Delany a great deal, not only because of his decade-long engagement with Stowe's work but because he had served as a health care worker in Pittsburgh during the city's 1833, 1849, and 1854 cholera outbreaks.[115] In 1837 Delany advertised himself in the *Pittsburgh Business Directory* as "Delany, Martin R., Cupping, Leeching and bleeding," and in

1849 the Pittsburgh City Council and Board of Health officially commended Delany's selfless contributions during the epidemic.[116] Delany understood the risks he took and knew he had been lucky. In 1852, he penned a tribute to a fellow African American physician of literary fame, Lewis G. Wells, who "effected more cures during the prevalence of the cholera in 1832, than any other physician" in Baltimore and who wrote some "fine original poems" but who finally fell prey to the disease himself while caring for others during a later outbreak.[117] Delany's years of medical work, particularly his experience with cholera, profoundly shaped his thinking, and *Blake* bears the imprint of cholera's epistemic crisis.[118]

Blake tells the story of a West Indian man enslaved in Mississippi. Blake decides to foment revolution when he learns his wife, Maggie, has been sold. He travels around the country from community to community inspiring a transatlantic revolution by entrusting a secret plan to a trustworthy individual in each location. In the second volume, Blake seeks Maggie in Cuba and grows close with his cousin Placido, a revolutionary Cuban poet. The novel's final words suggest the possibility of black revolt, with a character leaving to "spread among the blacks an authentic statement of the outrage: 'Wo be unto those devils of whites, I say!' "[119] If Delany ever wrote the end, it has never been found. If, as it appears, he did not, then the novel potently suggests that the momentum to topple oppressive systems the texts initiates must be carried out by Delany's readers.[120]

Blake is a novel deeply embedded in a scientific discourse. The January 1859 *Anglo-African Magazine* that introduced *Blake* couched Delany's authority in his scientific credentials, and the novel's first chapters were preceded by an essay by Delany titled "The Attraction of the Planets," which included an editor's prefatory remarks that emphasized the connection between Delany's scientific and literary pursuits.[121] The issue also featured an article by the prominent black physician James McCune Smith (1813–1865), which immediately preceded the first published chapters of Delany's novel. Together the works of these two black doctor-writers exemplify the monthly's intertwined aims: "literature, science, statistics, and the advancement of the cause of human freedom."[122]

Blake's plot and publication are both structured by the unexpected movement and radical geography that characterized the experience of cholera. Bucking a national frame, *Blake* tells the story of a West Indian in the United States and conjures a novel geography in its subtitle: "A Tale of the Mississippi Valley, the Southern United States, and Cuba." The first installment

imaginatively stretches from Canada to Cuba to Central Africa. The early
chapters trace a local geography made strange by the sudden disappearance
of Blake's wife. This event propels Blake into motion, traveling at an almost
dizzying pace from Louisiana to North Carolina and Virginia in a few pages.

As in *Dred*, *Blake*'s radical geography is shaped by the movement of disease. Blake describes his vision of the transmission of revolutionary discourse
early in the novel. "All you have to do is to find one good man or woman,"
he tells African Americans in huts across the American South.[123] "I don't care
which, so that they prove to be the right person—on a single plantation, and
hold a seclusion and impart the secret to them, and make them the organiz-
ers for their own plantation, and they in like manner impart it to some other
next to them, and so on. *In this way it will spread like smallpox among them.*"[124]
Delany's substitution of smallpox for cholera in his structuring metaphor seems
odd, especially when the movement he sought to describe much more clearly
resembled that of cholera. Furthermore, Delany had more immediate experience with cholera, and, as historian Charles Rosenberg has observed, fear of
smallpox had largely abated: "When cholera first appeared in the United States
in 1832, yellow fever and smallpox, the great epidemic diseases of the previous
two centuries, were no longer truly national problems . . . vaccination had de-
prived smallpox of much of its menace."[125]

Delany's substitution of smallpox for cholera was, thus, not incidental but
strategic. Smallpox was a rhetorically effective disease because it was clearly
communicable, whereas debates about cholera's contagiousness were still quite
unsettled, as far as the medical community and the public were concerned.
Smallpox was also more manageable than other epidemics, especially cholera,
because it was largely preventable if citizens were willing to act responsibly. It
offered a good model for thinking contagious disease as divine displeasure.
But the communication of knowledge about the disease, as Delany knew,
was a double-edged sword, which could be used both to stem the movement
of the illness and to propagate its circulation. This bifurcated legacy was
deeply racialized in the United States. On one hand, the history of smallpox
foregrounded black lives, bodies, and medicine: in New England, white colonists had learned about smallpox inoculation from Onesimus, an enslaved
black laborer who explained the African practice using his own scar, inoculation was verified by other enslaved workers, and it was first practiced on a
white boy and an enslaved father and son. In this way, the history of smallpox
and the history of black communities in America were already deeply entwined. On the other hand, as a doctor who spent years practicing medi-

cine in Pittsburgh, Delany was perhaps making a political point. Turning the sins of white Americans against them, Delany inverts the founding narrative of Pittsburgh in which the British captured the city by giving smallpox-ridden blankets to native opponents in the Seven Years' War.[126] The fantasy of revolutionary-discourse-as-disease may be nominally framed in terms of smallpox, but Delany's model of disease transmission strongly recalls both his personal experience with cholera and cholera's rapid transmission and vast circulation in the 1850s.

Even as Delany's revolutionary force draws on Stowe's use of cholera, Delany revises Stowe's fantasy to make revolution more possible. Practically paraphrasing *Dred's* terrible cholera prophesy, Delany describes, "From plantation to plantation did he go, sowing the seeds of future devastation and ruin to the master and redemption to the slave, an antecedent more terrible in its anticipation than the warning voice of the destroying Angel in Commanding the slaughter of the firstborn of Egypt."[127] Blake visits at the Great Dismal Swamp, but—unlike Dred, who gains his power from the swamp—Blake's relationship to the space is highly negotiated. On one hand, the novel reveres the area's long legacy of harboring fugitives and supporting black revolutionaries like Nat Turner and Denmark Vesey. Blake learns from the current inhabitants that "the Swamp contained them in sufficient number to take the whole United States."[128] On the other hand, Blake refuses to collapse his revolutionary energy with that of the swamp. Blake remains separate and wary of the obeah magic drawn from the area; he accepts the leaders' gifts and rituals but decides to slay their pet snake, should it choose to attack him. Seeming, perhaps, to understand this relationship, the community's priests make Blake a "conjuror of the highest degree known to their art . . . licensed with unlimited power—a power before given no one—to go forth and do wonders"; in having the Obeah grant Blake "unlimited power" and "place greater reliance in the efforts of Henry for their deliverance than in their own seven heads together," *Blake* respects but transcends the medical and religious work of these elders.[129] Distinguishing itself from *Dred*, *Blake* marks its place in the long history of black revolutionary action and gains sanction from the Great Dismal Swamp without reducing the novel's transnational revolution to the failed revolutionaries of the past. In this way Blake can move past the swamp as Dred ultimately cannot; unlike Stowe, who could not fulfill the revolutionary promise of cholera's devastation, Delany leaves open the possibility that Blake will return from Cuba to ignite the networks he has created into explosive, revolutionary action.

Since cholera wrought terrifying devastation and epistemic crisis in each decade of the antebellum era all over the country and beyond, we might consider expanding our understanding from what Rosenberg has called the "cholera years" to something more like an Age of Cholera. It is notable, for example, that the texts in this chapter were not written during American outbreaks of the disease but rather in the intervening years—and sometimes, in the case of stories like "The Sphinx," more than a decade later. These imaginative experiments thus suggest that the paradigm-rupturing experience of cholera remained with antebellum authors as a pressing epistemological problem long after the cholera bacteria had disappeared from U.S. shores. Americans were not immune from news stories that continued to trace cholera's movement out from India to the Middle East, Africa, and eastern Asia. The ease with which cholera continued to circulate reminded Americans how quickly it might return. This became especially clear in 1848 when the disease raged once more throughout Europe during a time in which Europeans were connecting cholera's return to the waves of revolution erupting across the continent. Such connections only augmented the case writers like Stowe and Delany were making for cholera's revolutionary potential.[130]

It would be easy to imagine cholera was an all-consuming medical concern during the antebellum era, but it was only one of the epistemic crises to upend American paradigms of health. As the *Vibrio cholerae* wended their way down the eastern seaboard of the United States, an assemblage of medical and political developments were also challenging the ways in which Americans thought about health. From the Nullification Crisis in South Carolina to the development of race science to an increasing interest in the science of sexual difference, a constellation of accumulating crises prompted a larger crisis. In this epistemic crisis, antebellum medical and political developments together conspired to challenge another central premise of medical epistemology: the notion of a single, representative American body.

CHAPTER 4

DIFFERENCE

SYMPATHY, *Sympathi'a, Compas'sio, Consen'sus, Sympathelis'mus, Conflux'io, Conspira'tio, Commer'cium, Consor'tium, Homoiopathia, Homoethnia, Adelphix'is, Sym. bolis'mus, Symboliza'tio,* from σύν "with," and πάθος, "suffering." The connexion that exists between the action of two or more organs, more or less distant from each other; so that the affection of the first is transmitted, secondarily, to the others, or to one of the others, by means unknown to us. A knowledge of the particular sympathies between different organs throws light on the etiology of diseases, their seat, and the particular organ towards which our therapeutical means should be directed.

—Robley Dunglison, *Medical Lexicon* (1839)

In 1826, two doctors and a medical student collaborated on a pamphlet about a hermaphrodite orangutan from Borneo that had recently died in Philadelphia. Richard Harlan (1796–1843), a physician and professor of comparative anatomy at the Philadelphia Museum, was the pamphlet's author, and he had Samuel George Morton, a young doctor, and Robert Montgomery Bird, a medical student, draw the illustrations; Harlan considered them essential to the essay. "Description of an Hermaphrodite Orang Outang, lately living in Philadelphia" provided details about the behavior and biology of the recently deceased animal, which they understood to shed light on human health.

In the right panel, Morton drew and labeled the animal's sex organs (Figure 11). With an eye toward objectivity, he represented them both as they could have been viewed from the outside of the orangutan's corpse and after

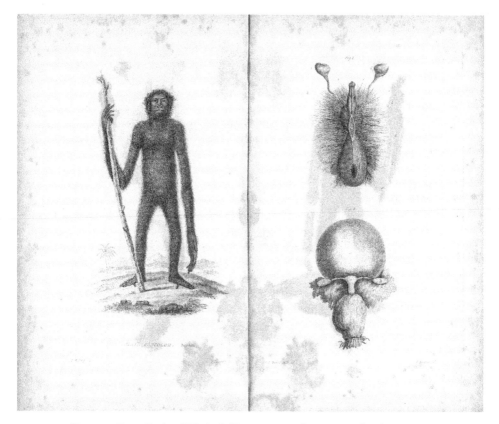

Figure 11. From Richard Harlan's "Description of an Hermaphrodite Orang Outang, lately living in Philadelphia," printed in *Medical and Physical Researches* (Philadelphia, 1835). The images were originally drawn for an essay delivered in Philadelphia on 17 October 1826. Left: Robert Montgomery Bird's "From a drawing of the animal, taken after death." Right: "External organ of generation" (top) and "Internal organs of generation, viewed from behind" (below). Courtesy of the American Antiquarian Society.

dissection. In a style that anticipated the medical illustrations in his later work, Morton details the body's particularity with regard to the emerging science of sexual difference through exacting ink lines and the meticulous labeling of parts using scientific nomenclature.[1] These illustrations experiment with objectivity and empiricism, emerging ways of knowing medical subjects in the nineteenth century.

In contrast, Bird's drawing in the left panel animates the orangutan corpse, imagining how it might have lived. Following a long medical tradition of illustrating active cadavers, Bird imagined life back into the corpse.[2] Bird augments this sense by picturing the animal as it could have existed in its natural habitat, flanked by the palm trees and mountains, presumably of Borneo. The lack of anatomical detail also shifts the viewer's attention from the orangutan's anatomy to its life. This drawing of the hermaphrodite orangutan illustrates Bird's burgeoning interest in using humanistic tools—here, visual narrative and the imagination—to produce medical knowledge. Bird relied on these techniques for his medical illustrations and remained committed to the value of imaginative inquiry for understanding medical difference throughout his life.[3]

Although not strictly a project about human bodies, Harlan, Morton, and Bird understood their work on the orangutan fundamentally as a contribution to medicine. Bird's drawing visually supports the pamphlet's claims, as his highly anthropomorphized ape stands upright, holds a tool, and meets the viewer's eyes. The orangutan's pose, open and even welcoming to the medical gaze, closely resembles the posture of human nudes in anatomy textbooks.[4] The hermaphrodite orangutan offered insight into human health by way of analogy: discoveries about the ape's body shed light on medical understandings of human sex organs. Because an orangutan's body was very close to— but not quite—a human body, Harlan believed he could use the ape to investigate issues that would be considered unethical with humans.[5] Such comparative anatomy, he wrote, was "intimately connected with the study of Medicine."[6] The medical community agreed. In the ten years that followed, the "Description of an Hermaphrodite Orang Outang, lately living in Philadelphia" would not only be delivered as a lecture, printed as a pamphlet (1827), and included in Harlan's *Medical and Physical Researches* (1835) but also appear in the *Journal of the Academy of Natural Sciences of Philadelphia* (1827) and in the *Lancet* (1836), England's premier medical journal.[7]

The deceased orangutan from Borneo provided an exciting and rare opportunity to investigate a growing issue for American medicine: the problem of knowing human difference. Over the first half of the nineteenth century, debates about monogenesis and polygenesis, increasing sexual bifurcation, more specific arguments about the effects of climate on human bodies, the rise of statistical differentiation, and ever more differentiated explanations about particular diseases, organs, and cells increasingly pulled apart the prevailing unitary models of health, prompting a epistemic crisis. In short, it was no longer clear whether all body parts operated according to the same principles or whether all bodies were, fundamentally, the same.

The hermaphrodite orangutan afforded Harlan, Bird, and Morton an opportunity to examine two facets of this politically initiated epistemic crisis in more detail. First, it augmented a growing body of research on sexual difference. Before the late eighteenth century, men and women were understood to be the same sex. Women were simply less perfect men. By the turn of the nineteenth century, however, Western culture was abandoning the "one sex" model for a "two sex" model; while men and women had once resided on a kind of sex continuum, *man* and *woman* were becoming diametrically opposed terms.[8] The hermaphrodite orangutan, then, offered a rare opportunity to examine this divergent biology up close through an intermediary. Second, in suggesting the close relationship between orangutan and human physiology, "Description of an Hermaphrodite Orang Outang" contributed to discussions of human speciation that had drawn increased scientific interest in the early nineteenth century. Orangutans played a central role in the scientific and cultural imaginaries of human speciation during the period. It was not just Harlan, Morton, and Bird who were interested in the orangutan. Harlan grounded his own inquiry in the work of the Comte de Buffon, who wrote that the species had "almost the human form," and doctors and writers around the Atlantic from Jean-Baptiste Lamarck to Edgar Allan Poe were fascinated by the ape's human-like physical and mental attributes.[9] The characteristics and behavior of the animal suggested to many that they might reside on a continuum with human species and might, given the right circumstances, even become human.[10] This inquiry into speciation dovetailed neatly with Harlan's early race science work. Although Harlan ultimately believed all humans were the same species, his mentee Morton would eventually come to a different conclusion.[11]

Through the hermaphrodite orangutan, Harlan, Morton, and Bird could attend to human difference on two important and related levels: the commensurability of bodies (orangutan and human) and the commensurability of body parts (sex organs). Theories of human differentiation in the period were largely grounded in the differences between body parts. Newly differentiated organs divided bodies into the two sexes; varying skull size and shape delineated both race and disposition; and the colors and contours of an array of body parts from lip to breast to limb mapped geographic and climatological differences between bodies. It was the differentiation of human body parts that laid a basis for the differentiation of human bodies.

A new collection of evidence and theory had been rapidly accumulating that challenged the prevailing universal models of the human body. That evidence and its related arguments suggested the incommensurable regional, racial, sexual, and even taxonomic differences between bodies, as well as an increasingly differentiated sense of the work of distinct body parts. This growing problem of knowing human difference prompted an epistemic crisis that forced Americans to reevaluate the basic premises of human health. In the first decades of U.S. medicine, a good deal of energy had been devoted to fashioning a unitary republican model for medicine. In that vision, a representative body, held together by a central, unifying feature of health—be it circulation, sympathy, or oxygen—provided a model for the health of all bodies as well as for society.

Accumulating ideas about human difference fundamentally altered the premises of American medicine, and, as a tricky, multifaceted problem, Americans employed a variety of epistemological tools to know it. Measuring, tabulating, and comparing different body parts formed the basis for widespread new ways of thinking about human anatomy, "the science of organization." Human physiology, "the science of life," was harder to know through quantification and empiricism. Thus doctors and writers also turned to practices including imaginative experimentation to know how these anatomical differences affected the life of different bodies.

Antebellum America was both medically and politically primed for this epistemic crisis. The crisis of knowing human difference made particular sense in the antebellum political climate. In the 1830s, a constellation of political changes rapidly took place that undermined republican models of governance, including the Nullification Crisis, Indian removal, the American colonization movement, and the proliferation of political constituencies. More radically democratic models that accounted for these increasingly distinct groups and constituencies were replacing republican visions in which a single representative could stand in for the whole. In other words, as Americans wondered whether eighteenth-century republican theories of health would hold, they were also grappling with whether the nation's different groups were commensurate (or commensurable), whether they were or could be joined with one another, and whether they could form a coherent whole. In short, the republicanism on which the first U.S. models of the body had been built was giving way to the rise of American democracy.[12]

As with earlier events in the history of American medicine, the medical and political were deeply entangled. The rapid geographical expansion of the United States, the sizable influx of immigrant bodies, and debates over slavery and indigenous territory all contributed to an increasing sense of the differences between bodies rather than a sense of their similarity. Cholera's dramatic unsettling of medical authority in the United States and the growing preference for empirical particularity typical of French medicine only further undermined the unitary theories that had dominated medicine in the early national period.[13] The synchronicity and entanglement of these shifts gave a particular urgency to the crisis of universality, setting in motion a paradigm shift.

Robert Montgomery Bird's career offers a useful window onto the problem of knowing human difference. Examining Bird's work in the context of his circle sheds light not only on the nuances of this epistemic crisis but also on how doctors and writers like Bird, who came of age in that period of uncertainty, used their imaginations to investigate the theories and questions of biological difference that emerged in the era. While the other chapters of this book explore an array of experiments performed in response to a single crisis, I focus here on the imaginative investigations of one individual during a variegated crisis. Examining Bird's work in the context of that of his mentors and friends—particularly Nathaniel Chapman and Samuel George Morton—shows how one representative figure experimented imaginatively with the thorny problems of knowing human difference.

Universal Sympathy

Robert Montgomery Bird would have been quite familiar with the medical model that privileged *sympathy* as the unifying feature of human health. While in medical school at the University of Pennsylvania, Bird learned from Nathaniel Chapman (1780–1853) that sympathy was the universal force that linked both bodies and body parts.[14] During his life, Chapman served as a professor of obstetrics and then materia medica (pharmacology) at the university. He had such influence over medicine in the Jacksonian period that historian Irwin Richman has called it "the Medical Age of Chapman."[15] His professional life spanned fifty years and included countless lectures, two books, fifteen edited volumes, a post as the eighth president of the American Philosophical Society, and election as the first president of the American Medical Association. Through Chapman's ideas, historians have observed, "one obtains a picture of the medical views actually subscribed to by a large number or even a majority of contemporary practitioners."[16] Trained by Benjamin Rush, Chapman believed in the importance of human differences but still held universal ideas of health. Individual differences were "of no small importance in the practice of medicine"; terms like "race" "implied modifications more profound, more essential differences, changes not confined to the surface, but extending to the very structure of the body."[17] Nevertheless, sympathy was a unifying concept flexible enough to accommodate the differences between distinct bodies and body parts. Defined as "the connexion that exists between the action of two or more organs, more or less distant from each other," sympathy in fact held the key to navigating those differences.[18]

While a number of doctors and writers of the early national period considered sympathy an element of health, Nathaniel Chapman spearheaded a shift that placed sympathy at the center of human health to the exclusion of other unitary theories. Eschewing Rush's teachings on the circulatory system, Chapman claimed his intellectual genealogy in Rush's Scottish mentor William Cullen. Cullen was a "solidist" who believed the body's health depended on distinct organs and the *sympathy* between them, even if he also held a more limited idea of sympathy than Chapman would come to embrace.[19] Chapman argued that the idea of sympathy had "hitherto been too much overlooked in our speculations as respects the phenomena of health and disease."[20] In 1810, Benjamin Rush complained to John Adams that through this position Chapman had "publicly renounced my medical principles, and said all that I have ever written 'is fit only to rot upon a dunghill.'"[21] Intently attacking Rush's theory that all disease stemmed from disturbed blood vessels, Chapman argued that the theoretical centrality of the circulatory system had dangerously skewed the perspective of early American medicine. Whereas Rush taught that medication "penetrate[d] into the circulation, and [acted] by a sort of chemical action," Chapman believed that the changed condition of solid organs initiated a set of actions through affiliation that promoted health.[22] Taking a dig at his recently deceased mentor a few years later, Chapman lectured, "It is not unknown to you that our own School denying the diversified nature of dise[ase] has attempted rather intemperately to put down all nosological distinctions—No one is more sensible than myself of the defects of the present arrangements."[23] Organs were distinct entities, Chapman argued, and the diseases arising from them should be treated according to those distinctions. In fact, Chapman continued, circulation was often dangerous; even healthy materials such as "the mildest fluid, as milk or mucilage," when introduced directly to the circulatory system, could be deadly.[24] Rather, materials needed to begin in the stomach, which altered medication so that it would be inert when it entered the blood for delivery to its intended organ. Once the circulatory system had been rightfully and "utterly deserted" as the means to health, doctors would be "forced to recur to sympathy, as affording the only explanation."[25]

Chapman may have learned about sympathy from the work of eighteenth-century physicians like Cullen, but he shifted its locus. Chapman held the stomach, not the nerves, most responsible for the connections between disparate body parts. "It would seem," Chapman wrote, "that in neither case [of sympathy] is it to be exclusively referred to the mediation of the nerves, as is commonly supposed. . . . There are many other sympathies, not less conspicuous, between parts, the nerves of which have not the slightest connection."[26] Rather, as a professor of materia medica, Chapman held that the stomach was "the centre of the greatest sphere of sympathy."[27] The stomach—not the brain, nerves, or blood vessels—was the major corporeal nexus. Chapman believed that through the stomach medication could be introduced to the body and spread sympathetically throughout the rest of the organs to promote health.[28] "Never am I called to a disease," Chapman lectured his students, "that I don't ask myself 'What concern has the stom[ach] to it?' "[29]

For a nineteenth-century version of medical sympathy, Chapman turned to French physician Anthelme Richerand, whose *Elements of Physiology* he edited and annotated for an American audience in 1813 in preparation to teach his medical students at the University of Pennsylvania.[30] In *Elements*, Richerand explained that the "links which unite together all the organs, by establishing a wonderful concurrence, and a perfect harmony among all the actions that take place in the animal economy, are known under the name of *sympathies*."[31] Nevertheless, he admitted that this non-neural version of sympathy was still quite vague: "The nature of this phenomenon is yet unknown; we know not why, when a part is irritated, another very distant part partakes in that irritation, or even contracts: we do not even understand what are the instruments of sympathy, that is, what are organs which connect two parts, in such a manner, that when one feels or acts, the other is affected."[32] Despite the inability to know much about sympathy, both Richerand and Chapman believed it to be the basis of life and health.

For Chapman, sympathy was a trans-organ quality that unified discrete parts both within the human body and between increasingly distinct bodies in the world. Chapman described the mechanism of sympathy as a "habit of concerted action"; this was the set of coordinated and repeated actions that John Locke, David Hartley, and Erasmus Darwin had called *association*.[33] More fully elaborating his capacious idea of sympathy in the early 1820s, Chapman triumphantly writes, "It is to this principle, whatever it be, which, uniting all the organs of the animal economy, that we are to impute the wonderful concurrence and perfect harmony observable in its complicated actions during health."[34] According to Chapman, sympathy worked when an element stimulated one part of the body, causing that part to be excited in a way that "extended more or less" to other parts "according to the diffusibility of the properties of the substance, or the degree of sympathetic connection which the part may maintain with the body generally."[35] Sympathy would not, however, produce the same effect in separate parts. It would produce one effect in a given system, "every one of which is precisely similar, provided they are confined to the same system, by which is to be understood, parts of an identity structure. If, however, the chain runs into other systems, it loses its homogeneous character, the actions being modified by the peculiar organization of the parts in which they may take place."[36] Thus sympathy behaved predictably within particular organs (e.g., a disturbance of the lungs causes coughing; emetics cause vomit), but when that disturbance transfers to other solid parts, "it loses its homogeneous character" and "the actions" of the stimulus or disturbance are transformed "by the peculiar organization of the parts." Fever may sympathetically connect with the stomach, but it causes diarrhea or vomit, not simply stomach fever. In an attempt to clarify these seemingly diffuse yet particular connections, Chapman defines sympathy more broadly by a phrase he borrowed from Richerand: the "consent of parts."[37] This politically inflected description would have resonated particularly in the antebellum United States where the growing problem of knowing human difference heightened the importance of the connection between distinct parts.

Chapman's discussion of sympathy may sound vague. It is. As a unitary mechanism, it seems to describe both everything and nothing at all. "It must be confessed, at present," Chapman admits, "we have no very distinct intelligence relative to its nature."[38] Nevertheless, he rallies his readers: "Are we, on this account, to question its existence?"[39] Listing other unquestionable yet vaguely conceived corporeal phenomena, Chapman argues for proof by effect rather than demonstrable mechanism: "In employing this term [sympathy], therefore, I mean only to denote like . . . many other such expressions, a principle, or power, of which we know nothing except from the experience of its effects, the precise essence or nature being occult, and concealed."[40] Choosing sympathy as his governing principle, he chose one of the eighteenth century's most highly contested and unstable terms.[41] To make sympathy universal, he also has to make it vague and mysterious, "occult, and concealed"—an issue the problem of understanding human difference would bring to crisis.

The rising empiricism of the nineteenth century made it more difficult to orient medicine around such vague notions. Sympathy was very difficult to test empirically for both ethical and physical reasons. Vivisection quite vividly illuminated the ethical issues posed by experimenting physically with sympathy. In the very first volume of the *Philadelphia Journal of Medical and Physical Sciences*, for example, Chapman published the work of William Horner (1793–1853), a colleague of his at the University of Pennsylvania, who used vivisection to know sympathy empirically. Seeking to determine sympathy's features more precisely, Horner performed a series of nine experiments on young cats and rabbits. To prove the relationship between the nervous system, organs, and principles of life, Horner "took a kitten, four days old, and divided the spinal marrow between the occipital foramen and first cervical vertebra, which instantly stopped respiration. The animal was much agitated, and gaped frequently. At the end of ten minutes, when sensibility had almost ceased, the larynx was divided from the *os hyoids*, and lungs artificially inflated."[42] He continued manually inflating the lungs before severing the spine. After half an hour, "each of the parts thus separated retained sensibility and motion: but all sympathy between them was destroyed, as an impression made upon the fore parts produced no effect upon the hinder, and *vice versa*."[43] After another ten minutes the kitten appeared to have lost sensation and by the time an hour had passed, Horner was sure the animal had died. In this experiment, Horner methodically deduced which parts of the spine connect to which organs and which parts control the major actions of life such as "sensibility and motion" from the order of his fatal incisions. His goal in this and the eight experiments that followed, he explained, was to determine exactly how nervous sympathy maintained life.

The practices of physical experimentation with sympathy like vivisection certainly posed ethical problems, but they were also not particularly effective for knowing sympathy. For one, vivisection hardly offered the "window of Momus" Robert Montgomery Bird had wished for; the practice provided only a partial view and one that necessarily rendered a healthy body unhealthy by the very act of cutting. As Bird would later explain to his students of physical experimentation more generally:

> The difficulty of arriving at truth in medicine, by mere experimental observation, though the observer be the most astute and

perspicacious of his race, is of a magnitude scarce conceivable by any but a physician. In the first place, we have no facilities and precise means of study, such as are offered in other paths of research. When any new fact is discovered in physics, it is capable of direct and immediate verification by the whole world. . . . No such testimony can be had in Medicine. The human economy is a complication of mechanism, to which Babbage's *Calculating Machine*, the most stupendously intricate of all human inventions, bears the same relation of simplicity that a smoke-jack does to a steam engine, a wheelbarrow to a chronometer or printing ma-chine. A thousand—a *million* agencies unite to make the little universe of life; and no human wit—not even the Calculating Machine itself—can compute the combinations of disease to which a single interruption in a single organ may give rise.[44]

The human body, Bird contended, resisted epistemologies based in sensory per-ception. Whereas natural sciences like physics were "capable of direct and immediate verification," physical research in medicine yielded little. Perhaps Bird had learned from Richerand's textbook that the body's physiology was "the model of the most ingenious productions of art," in which "a million agencies" baffled the attempts of physical experimentation to yield up the body's secrets.[45]

Practices like vivisection were also problematic for knowing sympathy because they ran up against other troubles of knowing human difference. If, particularly by the 1830s, Americans were increasingly coming to wonder what any body had in common with any other body, the commonalities human bodies shared with animals, which had been loosely grouped under the cate-gory "animal life," were yet more tenuous. Vivisection in particular *depended* upon argument by analogy, and analogy was problematically rooted in the imagination. Even Descartes maintained an "early conviction that the faculty of the imagination was the portal to the understanding [that] made analogies an indispensable part of his science," according to Park, Daston, and Gali-son.[46] Presumably, Horner could slowly torture and kill kitten after kitten because he believed his actions were immediately applicable to human medi-cine. "We are thus led to a beautiful and important conclusion in physiology," Horner writes, "one which, from the unequivocal character of the proofs brought to its support, is justly entitled to our greatest attention, and which ought to enter into all our reasonings upon the symptoms connected with apoplexy and other affections of the brain attended with compression of its substance."[47] Nevertheless, even Horner himself admitted, "one of the most striking circumstances in the nervous system is the variety which it exhibits in the different classes of animals."[48] Vivisection required an imaginative engagement that linked the bodies of kittens and rabbits to those of human beings precisely as the troubles of difference were being parsed.[49]

Finally, sympathy posed unique challenges as a subject for investigative practices like vivisection. By investigating one facet of universal sympathy, physical experimentation destroyed another. In working to learn about nervous sympathies, Horner destroyed what were understood to be natural sympathies between his body and his subject's, becoming the character of the unfeeling physician drawn to physical experimentation so common in novelistic critiques in the mid-nineteenth century. Physician-writer Bernard de Mandeville (1670–1733) argued early in the eighteenth century that "we are born with a repugnancy to the killing, and consequently the eating of animals. . . . Every body knows, that surgeons in the cure of dangerous wounds and fractures," he continues, "are often compelled to put their patients to extraordinary torments . . . their Practice itself is sufficient to harden and extinguish in them that Tenderness, without which no man is capable of setting a true value upon the lives of his fellow-creatures."[50] If this was true of lifesaving procedures, it was certainly more true of killing undertaken for medical research. In other words, in the process of trying to know sympathy, Horner risked destroying his own capacity for sympathy. Physically, this posed the following problem: How could he learn more about sympathy or feeling in others if he had lost a sense of "fellow feeling" himself? Or, thought differently: Could Horner be a trustworthy source for the production of knowledge if he had so troublingly altered his own constitution? Ethically, some nineteenth-century Americans were unsure the practice should be undertaken no matter the answer.

Chapman was less concerned with these empirical problems because he was committed to using humanistic tools to know medical phenomena like sympathy. The epigraph Chapman chose in 1820 for the *Philadelphia Journal of Medical and Physical Sciences* exemplified the close relationship between medical epistemology and the arts. Turning Scottish detractor Sydney Smith's famous critique of American culture toward more positive ends, Chapman rallied his countrymen: "In the four corners of the globe, who reads an American book? or goes to an American play? or looks at an American picture or statue? *What does the world yet owe to American Physicians or Surgeons?*"[51] His journal responded emphatically to Smith's sarcasm. Like many physicians in the period, Chapman believed humanistic inquiry to be closely related to the production of American medical knowledge.[52] Elsewhere he made the point more directly: "By the mythology of the ancients . . . we are instructed that the study and practice of physick was most conspicuously connected with the love of the liberal arts, and of polite literature."[53] However, Chapman's humanistic approach to medicine, unlike Bird's, relied most heavily on what he called "philosophizing."[54] For Chapman, observation was an initial step in knowing, but he was convinced that important medical principles like sympathy were best understood through philosophizing. He advocated "infusing into science the genuine spirit of reason and philosophy," which would "place medicine on a basis so solid as never again to be convulsed by the revolutions of opinion."[55] Because Chapman privileged his mind as the source of knowledge production, he was not worried about empirically proving that sympathy was the universal mechanism through which all distinct parts were unified.

Human Difference

Sympathy was a robust universal theory, but it could not ultimately stem or subsume the crisis emerging from the problem of knowing human difference. In retrospect, signs of the coming crisis had long been building. Chapman, for example, who was so invested in the idea of universal sympathy, nevertheless also lectured on human difference in some depth. Chapman cataloged American bodies for his medical students according to their humors, temperament, eye color, hair color, age, gender, and circumstance.[56] Climate and geography also determined corporeal differences and health. Chapman wrote, for example, that "the Sanguinous belongs to youth & to the Inhabitants of high latitudes, who are therefore subject to Inflamty. Diseases—Bilious appears in Manhood & in warm climates—The Plegmatic in low flat countries."[57] One should not expect hemorrhaging in flat Delaware, but towheaded Vermonters ought to beware.

This vision had obvious political corollaries. Rather than a republic-modeled representative system in which one body stood in for the nation, growing American democracy took stock of splintered demographics. When Andrew Jackson's success in the presidential campaigns of 1824, 1828, and 1832 threatened to and ultimately displaced an eastern, urban elite with the electoral power of western farmers and eastern laborers, these rising factional tides were rendered transparent. Furthermore, state-orchestrated secessionist flare-ups like the Hartford Convention (1814) and the Nullification Crisis (1832–33) increasingly drew attention to potentially irreconcilable differences between the not-so-united states. These tensions would only mount in the Jacksonian era, gesturing toward what seemed to some like inevitable civil war. Whereas Rush might have optimistically envisioned one body standing in for the nation, growing factions made that vision increasingly difficult to imagine.

Bird also invested in the idea of human difference early on. Not only had he worked for both Harlan and Morton, but his 1826 medical thesis evaluated the susceptibility of different kinds of bodies to tuberculosis. Bird began the study with the observation that individuals with a "congenital predisposition to consumption" could be identified by their "slender and delicate body; fair hair and complexion; a bright, tender, blue eye, with large pupils; a tumid upper lip, and clear white teeth."[58] Other features, including "long neck, and high shoulders; protruding scapula; a flat, constricted breast, with the xiphoid cartilage and bone lying hollow like a furrow; and in females, a particular leanness and laxity of the breasts [. . . and an] acuteness of feeling and intellect" also predisposed individuals to consumption.[59] Susceptible children were generally fair and thin with delicate bones and sharp minds. They were also prone to "capricious coughs, and fits of syspnoa [sic] from spasms."[60] Bird's interest lay in delineating the characteristics of attractive, intelligent white Americans who were most at risk. While reasonably confident about his physiognomic distinctions when it came to consumption, Bird nonetheless observed that the inquiries into "morbid anatomy . . . so sedulously and methodically cultivated" and physical experimentation on crabs, frogs, and rabbits had contributed little to medical knowledge about the disease.[61] As a result, Bird believed that physicians remained more generally "ignorant of the real origin and nature of tubercular consumption," which meant that medical "practice, like our thesises [sic], must be necessarily unsatisfactory."[62]

Though he would pursue more overt imaginative experiments in his later work, Bird's investment in the imagination and literary form as a way of knowing human difference is already apparent in this early text. For example, Bird begins the thesis with lines of verse from Horace's *Epodes* about the process and experience of becoming ill.[63] Bird likewise uses literary examples to understand why some individuals become prone to consumption: they do damage to themselves by inhaling "from too excessive an exercise" of their lungs, "especially like Falstaff, by hollering, and singing of anthems."[64] More generally,

Bird's thesis gathers narrative accounts of patients' lives and activities as well as more florid descriptions of individual characteristics to account for the differences between consumption patients and predisposed individuals, a phenomenon he felt was poorly explained by the physical experiments he and his peers undertook.

Even this early attempt to schematize human variation owed a clear debt to Samuel George Morton's work on difference. Bird's medical thesis was dedicated to Morton, who was a few years older and more advanced in his medical career. He inscribed the thesis to "An accomplished Physician, And, A warm Friend."[65] The writing bears the hallmarks of Morton's early thinking about the varieties of human bodies, and its discussion of humoral, characteristic, and environmental differences that predispose American bodies to consumption echoes the racial descriptions in Morton's work.

Bird continued to work with Morton on the topic of human difference through the 1830s. In 1833, Bird embarked on a trip through the West and South that was likely connected to the project that would become Morton's magnum opus on human difference, *Crania Americana* (1839).[66] On the night before he left, Bird apologized to Morton for leaving town before he could finish a promised sketch: "So great has been the bother of preparation for my journey," Bird wrote in his note to Morton, "that I have not been able to do anything of the least consequence to the sketch. I hope you will receive my apology, for really I was desirous of finishing."[67] Bird then promised to wait until midnight to see Morton before he departed, perhaps for Morton's advice on an undertaking that would have greatly interested him. Although no Bird sketches appear in *Crania Americana*, Bird seems to have been heavily influenced by, if not directly involved in, the production of the volume. As Bird's wife would later note, Bird's "accurate pencil was put in frequent requisition" for Morton.[68]

However, once more, Bird's techniques diverged from Morton's. The work Bird produced from the trip bore little relationship to the mechanical objectivity in which Morton would be interested for his skull project. Instead, Bird drew images of indigenous peoples in their natural habitats, living their lives. Whereas Bird's derogatory depiction of indigenous people in *Nick of the Woods* (1837) has guided scholarly interpretations of Bird's attitudes, these earlier sketches imagine the lives of the bodies he examined.[69] In the words of curator Daniel Traister, "Dr. Bird portrays real people, not anthropological data."[70]

While Bird was exploring humanistic epistemologies, Morton was hard at work on an empirical method for understanding human difference.[71] In the 1837 prospectus for the volume, Morton explained that the book would aim

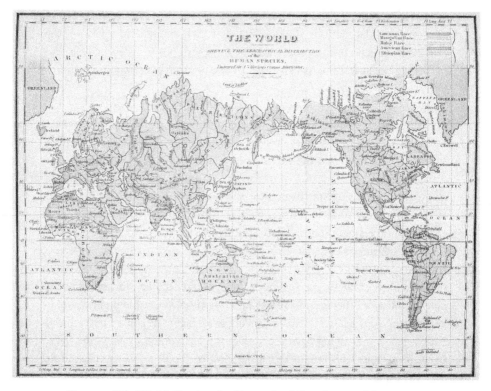

Figure 12. "The World, Shewing the Geographical Distribution of the Human Species" from Samuel George Morton's *Crania Americana* (1839). Courtesy of the American Antiquarian Society.

to allow "the general reader" to "investigate and compare the various analogies and differences, so remarkable in the several divisions of the human family."[72] The volume progresses from a frontispiece of the regal-looking Native American "Ongpatonga [Big Elk]" and a map of "The World, Shewing the Geographical Distribution of the Human Species" to an extensive set of quantitative data and lithographed skulls (Figure 12). Together, the frontispiece and map work to connect individual characteristics to a global medical geography—as the cholera maps of the 1830s did.[73]

The empirical problems that plagued the cholera maps also appeared in Morton's race map. One such problem was the ontological tension between the universal and the particular. Were the elements represented—in Morton's map, the human races—wholly distinct and incommensurable? Or were they, despite their apparent differences, a composite whole? It was a question Morton pondered for decades. In the map, Morton took a middle way between the cartographically traditional maps of climatists like Henry Schneck Tanner, who sought to distinguish different cholera epidemics by year, and the geographical radicalism of A. Sidney Doane and Amariah Brigham (see Chapter 3). The coloring, scale, and style of Morton's map resemble those of Tanner's map, while his refigured geography—which centered the globe on the Bering Strait rather than the Atlantic, as in the familiar Mercator project— partook of a more radical geography.

Spatial and temporal problems also hampered empirical knowing in the map. While Morton offered his map as a static and timeless representation of "the geographical distribution of the human species," he also claimed that the project celebrated the capacity of the human species to flout enormous environmental barriers; it represented the "peopling of the earth." The devil certainly was in the details for Morton, who found he had trouble drawing the lines that defined the putatively natural geographical boundaries between different kinds of human beings. "The boundary between the Caucasian and Mongolian races is extremely vague," he admitted, and deferred to the choice made by another race scientist: "Professor Blumenbach's line (which is an approximation to accuracy) runs from the Ganges in a northwestern direction to the Caspian sea."[74] Of the "Ethiopian line" drawn across the Atlas mountains, he likewise wrote, "little is known," and "many Negro nations inhabit to the north of them, at the same time that the Arab tribes have penetrated far beyond them to the south, and in some places have formed a mixed race with the native tribes."[75] The lines and colors on his map suggested a naturally bounded and static distribution of human difference that, he confessed, repeatedly defied the actual movement and mixing of people. If cholera maps sought to fix representations of a phenomenon that was too dynamic to map, Morton's map likewise struggled to represent the complete history of human difference as a static phenomenon, even when evidence proved otherwise.

Morton sought answers for what the map could not resolve empirically in data: in *Crania*, he collects, quantifies, and meticulously records anatomical measurements with charts, numbers, and statistics. The volume concludes with dozens of lithographs of human skulls that Morton links not to individuals but to types: "Peruvian," "Ottigamie," "From the Grave-Creek Mound Near Wheeling Virginia," "From a Mound in Tennessee." Even the frontispiece, it turns out, was a data point for larger claims about race. A small note on the image redirects the reader to the back of the volume wherein Morton explains that Big Elk is an ideal representation of a type; he "know[s] of no one that embraces more characteristic traits than this, as seen in the retreating forehead, the low brow, the dull and seemingly unobservant eye, the large, aquiline nose, the high cheek bones, full mouth and chin, and angular face."[76]

Morton's argument about the geographical distribution of human types hinges largely on the sets of numerical tables he includes in the back of the volume. In an impulse that would appeal to today's empirically minded scientists, Morton went to great pains to standardize his procedure and worked to have others verify his results: "That some errors may exist in so numerous a series of measurements is not merely possible but probable," he writes, "but the following facts show the reader how much care was taken to avoid them."[77] When he discovered an error in procedure, Morton's team discarded the mass of results they had accumulated. Morton's collaborator John Phillips additionally describes their method: "Dr. Morton took down all the measurements, the whole of which were made by myself; thus avoiding the inaccuracies which must necessarily have occurred, had several different persons contributed their aid."[78] Nevertheless, Morton acknowledges that "it may, perhaps, be thought by some readers, that these details are unnecessarily minute," but this abundance illustrates Morton's collection of "facts unbiassed by theory" to "let the reader draw his own conclusions."[79] Recording measurements to the tenth of an inch, he aimed for objectivity.

Morton hoped to eliminate the imagination from *Crania Americana*. Even as he continued to engage in humanistic pursuits like writing poetry, he sought to rid his volume of imaginative departures. Historian Ann Fabian describes Morton as "a fussy customer" who "sometimes rejected drawings with 'crabbed humor.'"[80] While common to the older styles of animated medical illustration, Fabian argues that such humor was troublesome to Morton's idea of his role as a "scientific naturalist": "To make 'objective' arguments about the differences among races, the book needed to sever readers' associations between the skulls depicted in *Crania Americana* and the human relics they might have seen in paintings."[81] These different tacks also align well with the epistemological differences between the nineteenth-century desire for "mechanical objectivity" and the eighteenth-century "truth-to-nature" ideal.[82]

In spite of this quantitative approach, *Crania Americana* did not draw definitive conclusions about the nature of human difference. In fact, the volume both argues for the unity of the human species and suggests that the "peopling of the earth" could not have occurred naturally and was only possible through divine intervention. Morton wanted it both ways. The different kinds of humans were distinct and should remain so, but he did not yet believe they were different *species* of human beings, a view called *polygenesis* that in 1839 Morton believed was heretical. The Bible, Morton wrote, supported a "literal and obvious interpretation" that "all men have originated from a single pair."[83] Nevertheless, he hedged, this difference could not be reduced to environmental factors. It would take another decade for Morton to embrace a polygenist position.[84]

Imagining Sympathy as Epistemology in *Sheppard Lee*

Bird experimented with the work of both Chapman and Morton in his 1836 novel *Sheppard Lee*, which investigates the topics of human connection and difference. *Sheppard Lee* is a picaresque novel based on Bird's travels in which he imaginatively explores a diverse set of American bodies. More so than any of Bird's other works, *Sheppard Lee* is a daring medical experiment in literary form.

The 1836 novel is the nominal autobiography of Sheppard Lee, a character who lives a dissatisfied life as a farmer before he accidentally kills himself digging for gold. In this novel that resists summary, Lee's death prompts his wandering spirit to tour the country in the host of distinct corpses he sequentially reanimates. Experimentally acquainting himself with the life of each body, Lee's soul tries and fails to find a happy resting place. Bird's protagonist tours the national body through a sequence of representative American bodies— Lee (yeoman farmer), Higginson (wealthy merchant), Dawkins (Northern dandy), Skinner (Jewish usurer), Longstraw (Quaker philanthropist), Tom (black slave), and Megrim (Southern gentleman)—driven by the twin desires for happiness and wealth.[85] Grounding American experience in dramatically different bodies, Bird explores the connections and divisions between Jacksonian types, testing the unifying mechanisms of life. Lee's propensities and beliefs change drastically within each, prompting recurring meditations about whether sympathy can hold together body parts or link increasingly different bodies through one unifying American spirit—a "Sheppard Lee."[86]

Bird's experimental question in *Sheppard Lee* amounts to this: If, as Chapman taught, sympathy is the unitary mechanism that structures our lives in the world, holding together increasingly distinct bodies and body parts, what exactly is it, how does it work, and how far do its powers extend? If sympathy is not the common experience of all bodies, what is? Since sympathy was understood to link body parts to one another and to cohere the body politic, the stakes of the answers were high—they promised to illuminate the basis of life and health. But Bird fretted about the capabilities of antebellum medical epistemology to provide answers and worried about the problem of commensurability: for Bird, American bodies were not interchangeable leaves of grass, and his questions about what bound the Southern gentleman to the Quaker philanthropist reproduced his concerns about what harmonized the body's distinct organs. Seeking to move past the limitations of Chapman's medical philosophy and Morton's quantitative methods, Bird turned to the literary to investigate the unitary mechanisms of life.[87]

Metempsychosis and the picaresque provided Bird with literary tools to test medical principles while avoiding the troubles of antebellum physical experimentation. Critiquing the increasing epistemological emphasis on the physical experiment, Bird has characters in *Sheppard Lee* perform unnecessary and disturbing experiments such as poisoning cats and electrocuting slaves.[88] As Arthur Megrim, Lee dreams his doctor "and his scientific coadjutors . . . were dissecting me alive," a nightmarish "torment" matched only by "those that beset me [by the doctors] while awake."[89] Most significantly, the novel is framed by a perverse physical experiment: Lee's original separation from his body occurs because, after Lee accidentally kills himself, the German doctor Feuerteufel steals his corpse for experimentation. Readers revel in the joke Bird's novel retributively plays on the scheming physician in reuniting Lee with his body when Feuerteufel's "thousand cares" for "the especial benefit of science and the world" work only "too well."[90] Willing himself back into his original body, Lee slips "off the pedestal and out of his hands [. . . while Feuerteufel] stare[s] upon [Lee] with eyes, nose, and mouth, speechless, rooted to the floor, and apparently converted into a mummy himself."[91] The return of the human (Lee's spirit) to the scientifically evacuated machine (Lee's body) disables Feuerteufel's scientifically honed senses and reanimates his "feelings."[92] Freed from the physical experiment, both Feuerteufel and Lee become human again. This scene is yet more damning of burgeoning medical epistemologies when we remember that in the 1830s many American doctors were increasingly heading to Germany for training. In an early draft, Bird imagines Lee's body shipped by Feuerteufel to Europe, from which Lee flees immediately upon reanimation.[93] The German Feuerteufel then embodies not only the incursion of foreign paradigms into American medicine but, more pointedly, the perils of American doctors' desire to acquire and reproduce the methods of dangerously dehumanized medical epistemologies in the United States.[94]

Turning to the novel, Bird charts another path. Declaring *Sheppard Lee* of interest to both the common reader and the "doctor of medicine and the physiologist," Bird announces the work's engagement in his medical project.[95] But the novel also plays coy. Bird's narrator declares he will "leave these learned gentlemen to discuss what may appear most wonderful in [the story's] revealments" and suggests the reader may skip the theorizing.[96] With bad doctors flitting in and out of the narrative, the novel appears to disavow medicine. One is an ineffective drunk and another a cruel, lovesick physician who prescribes to please his paramour. Feuerteufel is an alleged counterfeiter, conjurer, fortune hunter, and "devil" whose presence "torment[s]" Lee throughout from the death of his original body to the moment of his mind-body reunification at the novel's end.[97]

Nevertheless, these negative representations of doctors reflect Bird's growing ambivalence about the epistemological techniques and practices of medicine in the 1830s rather than a rejection of the medical enterprise. A cultural polymath (novelist, physician, playwright, draftsman, photographer, historian, poet, professor, congressional candidate, newspaperman), Bird understood well that genres were rhetorical strategies that could be used to explore different aspects of medicine and society. Beyond the objective and quantitative epistemologies promoted by peers like Morton, Bird used fiction to investigate physiological mechanisms that were difficult—if not "impossible"—to test physically and better pursued through humanistic methods.

Bird was intensely interested in sympathy as a possible force to unify the increasingly distinct bodies of human beings, but he was as wary of Chapman's vague "philosophizing" as he was of rising empirical methods. Of Chapman's epistemology, Bird wrote elsewhere, "Philosophy has not penetrated—she never can penetrate—the mysteries of mere vegetable life. . . . Need she blush to confess ignorance of the greater incomprehensibilities of animal life?"[98] To get around this difficulty, Bird engaged sympathy as both an epistemological tool and a subject of inquiry, grounding his inquiry in the local specificities Chapman eschewed. As Lee moves between bodies, the novel investigates the degree to which sympathy can link particular bodies and body parts and explores the possibility of a unifying American sympathy in a shifting Jacksonian world. In this Bird joined other medical theorists in believing that the body offered a metonym for a body politic that operated according to medical principles. Early plans for the novel reveal that Bird imagined Lee embodying a parson, Christian bigot, Mormon, schoolboy, schoolmaster, editor, critic, author, patriot, and physician; Christopher Looby writes that together the lists show "that [Bird] wanted to provide a map of the American society."[99] Through Lee, Bird sought to investigate the sympathies that linked these very distinct parts.

This experiment begins before Lee's death. Dissatisfied with his yeoman-farmer inheritance, Lee tries a variety of professions, eventually dragging his farming tools to an abandoned churchyard to dig for Captain Kidd's treasure. Enacting the fantasies of many Jacksonians, Lee hopes for speculative benefits in place of land-based rewards.[100] In an early sketch of the novel, Bird imagined it thus: "Sheppard Lee is confined in a madhouse (in Phil.) and a Penitentiary (Auburn, or Sing Sing). In these he hears the stories of men ruined by divers [sic] American propensities (chiefly the urge to grow rich)."[101] Lee's story compulsively repeats the "American propensit[y]" to confuse the pursuit of happiness with the "urge to grow rich."

Using sympathy as a mode through which to understand the national body, Bird's novel quickly reveals that the common connective force between American bodies is "chiefly" their speculative pursuit of happiness.[102] Stated another way, greed is the "sympathy" that propels Lee between bodies, despite vast social, economic, racial, and political differences. This sympathy is spurred by envy, the ability to imagine oneself in another's place and desire it. This affective state creates a closeness between bodies that often otherwise revile each other. In fact, it is the desire to attain wealth and happiness without hard work—the fantasy of the market revolution—that unites Lee's incarnations. Each new embodiment is a speculative venture. Weighing both the imaginative and the instrumental value of these bodies, Lee considers what they might feel like and what he stands to gain. In this sense, Bird's bodies are drawn together through a sympathy that is not empathy but a dark version of what Chapman called a "habit of concerted action."

More troublingly, if Lee's body-to-body sympathies are motivated by envy, they are made possible only by misrecognition; paradoxically, Lee's failures of imaginative sympathy are the precondition for physical sympathy. Lee-as-Higginson chooses Dawkins despite watching Dawkins commit suicide. Lee-as-Dawkins chooses the greedy usurer Skinner though Philadelphia reviles him. Entering Longstraw's mangled corpse Lee laments, "I took but little time for reflection; or perhaps I should not have been in such a hurry to attempt a transformation . . . it would have been wiser had I thought of [Longstraw's painful injuries]—but unluckily I did not: I was in too great a hurry."[103] Lee regrets most incarnations almost instantly. If Lee could properly sympathize—or rather, as we would understand it, empathize—with bodies as Adam Smith suggests a viewer does with the man on the rack, he would not leap so readily. But this failure of one facet of sympathy is the prerequisite for another. If Lee felt the misery of Dawkins, Higginson, or Longstraw, he would leave them to their fates. Lee *must* misrecognize the state of each new body to connect to it, a searing indictment of social and somatic sympathy in corporeal terms.

This imaginative experiment with medical sympathy finds its most serious ramifications in the medical understanding of the mind, which Bird renders first and foremost as an organ in the body.[104] Filling the distinct skulls of different corpses with his own mind, Lee's first discovery is that he needs to negotiate the former inhabitant's brain. But rather than developing sympathetic harmony through empathy (the ability to share feelings with another) or a seamlessly unified consciousness, uncomfortable frictions repeatedly emerge. The result is not a concordant union of brain and spirit but rather the effacement of the novel's sympathetic force, the spirit of Sheppard Lee.[105] As the novel continues to test lines of sympathetic association, this spirit-brain friction diminishes in the white bodies Lee inhabits not because the life he infuses into the body sympathizes most empathetically with Longstraw's benevolence, Dawkins's foppishness, or Megrim's privilege but because the bodies' habits take over in ways that align with Lee's original greed. This emphasis on sympathy as a "habit of concerted action" foregrounds the lack of empathetic or ideational consensus between Lee's incarnations. The novel makes a temporary peace by eliding the disjunctive spirit-brain fusions between Lee and his white embodiments, but it highlights the more disturbing failures of imaginative sympathy in Lee's other ventures.[106]

In these experiments, Bird reveals his interrogation of sympathy to be more richly specific and imaginative than Chapman's if more troubled in its articulation. One of the most significant and exciting examples is *Sheppard Lee*'s interracial experimentation. Bird's investigation of Chapman's theory that sympathy could exist, though "it loses its homogeneous character," between very different bodies and body parts here tests the limits of antebellum sympathetic imagination. In its willingness to fuse a white mind with Jewish and black bodies, *Sheppard Lee* offers a unique and vivid experiment in miscegenated sympathies if not shared feelings. In so doing, it imaginatively probes one of the most contested sites of Jacksonian medical and political thinking. Nevertheless, Bird cannot capitalize on the radical potential of his imaginative leaps, and only a forced and fraught physical sympathy emerges in Lee's non-white bodies.

Lee's third embodiment as the Jewish Skinner demonstrates sympathy's possibilities and its limits. Simultaneously engaging in one of the novel's most

creative and capacious acts of sympathy and illustrating the destructive nature of uneasy unions, Lee leaps into Skinner's body only to proclaim, "Abram
Skinner destroyed every trait that had belonged to Sheppard Lee; and as for
those [traits] I had taken from John H. Higginson and I. D. Dawkins, they
were lost in like manner. I was Abram Skinner and nothing but Abram Skinner."[107] Skinner's Jewish body "destroy[s]" the sympathy that had accreted between white bodies. Lee explains the impossibility of certain sympathies
thus: "strong minds may be indeed operated upon without regard to bodily
bias, and rendered independent of it; but ordinary spirits lie in their bodies
like water in sponges, diffused through every part, affected by the part's affections, changed with its changes, and so intimately united with the fleshly
matrix, that the mere cutting off of a leg, as I believe, will, in some cases, leave
the spirit limping for life."[108] When Bird inhabits heavily raced bodies the
"bodily bias" is so strong that the somatic life *becomes* the life of the "spirit,"
eradicating more meaningful notions of sympathy. Simultaneously adopting
and mocking language that could easily pass for Chapman's, Bird writes that
this now very diffused sympathy—Lee's "spirit"—is "affected by the part's affections, changed with its changes."

In his penultimate embodiment, Lee-as-Tom more decidedly articulates
sympathy's limitations for overcoming human difference. Getting over his
(white spirit's) initial revulsion to Tom's black body, Lee soon discovers he
is happiest as the unthinking Tom. Lee-as-Tom may be "the merriest and
happiest of them all," but his happiness is "foolish."[109] Lee decides, "My mind
was stupefied."[110] "I had ceased to remember," he writes, "all my previous
states of existence. I could not have been an African had I troubled myself with
thought of anything but the present."[111] Here Bird's language is instructive:
becoming "African" requires the deadening of Lee's spirit. Writing a sympathy between distinct parts that he then declares impossible, Bird imagines the
happiest state of sympathy is, paradoxically, the state of sympathy's destruction.
Lee can only join Tom if he is no longer Lee.

These scenes foreground sympathy's knotty complexities; they are simultaneously intricate and daring experiments in sympathy and forceful articulations of its limits. In racially marked bodies, Lee loses himself to the strength
of the body. For example, as Justine Murison observes, Bird resists melding
Tom's language with Lee's.[112] Despite the progressive potential of these scenes,
Bird retreats. As the failure of imaginative sympathy made corporeal sympathy
possible, in racially marked bodies, corporeal sympathy checks the possibility
of imaginative sympathy. Even within these parameters, Bird could not man-

age the radical possibilities, and, thus, the resurfacing of interracial sympathy ends in death. Lee-as-Tom finds an antislavery pamphlet meant to rouse white sympathies that revives Lee's spirit. Lee's ability to read leads to an insurrection that culminates in the second destruction of Tom's body. Like Skinner, whose sons kill themselves as a direct result of their father's reanimation, Lee's sympathy with Tom causes pain and devastation, rupturing putatively natural bonds between Tom and those around him; the sympathy between Lee's spirit and white bodies may be uncomfortable and ultimately untenable, but interracial sympathy is cataclysmic.[113] Recapitulating polygenist arguments about the incommensurability of different bodies, having Lee assume the minds of racially marked bodies produces catastrophe. In a jarring inversion of productive sympathetic social identification, interracial physical sympathy brings bodies and body parts together only for destruction. Murderous bloodshed underscores the limits of Chapman's unitary theory of sympathy.

Race and Human Difference in *Sheppard Lee*

In its illustration of the disastrous results of sympathy, *Sheppard Lee* invokes the work Bird and Morton undertook on the nature of human difference. Unsatisfied with Chapman's totalizing but too abstract sympathy, Bird explores the nature of human difference but displays deep ambivalence about the method and findings of empirical work like Morton's. Given their close medical and literary friendship, which spanned at least three decades, it is unsurprising that Bird and Morton pursued similar questions, if through divergent techniques. Over the years, both committed themselves to investigating the problem of corporeal distinction they had begun working on together in the 1820s. Nevertheless, while Morton experimented with new systems of empirical evidence, Bird used imaginative experimentation to explore the question of knowing human difference.

In imagining his protagonist into the skulls of different human bodies, Bird was experimenting imaginatively with methods that exceeded what empiricism could do to learn more about the nature of human difference. In particular, his technique challenged the new mechanical objectivity with which Morton was still very much experimenting in the 1830s. Morton used the relationship he observed between skull size and intellectual capacity to argue that Caucasians possessed "the highest intellectual endowments" and the "black complexion, black woolly hair[ed]" Ethiopians the lowest.[114] He used detailed maps and tables such as "On the Internal Capacity of the Cranium in the different Races of Men" to create a racial hierarchy based on indirect empirical evidence about the size and shape of human brains.[115] If "the brain is the organ of the mind" whose "different parts perform different functions," Morton reasoned, then different cranial measurements suggested the different capabilities of different human bodies.[116] Nevertheless, Morton knew his findings said more about the "science of organization" (anatomy) than the "science of life" (physiology). Morton had painstakingly recorded "elaborate measurements," but those numbers were an indirect measure of the differences between living human bodies.[117] Morton let a phrenological appendix written by his friend George Combe (1788–1858) do the work of connecting "the natural Talents and dispositions of Nations" to "the Development of their Brains" for him.[118] The most Morton could suggest was correlation.[119]

Morton may have been hesitant about his ability to know the relationship between different human bodies and the lives they made possible, but it was precisely this challenge that Bird took up in *Sheppard Lee*. Imagining Sheppard Lee into the brains and bodies of different types of Americans, Bird experimented imaginatively with the corporeal nature of human difference. Moving a step further than he had with the hermaphrodite orangutan, Bird imagines life into corpses, animating them to know human difference more intimately than epistemologies such as dissection and quantitative calculation made possible.

Bird made his engagement with Morton's theories of human difference clear. Parroting Morton's exclusionary taxonomies, for example, Lee-as-Longstraw describes the natural aversion of white minds to black bodies: Africans have "black faces, woolly heads, and an ill savour of body. For myself, verily, if they were not comely in my sight, nor agreeable to my nostrils, I said, 'Heaven hath made them so;' and although my nephew Jonathan insisted that Heaven had done the same thing with other animals . . . I perceived they were my brethren."[120] Picking up on Morton's language, Lee-as-Longstraw assesses African Americans' stark physical differences only to decide that Quaker teachings compel him to empathize with them as "brethren." Here Bird experiments with the tension that troubled Morton between Quaker beliefs and his polygenically suggestive skull measurements. Though his worldly nephew will prove right, Lee-as-Longstraw considers black men "brethren" despite their "repugnant" bodies and forges unnatural sympathies.[121]

Sheppard Lee exposes the error of empathetic sympathies that breach *Crania*'s racial divisions. Though Lee-as-Longstraw "laboured to do good to my fellows," he doubts that working "to injure and oppress" would have "rewarded [him] with more manifold outpourings of wrath and fury."[122] Lee-as-Longstraw's erroneous sympathy with black bodies is instructively literalized when crooks kidnap him and sell him down South to an angry lynch mob. In Tom, Bird cements the dangers of interracial sympathies. Lee learns the catastrophic effects of Morton's "joyous, flexible, and indolent" blacks by a direct engagement with their supposed scientifically small brains.[123]

We might conclude from Bird's novel that the races were so incommensurably different as to make any sympathy other than metempsychosis impossible were it not for Lee's handy, clever, and loyal slave Jim Jumble. Jumble appears to thwart these divisions. In an inversion of the Tom episode, the black Jumble steps into the role proscribed for Lee's white body, "planting and harvesting, and even selling what he raised, as if he were the master and owner of all things."[124] In Lee's indolence, Jumble plays the yeoman farmer, caring for Lee's patrimony and remaining Lee's only friend. Here interracial sympathies that verge on metempsychosis work to Lee's advantage; Jumble and his wife are the farm's most active inhabitants, ironically performing the work of the virtuous Jeffersonian citizens they cannot be. Jumble knows his value and powerfully inverts Morton's racial logic when he chastises Lee for having "no more sense than a nigger."[125]

Through the sympathy between Lee and Jumble, Bird experiments with alternatives to Morton's racial divisions, although he cannot convert his skepticism into a new order. Jumble's ability, loyalty, intelligence, and friendship should provide a harsh critique of developing theories of racial difference, but they do not. Bird manages the radical politics of this master-slave inversion by naming Jumble's desire the status quo: the "self-willed" Jumble declares his "extreme aversion to being made free" and threatens to call "the law" to enforce existing power structures.[126] The novel ends with this affirmation: "Jim Jumble is as independent and saucy as ever, but I can bear with his humours, he is so faithful, industrious, and . . . so happy to see his master once more prospering in the world."[127] Thus Bird naturalizes the shift in sympathetic bonds from friendship to master-servant.

While Jumble ultimately reaffirms the now scientifically established "natural" order, the specter of Tom troubles this logic. Theories are only satisfying if consistent. Either sympathies between white and black bodies reaffirm a natural order or they implode spectacularly. Either conclusion supports a coherent system, but Bird's refusal to settle on a consistent representation of race relations—his push/pull articulation of sympathy—underscores his uncertainty about available models of sympathy and division.

If the novel cannot quite shore up the boundaries of the Jacksonian white body (politic), neither can it reaffirm the sympathies within. What of the disparate parts? Can they develop meaningful or lasting sympathies? What connects the dandy to the philanthropist or the brewer to the Southern gentleman? The body to the mind? The tenuousness of even white sympathies reveals Bird's difficulty finding a sympathy that could articulate a coherent notion of the connection between parts.

Fiction allowed Bird to bridge distinct epistemological orientations and to inquire more deeply into the nature of sympathy and its limits. Intricacy and difficulty were the productive results of this literary approach, even if the complexity of what he discovered meant Bird could not yet articulate a comprehensive medical theory. Perhaps most productively, fiction let Bird dwell in this uncertainty and refuse premature conclusions.

What Bird's experiment did offer was a searing indictment of facile understandings of sympathy that collapsed its social, psychological, physiological, and political registers. After all, *Sheppard Lee* is a novel that literalizes the metaphor of empathy by placing Lee repeatedly in another's shoes—only to discover a sympathy that is not empathy. During the impending execution of Lee-as-Longstraw, no spectating character articulates the sympathies of Adam Smith's sympathizing citizen. Lee-as-Longstraw himself sympathizes with Tom only to escape his own imminent death. Lee finds no sympathy during his execution as Tom either. Bird's repeated distance from empathy in these scenes is not callous but instructive: in writing a humorous novel that chastises characters' empathetic errors, Bird disambiguates sympathy as a medical theory and epistemological tool from sympathy as empathy. In pursuing sympathy along this axis his comedic picaresque provides a more radical account of sympathy that investigates its finer points beyond the limitations of other medical epistemologies. Bird's suspension of empathy from his innovative research on the problem of human difference in *Sheppard Lee* makes a powerful case for the uses of humanistic inquiry beyond fellow feeling.

Unifying Pain

Sheppard Lee may resist premature conclusions about sympathy and human difference, but it finds a unifying force for the diverse features of corporeal life in sympathy's etymology. Bird's medical training taught him that, rather than "fellow feeling," *sympathy* had its root in the Greek "σύν 'with,' and πάθος, 'suffering.' "[128] Unable to find a coherent picture of sympathy in philosophical and empirical models, Bird looked to earlier articulations to pursue a unifying principle of life in suffering. Focusing on pain allowed Bird to return to an early moment in Morton's work where Morton might have pursued (but did not) a humanistic medical epistemology himself. Of Morton's 1823 medical thesis on bodily pain, a eulogizer observed that "the frequency of the poetical references and quotations" betrayed Morton as a physician "ambitious of the reputation of *littérateur*."[129] Here Morton examined some of pain's distinct qualities and hypothesized about pain's broader role in human life. Expressing more hesitation about empirical epistemologies than he did later, Morton wrote that there were instances of individual pain when physical observation and experimentation failed and "persons not equipped with the same idiosyncrasies are unable to judge."[130] He soon turned from such humanistic inquiry, but Bird circumvented the limits of physical experimentation by returning to these rhetorical modes to discover that pain alone unified the social and somatic lives of Americans.

In refocusing our reading on suffering, we discover that Lee seeks to avoid pain through his engagement with the bodies of others, and this constitutes their only common experience. His last feeling before leaving his original body is a "pain so horribly acute."[131] He awakens to "no pain" and "highly novel and agreeable" sensations, but before he can analyze them he spots his own corpse.[132] Lee's first lesson is that the body without pain is dead. Suffering from Higginson's excruciating gout, he kicks a chair: "crunch went every bone; crack went every sinew; and such a yell as I set up was never before heard in Chesnut-street."[133] "In anguish," Lee wills himself into Dawkins only to discover "a thousand pangs," so "horrible, that unless one were to have the toothache, gout, earache, gravel, rheumatism, headache, a stumped toe, and locked jaw all together, it would be impossible to form any just conception of the nature and variety of my torments."[134] The specter of pain prompts Lee to inhabit Skinner, where he immediately discovers "a thousand aches" in "a constitution just breaking up, if not already broken."[135] Longstraw's and Megrim's bodies are also quite painful. Only Lee-as-Tom, despite a broken neck, feels no pangs, though Lee's white spirit vividly imagines slavery's torments.[136] Both acutely particular (foot, eye, stomach) and quite general, pain is the common experience of the American body.

This unity through pain is not as grim as it sounds, since physical pain was integral to antebellum concepts of sympathy and health. Nineteenth-century doctors had an expansive view of pain, seeing it as fundamental to central features of human life, including romantic love, maternal affection, genius, manhood, and ethics. These physicians equated painful states with health, healing, and even life itself; the absence of pain signaled proximity to death. Some surgeons believed pain central to recovery, and, long after the development of anesthesia, many patients elected to undergo painful procedures to feel their own healing. Relying on the spectacle of pain to motivate audiences to reform through sympathy, many antebellum writers also felt pain was a powerful unifier, as reform writing from temperance novels and slave narratives to *Uncle Tom's Cabin* suggest. A medical contemporary of Bird's similarly understood this link: "Who can realize what is meant by intense pain and not feel himself called upon to relieve its victim? Surely no one who has a spark of sympathy within his breast."[137]

Sheppard Lee, of course, undoes this rosy understanding of a unifying sympathy through pain. The pain Lee discovers is decoupled from socially productive sympathy. "Peculiarities of the spirit are caused by certain peculiarities (congenital or accidental, +durable or temporary) of our physical structure," Bird explicates in an early draft. "The human may be pardoned by continued pain—(the danger of having <u>bad teeth</u> (!)) malignancy by deformity, +c. +c.. The story of the soldier who had an incurable+painful disease had rendered so recklessly viol[en]t until the king cured him. The souls of all men are therefore more or less influenced by their peculiar <u>physiques</u>."[138] While in the novel Bird writes that resilient minds can exist independent of the body's constitution, he initially posits that the "souls of all men" are the products of their bodies and that the pain of those bodies can fundamentally structure their affiliations. Here Bird's humor suggests an even more deeply unsettling vision for his readers. After all, if pain violently and pardonably disrupts a soldier's mandated affiliations, the voluntary affiliations of republican citizenship, bound primarily by sympathy, are doomed. Every one of Lee's citizen bodies experiences the kind of pain that should "pardon" acts of reckless violence. Here, as elsewhere in *Sheppard Lee*, the joke cannot dissipate the disturbing results of Bird's imaginative experiment. Ultimately tempering the radicalism of his position in the printed passage by softening his examples and omitting a direct discussion of pain, *Sheppard Lee* nonetheless follows the logic of this early draft wherein pain is a socially disruptive force providing the only common feature of bodily life.

Despite the commonality of pain, it is the intimate knowledge of others' suffering that drives Lee from other men. If sympathy is the force bringing people and parts together, it is a greedy one motivated by a desire to escape

pain and by the failures of "fellow feeling." Lee may declare the "impossib[ility]
to form any just conception" of another's pain without inhabiting the body
himself, but gaining this knowledge does not inspire sociality.[139] Instead, Lee
retreats: "be my body what it may, hardy or frail, stiff or supple, I am satisfied
with it, and shall never again seek to exchange it for another."[140] However medically and politically troubling, Lee's happiness depends upon retreating from
the sympathies and pains of other bodies, falling back only on the tenuous
"hardiness" of *his own* "constitution."[141]

Sheppard Lee provides a wonderful illustration of the uses of the imagination and literary form in producing nineteenth-century medical knowledge.
Bird's picaresque treatment of metempsychosis in *Sheppard Lee* allowed him
to push beyond the epistemological limits of medical philosophy and physical experimentation. The picaresque, which rhythmically moves its outsider
protagonist in and back out of distinct worlds, allowed Bird to engage in intimate experimentation through his various embodiments that was nonetheless contained within discrete episodes.[142] The imaginative tour of the landscape
that structures the picaresque's form allowed Bird to aggregate those episodes
into broader theory. And, because the picaresque does not require plot development or character growth, Bird could experiment with a diverse array of
bodies while forestalling hasty conclusions.[143]

Nevertheless, while *Sheppard Lee* demonstrates the vigorous role humanistic thinking has played in the production of medical knowledge, it also insists
on the limits of emotional sympathy often heralded as the ends of such work
today. In fact, Bird's novel usefully separates sympathy as a medical theory and
a way of knowing from the affective connection we now call *empathy*.[144] (Here
it is useful to remember that the twentieth-century term "empathy" is not the
same as eighteenth- and nineteenth-century sympathy, and while scholars
often root empathy in "fellow feeling," this yields a genealogy, not a definition.) Instructively literalizing empathy's most illustrative metaphor, Lee repeatedly finds himself in another's shoes only to discover forms of sympathy
that do not involve "the ability to understand and appreciate another person's
feelings [and] experience" ("empathy, n."). Bird's novel thus productively
complicates the premise that we *can* know another's body; rather, numerous
elements—race, age, class, climate, sex, diet, and so forth—might determine
the particular feelings and pains in an individual, many of which cannot be
empirically, philosophically, or empathetically known by another. Bird's distance from "fellow feeling" is edifying. Writing a humorous novel that chastises errors in feeling, Bird disambiguates emotional sympathy from sympathy

as a medical principle and a research device. In pursuing sympathy along this axis, Bird's comic picaresque creates a more radical account of sympathy that investigates its finer points beyond the limitations of philosophical and empirical epistemology.

Peter Pilgrim and the Problems of Knowing Human Difference

Sheppard Lee was a radical experiment with troubling conclusions. It was, perhaps, too daring, even for Bird. Six months after the pseudonymous publication of his novel, Bird's friend, the editor John Frost, wrote to tell him that the physician George McClellan, who would become Bird's medical colleague a few years later, had read *Sheppard Lee* and "taken up an absurd notion" that Bird had written it.[145] Sure that his friend "would be amazed at such an imputation and believing that [McClellan] would ha[ve] you to suspect if possible that I had countenanced the [idea]," Frost wrote "to clear myself of even giving the slightest intimation to that effect."[146] Whether Bird ever revealed his secret to Frost, McClellan, or any of his other medical or literary colleagues, he certainly got the message that readers considered *Sheppard Lee* a strange little book. Even Edgar Allan Poe, who expressed measured admiration for the novel, thought Bird's experiment did not quite work. Bird would never again experiment in quite so radical a form, but he did continue to investigate the problem of knowing human difference in his next picaresque, *Peter Pilgrim*.

Sheppard Lee and Peter Pilgrim form a kind of diptych.[147] Not only are both picaresque novels, but Bird also first planned to have *Peter Pilgrim* written and edited by Sheppard Lee with "an introduction, in which Sheppard accounts for his turning author." At least one sketch that later appeared in *Peter Pilgrim*—"My Friends in the Madhouse"—was originally intended for *Sheppard Lee*. And, on the back of his notes for the *Peter Pilgrim* story "Merry the Miner," Bird sketched the plot for a story much like *Sheppard Lee* in which "the Narrator acquires the power, at will, of leaving his body, and walking his spirit around—<u>invisible</u>, of course (except under certain <u>ghostly</u> circumstances,—to make observations on what he sees)."[148] In other words, the two novels were closely connected for Bird, not only in form but also in concept and content.

Peter Pilgrim was, nonetheless, a more conservative picaresque than *Sheppard Lee*. Whereas the latter took a radical approach to imaginative experimentation, purporting to be the real autobiography of a corpse hopper, *Peter Pilgrim* was less formally adventurous. Having failed to find satisfying solutions to the problem of human difference in *Sheppard Lee*, Bird focused more on the epistemological aspects of the epistemic crisis in *Peter Pilgrim*; in this latter novel, Bird used imaginative experimentation not so much to know human difference as to parse further the problems of knowing human difference.

To do so, Bird returned once more to regions both he and Morton considered valuable sites for this inquiry: the West and South. After his 1833 trip, Bird set a handful of novels in these regions: *Cavalar, or, The Knight of the Conquest: A Romance of Mexico* (1834) and *The Infidel, or, The Fall of Mexico: A Romance* (1835) took place in Mexico, and he attended more specifically to the U.S. West and South in *Nick of the Woods, or, The Jibbenainosay: A Tale of Kentucky* (1837) and *Peter Pilgrim* (1838). Morton likewise privileged these regions in *Crania Americana*, promising in the 1837 prospectus to have paid "particular notice of the Crania from the mounds and caves of the western sections of this country."[149] For both doctor-writers, these were important spaces for the investigation of human difference, but, while Morton's science worked to generalize about the bodies of the American West, using empirical practices that valued remains stripped of life and skin, Bird imagined living flesh back onto skulls and bones.[150]

The first portion Bird published of his picaresque was a short story called "The Mammoth Cave of Kentucky." It first appeared a year before the publication of *Peter Pilgrim* in the *American Monthly Magazine* in May and June 1837. Bird had visited the cave on his 1833 trip and was enough taken with the space to paint it repeatedly over the course of two decades.[151] The story offers an account of a tourist's visit to the famous cave in Kentucky and was a lightly fictionalized recounting of Bird's own 1833 experience.

Bird may have originally visited the cave hunting skulls for Morton's empirical project, but, in his picaresque return, Bird's protagonist values the cave for its imaginative potential. "Caves," Pilgrim begins, "have always formed a subject on which my imagination delighted to dwell; and to this day, the name seldom falls upon my ears without conjuring up a thousand grimly captivating associations—thoughts of the wild and supernatural, the strange and terrific."[152] His reaction is not idiosyncratic, Pilgrim explains; rather, it is in some measure universal, traceable "in the mind of the world at large."[153] Pilgrim is "certain there are few subjects on which men have given, and still continue to give, a greater loose to their imaginations than that of caves."[154] In the nineteenth century, Pilgrim laments that "Truth" has killed omens, devils, and "fairy Gnomes," but caves remain a final refuge.[155]

Pilgrim then descends into the Mammoth Cave, pursuing an imaginative investigation that troubles the line between fact and fantasy, particularly for questions of human difference. For example, Pilgrim claims as fact at one moment that the niter removed from the cave was "dug from among the bones of buried Indians," but then continues, introducing doubt, "*If* we can believe the account of those who should know best, many a generation of dead men sleeps among the vaults of the Mammoth Cave."[156] This account, he concedes, may be purely fantastical, a myth meant to conjure a particular reverence for the cave among its tourists. While other caves readily yield up their marvels, the Mammoth Cave "reveals no subterranean gardens, no Stygian lakes, no stupendous waterfalls; it discharges no volcanic flames, it emits no phosphoric sunlight; it contains no petrified pre-Adamites."[157] Invoking fantasy's presence by dwelling in detail on its absence, Bird implicitly critiques those who adhere too firmly to objectivity. Surveyors have "broken the heart of its mystery . . . with cruel scale and protractor," but intrigue and imagination still draw the narrator below.[158]

Bird's meditation on the relationship between empiricism and imagination is an engagement with Morton's ways of knowing human difference. Morton considered caves—and the Mammoth Cave in particular—an important site for the production of empirical knowledge about human difference. Morton, who "should know best," explains in *Crania Americana* that the caves are rich sources of measurable evidence because "it was a custom of many American nations to deposit their dead in caves."[159] He got a number of his skulls from such spaces. Caves were particularly useful sites for the study of human difference both because indigenous Americans buried their people there and because sometimes exhumed bodies were reburied in caves.

Bird's narrator finds nothing of this objective, quantifiable record of human variation in the Mammoth Cave, in spite of Morton's suggestion that caves like the Mammoth should be a plentiful source. Instead, Pilgrim spends his tour of the cave reminding his reader about the possible historical presence of indigenous peoples, waiting until the final pages to reveal that "no fossil bones have been discovered."[160] In *Crania Americana*, Morton uses a letter by John H. Farnham to support his belief about the historical record preserved in caves. According to Farnham, a woman had been found in the Mammoth Cave "in a state of complete desiccation. 'She was buried in a squatting form, the knees drawn up close to the breast, the arms bent, with the hands raised, and crossing each other about the chin.' "[161] Morton did not include an image of this woman, but he did include a lithograph of a corpse positioned in the style of the Mammoth Cave woman along with handful of drawings from skulls collected from various caves. Referencing the Farnham letter himself, Bird demurs, "Human bones in a recent condition were dug up near the entrance; but no mummies were found. The mummy in one of the public museums said to be from the Mammoth Cave, was taken, we were told, from a cave in the neighborhood . . . though deposited for awhile in the Mammoth Cave."[162] Playing with the cave's imperfect record of human difference, Bird restores some recent agency to the local natives who move the bodies of their ancestors.

Where bones are missing, Bird fills in life and the imagination. When *Peter Pilgrim* finally introduces native bodies to the caves, it is through an account of their living bodies rather than their corpses. In the cave, Bird's narrator finds torches, arrowheads, pottery, architectural work, and footprints—all evidence that, he emphasizes, "the original *inhabitants* of the cave . . . actually *lived* in the cave."[163] He continues, "I use the word inhabitants; for mere visiters [*sic*] . . . could never have left behind them so many vestiges."[164] As the signs of life multiply, no skulls or bones that can be transported, preserved, and measured appear. In the last three sentences of the lengthy account, Bird toys with the reader's desire for more tangible human remains: "The tribe has vanished," he announces, "and their bones (to what base uses we may return!) converted into gunpowder, have been employed to wing many a death against their warring descendants."[165] Here the mystique of empirical epistemologies, which might make much of old bones, is demystified. The history and historical bodies of native peoples collapse into current events, as Bird reminds us that the vanishing Indian is none other than the relative of current tribes. The distinctness of the "warring" Indian him/herself is further undermined by the white inhabitants' "base uses" of the historical record not to account for human difference, as Morton might, but for their own violent ends.

Bird more fully investigates his readers' desire for empirical evidence in "Merry the Miner." Unlike "The Mammoth Cave," "Merry the Miner" does not turn on the absence of human remains but rather indulges the reader's desire for a complete, observable record of human diversity. In this story, Bird returns once more to the West to tell the story of a miner named Merry who loses all his family and friends in a mad, twenty-year quest to find gold in the Tennessee hills. When Merry has, at long last, been truly abandoned by everyone, his dog leads him to the mouth of a cave filled with the gold he has been seeking. Here Merry discovers not only gold but a cave with a fully preserved record of an ancient civilization, more complete than any for which Morton or any other Mammoth Cave enthusiast could ever have hoped.

"Merry the Miner" offers up the ultimate fantasy of objectivity and empiricism: the cave provides a complete record of an extinct human civilization in which every aspect of corporeal difference might be known through observation and measurement. Looking in, he finds that the cave's empirical riches augment rather than banish the imagination. Entering, Merry finds "such fantastic shapes as both kindled the imagination and struck the spirit with awe."[166] Unlike the largely barren Mammoth Cave, Merry's cave is teeming with preserved scenes of life, "as if each rock was composed of animals, or parts of animals, each a congeries of limbs, heads, trunks, skeletons, cemented or incrusted together in one hideous organic mass."[167] Morton's skulls and bones, in contrast, were a fragile and very limited evidentiary base; there were fewer of them than Morton would have liked and some were inevitably chipped and broken during analysis. In contrast, Bird's protagonist finds "a petrified world," tantalizingly ready to yield up all the secrets of human difference.[168] The remains in Merry's cave are not merely skeletal; they are full human bodies preserved at the moment of death. Merry reaches out to touch the figures and finds "vast limbs, foully sheeted over with spar, a rough and rigid coat formed by the drippings and deposit of centuries, he could not but fancy a human body was sepulchered within."[169] The stone preserves the human bodies as close to life as possible. The record in the cave is not a new one, like the supposed mummy of Mammoth Cave, but rather a perfectly preserved record of ancient peoples, "the stony effigies and relics of pre-Adamitic ages."[170] In having Merry stumble on a world that predates the Garden of Eden, Bird asks his reader to invest in a vision of human difference premised on the distinct creation of different human species. This pre-Adamite vision was, at the time, closely aligned with the burgeoning ideas of polygenism with which Morton was also grappling.[171]

What if, Bird invites the reader to imagine, you could put "the remains and representatives of all races that had lived and perished" in one room together?[172] Conjuring the fantasy of a tantalizingly complete archive of human difference, Bird has Merry stumble upon "things of flesh . . . that *had* lived, and breathed, and walked the earth—all in their general sepulchre, not clad alone in the ordinary vestures of decay, in bones and ashes, but in form as when they lived, in body, and, it seemed, almost in substance."[173] These humans include those that coexisted with Mastodons and Dinotherium (ancient elephants) and lived in exotic cities that resemble "the ancient subterranean cities of the East."[174] From our privileged position as readers, we, like Merry, can see not only how these peoples died but also "how they lived."[175] Merry's cave should be able to solve, definitively, the problem of knowing human difference.

And yet, what Merry repeatedly learns about these seemingly distinct races of humans is how similar they are to nineteenth-century Americans. The first scene he encounters is one of war, of which he exclaims, "And so they do in the world above!"[176] The scene among the ancient environments is grue-some but "nothing that he might not have seen in a 'foughten field' in the world above."[177] While Merry at first invests in differences, he eventually comes to see only similarities between the pre-Adamite races and nineteenth-century Caucasian Americans. While he begins by critiquing these scenes of war and greed, demonstrating his distance from these ancient peoples, those differences quickly collapse. As in *Sheppard Lee*, Merry's greed aligns him with the bodies of others; he "moralized very prettily on the debasing effects of avarice" until "the very passion he saw thus variously personified, stole into his bosom."[178] Spotting easy money in a tantalizing tableau, Merry "long[s] to possess the bags of coin, so temptingly displayed."[179] He cannot remain the disinterested, objective observer but rushes to join the scene, running between gambling tables and pawnbrokers fueled by the same gold lust that animated the indi-viduals of these other races—even as he hypocritically judges them all the while. Decrying a greedy murder, Merry quickly shatters the perpetrator's coin-filled grasp to steal the gold for himself.

As the story unfolds, distinctions continue to collapse. Entering a mad-house, Merry observes that "among other bedlamites raving in stone, was doubtless the usual proportion of cases where the loss of gold, or the fear of losing it, had converted the children of God into gibbering monkeys."[180] Here, human and species differences give way entirely. Not only is the madhouse fully familiar to Merry, but in referring to pre-Adamite madmen as "children of God," he eliminates the essential categorical difference between the ancient peoples and his own race. Furthermore, when God's children become "gib-bering monkeys," Bird undermines essential differences between races and spe-cies that men like Harlan and Morton spent their lives delineating.

The sketch closes by suggesting that the cave may contain nothing novel at all. If what, at long last, assuredly separated Merry from these other races was not biology or society but time, Bird destroys that illusion, too, by the end of the sketch. Exhausted from collecting his gold and celebrating his wealth, Merry lies down to rest before leaving the cave. Attempting to rise a bit later, Merry finds he is quickly petrifying, becoming "a man of stone, like all around him!"[181] The terrified miner realizes that his body is as vulnerable to suffering as those that surround him, and he, too, risks becoming "a breathing corse [*sic*], a living fossil."[182] Poised to join the statuary, the last distinction between Merry and the frozen figures falls away: if Merry can petrify so quickly, he and the reader can no longer confidently date the stone bodies.

Thus, Bird uses imagination to investigate and extend the work of empiricists like Morton and also to suggest its limitations. The more Merry learns about this physical record, the more that information complicates and unsettles the very systems of empirical knowledge that make it valuable in the first place. In "Merry the Miner," paradoxically, completing the empirical record of human difference only highlights human similarity and undermines the very premises upon which such inquiry was being conducted by nineteenth-century skull collectors. Both stories furthermore insist on desire and imagination as necessary features of such empirical undertakings rather than on objective detachment. In his fiction, as in his medicine, Bird worried about relying too heavily on objectivity and empiricism. Human bodies remained tricky to know, but these difficulties of medical science could certainly be aided by the insights of imaginative inquiry.

Imaginative Experimentation and Empiricism

Despite their increasingly divergent epistemological orientations, Bird and Morton remained fast friends and collaborators. Morton secured Bird a job teaching at the Medical Department of Pennsylvania College in Philadelphia (which would come to be called Pennsylvania Medical College) with him for a time in the early 1840s. Bird accepted the post "with great pleasure," considering the invitation a "very distinguished testimonial of the regard and confidence of gentlemen, with whom I shall be most proud to be associated, in their labours for the promotion of Medical Science."[183] It was "doubly gratifying" coming directly from Morton.[184]

During these years, the two continued to conspire about both literary and medical topics.[185] In the spring of 1842, Bird sent Morton a letter indicative of their warm collaboration. Substituting his usual address to Morton, "My dear Doctor," with "Dear Poet," Bird writes to gossip about a dreadful new literary magazine: "I came up this morning to beg some vaccine matter," Bird begins, "and to show you the first number of a rascally fortnight magazine."[186]

Easily moving between literary and medical matters in his letter, Bird signs off, "Yrs. Poetically, RMB."[187] At the time, the two were also working together on more serious medical matters including the organization of and instruction in their medical school and, more urgently, how to keep it afloat.[188] The school was effectively disbanded in September 1843 for a combination of financial and interpersonal reasons, but Bird remained interested in the project and wrote Morton that he was willing to return if Morton and some of the other medical professors wanted to reassemble the college.[189] When a professional conflict with Benjamin Rush's son William proved irresolvable, they at last abandoned the school.[190]

Friends and colleagues for decades, Bird and Morton did not embody a before-and-after story of medical epistemology. As Bird and Morton's lifelong dialog demonstrates, imaginative experimentation and objectivity could work together, even if the best manner for doing so was not always clear. The two provided distinct but important ways of investigating pressing problems in human health. Morton's interest in empirical answers to the problem of knowing human difference was no wholesale condemnation of the imagination. He kept writing poetry and was praised for the artistry of his volumes. Likewise, Bird's warm relationship with Morton and eagerness to collaborate in the 1830s and 1840s indicates a respectful difference when it came to questions of epistemological orientation but not a wholesale condemnation of his friend.

Empiricism rose in prominence over the next decades of the nineteenth century, and this simultaneity of empiricism and imaginative experimentation became yet clearer. In the next generation, the work of doctor-writers like Oliver Wendell Holmes and S. Weir Mitchell did not oppose the two, even though it became professionally trickier to practice both. The imagination, objectivity, and physical experimentation were not mutually exclusive paradigms even in the late nineteenth century; rather, they continued to serve as tools to be used as the situation demanded.

CHAPTER 5

ANESTHESIA

[PAIN] The *morbid sensations* . . . are comprised under the term *pain*. In its enlarged signification, this word, as is well known, means every uneasy or disagreeable sensation or moral affection: thus including sadness, anger, terror, as well as the painful impressions, felt in the extremities or trunks of the nerves.

—Robley Dunglison, *Human Physiology* (1832)

ANAESTHESIA, *Anaesthe'sis, Insensibil'itas, analge'sia, Parap'sis expers*, (F.) *Anesthésie'* from *a*, privative, and Αισθάνομαι, "I feel." Privation of sensation, and especially that of touch, according to some. It may be general or partial, and is almost always symptomatic.

—Robley Dunglison, *Medical Lexicon* (1860)

On October 16, 1846, dentist William Thomas Green Morton (1819–1868) arrived at Massachusetts General Hospital's Bullfinch Amphitheater and administered ether to doctor John Collins Warren's patient Edward Gilbert Abbott, who was about to have a growth cut out of his jaw. Morton was late because the toolmaker had finished his ether inhaler only that day. Morton approached Abbott and asked, "Are you afraid?" Abbott answered directly, "No. I feel confident." Onlookers were likely more anxious. An experiment with ether in the very same auditorium had failed just the year before, and even Morton, who had experimented with the drug on himself, had not remained conscious long enough to record its effects. To everyone's great relief and joy, Abbott's surgery was successful—and pain free—inspiring Harvard's professor of surgery Henry Jacob Bigelow to announce, "I have seen something today which will go around the world." Just one month later, doctor, novelist, and soon-to-be dean at Harvard Medical School Oliver Wendell Holmes (1809–1894) would write to Morton to suggest a name for this revolutionary technique: "My dear Sir: Everybody wants to have a hand in a great discovery. All I want to do is to give you a hint or two as to names or the name to be applied to the state produced and the agent. The state should, I think, be called 'anaesthesia.' "[1]

While the successful administration of what would come to be known, after Holmes's suggestion, as *anesthesia* was met with enthusiasm and confidence by those in the amphitheater, its reception was more fraught with the wider public. The discovery of a substance that could prevent pain in surgery and childbirth immediately posed a series of difficult questions to antebellum Americans. These questions included: What is pain? What is its role in life and health? And when is anesthesia (literally the state "without feeling") useful—and when is it dangerous? The questions this new discovery prompted were so deeply unsettling because they were not only epistemological but ontological; in its aftermath, doctors and writers struggled not only to distinguish between the myriad types of pain they could enumerate but also to decide whether pain was bad, good, or useful. While U.S. doctors and writers sometimes distinguished between physical and mental pain, they often stressed how inseparable the two were.

Anesthesia initiated a crisis of knowing because, like prior epistemic crises, it unseated central ideas about the physiology of the human body. "Anaesthesia" was an insistently physiological term that framed pain and feelings as problems of the body-in-motion rather than anatomical concerns. When Holmes wrote Morton to encourage him to change the name of the substance from Letheon Gas to anesthesia, he highlighted the term's capacity to represent the actions of the drug on the living functions of the body. Holmes wrote, "Anaesthesia . . . signifies insensibility, more generally."[2] Terms like "anti-neuric, aneuric, neuro-leptic, neurolepsia, neuro-etasis, etc., seem to be anatomical; whereas the change is a physiological one."[3] Nevertheless, it was this physiological nature of the problems of pain and feeling that made them so difficult to know through physical experimentation.

Like other physiological processes understood to structure human health, such as circulation and sympathy, pain depended on an understanding of the body-in-motion that posed special problems for medical knowing. For a number of reasons, this meant pain could not be investigated particularly well through practices like physical experimentation. First, while doctors became increasingly interested in animal vivisection as a way of experimenting with the living body, many objected to the practice on moral grounds. The 1840s saw the rise of anti-vivisection reformers who sought to halt what they saw as an unethical and barbaric practice. Second, even if the practice had been uncontested, vivisection could not provide answers about pain other than what could be gleaned from interpreting the signs of distress in animals. Third, nineteenth-century doctors understood the basic epistemological problem inherent in studying the pain of another that Elaine Scarry has famously described as largely "inaccessible . . . to anyone not immediately experiencing it."[4] One writer in the early nineteenth century highlighted the problem through evasion. To the question "What is the nature of pain?" he replied, "To explain this is in no way necessary . . . since no one has not known pain."[5] Robley Dunglison concurred in his medical dictionary that pain was "a disagreeable sensation, which scarcely admits of definition."[6] But, of course, knowing pain *was* necessary—especially once it was possible to eradicate it.

In the wake of the discovery of anesthesia, doctors and writers employed imaginative experimentation to know the nature and value of pain. As the idea of "anesthesia," a term etymologically linked to the term "aesthetics," permeated U.S. culture it challenged what Americans thought they knew about pain and feeling.[7] While theories of pain and feeling have a long prehistory, the United States became a culture of pain in the antebellum period. This culture gave rise both to the discovery of anesthesia and to the crisis of that discovery. Although doctors turned increasingly to empirical methods to answer medical questions over the course of the nineteenth century, problems like pain and feeling—often considered constitutionally subjective—also demanded strategies like imaginative experimentation. No two figures better embody these responses to the discovery-initiated anesthesia crisis than Oliver Wendell Holmes and S. Weir Mitchell, who turned to the imagination and literary form to produce knowledge about physiology that was so difficult, if not impossible, to know through other practices.

Pain Before 1846

Antebellum Americans understood pain to be a central, constitutive feature of life. As one of the two principal feelings (the other was pleasure) that mediated the interaction of the body with the world, pain figured centrally in what it meant to be alive. In an early textbook translated by Nathaniel Chapman for use in U.S. medical schools, Anthelme Richerand writes, "It is only by our sensations that we are aware of our existence. Life, to make use of the figurative language of system, of a modern writer, consists in the action of stimuli on the vital powers."[8] Because of this need for feeling, "Sentient beings feel a continual necessity of renewed emotions; all their actions tend to the obtaining agreeable or disagreeable sensations; for in the absence of other sensations, pain is sometimes attended with enjoyment."[9]

And yet pain has long been difficult to know, and the ideas antebellum Americans inherited from the previous centuries of Western physicians were varied and vague. It is telling that early medical dictionaries frequently use the word "pain" to describe other conditions but do not include a distinct entry on the term. The seventeenth-century text *A Physical Dictionary* explained that pain was simply "a division of such parts as naturally ought to be united."[10] Early eighteenth-century London physician and lexicographer John Quincy similarly followed Galen, "It is commonly laid down that Pain is a Solution of Continuity" between "the Nerve, Membranes, Canals, and Muscles," a reaction to the displacement of body parts.[11] "But this is not a good definition," he admitted.[12] Edmund Burke averred that pain arose from "an unnatural tension in the nerves" but also confessed that "pain and pleasure are simple ideas, incapable of definition."[13] By the year Morton made his discovery, medical definitions of pain had become even more vague. Robley Dunglison explained that pain was rooted in the Greek for "to torment" but could not define it more specifically.[14]

Medical thinking remained split between the positive and negative aspects of pain. The negative aspects were most obvious: short term, pain could cause contortions of the face and body, physical contortions, alterations to the bowels, skin, and urinary tract, loss of control, and weakness (except in the case of reflex reactions in which incredible strength might be demonstrated).[15] Long-term consequences included personality alteration, madness, and death.[16] Nevertheless, pain was also an important feature of life. Physician William Dewees believed pain in childbirth signaled civilization, just as "the influence of domestication" on animals had resulted in "the mare and cow suffer[ing] extreme agony in bringing forth their young."[17] Benjamin Rush understood pain to be responsible for "conceptions and expression upon the most ordinary subjects, that discover an uncommon elevation of the intellectual powers" and considered it important for "rousing and directing the moral faculty."[18]

And Samuel George Morton believed pain played a part in love, maturity, morality, the development of the soul, and genius.[19]

One problem with defining pain was that it was notoriously difficult to pin down what exactly caused it—and the answer could be difficult to generalize. The "varieties and effects of pain," Samuel Morton lamented, are "numberless."[20] On one hand, pain was "the treacherous companion of our whole life," and on the other hand, pain was so infinitely variable that it varied by degree, location in the body, temperament, climate, age, sex, and weather.[21] Anthelme Richerand explained that things once considered painful could be diminished by repetition: "The habit of suffering, renders us in the end insensible to pain," though "every thing in this world is balanced, and if habit lightens our evils, by blunting sensibility, it on the other hand drains the source of our sweetest enjoyments. Pleasure and pain, these two extremes of sensation, in a manner, approximate to each other, and become indifferent to him who is accustomed to them."[22]

While pain could be diminished by repetition, rendering painful things dull or even pleasurable, too much pleasure could be painful. One definition of pain was the excess of feeling. To return for a moment to Alexander Pope's invocation of the "microscopic eye," Pope insisted then that humans lacked a "microscopic eye" because this excessive perception of beauty would produce incredible pain. Touch would cause "agon[y] at ev'ry pore" and a rose's scent would injure with "aromatic pain."[23] Succinctly capturing this view in his medical thesis, Samuel Morton writes, "Pleasure itself, carried to excess, ends in pain. And so heat, a most welcome sensation, becomes the cause of the bitterest pain when it increases beyond the right amount. It is likewise with all the other pleasures."[24]

To further complicate matters, the pain of excessive feeling could also be beneficial. First, as the Pope verses begin to suggest, pain was a powerful source of artistic inspiration. Without jest, Morton made a similar point about urinary tract infections: while they produce "the most severe pains of all," such infections had also "endowed the satirical poet Boileau with his wit."[25] Morton also believed that "the pains that precede death are often mingled with words and thoughts which reveal a remarkable capacity of the soul."[26] Feeling was certainly a source of pain, but pain, in turn, became a powerful source of productive feeling.

Second, such pain was also a foundational aspect of society. We need turn no further than Adam Smith's first famous articulation of sympathy to see how pain could prompt a necessary "fellow feeling" that connected citizens. Conjuring the image of a man on the rack, Smith writes:

> By the imagination we place ourselves in his situation, we conceive ourselves enduring all the same torments, we enter as it were into his body and become in some measure him, and thence form some idea of his sensations, and even feel something which, though weaker in degree is not altogether unlike them. His agonies, when they are thus brought home to ourselves, when we have thus adopted and made them our own, begin at last to affect us, and we then tremble and shudder at the thought of what he feels. For as to be in pain or distress of any kind excites the most excessive sorrow, so to conceive or to imagine that we are in it, excites some degree of the same emotion, in proportion to the vivacity or dullness of the conception. That is the source of our fellow-feeling for the misery of others.[27]

Smith goes on to list other causes of "fellow-feeling," including grief, joy, fear, and resentment, but he repeatedly returns to scenes of pain to illustrate instances of sympathy, as when he conjures the tableau of "the pangs of a mother when she hears the moanings of her infant that during the agony of disease cannot express what it feels."[28] Medical definitions of sympathy, of course, were etymologically rooted in the Greek phrase for "with suffering."[29]

In spite of these confusing and contradictory aspects of pain, one thing antebellum Americans inherited from the early modern period was the idea that all kinds of pain were at some level physical. As Jans Frans Van Dijkhuizen and Karl Enenkel explain, "Early modern culture construes intense emotions as inherently physical; their physicality even serves as an index of their intensity. Paradoxically, then, it is precisely through the importance of the body in early modern notions of pain that the cultural dimensions of pain become clear."[30] Descartes's influential model of pain also privileged its physical nature while acknowledging the messiness of pain's relationship to the mind and culture. His system depicted animal spirits controlling threads that emanated from the pineal gland to respond to perceptions of peril. Despite common glosses of this vision as an instance of Cartesian mind-body dualism, Descartes used pain to work out the relationship of mind to body.[31]

This close connection between the mind and body in pain secured a central role for the imagination in the experience and treatment of pain. Robley Dunglison wrote in his comprehensive *Human Physiology* that pain encompassed both physical and psychological pain: "In its enlarged signification," he wrote, "this word, as is well known, means every uneasy or disagreeable sensation or moral affection: thus including sadness, anger, terror, as well as the painful impressions, felt in the extremities or trunks of the nerves."[32] Pain was, simultaneously, a somatic and a psychological reaction to phenomena as diverse as physical, social, and political stimuli. Theorists like Rush and Morton describe the painful horrors that might be stimulated by the imagination. "It is no less remarkable than true," Morton writes, "that there is a sort of pain, arising from the imagination, which exists as much in the mind as in the body. . . . The mind's power over the body is so remarkable that it is quite plausible to believe that the soul's attention to a given cause, existing only in the soul, if long sustained, may result in disease or pain at last actually manifesting itself in the body."[33] The idea that the imagination was so intimately linked to bodily pain was not all problematic, however. Morton turns back to an example from Rush that proves "if the motions of the soul are remarkably effective at generating disease and pain, they must be likewise efficacious in removing either."[34] Rush's bibliotherapy was rooted in precisely this idea.

The Culture of Pain in Antebellum America

Because the phenomenon of pain was notoriously difficult to know, many of these ideas about pain persisted well into the nineteenth century; nevertheless, as Karen Halttunen has elegantly argued, cultural attitudes toward pain shifted dramatically in the half decade preceding the discovery of anesthesia. The Anglo-American world came to see pain as a social problem rather than a foundational element of society. The culture of sensibility, she argues, "redefined pain as unacceptable and indeed eradicable and thus opened the door to a new revulsion from pain, which, though later regarded as 'instinctive' or 'natural,' has in fact proved to be distinctly modern."[35] While the crisis emerging from anesthesia's discovery suggests that pain was not understood in purely negative terms, there was a marked shift during the period toward a concerted effort to diminish or eradicate pain. One effect of this new culture of pain was a more global effort to lessen pain not only in medicine but across the professions: as Martin Pernick suggests, the period saw a decline in phys-

ical punishment in jails and classrooms as well as the development of anesthetics.[36]

It is no surprise that this focus on pain was closely related not only to the
discovery of anesthesia but to the evolving discourse of aesthetics in the antebellum era. As Edward Cahill has persuasively argued, the language of aesthetic theory was everywhere in early U.S. culture; Americans insistently
framed their own cultural and political pursuits through questions of truth,
beauty, goodness, and the imagination that were grounded in the mind and
in the body.[37] By the antebellum period, the language of aesthetics became
ubiquitous, even if the word "aesthetics" grew diffuse and muddled. Competing definitions from around the Atlantic had confused the matter to such
a degree that in 1849 Elizabeth Peabody wrote about "the word 'aesthetic'" in
her journal the *Aesthetic Papers*, "Of all the scientific terms in common use,
perhaps no one conveys to mind a more vague and indeterminable sense than
this, at the same time that the user is always conscious of a meaning and ap-
propriateness; so that he is in the position of one who endeavors to convey his
sense of the real presence of an idea, which still he cannot himself fully grasp
and account for."[38] Moreover, whereas aesthetic ideas permeated early national
culture, the term "aesthetics" became commonly used only in the 1840s. This
emerging and widespread discourse of the aesthetic was deeply concerned with
the nature and value of feeling at the levels of personal experience, health, and
society. As such, these fraught discussions of aesthetics were inextricable from
the American discourse of pain, and it is perhaps unsurprising that Holmes
coined the term "anaesthesia" in the very decade when Americans had grown
enamored with the word "aesthetics."[39]

In fact, it might be said that in the antebellum era, American culture was
becoming fixated on pain or, to borrow a phrase, a "culture of pain."[40] We
might recognize this culture of pain by some of its associates: the eighteenth-
and nineteenth-century cultures of sympathy and sensibility that were built
into a culture of sentiment by the mid-nineteenth century; its embodiment in
the mid-nineteenth century was the "man of feeling."[41] In fact, the term "hyperaesthesia," which described a condition of suddenly feeling too much,
only began to gain currency in the year that its opposite, "anaesthesia," was
discovered.[42] The proliferation of sentimental novels, sensational fiction, and
reform literature and lecturing (temperance, antislavery, anti-vivisection,
etc.) that put the spectacle of pain on display amply illustrate the moment:
the fascination of George Lippard's Devil-Bug with the slow suffering of his
victims, Harriet Beecher Stowe's dying little Eva, John Gough pleading his

temperance case before a lecture hall, and the detailed descriptions of animal torture available from children's literature to anti-vivisection tirades in antebellum novels. Literary forms like the short story and the novel, which invited readers to experience the lives and sensations of others, were an especially effective means of exploring the pain. Fictional tableaus like these reached an apogee in the 1840s and 1850s.[43]

Developments in literary forms over the first half of the nineteenth century and a popular investment in aesthetics made forms like fiction an increasingly useful site for communicating and investigating this new culture of pain. The introduction of Romanticism to the United States was central to this shift; Romantic forms of representation provided a grammar for articulating the particularity of pain men like Morton had begun to insist upon. The delayed introduction of the Romantics into the United States meant that early fictional representations of individuals were not imbued with corporeal specificity until the 1810s, and, even then, the specificity of bodies we see in Nathaniel Hawthorne's Georgiana ("The Birthmark," 1843), Herman Melville's Ahab and Queequeg (*Moby-Dick*, 1851), and Rebecca Harding Davis's Deb (*Life in the Iron Mills*, 1861) did not arise until (what scholars at least once called) the American Renaissance. Here we might think of the difference between the rare descriptions of physical pain in earlier American novels like Rebecca Rush's *Kelroy* and Charles Brockden Brown's *Arthur Mervyn* that are so full of ailing bodies but so absent corporeal detail, as compared with the (sometimes excruciatingly) detailed descriptions in later novels. For example, George Thompson describes a woman's torture in detail in *City Crimes* (1849): her evil antagonist douses her in acid, which "ran in her eyes and down her face, burning her flesh in the most horrible manner. She shrieked with agony the most intense, and the Doctor rushed into the room, followed by Mrs. Franklin. They both stood aghast when they beheld the awful spectacle. The Doctor . . . rushed to the aid of the burning wretch, and saved her life, though he could not restore her lost eyesight, or remove the horrible disfigurement of her burned and scarred visage."[44] Or Ahab's near castration in *Moby-Dick*: "he had been found one night lying prone upon the ground, and insensible; by some unknown, and seemingly inexplicable, unimaginable casualty, his ivory limb having been so violently displaced, that it had stake-wise smitten, and all but pierced his groin; nor was it without extreme difficulty that the agonizing wound was entirely cured."[45] These descriptions were unimaginable for the fiction of the early national period.[46]

Other literary genres like the slave narrative also invited their readers to imagine pain for humanitarian ends.[47] In his 1847 slave narrative, for example, William Wells Brown (1814–1884) meditates on the cowhide-and-wire whip held like a threat at all times by the overseer. "I have often laid and heard the crack of the whip and the screams of the slave," Brown remembers.[48] On one day in which his mother was late to the fields, Brown witnesses her whipping: "She cried, 'Oh! pray—Oh! pray—Oh! pray'—these are generally the words of slaves when imploring mercy at the hands of their oppressors . . . I could hear every crack of the whip, and every groan and cry of my poor mother. . . . The cold chills ran over me, and I wept aloud."[49] Here Brown uses the spectacle of pain to draw readers toward sympathy at a variety of levels: with his mother at the repeated landing—"Oh! pray"—of each lash, with him as a son witnessing his mother's abuse, and with all tortured and enslaved people in this all-too-common scene. Though pain itself cannot speak, the em dashes between her cries grammatically translate the agonizing anticipation of each lash, drawing the reader into the immediacy of her pain. Frederick Douglass (1818–1895) depicts similarly unconscionable scenes of pain in his 1845 memoir. Describing the actions of his master, who "was not a humane slaveholder," Douglass recalls "hav[ing] often been awakened at the dawn of the day by the most heart-rending shrieks of an own aunt of mine, whom he used to tie up to a joist, and whip upon her naked back till she was literally covered with blood. No words, no tears, no prayers, from his gory victim, seemed to move his iron heart from its bloody purpose . . . where the blood ran fastest, there he whipped longest. He would whip her to make her scream, and whip her to make her hush; and not until overcome by fatigue, would he cease to swing the blood-clotted cowskin."[50] Such gut-wrenching descriptions of unacceptable pain were crucial to the persuasive logic of antislavery. Inviting the reader to sympathize with his aunt's suffering as the inhumane master cannot, Douglass details the particularities of her agonizing experiences. Emphasizing the connection between slavery and pain, Douglass describes this scene as a "blood-stained gate, the entrance to the hell of slavery through which I was about to pass."[51] This graphic revision of Adam Smith's famous description of a viewer's feelings for a man on the rack powerfully argues for a humanitarian impulse inspired by the spectacle of suffering.[52] Nor were slave narratives alone in these tactics; the temperance and anti-vivisection movements also used pain to effect social and political change, partaking in the broader mid-nineteenth-century fixation on pain and suffering.[53]

Developments in literary form made genres like the novel and slave narrative important sites for investigating pain precisely as it became more difficult to investigate pain through physical experimentation. If the humanitarian imperative to speak the unacceptable nature of pain was augmented by the developments in literary form, that same humanitarian imperative clashed forcefully with emerging practices of physical experimentation. Paradoxically, the new humanitarian concerns about pain troubled physical investigations into pain, even though both emerged from the new culture of pain and were ultimately invested in diminishing suffering; because physical experiments with pain were painful, they were unacceptable. Attempting to reconcile the tautological problem of trying to understand and alleviate pain by causing it, Robley Dunglison invoked human exceptionalism: "Nothing is, indeed, more erroneous than the notion, that even sensibility to pain is equal in every variety of the animal creation . . . we have the strongest reasons for believing, that [animal] sensibility diminishes as we descend; and that the feeling, expressed by the poet, that the beetle, which we tread upon—'In corporal sufferance finds a pang as great, / As when a giant dies'—however humane it may be, is physiologically untrue."[54] Dunglison provides examples from vivisection: "The frog will continue sitting, apparently unconcerned, for hours after it has been eviscerated; the tortoise walks about after losing its head; and the polypus, when divided by the knife, forms so many separate animals."[55] This line of argument about differential experiences of pain was also extended to other human bodies that were imagined to be less sensitive to certain kinds of suffering. Nonetheless, objections to practices like vivisection remained strong and the humanitarian troubles with physical experimentation made literary form and the imagination less problematic tools for medical experimentation.[56]

The use of literature to know pain was not new in the antebellum era. In his description of the pain of madness, for example, Rush grounds his views in "the authority of Shakespeare."[57] After quoting eight lines from *King Lear*, he continues to quote the play for its "language still more expressive of suffering" to which he offers "no objection to the correctness of this description of the distress": "I am bound / Upon a wheel of fire, that mine own tears / Do scald like molten lead."[58] In fact, as Benjamin Reiss has shown, "in the first three decades of American psychiatry, no figure was cited as an authority on insanity and mental functioning more frequently than William Shakespeare."[59] Thus it comes as no surprise that Samuel Morton, in a medical thesis replete with literary allusions and aspirations, also turned to *King Lear* to describe the intimate experience of pain.[60] A posthumous evaluation of this thesis in

1854 noted that Morton's work "takes up the subject of bodily pain, and considers it in regard to its causes, its diagnostic value, and its effects, both physical and psychical, leaving very little more to be said with regard to it."[61] It was, moreover, clear to this essay's author, Henry S. Patterson, that Morton hoped his thesis would be lauded for its literary value as well as its medical content. Noting "Morton's literary turn and studious habits," Patterson continues to describe the sentences in his pain thesis, "march[ing] sometimes with a didactic solemnity almost Johnsonian, while the frequency of the poetical references and quotations,—Latin and Italian as well as English,—and the facile fitness with which they glide into the text, show how familiar they must have been to the mind of the author."[62]

Pain in the Wake of Anesthesia

Anesthesia did not resolve the problem of knowing pain; rather, the discovery drew attention to it. The uncertainty about the purposes and experience of pain made its elimination fraught. The responses to anesthesia were mixed and complicated, and, while anesthesia was generally heralded as an extremely important medical breakthrough, it was adopted in less than half of surgeries performed in the coming decades.[63] Americans argued over its safety, its morality, and the extent of its recommended usage. It took thirty years for the administration of anesthesia to become a ubiquitous practice in American surgery.[64] In the meantime, Americans set about writing fiction to experiment imaginatively with feeling and pain to understand their value and nature in the wake of a discovery that made sensation optional.

John Collins Warren was vociferous in his warm support for the practice of anesthetization he had helped first demonstrate. In his volume on the practice, Warren begins by lamenting the unnecessary amount of suffering surgeons had long inflicted. "What surgeon is there," he asked, "who has not felt, while witnessing the distress of long painful operations, a sinking of the heart, to which no habit could render him insensible! What surgeon has not at these times been inspired with a wish, to find some means of lessening the sufferings he was obliged to inflict!"[65] In his impassioned language, Warren calls upon on antebellum Americans to be in sympathy—or, by definition, "with suffering"—with surgery patients. He wondered what medical practitioner, upon witnessing and sympathizing with sufferings that could not be dulled by exposure, could question the first viable anesthetic.[66]

Nevertheless, the mitigation of pain using ether *was* a contentious practice, as its administration in childbirth made very clear. Because it involved a
natural process, unconscious women, and men touching the genitalia of those
women, childbirth served as a kind of lightning rod for a host of concerns
about anesthesia. Some Americans worried that childbirth was not sufficiently
painful to merit the risks, that etherization itself was dangerous, that the practice was profane, that it was unethical, and that it put the child in unnecessary danger.[67] Others argued that "no pains can be worse than those which
women suffer in childbirth," but, a common line of inquiry continued, pain's
"companion love, which nature placed in their breasts, provides comfort."[68]
Religious objections proceeded from the Genesis passage "Unto the woman
he said . . . in sorrow thou shalt bring forth children," which embroiled anesthesia proponents in hermeneutical debates as well as scientific ones.[69]

Despite the clamor of early objections, proponents like literary physician
Walter Channing (1786–1876) championed the use of anesthesia in childbirth.
Channing had held the post of Professor of Obstetrics and Medical Jurispru-
dence at Harvard for more than thirty years by the time he witnessed Morton's
demonstration in the Bullfinch Amphitheater.[70] Not two years later, Channing had accumulated 581 cases of etherized childbirth and published a four-
hundred-page tome on the subject. In it, Channing explained that he had
rushed his volume to print because the exciting news that pain had been abolished by William Morton deserved to be made public. "The remedy of pain
was discovered in this city," he wrote to medical professor emeritus James
Jackson in his dedication, and "[it] is due to it, that what it has accomplished
should have its earliest embodiment in our own literature."[71] The New York
review offered similar praise, quoting Channing back to himself: "After ages
of suffering, and of frequently and long intermitted pursuit of such a remedy,
one has been discovered. It remains with the profession to say, whether it shall
take its place among the permanent and most important agents in the treatment of disease, and in abolishing pain; or whether it shall pass away, till another and a truer age shall revive, and give it a wider sphere of usefulness and
a surer perpetuity."[72] The *Providence Daily Journal* described the work as "a
very handsome volume" treating the "marvellous [invention] of the age . . .
the application of ether for the prevention of suffering."[73]

For the staunch empiricist Channing, numbers spoke.[74] Whereas about
half of patients died from thigh amputations without ether, that number was
halved with its use.[75] He reasoned the diminished number thus: "I see no other
explanation than that which is furnished by the established fact, that in [the

etherized patients] sensibility was abolished, and that the nervous power experienced no waste, and the great centres whence proceeds that power, no disturbance in their important functions."[76] Pain exhausted the mind and body of the patient, leaving him or her with fewer resources to do the work of healing, and Channing found his patients recovered more quickly.[77]

In the decades that followed the discovery of anesthesia, people meditated widely on pain, as they did on anesthesia itself. One of the last conversations Silas Weir Mitchell had with his father, John Kearsley Mitchell, suggests the immediacy of this knowledge conundrum even for prominent physicians. Knowing he was dying on the first of April 1858, John Mitchell talked with his son about the possible reasons for bodily pain and how much medicine stood to gain if doctors could know more about how their patients felt. This tableau, the dying physician-writer father attempting to communicate the incommunicability of pain to his physician-writer son, poignantly illustrates the limitations of the moment's medical knowing. Echoing earlier beliefs about the mental acuity brought on by pain, Weir Mitchell wrote that his father's "brain never acted more clearly."[78] That night John Mitchell suggested to his son that perhaps advances could be made if there were "more autobiographie of disease in our literature."[79] He died three days later.[80]

For some, the discovery of anesthesia appeared as if out of a dream. "Among the discoveries of the present age," Peter Van Buren wrote for the State Assembly of New York, "nothing, in its power to relieve human suffering, equals in importance that of chloroform, and its kindred compounds. If it be not the 'elixir of life,' so eagerly sought for by the ancient visionary, it is at least the prompt assuager of pain, the mitigator of suffering, to an extent unequaled."[81] With anesthesia the generation can "behold, converted into realities, those phenomena which heretofore have been regarded as only amongst the pleasing illusions of mythological fiction."[82] Van Buren concluded by insisting that the proper use of anesthesia would entitle the assembly "to the gratitude not only of the suffering, but of sympathising humanity."[83]

For others, the discovery of anesthesia unsettled longstanding ideas of pain and suffering. In the July 1851 issue of the *New-York Journal of Medicine*, physician Valentine Mott reflected this changing notion through a pessimistic declaration: "Pain reduces all ranks to a level—it makes all men cowards."[84] Whereas pain had been a regular feature of life before the 1840s, by 1860, a broadside for Perry Davis's patented painkiller in Providence, Rhode Island, could declare "It is not unfrequently said of it,—'*We would as soon think of being without flour in the house as without* PAIN KILLER.'"[85] Other changes were subtler. For example, the medical definition for "sympathy" had been tied to its Greek root "with suffering," but as early as 1848, Robley Dunglison purged the word "suffering" from sympathy's definition.[86] Among the reasons Dunglison altered his definition was likely the profound shift in ideas of pain and suffering since the 1839 edition of his medical dictionary. In other words, in the wake of the discovery of anesthesia it became possible—if not crucial— to imagine sympathy separated from its origins in pain. Once pain could be imagined as an elective state rather than a constitutive feature of life, sympathy, the great connector of body parts and human society, had to be imagined without it.

Holmes's Anesthetic Experiment: *Elsie Venner*

Oliver Wendell Holmes may have named "anaesthesia" and served as a fervent advocate of Morton's gas; nevertheless, after a decade and a half of debates he was still unsure about the ramifications of living "without feeling." After all, one could not use anesthesia without eradicating both pain *and* feeling. Holmes used his novels over the next few decades, most notably *Elsie Venner* (1860–1861), to imaginatively experiment with anesthetized states and better understand what it might mean to live "without feeling."

Holmes committed himself to a life of both medicine and literature. He wrote poetry while studying medicine and published his first book of poems in the same year he received his Harvard medical degree.[87] These dual commitments were professionally fraught for Holmes, who, from the time of his first poetry book, met with resistance from Bostonians who believed such a volume "militated seriously against this respectable and abstemious physician."[88] Nevertheless, Holmes continued to write poetry, popular vignettes (most famously in his "Breakfast Table" series), and medically oriented fiction as his medical star continued to rise. Between the early 1830s and early 1850s he went to Paris for training, joined a number of medical societies, founded the Tremont Medical School, joined the Dartmouth and Harvard medical faculties, was appointed to the American Academy of Arts and Sciences, and served as dean at Harvard's medical school. He also contributed enormously to American medical knowledge in this period; among other accomplishments, he introduced the stethoscope to American doctors, published a landmark study on puerperal fever, and, of course, renamed Morton's Letheon Gas *anesthesia*.[89]

Throughout this time, Holmes continued to write in both literary and more recognizably scientific modes. Holmes certainly employed literary forms because he loved them, but he also did so because he had reservations about the ability of other practices of medical science to yield all the answers it sought. In an 1857 essay, "The Mechanism of Vital Actions," he observed, "Experimental physiology teaches how to stop the wheels of the living machinery, and sometimes how to start them when their action is checked; but no observation from the outside ever did or ever will approach the mystery of that most intense of all realities."[90] Holmes's proclamation of the limits of physical experimentation bore a clear theological bent, but it also suggested a broader critique of experimental physiology's inability to parse the "science of life."

In contradistinction, Holmes explained that different epistemological tools made distinct forms of knowledge possible. "Physiologists and metaphysicians look at the same objects with different focal adjustments," he wrote, "but if they deny the truths out of their own immediate range, their eyes have got the better of their judgment."[91] The "microscope, or balance, or scalpel" could not probe the deeper mysteries of human life.[92] It is here that imaginative forms could help. Holmes was not interested merely in the "mechanism" of human life but, like many pursuing physiological inquiry before him, in what exceeded descriptions of human machinery. That is, after all, what physiology had in common with literature and metaphysics.[93]

Like a number of other nineteenth-century physicians, Holmes understood fiction, and novels in particular, to bear a particularly close relationship to the bodies and imaginations of their readers. After the discovery of a new painkiller, for example, Holmes playfully remarked, "The new local anesthetic, cocaine, deadens the sensibility of the part to which it is applied, so that the eye may have its mote or beam plucked out without feeling it,—as the novels of Zola and Maupassant have hardened the delicate nerve-centres of the women who have fed their imaginations on the food they have furnished."[94] Since pain itself sat at the nexus between the body and the imagination, fiction was a particularly good way of approaching it.

Nevertheless, the first published installment of the novel that would come to be called *Elsie Venner* playfully disparages the work of fiction. Appearing serially as *The Professor's Story* in the *Atlantic* beginning in 1860, Holmes opens his story with a humorous anti-fiction preface. Refusing his editor's request for a fictional story, Holmes's author writes that he can "under no circumstances . . . entertain your proposition to write a *fictitious* narrative."[95] Compromising, he offers a collection of true stories that "might undoubtedly be taken by the public for a world of fiction," while still reproaching writers who "go to work, in cold blood, to draw, out of what they call their *imagination*, a parcel of impossible events and absurd characters."[96] As the letters continue, the author categorically dismisses romance, fiction, novels, and the imagination—a set of terms that, of course, describe the very task he is already undertaking. "I have been more intensely bored with works of fictions," the fictitious narrator declares, "than I ever was by the Latin Grammar or Rollin's History," and, sharing a joke with the reader, he continues, "no one can accuse me of writing a *novel*,—a thing which I never meant to do, under any circumstances."[97] Holmes would, of course, have likely expected readers of the *Atlantic Monthly* to have recognized *The Professor's Story* as fictional, drawing on his popular persona from *The Professor at the Breakfast-Table*, which he had begun serializing the year before.[98] *The Professor's Story* opens as a work of fiction by a fictional author for a fictional magazine that, nonetheless, pretends to reject fiction in an elaborate joke. Playing with what constitutes truth, Holmes prepares his reader to accept new relationships between fact and fiction.

In the 1861 revision he called *Elsie Venner*, Holmes changed his tack. The new preface features an authorial persona who directly claims his literary tools. He calls the work a "romance" to "make sure of being indulged in the common privileges of poetic license."[99] This story in the "disguise of fiction" offers

> a grave scientific doctrine [that] may be detected lying beneath some of the delineations of character. [The author] has used this doctrine as a part of the machinery of his story without pledging his absolute belief in it to the extent to which it is asserted or implied. It was adopted as a convenient medium of truth rather than as an accepted scientific conclusion. The reader . . . must decide how much of what has been told he can accept, either as having actually happened, or as possible and more or less probable. The Author must be permitted, however, to say here, in his personal character, and as responsible to the students of the human mind and body, that since this story has been in progress he has received the most startling confirmation of the possibility of the existence of a character like that which he had drawn as a purely imaginary conception in Elsie Venner.[100]

Here Holmes is arrestingly forthright about the relationship between the novel and medical science. Abandoning facetious claims from the first preface about what fiction writers "call their *imagination*, a parcel of impossible events and absurd characters," this second preface commits to "a purely imaginary conception"—if one "startling[ly]" verified by fact. Fiction allows Holmes to enter a mode of inquiry "without pledging his absolute belief in it"; it allows readers to become co-producers of medical knowledge who can "decide how much of what has been told he can accept"; and it provides a form to pursue medical inquiry through a "purely imaginary conception." Finally, Holmes anticipates his readership including "students of the human mind and body," a pointedly undisciplined category that includes both his own Harvard medical students and any person interested in physiological and psychological questions.

Holmes's novel was a serious scientific investigation. *Elsie Venner* is the story of a medical student's encounter with Elsie Venner, a wholly unique woman, made snakelike in the womb after a rattlesnake bit her mother. The student's professor narrates the story, which begins with the promising young medical student Bernard Langdon leaving school to make money teaching in a small New England town. After a false start, Bernard lands at the Apollinean Female Institute where he meets the strange loner Elsie. Elsie spends time only with her father, Dudley, cousin Dick, and black governess, Old Sophy. Dudley loves but does not understand her, Dick tries to marry her for money but is rebuffed, and Sophy is Elsie's one true confidant. Elsie falls for Bernard (as much as she can for anyone), but he eventually comes to see her only as a friend and subject of inquiry. Only as she is dying does Elsie begin to become human and grow the capacity to love for the first time. The narrator finds himself interested enough in Bernard's account to "avail myself of all those other extraordinary methods of obtaining information well known to the writers of narrative."[101]

Despite this seemingly straightforward account of what the novel will be about and what tools Holmes will use, the subject of the novel has long been debated. Scholars have located *Elsie Venner*'s "grave scientific doctrine" in any number of contemporary discourses including early psychiatric inquiry,[102] rising statistics, contagion, childbed fever,[103] race science,[104] nervous disorders, research on snake venom, and a critique of homeopathy.[105] As a prominent and broad-ranging thinker, Holmes may well have had all of these issues in mind, but he also uses *Elsie Venner* to address a question raised by the discovery of anesthesia, which by 1860 had prompted a series of nightmarish questions for Holmes about what it meant to live without feeling.

For Holmes, rattlesnakes were useful for getting to the heart of these concerns. Holmes had likely read Robley Dunglison's popular textbook *Human*

Physiology, from which he would have learned that that while "it is impossible to change places with the animal," rattlesnakes likely lived their lives largely without feeling.[106] Philadelphia physician Richard Harlan had likewise explained that simpler animals like rattlesnakes simply felt less. Harlan claimed to have proven rattlesnakes' freedom from pain by beheading one. In his experiment, both halves of the animal acted as he believed they would have while whole (the body wriggling and the head looking to strike), so Harlan reasoned the animal could not possibly have felt the injury.[107]

Holmes had also avidly read his friend Silas Weir Mitchell's experiments with rattlesnake venom, which were published as Holmes was serializing *Elsie Venner*. Holmes himself was so taken with the subject, the study, and Mitchell's method that he housed a rattlesnake for a few weeks to acquaint himself with the animal.[108] Of his intellectual method in the rattlesnake study, Mitchell wrote, "Ideas about snake poison, how to do this or that, the phenomena it causes in animals, occupied my mind incessantly. I took it to sleep with me and woke to think about it and found it hard to escape it even when in church or conversing with people. It is something like being haunted, this grip a fruitful research gets upon you. You come upon a difficulty, try to think a way out of it. This happens continually."[109] Mitchell described this method of work in words that recall those of Benjamin Rush, whom he greatly admired: it is "not very unlike that which is present when in fiction or verse you wait, watching the succession of ideas which come when you keep an open mind."[110] Holmes employed this method more directly in writing *Elsie Venner*.

Elsie Venner is an imaginative experiment with anesthetization, a state "without feeling." A young woman poisoned by snake venom in the womb, Elsie is both an anesthetizing and anesthetized character. She is a fascinating, "strange, wild-looking girl" with a cold touch who produces strikingly strange effects on others that range from chills to imprecise sensation: her doctor, for example, "fe[els] oddly as she looked at him; he did not like the feeling."[111] Elsie's look likewise affects Bernard "strangely. It seemed to disenchant the air, so full a moment before of strange attractions. He became silent, and dreamy, as it were."[112] Like anesthesia, Elsie's gaze disrupts Bernard's feelings and connection to his immediate surroundings, drawing him into a silent, "dreamy" world. This peculiar feeling Elsie produces in others accords well with contemporary accounts of anesthetics: "Perhaps, as a general rule, the intellectual faculties first feel their influence,—a sort of intoxication supervening, with imperfect power of regulating movements," and, if too much was inhaled, anesthesia could kill.[113]

Elsie both produces strange, anesthetic feelings in others and is incapable of proper human feeling herself. Though still a girl, Elsie refers to her father formally (as Dudley) and shows little affection for those who care for her. Early in the novel she brags to the family doctor that she ran away for a night: "You should have heard the horns blowing and the guns firing. Dudley was frightened out of his wits. Old Sophy told him she'd had a dream, and that I should be found in Dead-Man's Hollow, with a great rock lying on me. They hunted all over [the mountain], but they did'nt [sic] find me,—I was farther up."[114] Her disinterested amusement and apathy disturbs Dr. Kittredge, who "forced a pleasant professional smile" and diverts the conversation "as if wishing to change the subject."[115] Characters repeatedly worry that Elsie might harm them.

Later in the novel Elsie reveals herself as a person who, constitutionally, cannot feel. Near the story's end she confesses to her governess, "I cannot love anybody. What is love, Sophy?"[116] Sophy tries to assuage Elsie by vowing her own love, but the physician-narrator describes their shared emotion in a circumscribed way: "What strange intelligence was that which passed between them through [Elsie's] diamond eyes and [Sophy's] little beady black ones?—what subtile [sic] intercommunication, penetrating so much deeper than articulate speech? This was the nearest approach to sympathetic relations that Elsie had ever had: a kind of dumb intercourse of feeling, such as one sees in the eyes of brute mothers looking on their young."[117] Elsie's lack of love is not a failure of nurture—her father and her governess care for her very much. This limited sense of "sympathetic relations," rather, emerges from Elsie's nature.

Her anesthetized and anesthetizing character is most strikingly tested through her desire to love. Increasingly panicked about her inability to feel, Elsie looks for a cure in Bernard; she hopes he will love her. "I have no friend," Elsie confesses to him. "Nothing loves me but one old woman. I cannot love anybody. They tell me there is something in my eyes that draws people to me and makes them faint."[118] Attempting to use her anesthetizing powers to dominate Bernard's physiology, she looks into his eyes and commands, "*Love me!*"—but passion cannot be produced anesthetically.[119] While her eyes can produce certain sensations—tingling, fascination, and even fainting—they cannot force love.

In the novel's logic, love is the highest order of feeling, which must be articulated in a language Elsie cannot access.[120] Elsie's "dumb intercourse of feeling" with Sophy is not love but a "narrow and individual" animalistic expression.[121] "An emotion which can shape itself in language opens the gate for itself into the great community of human affections," the physician-narrator explains, "every word we speak is the medal of a dead thought or feeling, struck in the die of some human experience, worn smooth by innumerable contacts, and always transferred warm from one to another. By words we share the common consciousness of the race, which has shaped itself in these symbols. . . . The language of the eyes runs deeper into the personal nature, but it is purely individual, and perishes in expression."[122] Lacking the language that comes out of the experience of affect, Elsie can only reach the first level of human feeling—not the sympathy that forms the connective tissue of human society. Holmes describes this higher order of feeling through the metaphor of print: the language of feeling is the "medal" of a feeling past, cast in the mold of "human experience" and "worn smooth" by repeated used. This language derives its form from the "mosaics of vocabulary" to which Elsie does not have access for much of the novel—but which Holmes shares with the reader through his words on the page.[123]

It is here that we can see Holmes experimenting with the relationship between anesthesia and aesthetics. Using the body of a woman physiologically altered by anesthetizing chemicals, Holmes investigates the physical, social, and aesthetic effects of anesthesia. Physically, anesthesia does not seem to have done damage to Elsie. She is not only healthy but hearty. Her anesthetic physiology has, however, done her great harm at social and aesthetic levels. Disrupting the processes of judgment and emotion, Elsie's inability to feel destroys her relationships with people and the world around her. She cannot perceive or be affected by the world as a human might but rather anesthesia renders her like an animal, incapable of proper sensibility or sentiment. Holmes's anesthetic experiment also weighs in on debates in aesthetic theory. In writing the story of a woman whose feelings are inexplicable to those around her, Holmes experiments in his story with assertions made by aesthetic philosophers like Kant that aesthetic perceptions have only the feeling of universality but are not, in fact, universal. Elsie's inability to access some sense of universal feeling is, in the end, her tragedy.

Only as she is dying can Elsie achieve higher levels of feeling. A fever caused by heartbreak (the result of her inability to feel properly) destroys the anesthetizing effects of the snake venom on her body. With an unexpected shock—what Holmes would refer to in a later novel as a "mortal antipathy"—her body transforms: "From this time forward," the physician-narrator describes, "there was a change in her whole expression and manner."[124] With the death of her poisoned part, Elsie at last gains a capacity for more complex feeling and love. One evening, after her father kisses her goodnight, she "rose by a sudden effort" and unexpectedly "threw her arms round his neck, kissed him, and said, 'Good-night, my dear father!' "[125] Speaking the language of filial feeling for the first time, Elsie expresses her love for Dudley Venner and dies. She has already lost Bernard.

While Bernard begins the novel as a possible love interest for Elsie, he becomes a more explicit agent of Holmes's imaginative experiment by the novel's end. The anesthetizing spell Elsie once held over Bernard breaks, and he sublimates this dangerous fascination into medical interest. Bernard's epistemological orientation toward his study (taking on Elsie as the subject of his medical thesis) nonetheless shares much with Holmes's own experiment in *Elsie Venner*. While his "professional training made him slow to accept marvellous stories," Bernard commits to the part-snake girl as an appropriate subject of medical inquiry: "As a man of science, he well knew that just on the verge of the demonstrable facts of physics and physiology there is a nebulous border-land which what is called 'common sense' perhaps does wisely not enter, but which uncommon sense, or the fine apprehension of privileged intelligences, may cautiously explore, and in so doing find itself behind the scenes which make up for the gazing world the show which is called Nature."[126] Here Holmes emphasizes the "privileged intelligences" of imaginative experimentation, which can make sense of phenomena "on the verge of demonstrable facts" where pure objectivity cannot. As a subject of study, Elsie Venner occupies this "nebulous border-land" of knowing, which Bernard will parse in his yet-to-be-written medical thesis, "Unresolved Nebulae in Vital Science." In this metafictional moment, Bernard commits to investigating the topic that the novel itself parses, using a title that recalls those used by Holmes, such as "Border Lines of Knowledge in Some Provinces of Medical Science." Significantly, then, it is "perhaps with some degree of *imaginative exaltation*" that Bernard "set[s] himself to solving the problem of Elsie's influence . . . [to the] alien current of influence, sinuous and dark," that ran through her "rich nature." Bernard marshals "the images which certain poets had dreamed of" to identify what "seemed to have become a reality before his own eyes."[127] As in Holmes's prefatory remarks, Bernard's imagination precedes what can be otherwise known.[128]

Medicated Novels

Fiction was a particularly useful form for pursuing the fraught questions raised by the discovery of anesthesia. It offered at least five benefits as a form for inquiry into pain and feeling. First, as Holmes noted in the 1861 preface, there were the "common privileges of poetic license" that "romance" allowed, along with the ability to present a "grave scientific doctrine" as a "part of the machinery . . . without pledging [the author's] absolute belief in it." Second, there was the possibility of imagining a perfect test case for problems of feeling beyond what empirical observation could provide. Third, fiction was a better venue for pursuing his inquiry because of notorious limitations of knowing the pain and feeling of another. Following in the footsteps of physician-writers like Bird, Holmes imagined himself into the bodies of characters, which allowed him to get closer to phenomena that defied physical experimentation. Fourth, since issues like pain and feeling sit at the border of physiology, politics, philosophy, and the social, fiction allowed Holmes to engage the problem of feeling in its fuller sense through a complex narrative, whereas truth claims would immediately force him to divide his inquiry between these fields. And, finally, imaginative inquiry was helpful especially because of the centrality of any findings about feeling and pain to ethical questions in medicine.[129]

Holmes was invested in fiction's usefulness for medical questions, but it had to be good to be effective. *Elsie Venner*'s literary merit was central to its value as a work of medical theory. In 1883, Holmes reflected on *Elsie Venner* through an amusing anecdote in which a "very good friend, spoke of [*Elsie Venner*] as 'a medicated novel,' and quite properly refused to read. . . . It *is* a medicated novel," he continued, "and if she wished to read for mere amusement and helpful recreation there was no need of troubling herself with a story written with a different end in view."[130] Scholars have largely taken this comment about "medicated novels" as a straightforward description of *Elsie Venner*'s medical work.[131] It was, and it wasn't. Although Holmes here accepts the term "medicated novel" as a description of *Elsie Venner*, it was a term he both returned to and worried about over the decades. For example, he had described medicated novels disparagingly a decade earlier in *The Poet at the Breakfast-table* (1872) as works whose moralizing undermined their art. Dwelling on the idea of a "book infirmary" where "many books, invalids from their birth," and other "unpresentable cripples" find a home, Holmes's poet protagonist explains, "I always, from an early age, had a keen eye for a story with a moral sticking out of it, and gave it a wide berth, though in my later years I have myself written a couple of 'medicated novels,' as one of my dearest and pleasantest old friends wickedly called them . . . I forgave the satire for the charming *esprit* of the epithet."[132] *Elsie Venner*, he hoped, was not too much in this latter category. In 1891, Holmes worked to clarify this position once more: discussing *The Guardian Angel* (1867), Holmes writes that "like 'Elsie Venner,' [it] depends for its deeper significance on the ante-natal history of its subject. But the story was meant to be readable for those who did not care for its underlying philosophy. If it fails to interest the reader who ventures upon it, it may find a place on an unfrequented bookshelf in common with other 'medicated novels.'"[133] *Elsie Venner*, *The Guardian Angel*, and *A Mortal Antipathy* were serious, imaginative experiments, not, he hoped, overly prescriptive novels killed by dry morals and overly structured form.

A well-written novel could do things that physical experimentation could not. As Holmes was publishing the first complete edition of *Elsie Venner* in 1861, he was also mourning limitations of experimental physiology and "recognizing the fact, then, that we have learned nothing but the machinery of life, and are no nearer to its essence."[134] This limitation is precisely where Holmes's belief in the imagination and literary form could help. Returning to *Elsie Venner*'s claim that words were essential to human feeling, Holmes's own book becomes a useful venue for experimenting with the more difficult aspects of human life within and between bodies. For if the deepest feelings are "struck in the die of some human experience, worn smooth by innumerable contacts, and always transferred warm from one to another," then language is a powerful medium through which to understand human feeling. This recursive practice of feeling-making through language dovetails with the practice of meaning-making Mitchell described for his own rattlesnake study. "I think best," Mitchell explained, "when, having come to a critical point, I state a theory which I am going to accept or reject as experiment decides. I must always write it out, sometimes again and again. This is a favorite method with me for fruitful thought."[135] Still, Mitchell did not know exactly how it happened: "As to the mechanism of this process, beyond a certain point it is an absolute mystery . . . there comes to me from some inward somewhere criticisms, suggestions, in a word, ideas, about the ultimate origin of which I know nothing."[136] Later, Mitchell would name that origin "poetic imagination."

Pain in the Civil War Hospital

When Mitchell discussed pain with his dying father in 1858 the two foresaw the coming war, but Mitchell could little imagine the more intimate acquaintance he would make with bodies in pain in Civil War hospitals. An ambivalent unionist with strong Southern ties, Mitchell initially avoided involving himself in the war. Nevertheless, like many physicians of the period, he could not long escape service; by 1864, 130 of the 174 fellows at the College of Physicians in his hometown of Philadelphia were involved with the war effort.[137] Mitchell eventually worked for a series of local hospitals that provided him ample opportunity to witness injuries in greater numbers and varieties than would have otherwise been possible; this was especially true at the makeshift hospital on Turner's Lane that specialized in the injuries and diseases of the nerves, where Mitchell saw pain assembled and displayed as never before.[138] "Here at one time," Mitchell wrote, "were eighty epileptics, every kind of nerve-wound, palsies, singular choreas, and stump disorders. . . . That hospital was, as one poor fellow said, a hell of pain."[139] This superabundance of pain led Mitchell and his fellow physicians to administer forty thousand injections of morphine in just one year.[140] Some of his descriptions of pain "were received in England with critical doubt," but this was due to the uniqueness of the situation rather than the veracity of his account: "I have never encountered such cases since, nor shall we again until we see diseased men the victims of wounds."[141] Whereas just a short time before Americans might have felt it necessary to travel to Europe for their medical training, during the Civil War medical men and women got all of the clinical experience they could want at home. This is not a book about the Civil War, but dipping a toe into the war years through the eyes of one literary physician allows us to understand how Americans began to grapple with the epistemic and ontological difficulties of pain in the face of radically altered circumstances.

The Civil War and rising professional communities in the 1860s had a profound effect on American medicine. One paradigm-shifting phenomenon was that during the Civil War, for the first time, large numbers of Americans received care outside of the home.[142] Before the war, doctors mostly visited patients in their homes; hospitals and almshouses housed individuals who did not have family members or a church community to care for them.[143] During the war, union hospitals alone cared for more than a million men.[144] This shift from a fundamentally domestic and deeply relational U.S. medicine to a more clinical practice could not but fundamentally alter the nature of the profession. The rise and reorganization of the hospital in this period altered doctors' daily work, but the experience the war provided made possible a kind of medical training that not only rivaled the clinical experience Americans had long sought in Europe but also offered unique exposure to the bodies of injured citizens.

For Mitchell, the Civil War hospital provided a good deal of experience from which to ground his own investigations into the nature of pain, an interest he pursued throughout his life.[145] First, he used anesthesia to discover soldiers dodging military service. "I could interest you long," he told the Physicians' Club of Chicago decades later, "by our devices to trap these young fellows, commonly by the use of anesthetic," presumably administering a drug that eradicated pain to test its existence in the first place.[146] But Mitchell went beyond individual cases, inquiring into the nature of pain and eventually coining his own terms for phenomena of pain and feeling he would introduce to the medical world as *causalgia* and *phantom limb*. In a lengthy discussion of pain, Mitchell first describes causalgia in a collaboratively written volume on gunshot wounds in 1864, though he would not name it until later. In some "pain was of that strange burning nature," a "peculiar and agonizing form of suffering."[147] This "burning pain" was "a form of suffering as yet undescribed, and so frequent and terrible as to demand from us the fullest description. In our early experience of nerve wounds, we met with a small number of men who were suffering from a pain, which they described as 'burning,' or as 'mustard red hot,' or as 'a red-hot file rasping the skin.' In all of these patients, and in many later cases, this pain was an associate of the glossy skin. . . . In fact, this state of skin never existed without burning pain."[148] Words failed in describing the pain. Mitchell and his coauthors wrote of the "unendurable anguish" they sought to describe, "the terms here used may seem strong to those who have not encountered these cases; but no one who has seen them will think that, as regards some of them, it would be possible to overstate their most wretched condition."[149] In 1872, he coined the term "causalgia" to name this "burning pain."[150]

Mitchell and his collaborators relied largely on thirty-one case histories of patients, some of them extending for a number of pages, to know the "yet undescribed" instances of pain. An excerpted version of the final "CASE 31.— A. D. Marks, sergeant," admitted May 3, 1863, illustrates the prose style they used to marshal their evidence:

> During the first week, the arm, though palsied, was painless. Then
> he began to feel a knife-like pain from the wound down the inside
> of the limb, and also on its front, and on the ulnar side, half-way to
> the wrist. With these pains came a tingling and burning sensation,
> as when the blood returns into a limb said to have been asleep, but
> more severe . . . [July 5,] He lies on his back, anxious-looking and

pain-worn. The left arm rests on a pillow. It is cold, mottled, and swollen. The skin of his hand is thin, and dark-red, but presents no eruption. . . . The whole arm and hand, except its back part, is, as he says, alive with burning pain, which warmth and dependence of the limb increase, and which cold and wetting ease considerably. It is subject to daily exacerbations about mid-day . . . [July 21,] Probably the muscles still had sensation, since pressure on them was agonizing . . . August 14.—The recent warm weather has increased the pain, so that he moans and weeps incessantly.[151]

The record of Marks's life and physical condition continues until, at long last, on April 10, 1864, Marks is discharged, "free of pain," though the motion in his arm is still limited.[152] This description, if not quite intimate, still gives a more robust sense of the patient than many earlier case histories did. In its legitimizing of the patient's own description of his pain and detailing of sentimental moaning and weeping, the case history shares much with the literary forms Mitchell spent his summers writing.[153]

When "The Case of George Dedlow" appeared in the *Atlantic* in July 1866 with no introductory apparatus, it looked very much like one of these case histories.[154] The narrator begins "The Case of George Dedlow" by describing his story as a case history: while "the following notes of my own case have been declined on various pretexts by every medical journal to which I have offered them," at the request of friends, he has decided "to print my narrative with all the personal details, rather than in the dry shape . . . I shall publish it elsewhere."[155] (Further confusing matters, Mitchell himself claimed never to have intended to publish "George Dedlow."[156] Rather, he gave the story to Reverend William H. Furness [1802–1896], who passed it to Edward Everett Hale [1822–1908], who sent it to the *Atlantic*.[157] Mitchell declared he was quite surprised when he got the page proofs and a check.[158])

The story gives an account of a wartime physician who loses his limbs one by one until he is left a torso in an army medical hospital; it is also an imaginative inquiry into the nature and mechanism of pain. In the first extended scene Dedlow injures his left arm and loses his right arm to a bullet; after a period of insensibility, the arm begins to acquire "a strange burning, which was rather a relief to me" until the pain increased so that Dedlow feels "as if the hand was caught and pinched in a red-hot vise. Then in my agony I begged my guard for water to wet it with."[159] Continuing with phrases that very much recall the language of his earlier pain case histories, Mitchell has

Dedlow continue, "At length the pain became absolutely unendurable, and . . . I screamed, cried, and yelled in my torture" over his arm "which is dead except to pain."[160] Here the narrative takes a turn from Mitchell's medical work, as a local preacher instructs Dedlow on the value of pain. The pain in his arm teaches Dedlow about his future "if you die in your sins: you will go where only pain can be felt. For all eternity, all you will be as that hand,—knowing pain only."[161] While Dedlow doubts the preacher's authority, the words take effect, as he feels a second kind of pain—"a sudden and chilling horror of possible universal pain, and suddenly fainted."[162] This discussion of the meaning of pain gives way to the next stage of causalgia, his arm "red, shining, aching, burning, and, as it seemed to me, perpetually rasped with hot files."[163] Again, the precise repetition of Mitchell's language from *Gunshot Wounds* blurs the boundaries between fact and fiction, lending credibility to the story as a medical text. No morphine can cross the Confederate lines and the doctor suggests amputation as the solution to the damaged limb that might also provide "some chance of arresting the pain," which "was so awful, that I made no more of losing the limb than of parting with a tooth on account of toothache."[164] Emphasizing the incommunicable nature of pain, Dedlow explains, "brief preparations were made, which I watched with a sort of eagerness such as must forever be inexplicable to any one who has not passed six weeks of torture like that which I suffered."[165] But, of course, there is no ether across enemy lines either, and Mitchell narratively inhabits the position of a surgery patient undergoing an amputation without painkillers: "The pain felt was severe; but it was insignificant as compared to that of any other minute of the past six weeks. . . . As the second incision was made, I felt a strange lightning pain play through the limb, defining every minutest fibril of nerve . . . followed by instant, unspeakable relief."[166] Dedlow recalls only "pointing to the arm which lay on the floor: 'There is the pain, and here am I.' "[167]

A few months later, Dedlow loses his legs. Though the scene of injury is "scarred" upon his memory and his legs are irreparably damaged, he feels "no pain."[168] This time the doctors use chloroform for the amputation: "In a moment the trees began to move around from left to right,—then faster and faster; then a universal grayness came before me, and I recall nothing" until he wakes up with "a sharp cramp in my left leg."[169] Unable to reach the pain, Dedlow asks an attendant to rub his left calf. The attendant responds, "You ain't none, pardner. It's took off," but Dedlow retorts, "I know better . . . I have pain in both legs."[170] Inverting the scene of arm loss, where Dedlow is relieved to find the pain physically separated from him, in this scene Dedlow only acquires pain at the moment that his limbs go missing.[171] Whereas in the depiction of Dedlow's right arm Mitchell attempts to know the pain of causalgia, he uses the case of Dedlow's legs to theorize, for the first time, what he would come to call "phantom limb" syndrome.

In the next scene Dedlow loses his left arm to gangrene, and the remainder of the story is dedicated to understanding the "relation of the mind to the body" in his new state at the Stump Hospital in Philadelphia and finally at the "United States Army Hospital for nervous diseases," very much like the one Mitchell himself worked in.[172] Here he finds that "the great mass of men who had undergone amputations, for many months felt the usual consciousness that they still had the lost limb. It itched or pained, or was cramped."[173] In painful cases, "the conviction of its existence continued unaltered for long periods; but where no pain was felt in it, then, by degrees, the sense of having that limb faded away entirely."[174] Dedlow theorizes the phenomenon thus: "The knowledge we possess of any part is made up of the numberless impressions from without which affect its sensitive surfaces, and which are transmitted through its nerves to the spinal nerve-cells, and through them, again, to the brain. We are thus kept endlessly informed as to the existence of the parts," which, in the case of amputation, have "nerve-trunks" that "[remain] capable of being impressed by irritations . . . referred by the brain to the lost parts, to which these nerve-threads belonged."[175] The pain prompts an existential awareness, reminiscent of Bird's musings about pain in *Sheppard Lee*, that "keeps the brain ever mindful of the missing part, and, imperfectly at least, preserves to the man a consciousness of possessing that which he has not."[176]

Pain prompts, then, both medical and philosophical meditations. Of his own experience with this, Dedlow continues, "Before leaving Nashville, I had begun to suffer the most acute pain in my left hand, especially in the little finger; and so perfect was the idea which was thus kept up of the real presence of these missing parts, that I found it hard at times to believe them absent. Often, at night, I would try with one lost hand to grope for the other. As, however, I had no pain in the right arm, the sense of the existence of that limb gradually disappeared, as did that of my legs also."[177] On one hand, this allows Mitchell to detail the different ways an individual might feel the missing parts. On the other hand, pain provides wholeness to the body, if a phantom wholeness, that offers a unitary explanation of corporeal existence.

Nevertheless, the experiences of pain offered in "The Case of George Dedlow" are also widely disparate. When Dedlow's pain is eased by morphine he "beg[ins] to be disturbed by the horrible variety of suffering about me."[178] Describing a man who walked only sideways, a man with shoulder blades projecting oddly, and others who lost the use of their senses, Dedlow concludes, "In fact, every one had his own grotesquely painful peculiarity."[179] It was this variety, which Mitchell had personally witnessed, that excited him, but it was also problematic for theorizing pain—or understanding the pain of others—when each instantiation was so deeply particular.

As these painful sensations cease, Dedlow is faced with a much greater psychological pain. Having lost "four fifths" of his body weight, he finds he has lost that much of himself.[180] "I found to my horror that at times I was less conscious of myself, of my own existence," Dedlow narrates. "I felt like asking some one constantly if I were really George Dedlow or not . . . [and a]t times the conviction of my want of being myself was overwhelming, and most painful."[181] This second psychical pain results from a loss of feeling, a state that Dedlow worries obliterates his subjectivity: "About one half of the sensitive surface of my skin was gone, and thus much of my relation to the outer world destroyed. . . . This set me to thinking how much a man might lose and yet live."[182] In language that might have been written by Robert Montgomery Bird, Dedlow "reach[es] the conclusion that man is not his brain, or any one part of it, but all of his economy, and that to lose any part must lessen this sense of his own existence."[183]

As in some other medical novels, like *Sheppard Lee*, these meditations are cloaked in absurdist fantasy. While Dedlow does not will himself into other bodies, he does go to a spiritualist meeting in which a spirit rapper locates his lost legs by number in the army medical museum. "Suddenly," Dedlow finds "a strange return of [his] self-consciousness. I was reindividualized, so to speak."[184] Dedlow rises up on phantom limbs, "and, staggering a little, walk[s] across the room on limbs invisible to them or me."[185] Ending with a joke about Dedlow's "spirit" limbs stumbling, having "been for nine months in the strongest alcohol," Mitchell signals to his reader that the case history is a fantasy, or something of an extended joke.[186]

Nevertheless, readers took Mitchell's case history for fact. Mitchell would remember his readers' responses thus: "It was at once accepted by many as the description of a real case. Money was collected in several places to assist the unfortunate man, and benevolent persons went to the 'Stump Hospital,' in Philadelphia, to see the sufferer and to aid him."[187] This preface to the new publication of the story simultaneously marks the "George Dedlow" as fiction for future readers and signals its medical value. For while Mitchell himself may have been shy about offering his story as medical inquiry, the story repeatedly used phrases Mitchell recorded elsewhere as medical language. In this way, "George Dedlow" was a serious investigation of the nature of pain.

It was not until 1871 that Mitchell would rewrite his findings as medical nonfiction in an essay titled "Phantom Limbs," published in *Lippincott's Magazine of Popular Literature and Science*.[188] Picking up on his description in "George Dedlow," Mitchell begins his account with a description of the "Stump Hospital" and reproduces many of the details of his fictional story.[189] Recognizing, perhaps, that some of his readers might recall the particulars, Mitchell clarifies: "Some years ago an article was published in the *Atlantic Monthly*" that "gave an account of the sensations of men who have lost a limb or limbs, but the author, taking advantage of the freedom accorded to a writer of fiction, described as belonging to this class of sufferers certain psychological states so astounding in their character that he certainly could never have conceived it possible that his humorous sketch, with its absurd conclusions, would for a moment mislead any one."[190] His earnest medical text, "Phantom Limbs," was, then, written to present a "description of what the amputated really feel and suffer," in the hopes that it would "serve to correct such erroneous beliefs as were caused by this *jeu d'esprit*."[191]

In spite of Mitchell's disavowal of his account in "George Dedlow," much remains the same. In words that specifically recall Dedlow's, Mitchell writes, "It has long been known to surgeons that when a limb has been cut off the sufferer does not lose the consciousness of its existence."[192] In 95 percent of cases, he continues, the patient keeps some feeling of the missing limb, which usually does not dissipate. "A person in this condition," Mitchell writes, "is haunted, as it were, by a constant or inconstant fractional phantom of so much of himself as has been lopped away—an unseen ghost of the lost part. . . . There is something almost tragical, something ghastly, in the notion of these thousands of spirit limbs haunting as many good soldiers, and every now and then tormenting them with the disappointments which arise when, the memory being off guard for a moment, the keen sense of the limb's presence betrays the man into some effort, the failure of which of a sudden reminds him of his loss."[193] This description and that which follows it closely reproduce the scenes depicted in "The Case of George Dedlow." Even Mitchell's language cannot resist literary articulation as he lapses into gothic language (reminiscent of his father's gothic medical writing), imagining the "tragical" and "ghastly hauntings" of phantom limbs. These "spirit limbs," as Mitchell calls them in his scientific article, specifically recall the joke in "George Dedlow." Perhaps, then, what disturbed Mitchell was not that readers had taken his accounts of pain in the story to be true but that "the spiritualist incident at the end of the story was received with joy by the spiritualists as a valuable proof of the truth of their beliefs."[194] Mitchell had strong feelings about spiritualism: after a séance he witnessed with William James, he wrote, "The impression made upon me was of a fraud and I thought a very stupid one."[195]

In contrast, Mitchell's explorations into causalgia and phantom limb through fiction were rigorous inquiry. Perhaps adopting his father's deathbed suggestion that first-person accounts of pain might provide the best insight for physicians, Mitchell imagined himself into a painful body to explore what a life in pain and then "without feeling" (or with a diminished capacity for feeling) might mean. If it was the "psychological states" that Mitchell found so improbable—the ones that made spiritualism possible—he did not disavow the physiological descriptions in "George Dedlow." Even then, the psychological and philosophical meditations in the story were undertaken in earnest. Mitchell describes the state of injured soldiers in his medical text as "haunted, as it were, by a constant or inconstant fractional phantom of so much of himself as has been lopped away—an unseen ghost of the lost part." Mitchell's inquiry into pain in "George Dedlow," then, was an experiment based in his medical imagination.

Nevertheless, Mitchell's caution about writing medicine through fiction should be taken seriously. He recognized that the genres were being disciplined. His concern about these emerging epistemological and formal boundaries appears from the very beginning of "George Dedlow," when Dedlow opens with the declaration that "the following notes of my own case have been declined on various pretexts by every medical journal to which I have offered them." Mitchell could best articulate the value of "the wild-winged thing, poetic imagination (mine)" for science because he saw so plainly how it might be lost. That it was Oliver Wendell Holmes, of all people, who cautioned Mitchell to mind the gap between literature and medicine signals the shifting terrain of medical epistemology. Figures like Mitchell and Holmes were most articulate about the value of imaginative thinking for medical inquiry because they saw so clearly how it was being threatened.

CONCLUSION

HUMANISTIC INQUIRY
IN MEDICINE,
THEN AND NOW

In an 1872 essay on Johann Wolfgang von Goethe's scientific thought, the aging Ralph Waldo Emerson observed, "Science does not know its debt to imagination."[1] In contrast, a hundred years earlier, "Goethe did not believe that a great naturalist could exist without this faculty. He was himself conscious of its help, which made him a prophet among the doctors."[2] Emerson's remarks encapsulate a shared feeling of regret echoed by a number of doctors and writers around the Atlantic in the late nineteenth and early twentieth centuries. As the century drew to a close, prominent Canadian doctor-writer William Osler (1849–1919), often called the Father of Modern Medicine, urged students and patients alike to pick up literature and philosophy once more.[3] Scottish physician-poet Ronald Campbell Macfie also lamented medicine's unacknowledged debt in his book *The Romance of Medicine* (1907), which he wrote to demonstrate "the imaginative aspect and romantic character of medical discovery."[4] And, of course, it was during these years that Weir Mitchell articulated the relationship of his own "poetic imagination" to the production of scientific and medical knowledge.

Perhaps Emerson might have said more accurately that science *no longer* knew its debt to the imagination. Or, at least this is what many feared. Like Emerson, a number of turn-of-the-century doctors and writers struggled to be more explicit about the value of the imagination and literary form for producing medical knowledge during this moment when professionalization was actively limiting ways of medical knowing. Whereas at the turn of the nineteenth century professors wanted medical students to have a working knowledge of classical languages and literatures, by the turn of the twentieth century medical education was being concentrated around much more narrowly defined scientific topics.

Two events formalized this shift. These were the founding of the American Medical Association (AMA) Council on Medical Education in 1904 and the publication of the Carnegie Foundation's 1910 report on medical education in the United States and Canada, popularly referred to as the Flexner Report, which was supported by the AMA.[5] One of the very first acts of the newly formed AMA Council on Medical Education was to change the structure of medical learning. In the first few years of its existence, the council set out new rules for medical education: doctors now needed four years of secondary education, four years of medical school, and a passing grade on a licensing exam to be certified.[6] The Flexner Report made these new requirements yet more specific, placing the emphasis for a new medical training system on particular kinds of scientific knowledge.

The Flexner Report authorized an official version of medical history, evaluated the current state of medical education, and effected the reform of that education. The report's author, Abraham Flexner (1866–1959), understood the long nineteenth century of American medicine as a declension narrative.[7] One goal of Flexner's report, then, was to make medical instruction more scientific, more based in empirical research, and confined to a more limited set of professionals. In his introduction to the report, president of the Carnegie Foundation Henry S. Pritchett summarized two central problems of medical education in the United States: that it had not previously done enough to distinguish the work of highly trained medical professionals from other kinds of medical practice and discourse and that "a vast army of men is admitted to the practice of medicine who are untrained in sciences fundamental to the profession."[8] The report did not imagine these sciences capaciously but rather understood them through a rigid disciplinarity. Instead of Greek and Latin, entering medical students were now expected to arrive with "a competent knowledge of chemistry, biology, and physics" and pursue a four-year curriculum of clinical and laboratory work based on the German empirical models that earlier doctor-writers like Robert Montgomery Bird had eyed with intense suspicion. There was some irony in this given that Flexner was not himself a physician but rather an educator trained in the old tools of the trade: Latin, Greek, and philosophy. Flexner had never stepped foot in a medical school before he was tasked with preparing the report.[9]

The changes in medical epistemology that culminated in the Flexner Report were uncomfortable for doctors and writers who believed in both empiricism and imaginative experimentation. Into the twentieth century, doctors at the forefront of modern medicine like William Osler and S. Weir Mitchell continued to insist on the value of literature and philosophy for a doctor's education in addition to the scientific subjects that were taught in medical school. In a lecture he delivered at Harvard in 1906, Osler clarified this educational necessity for physicians: "To keep his mind sweet," he explained, "the modern scientific man should be saturated with the Bible and Plato, with Shakespeare and Milton."[10] In a resonant address titled "Imagination and Idealism in the Medical Sciences," Columbia University medical professor Christian Herter concurred. Published in *JAMA* in 1910, Herter's address identified what he hoped was a new energy for imaginative experimentation: "It is a cheering sign of the times," he wrote, "that the cultivated classes are beginning to recognize the essential role of imagination in the progress of biological and medical sciences."[11] Flexner cited Herter's work in his report, begrudgingly acknowledging that there was some space in medical schools for professors of "wide learning, continuous receptivity, critical sense, and responsive interest"—even if he positioned these figures in opposition to the "genuinely productive scientist."[12] There was, of course, no route for training such imaginative professors in the new world Flexner imagined.

The perspectives of physicians like Osler, Mitchell, and Herter were part of a more general discomfort with the new epistemologies demanded by modern medicine around the Atlantic. In an address to the 1,500 new English students entering medical school in the fall of 1901, for example, the *Lancet* stressed the need for a doctor's general erudition and featured a distinct section titled "The Role of Imagination."[13] It began, "There are many branches of the complex science of medicine in which a mental quality is needed which is often considered to be antagonistic to accuracy. This quality is 'imagination.'" The writer cautioned against the hubris of the contemporary moment. While it was tempting to dismiss the historical uses of the imagination in medicine, he continued, quoting Tennyson, "Our little systems have their day. / They have their day and cease to be." He cited the tuberculosis discoveries for which Robert Koch would win the Nobel Prize in 1905 as evidence of "a valuable use to which the imagination can be put."

Oliver Wendell Holmes dramatized this shift in medical epistemology in his novel *A Mortal Antipathy* (1885), which featured a lament for the increasing separation of the imagination and literary form from medicine. One of the novel's central characters is a brainy young heroine named Lurida Vincent, who approaches the local physician, Dr. Butts, for advice on becoming a doctor. Admired for her sharp intellect, this "imaginative friend" of Holmes's protagonist Eumythia is known in town for her scientific interest, keen observation, and work for the local literary society. Wishing to start herself on a course of study, she approaches Butts: "I read in one of your books that when Sydenham was asked by a student what books he should read, the great physician said, 'Read "Don Quixote."'" I want you to explain that to me."[14] She has the story right: in the seventeenth century, Sydenham (1624–1689) had suggested Cervantes's novel to physician-poet Richard Blackmore. Lurida's query is, among other things, one about the role of humanistic inquiry in medicine, but in the medical world of Holmes's novel, there is little room for such a question. Instead of engaging her curiosity, Butts writes a public lecture to correct what he perceives to be dangerous misperceptions about the relationship between literature and medicine. Reframing the Quixote vignette for the community as "a convenient shield for ignorant pretenders," Butts insists, "Sydenham left many writings in which he has recorded his medical experience, and he surely would not have published them if he had not thought they would be better reading for medical students than the story of Cervantes."[15] Poised to be a young Holmes, Lurida inspires admiration in the novel's readers, even as *A Mortal Antipathy* makes clear that the world is ever more populated by men like Butts. The scene perhaps explains why literary physician Charles Walts Burr (1861–1944) would later recall Holmes's advice to Weir Mitchell "not to go seriously into literature until his professional position was established, telling him if he did it would injure him as a physician, because people would say he had lost interest in his medical work."[16]

All this is not to say that literature and medicine suffered an irrevocable split at the turn of the twentieth century, but the contributions of the imagination and literary form to the production of medical knowledge in this period became harder to do and harder to see. Charlotte Perkins Gilman's (1860–1935) "The Yellow Wallpaper" (1892) offers a particularly clear example of this. Gilman penned her story as a thinly veiled autobiographical tale of a woman driven mad by her physician-husband, whose disastrous medical theory traps her in a nursery until she comes to identify with a woman she sees in the wallpaper. Gilman's physician, Weir Mitchell, had prescribed his famous rest cure for Gilman, forbidding her to write and bringing her "so near the borderline of utter mental ruin that I could see over."[17] Mitchell himself may have struggled with the new epistemological limitations of professional

medicine, as "The Case of George Dedlow" illustrates, but Gilman counted
on his continued investment in imaginative experimentation when she published "The Yellow Wallpaper." The autobiographical nature of Gilman's story
would have held further purchase on Weir Mitchell, who must still have re-
membered his father's deathbed injunction to consider more autobiographies
of illness in medicine. Publicly declaring the story's medical work, Gilman
wrote, "The real purpose of the story was to reach Dr. S. Weir Mitchell, and
convince him of the error of his ways."[18] Reflecting back on these events in
1913, Gilman was confident of her success: she wrote the story "to save people
from being driven crazy, and it worked."[19] Despite Gilman's forthright declaration, it took until the twenty-first century—an age in which medical and
health humanities programs are flourishing—to see the story as a medical text.

Gilman's claims have led recent scholars to celebrate "The Yellow Wallpaper" as an example of the growing power of stories in medicine and the
ability of late nineteenth-century fiction to bridge a perceived medico-literary
divide.[20] In fact, something altogether different was occurring. By the end of
the century, literature had ever less of a role in medicine. Rather, literature and
the imagination were increasingly confined to the new study of the mind,
psychology, rather than addressing medicine and human health more broadly.
This was the era of the celebrated James brothers—William James, the literary
physician and founder of American psychology, and his brother, psychological
novelist Henry James.[21] As in the work of the Jameses, Gilman's story experiments imaginatively more with psychology than with medicine broadly conceived. During the late nineteenth century, literature's role was increasingly
circumscribed to medical conversations about the mind—but not the body.

Thus the Progressive Era saw the curtailing of literature's role, and modern
medicine was born. By the early twentieth century the medical establishment,
through the Carnegie Foundation and the AMA, had formalized medicine's
shift away from humanistic inquiry. In 1920, Osler's death provided Charles
Walts Burr a platform for publicly mourning the old system of medical education; doctors like William Osler, he explained to the College of Physicians
of Philadelphia, "belonged to a generation which followed the old tradition
that the physician ought to be a scholar," whereas the "theoretical pedagogues
of the newer school" like Flexner who operated "under the pernicious influence
of the so-called efficiency" had discredited the role of humanistic inquiry in
medicine.[22] Burr referred to this increasingly scientized and specialized vision
of medical education as an "experiment of vocational training" that he was sure
would "do much injury for many years."[23]

Even Flexner himself came to lament the changes he had set in motion.[24] "Scientific medicine in America—young, vigorous, and positivistic—is today sadly deficient in cultural and philosophic background," Flexner wrote fifteen years after the publication of his famous report; "something more intellectual is also needed."[25] The requirements and accreditation he helped institute were "making the medical curriculum a monstrosity," he further reflected.[26] Students traveled "through medical school in tight lock step, and have little time to stop, read, work, or think."[27] The damage was already done. Almost since the moment the ink dried on Flexner's report, doctors have been trained more firmly in the science—rather than the art and science—of medicine.

It is now one hundred years since this split, and yet the work of doctors and writers like William Carlos Williams, Oliver Sacks, Rafael Campo, and Vincent Lam attests to the continued entanglement of literature and medicine. The international excitement over the medical and health humanities in the last decade further suggests a renewed energy for humanistic ways of knowing. We should draw our inspiration from the epistemological contributions of imaginative experimentation in the past to illuminate the potential of the humanities for health in the present. Many of the figures in this book undertook imaginative experiments as rigorous practices of knowing. Our current disciplinary configurations are distinct from theirs, but these doctors and writers understood their work, as contemporary humanists understand ours, to use creative analytical thinking toward the ends of new knowledge. It is time we returned once more to this vibrant history of imaginative experimentation to learn what more humanistic inquiry can do for the study of health and practices of health care today.

Reimagining the Medical and Health Humanities

The Flexner Report evaluated just over a century of medical education, fundamentally altering the production of knowledge in ways that continue to structure American medicine. Flexner's report made medicine more scientific, but it also erected significant barriers to humanistic training in health that remain today.[28] In recent years, doctors, humanists, and educators have advocated for a reevaluation of medical training, especially through the fields of medical and health humanities, pushing once more for an expansion of humanistic approaches.[29] It is exciting and invigorating to see so much energy and enthusiasm for this fast-growing enterprise. But though some excellent work has been done, most current efforts remain vague about the value of the humanities for medicine and other health professions. They are also limited in their ambitions. More can and should be done—and the history of imaginative experimentation provides a usable past for this work.

For the most part, today's programs, especially those that call themselves medical humanities, are well-meaning but weak attempts to reclaim the humanistic tools of medicine's past.[30] Programs situated in and funded by medical schools have fought for modest gains, mostly aiming at improving physician empathy rather than at shaping and expanding medicine's ways of knowing. Those situated in and funded by undergraduate colleges (rapidly proliferating across the United States in the last decade) are, for the most part, also limited in their objectives. Designed mainly for aspiring doctors looking to improve their medical school applications, these programs may be run by humanists, but their terms are still largely dictated by the perceived and articulated needs and interests of medical schools.[31] Both work to bring a sense of the human back to a medicine that risks being too governed by dispassionate science, routinized procedure, and market logic. Many medical humanities programs combat this by working primarily to improve care by nurturing empathy. "Developing and preserving empathy is often at the center of medical humanities programs, which have become a common offering at medical schools throughout the nation," the Association of American Medical Colleges recently explained.[32]

This emphasis on feeling foregrounds an epistemological problem: the medical humanities all too often emphasize the arts and humanities as ways of feeling rather than methods of knowing and conflate the humanities with a hazier notion of humanity. This confusion is best illustrated in the field's misleading name. While the phrase "medical humanities" grammatically suggests that the field is a branch of the humanities focused on medical questions, in practice the field might more properly be called something like "human-interest medicine." Borrowing the intellectual and institutional authority of the humanities, medical humanities programs too often use feel-good narratives to describe their work instead of taking up the more rigorous analytical tools of humanities disciplines. As Caroline Wachtler, Susanne Lundin, and Margareta Troein explain, "The ideological language used to describe the program calls it an interdisciplinary learning environment but at the same time shows that the conditions of the program are established by the medical faculty's agenda. In practice, the 'humanities' are constructed, defined and used within a medical frame of reference. Medical students have interesting discussions, acquire concepts and enjoy the program. But they come away lacking theoretical structure to understand what they have learned. There is no place for humanities students in the program."[33] The challenge that remains for the medical humanities, they conclude, "is creating an environment where the disciplines have equal standing and contribution."[34] Instead of creating curricula that are truly interdisciplinary, such programs regularly oversimplify the work of the humanities, keeping the discipline-specific knowledge, skill, and authority of trained humanists at arm's length. Thus humanities teaching, training, and scholarship become the purview of all empathetic and thoughtful people—not trained experts.[35] This misunderstanding of humanities work is so broadly pervasive in medicine that the submission category "Humanities" in *JAMA* describes the publication venue for "personal vignettes," "original poems," and art appreciation.[36] A humanist seeking to publish his or her analytical work on health in *JAMA* would need to do so instead under the submission category "Opinion."[37]

Nevertheless, we ought not to abandon the troubled terms "medical humanities" and "health humanities." Rather, we should insist on them. The number and breadth of medical and health humanities programs offer a terrific opportunity not to start over but to sharpen the fields, encouraging them to offer what they nominally suggest they might—a strong set of humanistic approaches to medicine, health care, and the study of human health. In other words, we should insist that the humanities' distinct ways of knowing have enriched and can continue to enrich medicine and the health professions, especially in their more rigorous application. Incorporating the humanities into health care and health research in this way will require *epistemological humility* on both sides: the recognition that humanists have an important and distinct set of tools for knowing the world, as do health professionals. Being rigorous about the tools particular fields bring while also being humble about what each field cannot do or know is crucial for improving health care and the study of human health. It will expand the horizons of our health knowledge and has the potential to build a more dynamic, multifaceted, and ethical set of approaches to health in the future.

Humanistic Competencies

In recent years, health professionals and scholars have begun proposing methods for bringing a stronger version of the humanities into medicine. Scholars such as Jacqueline Dolev, Linda Friedlaender, and Irwin Braverman, for example, have shown that art history training can improve the observational skills of physicians, aiding in more accurate diagnoses and comfort with ambiguity.[38] Rita Charon has likewise advocated literary training for physicians, calling for doctors to acquire "narrative competence."[39] The clinical encounter, she argues, is based on the production of, reception of, and engagement with narrative, and, she suggests, if doctors were better trained to handle narrative, they would be better practitioners.[40] Jonathan Metzl has encouraged going beyond the individuated focus of health care, suggesting that health professionals are sorely in need of "structural competency," an understanding of how social, cultural, and political contexts structure medicine, which is best approached through the humanities and social sciences.[41]

Building on the work of these thinkers, I propose expanding medical and health humanities work beyond the indistinct and often elusive idea that medicine needs more humanity to highlight the more powerful and precise contributions the humanities can make to health. We need to insist more generally on the expertise of the humanities and its distinct and powerful ways of knowing. To do this, we need to be more precise about what the humanities are and what they do; we can do this by attending to the collection of competencies the humanities train—what I am calling here *humanistic competencies*— which include narrative, attention, observation, historical perspective, ethics, judgment, performance, and creativity.[42] When approached through a strong commitment to the humanities, all of these competencies can prepare health professionals to engage in what the humanities cultivate best: creative analytical thinking.

The language of competencies is powerful for this work because it offers medical and health humanists common ground with medical educators and health professionals while insisting on the distinct intellectual insights of humanists.[43] Medical schools have increasingly turned to competency-based education in the last decade, investing in medical knowledge, patient care, professionalism, interpersonal and communication skills, practice-based learning, and systems-based practice as "competencies" students ought to acquire before they graduate.[44] Nevertheless, the notion of competencies provides room for humanistic articulation, since, while the language of competencies is very powerful, the idea itself is not yet well-defined and is often difficult to measure empirically.[45] This concept is useful for medical and health humanists, even if we ought not squeeze humanistic competencies into categories designed by and for medicine; rather, we ought to insist on the distinct competencies that the humanities can offer the health professions.[46]

Humanistic competencies have the potential to organize and articulate the humanities' contributions to study, practice, and research in human health at all levels, from undergraduate programs and medical schools to fields such as nursing, health policy, public health, and global health. In pedagogical spaces they offer a practical tool kit for assessing health professionals' preparation. Beyond pedagogy, they offer a set of organizing terms that are widely useful—for sharpening clinical skills, for promoting thoughtful and ethical engagement, for historicizing encounters, for encouraging collaboration through a shared language, for developing inventive responses in areas with limited resources, and for pushing research in new directions through the training and practice of creative analytical thinking. The capacious aims and incomplete definitions of competency—concerned as they are with knowledge production and human experience—invite interdisciplinary work. If humanists are open to this kind of collaboration, we will find that shared language of competencies can help expand the horizons of humanistic inquiry, sharpen and embolden its work, and craft a space for more equitable and exciting collaboration. In this context, humanists with a strong sense of what the humanities offer the study of health and practices of health care can shape what it means to be not only a competent but a skilled health professional.

Observational and creative competencies offer two good examples of how this might work. Observation is an indisputably central component of health work. It is also a faculty whose history has already been richly complicated in the preceding pages. A foundational yet fraught practice in early U.S. medicine, observation is even more fundamental to the study of health and to health care now. Contemporary medicine, for example, is based in bench science, evidence-based medicine, and routine clinical practices, all of which depend on observation. Nevertheless, observation is not an innocuous, untrained, or ahistorical act. Thinking more deeply about the nature, structure, and stakes of observation can make for better research and care by training doctors and health professionals to be more careful, thoughtful, and informed about the act of observing.

In acknowledging the expertise of humanists in thinking about observation, we begin to see how disciplines—not only art history but also literature, history, and interdisciplinary fields like gender and sexuality studies, critical race theory, and disability studies—can make more robust contributions to the study of human health. Certainly art history provides an excellent set of tools for educating doctors and other health professionals in the art of observation. Some medical humanities programs already take medical students to museums to sharpen their observational skills by teaching them techniques for looking at artwork.[47] But we might accomplish even more by expanding our understanding of the disciplines that can contribute to a competency in observation. The close-reading skills of literary scholars hone the aptitude for observing detail, for understanding how language informs perspective and interpretation, and for attending carefully to the relation between a part and the whole. Historians of science teach us to better situate our own ways of looking. Observation, they demonstrate, is not the innate and natural act it might seem, but rather our ways of looking are deeply contingent on time and place—shaping and limiting what we see and how we see it.[48] Disability studies scholars provide another perspective, teaching us to investigate how and why we observe bodies and minds as we do and showing us how we might learn to look differently.[49] The ends of such work range from improving diagnosis to practicing social justice and from the classroom to the clinic and the laboratory. Given how powerful this rethinking of observation is, we can readily see how other humanistic competencies—like attention and judgment—can improve study, treatment, and research in the health professions today.

Creativity is another humanistic competency that can help health professionals improve their work. This book traces the long history of the medical imagination and the varied ways in which doctors and writers employed their imaginations and literary form in the service of human health. Imagination may at first seem distant and distinct from creativity until we realize there was no word "creativity" in common parlance before the 1970s when the concept of creativity was carved out of what had once been understood as the imagination.[50] With this rise of creativity, "imagination" came to refer not only to the ability to make new things out of existing ones but also to create things that were not necessarily real (what had, in the past, been more the domain of fancy).[51] The faculty, once understood as imagination and frequently now as creativity, is one that health professions continue to prize today.[52] Creativity, we hope, will teach us new ways of seeing and knowing that can reveal more about health and diminish human suffering; potential benefits of more creative health work range from better care with limited resources to better diagnoses and groundbreaking discovery. It is how we envision the future of human health. But if diagnosing new diseases and achieving medical breakthroughs require us to see what others do not and to develop original understandings of new and known phenomena, then we want to think better about how we train creativity. Leaving it to a vague sense of genius or innate ingenuity will not do.

It is time, then, to ask how we might recuperate some of the spirit of this earlier work to train creativity in health work.[53] Here, again, the humanities can help. While many medical humanities programs use paintings, literary texts, historical documents, and philosophy to cultivate a vaguely conceived sense of human interest or empathy, the humanities use those same objects to train creative analytical thinking. Reassembling knowledge, experience, and observation creatively toward new discovery, the humanities privilege the unexpected, unanticipated, and precise rather than the routine and strictly procedural. Informed by historical precedent, structural understanding, and an ability to dwell in ambiguity, the humanities can also help students develop an ethical dimension to that analytical creativity, educating future health workers toward new insights while also bearing in mind the potential stakes and consequences of such work. Here, again, the more rigorous and specific we can be about what the humanities do, the better medical and health humanities can be.

Humanistic perspectives can and should contribute more fully to medicine and the health professions than they currently do. They have been sidelined because, in addition to the reasons already outlined, "the unwieldy, ever-complicating humanities do not lend themselves to neat randomization in a clinical trial, not to mention remuneration according to *CPT* coding," physician-poet Rafael Campo explains.[54] Nor should they. Rather than attempting to fit the humanities strictly into empiricist epistemologies, we should clearly define the value of the humanities on their own terms. Here the history of imaginative experimentation can help: we ought to insist vociferously on the historical contingency of disciplinary structures and draw lessons and inspiration from earlier medical work that valued humanistic inquiry in health to craft stronger visions of the medical and health humanities for the future. Epistemologies relying on physical experimentation and objectivity—which gave way to the hegemony of scientific medicine—emerged as one way of knowing, but doctors have long used a variety of knowledge practices alongside and as a complement to empiricism.[55] A broader consideration of such strategies should be combined with an articulate insistence on what they can offer to improve health care, to advance health research, and to expand our repertoire of useful and humane ways of knowing. Reinvesting in the value of humanistic competencies is one way forward. More generally, however, humanists and health professionals ought to meet in the spirit of openness, disciplinary flexibility, and, most important, epistemological humility to imagine new ways of knowing health together.

NOTES

INTRODUCTION

Dunglison, *Medical Lexicon* (1839), n.p. Robley Dunglison (1798–1869) was a British physician who immigrated to the United States at the request of Thomas Jefferson to serve on the medical faculty of the University of Virginia. For an expansive discussion of encyclopedias, dictionaries, and the ordering of knowledge in the eighteenth and early nineteenth centuries, see Yeo, *Encyclopaedic Visions* and Valenza, *Literature, Language, and the Rise of Intellectual Disciplines*.

1. Bird, *Difficulties*, 15.

2. Ibid., 9, original emphasis.

3. Ibid., 6, 15. Medicine's goal was only "the relief and diminution of human suffering. . . . Can that be said of any *other* science?" Ibid., 6, original emphasis.

4. Ibid., 15–16.

5. Lucian of Samosata, *Lucian of Samosata*, 285.

6. See Starr, *The Social Transformation*, especially 156, for an overview. Of course, physicians on very rare occasion did open up bodies, but this kind of invasive surgery would not be practiced with any regularity until the very end of the nineteenth century.

7. Sterne, *The Works*, 128.

8. See Rosner, "Thistle on the Delaware" for more on medical education in Philadelphia in the early republic.

9. E.g., Bird, *Difficulties*, 13; Bird, "Notes on Pulmonary Consumption," 1, in the University of Pennsylvania's Collection of Medical Theses on Pulmonary Consumption.

10. Kilman, "Robert Montgomery Bird," 38; University of Pennsylvania's "Miscellaneous Manuscripts" collection, Box 2, Folder 13.

11. Ibid. These can be found on manuscript pages of *The Infidel* and *Peter Pilgrim*.

12. Bird, *Sheppard Lee*, 8. For more on *Sheppard Lee*, see Chapter 4.

13. John Gilmore writes, "Eighteenth-century medical men often were, or at least aspired to be, gentlemen of wide general culture as well as practitioners of a specific scientific discipline" (*Poetics of Empire*, 11).

14. For more on Grainger, see Gilmore, *Poetics of Empire*.

15. Jenner's poem "Signs of Rain" (also called "Weather Signs") first appeared in the early 1820s but continued to be cited in medical contexts into the twentieth century. See quoted passages in physician William Whitty Hall's *Hall's Health Tracts*, 178 and Mitchell, "The Relations of Pain to Weather," 305. Elsewhere Hall writes that Jenner's "poems exhibit the life and spirit of true genius, a close observation of nature and a weird and unique style of expression that remind one of the short fragmentary poems of Shakespeare" ("Dr. Edward Jenner," 175).

16. "The double role of Apollo as god of medicine and poetry was something of a cliché: an anonymous contemporary versifier, for example, hailed Akenside as 'Twofold Disciple of APOLLO!' " (Gilmore, *Poetics of Empire*, 11).

17. For a terrific account of the epistemological work of British literature in nonmedical science in the late eighteenth and nineteenth centuries, see Smith, *Fact and Feeling*. Janis McLarren Caldwell (*Literature and Medicine*) develops a wonderful argument for the epistemological work of narrative in medicine between 1800 and 1859, but, for Caldwell, medical narrative still works largely in contradistinction to a firmer notion of medicine based in physical observation and experimentation. Drawing on Gillian Beer's notion of "romantic materialism" (which Beer locates later in Charles Darwin's epistemology), she argues that "romantic materialists . . . called for an interpretive method which tacked back and forth between physical evidence and inner, imaginative understanding. This dialectic hermeneutic yielded innovations in both medical diagnostics and literary representation" (1). Nevertheless, in preserving the two as a dialectic, Caldwell describes a world where a "doctor's scientific observation" and "medical knowledge [*co-exist*] . . . *with* the story of human pain and courage," rather than a world where imaginative practices can produce medical knowledge and are more intimately connected to empirical work (144, 146, emphasis added).

18. Rush, *Lectures on the Mind*, 506.

19. Rush, *Medical Inquiries and Observations Upon the Diseases of the Mind*, 160, emphasis added (hereafter this volume will be referred to as *MIODM*). Thus, in his definitive text on mental illness, Rush supported his work with evidence from "an ingenious modern poet" and "the authority of Shakspeare [*sic*]" (41, 246).

20. With its origins in the natural science of the seventeenth century, the figure of the "microscopic eye" was employed by many writers from Jonathan Swift to John Locke. See Goodman, *Georgic Modernity*, 40. For an excellent genealogy of the "microscopic eye," see Goodman, "The Microscopic Eye," in *Georgic Modernity*. The eighteenth-century poet Alexander Pope, whom Rush cited with some frequency, famously disavowed the poet's "microscopic eye" in his *Essay on Man*. Taking up a familiar line on the tyranny of detail, Pope asks, "Why has not man a microscopic eye?" (9). The answer, according to Pope, is that God denies humans the microscopic eye because it would doom them to see the miniscule but miss the divine. Our measured perception, Pope continues, also saves us from the extraordinary pain of too much stimulus—the agonies of a "nature thunder'd in his op'ning ears" (10). Pope's language nevertheless imaginatively appropriates the powers it physically denies poets using medical terms. Microscopic perceptions would cause touch to "smart and agonize at ev'ry pore," while the sweet smell of a rose would turn "effluvia" that kills with "aromatic pain" (9–10).

21. Mitchill, "Outlines," 40. It is also no surprise that these early republican doctors would turn to Pope, a poet renowned for his medical and scientific observations. For more on Mitchill's uses of poetry to write medicine, see Chapter 1. Young writes, "It has been suggested that I have assumed some fundamental principles without proof: I freely confess that there are some phenomena in astronomy which oblige us to have recourse to analogy: but I have endeavoured to confine myself to a rule similar to that which Pope prescribed to himself in his *Essay on Man*, " 'Say, first of heav'n above or earth below, / What can we reason but from what we know?' / We see that power and motion every where / Are caus'd by fire or water, gas or air: / We also see all heavy bodies tend / To earth, where all factitious motions end: / Stones neither fly nor leap, nor walk nor crawl, / But must be raised before they fall" ("Correspondence," 361).

22. Caldwell, introduction to Darwin, *Zoonomia*, part 2, 1:xi, emphasis original.

23. Ibid., part 2, 1:xii.

24. I do not mean to suggest here that formal rigor produces poetic mediocrity; it is clear that the doctors and writers of the period thought no such thing. Rather, it is contemporary literary scholars and the public alike who have paid less attention to this kind of nineteenth-century U.S. poetry. Once-famous poets like John Greenleaf Whittier are underappreciated today, especially relative to novelists of the period like Herman Melville and Nathaniel Hawthorne, as well as more formally innovative poets like Emily Dickinson and Walt Whitman. (Some, like Whitman, still contributed to U.S. medicine.) Of course, it is also true that because so many doctors wrote poetry during the nineteenth century a good amount of it was necessarily mediocre.

25. Brown, *Ormond*, 55; Brown, *Arthur Mervyn*, 3. All references to *Arthur Mervyn* refer to the 1980 edition unless otherwise noted. See Chapter 2 for more on Brown and *Arthur Mervyn*.

26. Altschuler, "Prescient Description." In 1989, Leland Rickman and Choong Kim expressed their surprise in *JAMA* that Poe "apparently observed and described porphyria 50 years before the first reported case in the medical literature" ("Poe-phyria," 864). Likewise, in 2004, Eric Lewin Altschuler wrote in Britain's preeminent medical journal the *Lancet* that Poe's story "The Business Man" "contains an accurate description of frontal [lobe] syndrome and its features—only appreciated this century—or neuropsychiatric pathology resulting from paediatric injury" ("Prescient Description").

27. "Morton found time to indulge a taste for poetry; and his occasional effusions show that united a fine imagination, and refined appreciation of the beautiful, with his more solid powers and attainments" ("Death of Samuel George Morton, M.D.," 384).

28. "Fiction Anticipates Science."

29. Warner and Tighe, "What Is the History of Medicine and Public Health?" in *Major Problems in the History of American Medicine*, 2. See Reverby and Rosner, "Beyond the 'Great Doctors'" for the beginning of the social history of medicine turn.

30. For an overview of this history, see Warner, "The History of Science and the Sciences of Medicine"; Worboys's later evaluation of that essay in "Practice and the Science of Medicine in the Nineteenth Century"; and Warner and Tighe, "What Is the History of Medicine and Public Health?"

31. See Starr, *The Social Transformation* and Warner, *The Therapeutic Perspective*.

32. For example, in the mid-twentieth century, Martin Kaufman glossed the nineteenth century in the *Bulletin of the History of Medicine* as "an age of 'heroic' medicine. Treatment consisted of bleeding, blistering, vomiting, sweating, purging, and administering massive doses of calomel, often until the patient was on the threshold of acute mercurial poisoning" ("The American Anti-vaccinationists," 468). In a 2004 issue of *American Literature*, Kristin Boudreau likewise summarized the period as "an age when medicine was random, unscientific, and caustic" (review of *Rehabilitating Bodies*, 891); and, in 2010, Ira Rutkow wrote in his popular history of American medicine, "Rush's point of view so blinded physicians that they readily believed that illness would certainly worsen and lead to death without heroic therapy. Rush's smug advice became even more disconcerting when he rejected reliance upon Mother Nature as part of the healing process" (*Seeking the Cure*, 39).

33. Current scholarship offers two descriptions of medicine in the early republic. Starr, *The Social Transformation*, Vogel and Rosenberg, *Therapeutic Revolution*, and Rothstein, *American Physicians* chart the rise of heroic medicine—bloodletting, blistering, and purging—and suggest that little innovation or change occurred after Rush's medical treatises. Histories following Foucault's *Birth of the Clinic* trace a Western shift from medicine that started with ideas to one that began with bodies and assume Americans practiced European medicine. Burbick,

Healing the Republic and Warner, *The Therapeutic Perspective* and *Against the Spirit of the System* are terrific alternatives to these narratives of American medical history.

34. Flexner, *Medical Education in the United States and Canada*, 5, 19.

35. Ibid., 10.

36. Warner, *The Therapeutic Perspective*, 42.

37. Ibid., 43–44. "Empiric" became a damning term in seventeenth-century England but retained that sense through at least the early twentieth century (44). Surprisingly, even Abraham Flexner used the term this way in his famous report, when he wrote that in the mid-nineteenth century "medicine, hitherto empirical, was beginning to develop a scientific basis and method" (*Medical Education in the United States and Canada*, 8).

38. Ibid., 4.

39. Webster, Matthews, and Remington, *The Medical Recorder*, 457.

40. Eve, "Professional Qualifications and Character," 706.

41. The twentieth-century break refers to events I cover more fully in the conclusion. This vision, of course, only tells part of the story. While a humanistically inclined medical education was considered ideal, Americans became doctors in a variety of ways, only some of which involved a complete and rigorous medical education. For more on medical education in the period, see Starr, *The Social Transformation*; Warner, *The Therapeutic Perspective*; Vogel and Rosenberg, *The Therapeutic Revolution*; and Rosner, "Thistle on the Delaware."

42. For excellent recent work on the imagination in the early republic, see Cahill, *Liberty of the Imagination*. Taking "literary culture" broadly to encompass poetry, natural history, political writing, novels, criticism, newspapers, magazines, commonplace books, sermons, polite conversation, etc., Cahill argues, "Early U.S. literary culture speaks the philosophical language of the imagination fluently and vociferously. Despite the extraordinary political demands of the day, literary texts of all kinds invoke the concepts of aesthetic theory with erudition and persistence . . . in nearly every genre and medium of expression, the rhetoric of aesthetic theory is ubiquitous and insistent" (1).

43. Dunglison, *Medical Lexicon* (1839), n.p.

44. Readers will note that my account of medical epistemology diverges significantly from Foucault's in *Birth of the Clinic*.

45. Dunglison, *Human Physiology* (1832), 2:427.

46. Mitchell to Mason, March 24, 1912. College of Physicians of Philadelphia, Weir Mitchell Papers, Box 9, Folder 24.

47. Mitchell to Mason, April 2, 1912. Ibid.

48. Ibid.

49. Mitchell to Mason, March 24, 1912. See biographer Nancy Cervetti's discussion in *S. Weir Mitchell*, 158.

50. For the epistemological uses of history in medicine, see, e.g., Valenčius, *Health of the Country*, 181–83 and Apel, "The Thucydidean Moment."

51. For the history of objectivity, see Daston and Galison, *Objectivity*.

52. Quoted in ibid., 59.

53. Dunglison, *Medical Lexicon* (1839), 245, emphasis added. For the French influence on medicine of this period, see Warner, *Against the Spirit of the System*.

54. Dunglison, *Medical Lexicon* (1848), 335, emphasis added.

55. Dunglison, *Medical Lexicon* (1860), 363.

56. Daston and Galison, *Objectivity*, 17.

57. See this book's conclusion. For science more generally, see Walls, *Passage to the Cosmos*.

58. Bird, *Difficulties*, 22, original emphasis. For more on the widespread practice of self-experimentation, see Altman, *Who Goes First*; Kerridge, "Altruism or Reckless Curiosity?"; Schiebinger, "Human Experimentation"; and Strickland, "Ideology of Self-Knowledge."

59. See Schiebinger, "Human Experimentation."

60. In the eighteenth and early nineteenth centuries, access to bodies was also limited. See Sappol, *A Traffic of Dead Bodies* and Porter, "Rise of Physical Examination."

61. There are a number of contemporary texts about this event. See, e.g., Manningham, *An Exact Diary*; St. André, *A Short Narrative*; and the anonymous *Much Ado About Nothing*.

62. Darwin, *Zoonomia* (1794), 520, 519.

63. Cullen, *Works*, 2:418.

64. For more, see Shorter, *From Paralysis to Fatigue*, 234.

65. Rush, *MIODM*, 21.

66. For other scholarship on the relationship between literature and the body in nineteenth-century America, see Davis, *Bodily and Narrative Forms*; Millner, *Fever Reading*; Murison, *The Politics of Anxiety*; Silverman, *Bodies and Books*; and Thrailkill, *Affecting Fictions*. As late as 1870, Noah Porter could still write about this connection quite literally: it was "not in the least surprising that so many have cleaved to their libraries with so fond an affection and have learned to conceive of them as parts of themselves, as in a sense visible and tangible embodiments of their own being" (quoted in Silverman, *Bodies and Books*, 13).

67. For more on this, see Silverman, *Bodies and Books* and Millner, *Fever Reading*.

68. See, most famously, Sappol, *A Traffic of Dead Bodies*.

69. Richerand, *Elements of Physiology*, 1, original emphasis. In this 1813 textbook, Richerand defines physiology more fully as "the science of life. The term life is applied to an aggregate of phenomena, which manifest themselves in succession, for a limited time in organized bodies" (1). Nathaniel Chapman produced this volume of Richerand's for an American audience when he prepared to teach the Institutes of Medicine at the University of Pennsylvania. I offer Richerand/Chapman's perspective in contrast to views like Michael Sappol's that "anatomical dissection, far from being butchery, was the quintessential epistemology of scientific, 'civilized' man, a systematic and careful division and reduction of the material world, a triumph of mind over matter, reason over emotion" (*A Traffic of Dead Bodies*, 6).

70. Holmes, *Border Lines*, 31. Robley Dunglison would also write that "it has been well remarked, by an intelligent writer . . . that the crying defect of the British anatomical schools—and the remark is applicable elsewhere—is, that they teach anatomy as if a knowledge of the *dead* body were the sole foundation of medical study; whereas it is a knowledge of the *living* body, which constitutes that foundation; and, therefore, it is not the parts of the body themselves, as they lie exanimate on the dissecting table, which are of importance, but the actions and functions of those parts, as they administer to the wants of the living man; and, hence, that physiology, or 'living anatomy'—*anatome animata*, as Haller appropriately termed it—is the real foundation of medical knowledge" (*Medical Student*, 157–58).

71. Dunglison, *Human Physiology* (1856), 1:v.

72. Ibid., 1:33.

73. See Porter, "Rise of the Physical Examination."

74. For a useful summary of the transition from patient description to the combined medical history narrative and physical examination model in Britain, see Caldwell, *Literature and Medicine*, especially chap. 7. As she helpfully summarizes, "Before the nineteenth century, doctors relied for diagnosis primarily on the patient's report of his or her illness—so much so, that it was not uncommon to treat patients via correspondence" (143). Caldwell goes on to narrate

the rise of physical examination (in addition to patient histories) through practices like taking the pulse and auscultation (listening to the body), while linking the rise of the physical examination to an 1840s privileging of morbid anatomy. Here my argument diverges from hers in emphasizing the limits of these ways of knowing for understanding the physiology or pathology of the living body.

75. See endnote 33 in the following chapter for more on this misconception.

76. Dr. William Beaumont's experiments, published in 1833, drew the question of ethics in physical experimentation into relief. Whereas vivisection relied on torture, Beaumont stumbled upon a very rare opportunity to experiment with healthy human physiology without such horrifying disruption. In the summer of 1822, Alexis St. Martin was accidentally shot in the stomach at close range while working for the American Fur Company in the Michigan Territory. Beaumont did what he could, but as St. Martin's organs were perforated and protruding it looked likely that he would die. (For the story of St. Martin's condition, see Beaumont's introduction to his *Experiments*, 10–17.) Instead, St. Martin healed, but with a small hole that opened from his stomach to the outside. Between 1825 and 1833, then, Beaumont took St. Martin with him from Michigan to New York and Vermont. During that time Beaumont experimented on St. Martin repeatedly, usually by inserting food directly into the stomach through St. Martin's hole and then extracting it and experimenting with it. Beaumont discovered that the stomach digested food by physical as well as chemical means, but even this experiment pushed the boundaries of ethics. Some tests left St. Martin "complaining of considerable distress and uneasiness at the stomach, generable debility and lassitude, with some pain in his head," and a fever (126). And, thus, it is not entirely surprising that at times St. Martin left Beaumont "without obtaining [his] consent" (18). This was physical experimentation with living physiology under the very best circumstances. J. Marion Sims's brutal gynecological experiments on enslaved women, offer an example of unambiguously unethical testing (see Harriet Washington's *Medical Apartheid*).

77. Medical texts in this period are full of descriptions of the pulse. For example, in the second volume of *Medical Inquiries and Observations*, Benjamin Rush considers the pulse to offer essential information about the body in fifty-five separate instances. Employing a different sensory way of knowing, the Parisian René-Théophile-Hyacinthe Laënnec (1781–1826) invented the stethoscope in 1816.

Other senses—especially smell and taste—were also used in medical inquiry. Smell was commonly recorded to understand substances. In 1805 Rush took John Hunter's experiments with semen as crucial evidence for the uses of sperm in reproduction: "The pungent taste which John Hunter discovered in the male seed renders it peculiarly fit for this purpose" (*Medical Inquiries and Observations*, 4:404). (This use of taste-as-epistemology was especially significant since John Hunter made his fame as an anatomist.) The epistemology of taste also has a longer, storied history in the Atlantic world. For example, Portuguese slave traders "sometimes ran their tongues across the faces of the enslaved . . . [they] believed they could discover illness or disease by the taste of the captives' sweat" (Sweet, *Domingos Álvares*, 29). For more on taste as a method for producing medical knowledge, see Ragland, "Experimenting with Chemical Bodies."

78. This work began in the 1930s with Ludwik Fleck, who identified the social forces involved in the production of and shifts in scientific knowledge, although he was less interested in the precise nature of the crises or in the process of scientific revolution. See Fleck, *Genesis and Development*. As Thaddeus Trenn writes in his introduction, Fleck does not "[dwell] upon the controversial concept of revolutions; indeed, Kuhn's sharp distinction between so-called normal and revolutionary science has no direct counterpart in Fleck's theory" (xiv).

79. See Fleck, *Genesis and Development*; Kuhn, *Structure of Scientific Revolutions*; and Foucault, *Order of Things*.

80. Kuhn, *Structure of Scientific Revolutions*, 67.

81. Ibid., 77.

82. Ibid., 6.

83. I hesitate to use Fleck here because his moment is so close to the one at which this book ends, but for an interesting take on medical thinking and its departures from scientific thought, see Fleck's 1927 essay "Some Specific Features of the Medical Way of Thinking."

84. Latour's work on nature and culture is particularly relevant. Here my thinking about nonhuman agents and new paradigms of medical thought is particularly indebted to Latour, *We Have Never Been Modern* and *The Pasteurization of France*.

85. The term "epistemic crisis" is also related to one coined by Owen Whooley, who develops the related concept "epistemic contest" to describe a situation "in which actors, advocating competing understandings of reality and the nature of knowledge, struggle in various realms to achieve validation for their epistemological systems" (*Knowledge*, 16).

86. Definition for "crisis" in Webster, *American Dictionary*, 1:n.p.

87. Ibid.

88. Dunglison, *Medical Lexicon* (1839), 171; Dunglison, *Medical Lexicon* (1848), 235.

89. Kuhn, *Structure of Scientific Revolutions*, 79.

90. See MacIntyre, "Epistemological Crises." Fleck goes so far as to claim all medical knowledge involves some degree of the nonobjective and the imaginative: "morbid phenomena are grouped round certain types, producing laws of a higher order, because they are more beautiful and more general than the normal phenomena which suddenly become profoundly intelligible. These types, these *ideal, fictitious pictures*, known as morbid units, round which both the individual and the variable morbid phenomena are grouped, without, however, ever corresponding completely to them—are produced by the medical way of thinking, on the one hand by specific, far-reaching abstraction, by rejection of some observed data, and on the other hand, by the specific construction of hypotheses, i.e., by guessing of non-observed relations" ("Some Specific Features of the Medical Way of Thinking," 40, emphasis added).

91. See Arner, "Making Yellow Fever American."

92. "Medical Humanities." Some programs are, of course, more expansively conceived. They work not only to foster "empathy, altruism, compassion, and caring toward patients" but also to "hone clinical communication and observational skills" (Shapiro and Rucker, "Can Poetry," 953). For field-structuring work, see Frank, *The Wounded Storyteller*, esp. 53–74; Arthur Kleinman, *The Illness Narratives* (1988), esp. 227–51; and Charon, *Narrative Medicine*, esp. 3–64. For recent developments, see Holloway, *Private Bodies, Public Texts*, esp. 1–24; Shapiro and Rucker, "Can Poetry"; Jurecic, "Empathy"; and Woods, "The Limits of Narrative." I discuss this more extensively in the conclusion.

93. Others have remarked on the absence of a coherent theory in medical inquiry almost since the moment of its exclusion. In 1923 F. G. Crookshank lamented "there is to-day no longer any Science of Medicine . . . there is no longer any organized or systematized *corpus*, or formulated Theory . . . to form an integral part of Natural Philosophy" ("Importance of a Theory," 337). While systemic thinking was the hallmark of much medical thinking in the first decades of the nineteenth century, it declined as rising medical empiricism articulated itself in opposition to unitary theories. Thomas Long provides a useful discussion in "Legible Signs," and Arthur L. Caplan recently explored what he terms the current "epistemological crisis" of evidence-based medicine in an article titled "No Method, Thus Madness?" 12.

94. Bioethicists and other researchers concerned with medical ethics have covered this territory extensively. For examples, see Carper, "Fundamental Patterns"; Kodish, Lantos, and Siegler, "Ethics of Randomization"; Crouch and Arras, "AZT Trials and Tribulations"; Benatar, "Imperialism, Research Ethics, and Global Health"; and Levine, "Clinical Trials and Physicians as Double Agents."

95. The more recent field of the health humanities is more expansive, useful, and provocative than the medical humanities and understands its purview as extending beyond medical schools; nevertheless, the field's uses of the terms "medicine" and "humanities" are often similarly limited or vague.

96. I do not mean to gloss over the differences between writing poetry and writing literary criticism here. What I am suggesting, rather, is that we take the spirit of this early work and its sharper vision of what the arts and humanities can help us know to craft a stronger medical and health humanities vision.

CHAPTER I

1. Rush, *Lectures on the Mind*, 450.

2. Ibid.

3. Ibid. Especially in his views on the imagination, Rush is best understood as a medical philosopher. For example, in their commentary on Rush's *Lectures on the Mind*, Carlson, Wollock, and Noel compare his work to that of Scottish philosopher Thomas Reid (1710–1796): "Reid too believed the non-rational operations of the mind could be used creatively; he regarded flights of imagination as opportunities to project oneself into new roles or situations in order to explore possibilities and to judge their promise. The process was a controlled one, however, to be tempered by waking reason and judgment, for dreams which could serve directly as fables, as Beattie suggested, were rare" (*Lectures on the Mind*, 398).

4. Ibid., 450–52. Rush compared memory to history while imagination resembled artistic forms like "painting, which presents a number of objects at the same instant to the eye" (450).

5. Ibid., 451.

6. Rush also draws on Dugald Stewart's literary distinction between fancy and imagination: fancy "supplies the poet with metaphorical language, and with all the analogies of his allusions, but imagination creates the complex scenes he describes, and the fictitious characters he delineates. To fancy we apply the epithets rich and luxuriant; to the imagination, those of beautiful and sublime" (quoted in ibid.).

7. Ibid. The imaginative faculty was then not opposed to mental faculties like reason. Rather, imagination was a tool of reason and understanding as well as the source of almost all discovery. See ibid., 452–53, 510.

8. Ibid., 450–51.

9. Ibid., 451.

10. Rush, *Medical Inquiries and Observations*, 1:337.

11. Ibid., 1:337–38.

12. Rush, "Observations and Reasoning in Medicine," in *Selected Writings*, 252–53.

13. Rush, *Medical Inquiries and Observations*, 2:vi–vii.

14. This article and "Observations on the duties of a physician, and the methods of improving medicine. Accommodated to the present state of society and manners in the United States" appeared in the first volume of *Medical Inquiries and Observations* published in 1789.

15. Quoted in Rush, *Selected Writings*, 331. See ibid., 328–33 for a more complete list.

16. The republic was a widely sought-after ideal on both sides of the Atlantic. It was the articulation of republicanism in the colonies—as opposed to monarchy—that was contentious. As Gordon Wood explains, "Perhaps everyone in the eighteenth century could have agreed that in theory no state was more beautiful than a republic, whose whole object by definition was the good of the people"; it was "a beautiful but ambiguous ideal" (*Creation*, 65, 73).

17. For Rush's republicanism, see Michael Meranze's 1988 introduction to Benjamin Rush's *Essays*. There is less scholarship on Rush than one might expect. Most recent scholarship on him does not treat him as a central figure but rather uses him principally as a device to make broader cultural, medical, and political points about the era. The most recent biographies by Alyn Brodsky (*Benjamin Rush*, 2004) and David Barton (*Benjamin Rush*, 1999) are not scholarly works. The latter is irresponsibly presentist, written in the service of a current political project. For older scholarly work on Rush, see Hawke, *Benjamin Rush* (1971); Dagobert Rune, introduction to *Selected Works* (1947), and Corner, introduction to Rush, *Autobiography* (1948). For more recent scholarship on Rush, see Carlson, Wollock, and Noel, introduction to *Lectures on the Mind*; Meranze, introduction to *Essays*; and the spring 2017 issue of *Early American Studies* titled "The Republics of Benjamin Rush," which Christopher Bilodeau and I coedited.

18. For example, Thomas Paine wrote in *The Rights of Man*, "What is called a republic is not any particular form of government. It is wholly characteristical of the purport, matter or object for which government ought to be instituted, and on which it is to be employed, Res-Publica, the public affairs, or the public good; or, literally translated, the public thing" (229). Republicanism, its nature and scope in the late eighteenth century as well as its effects on U.S. political and cultural history, has been a subject of debate among historians for decades. Insofar as it represented a Kuhnian paradigm shift in the eighteenth century, it was likewise one for mid-twentieth-century historiography. In 1992, Daniel T. Rodgers described the "process by which republicanism burst onto the scene" in the 1960s as less a product of "intellectual fashion" or "a discovery, driven by newly unearthed evidence," but "a conceptual transformation, a reconfiguration of the largely known, a paradigm shift of Kuhnian scale and Kuhnian dynamics" ("Republicanism," 11). It was, for Rodgers, no accident that the shift occurred at the moment that such shifts were being theorized by Kuhn. For classics in this tradition, see Bailyn, *The Ideological Origins of the American Revolution*; Wood, *Creation*; and Pocock, *Machiavellian Moment*. For historiographical accounts of republicanism in U.S. history, see Rodgers, "Republicanism"; Weithman, "Political Republicanism and Perfectionist Republicanism"; and Wood's reevaluation of the concept in his 1998 introduction to *Creation*.

19. On July 21, 1789, shortly after the election of George Washington, Rush wrote John Adams that "republicanism has never yet had a fair trial in the world. It is now likely to be tried in the United States. Had our government been more completely balanced, that is, had the President possessed more power, I believe it would have realized all the wishes of the most sanguine friends to republican liberty" (*Letters*, 1:522). Nevertheless, having failed the ideal, Rush resigned himself to the idea that "an hundred years hence, absolute monarchy will probably be rendered necessary in our country by the corruption of our people" (ibid.).

20. See Rush, "Of Physiology," in Carlson, Wollock, and Noel, *Lectures on the Mind*, 67–361 (hereafter "Of Physiology"), 73.

21. As historian Mark Brake writes, "Copernican cosmology . . . gave fresh impetus to the role of the imagination, even as it implied its moment of crisis . . . Copernicus' reorganisation of the cosmos, in which the Earth had been demoted to a mere planet, implied the possible

existence of other Earths in a vast and boundless universe. It pulled the cosmos down to Earth, so to speak, bringing it into the realm of the imagination" (*Alien Life Imagined*, 59). For more on the long history of such work, see Brake, *Alien Life Imagined*.

22. Rush, "Of Physiology," 75. While Rush would later delete this extended account from his lectures, it formed the basis of the physiological instruction he delivered to more than two decades of American medical students.

23. Ibid., 76–77.

24. Ibid., 77.

25. Ibid.

26. Ibid.

27. Ibid.

28. Ibid., 77–78.

29. Ibid., 86.

30. Ibid., 70.

31. Ibid., 82n2.

32. Rush, *Medical Inquiries and Observations*, 4:389, 2:377.

33. Rush's description of "republican machines" was anything but a mechanistic decree about the nature of American bodies; instead, his vital materialism insisted on the dynamism of physiology. In an effort to support mechanistic descriptions of the early republic scholars twisted Rush's words both by selectively quoting and by altering Rush's language. Scholars have either neglected or, more than once, dropped the word "not" from the preceding quotation to have Rush declare "the human body is an automaton." For the automaton misprint, see Terrell, "Republican Machines," 104 and Haber, *Quest*, 51. This second omission, were it supportable by a misprinted Rush original, renders the full sentence illogical. The full sense of Rush's statement about citizen bodies—that Rush *"considers it possible"* to make Americans into "republican machines" and thus that he believed that men could be educated toward salubrious sympathies—is the subject of the next chapter. What is relevant for this chapter, then, is that "the human body" was "not an automaton" and that Americans understood the dynamism of the circulatory system to be the key system of American health in the early republic.

34. Rush, *Medical Inquiries and Observations*, 4:389. Cullen was not only his mentor but, as Rush noted, the guiding light for American physicians in the 1760s.

35. Rush explained to his students that he had notes that proved Cullen had once thought otherwise. "It is true Dr. Cullen afterwards deserted this opinion," he lectured, "but is equally true I never did, and the belief of it has been the foundation of many opinions and modes of practice in medicine which I have since adopted" ("Of Physiology," 86).

36. "Introduction to the Lectures on Animal Life," in Carlson, Wollock, and Noel, *Lectures on the Mind*, 52–66.

37. See Harvey, *Exercitatio Anatomica*.

38. Ibid., 3.

39. Harvey continued to explain in his dedication to Charles I: "The King, in like manner, is the foundation of his kingdom, the sun of the world around him, the heart of the republic, the fountain whence all power, all grace doth flow . . . the motions of the heart I am the more emboldened to present to your Majesty . . . [because] many things in a King are after the pattern of the heart" (ibid.).

40. Rush, *Notes on Physiology*, 112.

41. Ibid.

42. Rush, "Of Physiology," 84.

43. Ibid., 85.

44. Of Rush's early commitment to what would become a more widespread set of early ideas about U.S. republicanism, Michael Meranze summarizes, "Rush was a federalist before there were federalists"; he opposed direct democracy and feared "mobocracy" (*Essays*, iii). For an excellent summary of Rush's vision of republicanism, see Meranze, "Introduction to Benjamin Rush," in Rush, *Essays*.

45. Rush, "Of Physiology," 188.

46. Brodsky, *Benjamin Rush*, 89–90. Here Rush follows John Brown's sthenic and asthenic diseases. For Brown and Rush and the uniqueness of Rush's vision, see Rees, "Remarks on the Medical Theories of Brown, Cullen, Darwin, & Rush."

47. Rush, "On Securities for Liberty," in *Selected Writings*, 32–34.

48. Ibid., 33. For more on anarchia, see Meranze, "Introduction to Benjamin Rush," in Rush, *Essays*, ii–iii.

49. Editors' notes in Rush, "Of Physiology," 162.

50. "Sympathy" was key to eighteenth-century thought, though it lacked stable meaning. Evelyn Forget claims, "It is no wonder that eighteenth-century characterizations of social sympathy have been called ambiguous . . . despite its apparent universality, the definition of sympathy varied among writers and within the body of work of any single social theorist" ("Evocations of Sympathy," 288). Its centrality and indeterminacy fostered lively debate over a term that grounded Enlightenment models of state and society. Jason Frank writes, "Sympathy was understood both as the 'cement' that cohered social order and as a perpetually destabilizing threat to that order" ("Sympathy and Separation," 30). Edmund Burke, Frances Hutcheson, Adam Smith, and David Hume all considered the term essential. Physicians like Robert Whytt linked philosophical discussions of sympathy to medical ones. Rush was highly attuned to these discussions, not only because he studied in Edinburgh but also because he was fully immersed in the circum-Atlantic Enlightenment world. Excellent discussions of eighteenth-century sympathy include Barker-Benfield, *Culture of Sensibility*; Marshall, *Surprising Effects of Sympathy*; and Stern, *Plight of Feeling*.

51. Rush, "Of Physiology," 238.

52. Ibid.

53. Rush's sympathy was Humean. Rush had met Hume, and Rush's teachers John Gregory and Cullen were intimates of Hume who mapped medical sympathy along Humean lines. Hume saw sympathy as resulting from the interaction between external impressions and innate response. Hume describes passionate sympathy as "directly related to the object, which nature has attributed the passion; the sensation, which the cause separately produces, is related to the sensation of the passion: From this double relation of ideas and impressions, the passion is deriv'd" (*Treatise*, 286). Following Hume, Rush views sympathy as the body's reaction to circulating stimuli; Gregory and Cullen used Hume's "double relation." Gregory based his medical ethics on Hume, and Cullen was Hume's friend, advocate, and physician. For Cullen's relationship to Hume and Smith, see Thompson, *An Account of the Life, Lectures, and Writings of William Cullen*. For Gregory's indebtedness, see McCullough, "Hume's Influence." Rush met Hume (see Rush, *Travels Through Life*, 28–29, 43 [meetings], 87 [indebtedness]).

54. Rush, *Notes on Physiology*, 128.

55. Rush, *Letters*, 1:523.

56. Rush, "Of Physiology," 238.

57. Ibid.

58. These modes included *continuity* and *contiguity* to describe direct sympathy (organ to organ) as well as indirect (organ-brain-organ) sympathy connections. *Reciprocal, nonreciprocal,* and *inverse* reactions describe directionality and type of sympathetic response. See Rush, "Of the Nervous System," in *Lectures on the Mind,* 241. For example, sympathetic response might be *contiguous* and *inverse*: if one organ became hyperactive, the brain might enervate a spatially removed organ. Rush's sympathetic taxonomy was exhaustive, delineating sympathetic pathways between all organs.

59. Rush, *Notes on Physiology,* 153.

60. Rush, "Of Physiology," 240. The brain remained central, even if he understood that "sympathy often takes place independently of the nerves" (ibid.).

61. "The contraction of every muscle fibre, diastole and systole of the heart, the pulsation of the arteries . . . and the sense of touch, *nay more, thought itself,* all depend upon the action of stimuli upon organs of sense and motion. *These stimuli are external, and internal*" (Rush, "Animal Life" in *Lectures on the Mind,* 87–88, emphasis added.

62. Rush, *Notes on Physiology,* 124.

63. Ibid., 133, 124.

64. Rush, "Lectures upon the Mind" in *Lectures on the Mind,* 403.

65. Rush, *Medical Inquiries and Observations,* 2:37.

66. Ibid., 1:331–32. See, e.g., Wood, *Radicalism of the American Revolution* for the connection between revolution and the Enlightenment.

67. Frank, *Constituent Moments,* 108. Here he refers largely to Rush's social and political work, but I am extending it to his medical work. Frank is indebted to John B. Radner for this term.

68. Rush, *Autobiography,* 113–14. Rush explained that Paine, who fashioned himself a global citizen, had "nothing to fear from the popular odium which such a publication might expose him, for he could live anywhere," but Rush had an established life and career in Philadelphia, which he explained "forbade me to come forward as a pioneer in that important controversy" (114).

69. Adams, *Works,* 3:507.

70. For Rush's account, see *Travels Through Life,* 113–15, and see Hawke, *Benjamin Rush* for a version of this story (137–38). For more on common sense in general and in relation to Rush, see Sophia Rosenfeld, "Benjamin Rush's Common Sense."

71. Rush, *MIODM,* 27. Rush called the brain's blood vessels "the primary seat of madness" (ibid.).

72. Rush, *Medical Inquiries and Observations,* 4:426.

73. Ibid., 4:424.

74. Ibid., 1:324.

75. Ibid.

76. Ibid.

77. Rush, *MIODM,* 94, 96.

78. Ibid., 97.

79. Ibid., 162.

80. Rush, *Selected Writings,* 217, 224, 217. Rush describes "dress mania" as the insanity of impractical fashion invading every city street and "place of public resort" and "church phobia" as the phenomenon in which sunny weather spurs "chariots, phaetons, chairs, and even stage-waggons" to flee churches "every Sunday in summer, as soon as they are open for divine worship" (217, 224).

81. For another example, see my discussion of "Negro Mania" in Altschuler, "From Blood Vessels to Global Networks of Exchange," 208–9, 231.

82. Rush, *Selected Writings*, 90.

83. Ibid., 223.

84. Ibid.

85. Ibid., 217.

86. Rush, *MIODM*, 315.

87. Ibid.

88. Rush, *Medical Inquiries and Observations*, 4:422–23.

89. Ibid., 4:423.

90. For an account of early bibliotherapy, see Weimerskirch, "Benjamin Rush and John Minson Galt."

91. See Rush's lecture "On the Construction and Management of Hospitals" (1802) in Rush, *Sixteen Introductory Lectures*, 182–209, especially 192.

92. Ibid., 192.

93. Ibid.

94. Rush, *MIODM*, 123. This was especially for diseases of the mind and physical pain. While physicians should first offer patients the Bible, "where there is no relish for the simple and interesting stories of the Bible, the reading of novels should be recommended to patients" (ibid.).

95. Ibid., 117.

96. Ramsay, *Eulogium*, 26–27. To get a sense of how widely read this essay was, the volume held by Harvard was "written at the request of the Medical Society of South Carolina," published in Philadelphia, "Bought in Baltimore," and donated to Harvard at "the request of Convers Francis, of Cambridge (Class of 1815)." I will cite from this edition.

97. Ibid., 27.

98. Staughton, *Eulogium*, 32.

99. For excellent work on the Friendly Club, see Waterman, *Republic of Intellect* and Kaplan, *Men of Letters*.

100. In support of Rush's work, Smith circulated a manuscript copy of the notes he took in Rush's lectures and continued to seek Rush's advice throughout his life. Smith's copy of Rush's *A Course of Lectures on the Theory and Practice of Medicine* is held at the Cushing/Whitney Medical Historical Library, Yale University.

101. Smith, *American Poems*, iv. Though Smith died young, his literary accolades include a staged play, an opera, and a number of acclaimed poems. See Bennet, "A Poetical Correspondence" for his thirty-five-poem collaboration with Charles Brockden Brown and Joseph Bringhurst Jr.

102. Darwin, *The Botanic Garden* (1790), iii. For more on Darwin's science and poetry, see, e.g., Griffith, "The Institutions of Analogy in Erasmus Darwin's Poetics"; Bewell, "Erasmus Darwin's Cosmopolitan Nature"; and Emery, "Scientific Theory in Erasmus Darwin's 'The Botanic Garden.'" The first part, *The Loves of Plants*, was published anonymously in 1789.

103. Darwin, *Botanic Garden* (1789), vii.

104. Ibid., 8, 14.

105. They teach "mysterious BACON, to explore / Metallic veins, and part the dross from ore" (the discovery of gunpowder) and "call'd delighted *Savery* to your aid; / Bade round the youth explosive *Steam* aspire" (the discovery of steam power) (ibid., 15, 16–17).

106. Smith's 1798 edition was published in New York while Caldwell, who only worked on the second volume, published his the same year in Philadelphia. Nevertheless, Caldwell's

introduction is dated January 10, 1797, while Smith's introduction is dated March 20, 1798, fourteen months later.

107. Smith, "Epistle," in *Botanic Garden*, n.p.

108. Ibid.

109. In arguing for the differences between Smith's and Rush's visions, I respectfully depart from Catherine O'Donnell Kaplan, who views them as aligned in *Men of Letters*, especially chap. 3, and from Bryan Waterman, who writes that "Benjamin Rush received Smith's unending loyalty" (*Republic of Intellect*, 202).

110. Here I have opted for the title at the heading of Smith's piece rather than "The Institutions of the Republic of Utopia," which Kaplan uses. For more on the discourse of Western health into the nineteenth century, see Valenčius, *Health of the Country*.

111. Kaplan, "Elihu Hubbard Smith's 'The Institutions of the Republic of Utopia,'" 310 (hereafter "EHS").

112. Ibid.

113. Ibid.

114. Ibid., 311.

115. Ibid.

116. Ibid., 298.

117. Ibid., 298. An even more revealing comparison is Smith's essay "The Plague of Athens," a treatise he was writing at the same time in response to the yellow fever epidemics that had struck the eastern seaboard almost every year since 1791. ("The Plague of Athens" appears to have been written in June 1797, and "The Utopia" was written in two moments, between August–September 1796 and September 1797; Kaplan, "EHS," 304.) The two works are remarkably similar, especially in the beginning, but while "The Utopia" presents an ideal, "The Plague" presents a dystopian version of health that Smith hoped could provide answers for the yellow fever outbreaks in New York. Both begin with an introduction to the general state of the society at the moment of investigation in the place it examines. They then proceed to a second paragraph that details the size, location, longitude, and latitude of the place, followed by paragraphs about the soil quality and its relationship to farming, and the state of plants and general climate of each place. In the pages that follow, Smith details the living conditions of each place, the employment of the citizens, the habits of the people, and the general organization of the society and outline of the built environment.

118. I made this calculation by identifying the number of health care professionals Smith distributes across each of the nine counties in Utopia (three per parish, forty-five parishes per county). I doubled the number for the central "Mid County," where Smith estimated the number of participants in the medical society should be increased from sixty to eighty or ninety. I did not add any numbers for the cities of the surrounding counties, which Smith imagines will have more medical men. See *Catalogue of the Medical Graduates* for more on the numbers of graduates, esp. p. 96, and early medical education.

119. Kaplan, "EHS," 326.

120. Ibid.

121. Smith's portrayal is hyperrational, and no absence is more striking than that of sympathy. Information rather than sympathy controls Smith's Utopia. Especially in comparison with Rush's prose, Smith's vision of republican health is penned in language strikingly free of affect; words like "sympathy," "empathy," "feeling," and "emotion" are missing from the text. The omission of the language of sympathy is especially surprising in a work of eighteenth-century political philosophy and medical theory. This exclusion is likely the result of the trouble Smith

had with sympathy. Whereas Rush considered sympathy paramount for republican health, Smith struggled with it. In truth, Smith believed in the power of sympathy, but he often found it too dangerous. In "The Utopia," Smith flirts with feeling only once, and even then the reader's sympathies are tightly policed. Smith observes in his opening passage that the description of his republican utopia "can not fail to inspire every considerate mind with an eager disposition to search into & discover what are the foundations of a prosperity so novel & affecting" (ibid., 309). But even in invoking affect, Smith patrols it, dictating that the reader "can not fail" to respond to his text in very particular ways. Utopia's remarkable vibrancy may be "affecting," but this mandated affect has nothing to do with feeling; rather, it spurs a "curiosity" that is "at once rational & natural" (ibid.). Smith rejects the art of sympathy as a means to republican health.

The utopian form of "The Utopia" helps structure this rejection of sympathy. Unlike sentimentality, satire, or the gothic, utopian fiction readily lent itself to dispassionate description. Since Smith was deeply passionate about the subject matter of "Institutions," a reader might expect enthusiasm, excitement, or at least rhetorical flourish from the literary physician, but, unlike Rush, Smith proceeds simply and without affect or ornament. The sentences are factual, direct, and dry. Smith's enthusiasm is legible only in asides to himself to provide more details on health reports ("//Many explanations remain on this article//"), in the lengthy, breathless procedural detail, and in his inability to conclude his section on "Medical Institutions" (ibid., 322). His dispassionate style otherwise reveals nothing of his zealous, lifelong commitments to literature and to health.

122. Ibid., 310.

123. Ibid., 329. Kaplan wryly notes of the problems with Smith's negotiation between an isolated republic and a global vision: "Those rivers too narrow to carry dangerous luxuries are apparently broad enough to bear medical communications from all corners of the globe" (301).

124. Smith, "Epistle," in *Botanic Garden*.

125. For more on the relationship between "The Utopia" and the *Medical Repository*, see Kaplan, *Men of Letters*, chap. 3, "Two Visions of Circulation." Kaplan, however, emphasizes Smith's vision of circulation and alignment with Rush in her reading, whereas I am interested in their differing visions of republican health.

126. Smith, "Introduction," 1.

127. Smith, Miller, and Mitchill, "Circular Address," ix–x.

128. Ibid., x.

129. Numbers from Apel, *Feverish Bodies*, 49.

130. Kaplan, "EHS," 326.

131. Smith, Miller, and Mitchill, "Circular Address," viii.

132. Ibid.

133. Ibid., xii.

134. Ibid., xi. St. Mary's is an island in southeastern England and St. Croix did not become a U.S. territory until 1917.

135. For detailed accounts of print circulation, see Warner, *Letters of the Republic* and Davidson, *The Revolution and the Word*.

136. Smith had corresponded with Rush previously about the *Repository*, hoping Rush would assist in its success in Philadelphia. On December 1, 1797, Smith wrote to Rush, "With regard to the Medical Repository, in the success of which I make no doubt of your feeling some interest," and followed by asking Rush to recommend it to "Mr. Dobson, or any respectable Bookseller in Phila." (*The Diary*, 400). "May we not hope," Smith concluded, "that it will deserve your recommendation?" (ibid.). He could not.

137. Ibid., 410. At the moment Smith sought Rush's endorsement, Rush was personally embroiled in a nasty and personal set of medical disputes. It was not ideal timing for Smith to propose a compendium of medical opinions from across the country. Smith was more than aware of these circumstances, having spent the first part of his letter apologizing for the hostility toward his mentor from Smith's own medical institution, which had recently decided not to hire Rush to teach the following fall. These circumstances likely added to Rush's feelings about the journal produced by a set of New York physicians—even if they were his students and colleagues.

138. Ibid. Smith's fears about the journal's failure in Philadelphia were especially troubling to him, since he considered the city "the emporium of American science" (ibid., 398). Nevertheless, the journal was a success. The first volumes were quickly reprinted, and new volumes were published regularly until 1824.

139. The poem spans pages 189–93 in the November issue of the *Medical Repository*. This was by no means Mitchill's only imaginative foray into science. In his poem "Elegy on a Shell—The Nautilus," Mitchill traces the shell's life from Manilla "on the surface of the placid wave, / With guiding oars and elevated sail" until a storm took the life of the Mollusca who lived within. Merging science and art, Mitchell muses on its life history and beautiful symmetrical form (Stedman and Hutchinson, *A Library*, 193–94).

140. Mitchill, "The Doctrine of Septon," 189. In its circular address, the *Medical Repository* declared its commitment to reason and fact, giving "little flattering to indolence, to vanity, and to a creative fancy," but, as a collective venture, it was not as distanced from fancy as Elihu Hubbard Smith might have hoped (Smith, Miller, and Mitchill, "Circular Address," vii). Despite the intent of the journal to debunk "Philosophers" who "descend[ed] from generals to particulars, shaping them according to preconceived notions of their intimate relations" in favor of "rigid examination and cautious assemblage of particulars," the *Medical Repository* still took a truth-to-nature approach to the development of medical knowledge ("Circular Address"). See, e.g., Noah Webster, "A Collection of Phenomena, relative to the Connection between Earthquakes, Tempests, and Epidemic Tempers; and a Vindication of the Doctrine of Equivocal Generation" in the fifth volume in which Webster claims to simply provide "scraps" and "unusual facts" but in fact seeks to prove "the connection between electricity and earthquakes, and violent tempests" using "a singular concurrence of facts to confirm the opinion" (25). A botanical drawing from the same volume makes the visual point about the *Repository*'s truth-to-nature orientation (160–61). Finally, the Circular Address's avowed rejection of medical philosophy was perhaps meant to pointedly distance it from Benjamin Rush and his circle.

141. Smith, *The Diary*, 366. Also see Waterman's discussion of "The Doctrine of Septon" in *Republic of Intellect*, 209–11.

142. The scant scholarship on "The Doctrine of Septon" that exists treats it as entertainment or as an "effective [vehicle] for delivering his arguments to general readers" but not as an act of scientific inquiry (e.g., Waterman, *Republic of Intellect*, 203). While Mitchill did develop the idea of septon in a number of places, as a poem, "The Doctrine of Septon" allowed Mitchill to experiment with septon more capaciously and imaginatively than he could in more formal medical and scientific writing and to articulate his vision in more explicitly republican terms. That Mitchill circulated the poem repeatedly also suggests his investment in this particular articulation of his theory.

143. Mitchill, "The Doctrine of Septon," 189.

144. Ibid.

145. Ibid., 189–90.

146. Ibid., 190. Rush was, at least partially and belatedly, won over to this view of oxygen. By 1809, Rush changed his lectures to reflect his new belief that the first external stimulus to promote life was air rather than water. See Rush, *Lectures on the Mind*, ed. Carlson, Wollock, and Noel, 88n2.

147. Mitchill, "The Doctrine of Septon," 190; Valenčius, *Health of the Country*, 114. Conevery Bolton Valenčius usefully summarizes various understandings of miasma: the nature of miasma, she writes, is "difficult to capture" and, "in many ways, the concept of miasma functioned usefully precisely because it was so flexible and protean. . . . Like malevolent sprites, miasmas were at once wispy and possessed of great power, ethereal in nature but chillingly tangible in effect. Miasmas emanated from harmful or degraded places or things, infiltrating their surroundings with illness. They carried the essence of decay and putrefaction" (114). For a useful general overview of the idea of miasma, see Valenčius, "Airs," in *Health of the Country*, esp. 114–17.

148. Mitchill, "The Doctrine of Septon," 190.

149. Ibid.

150. Ibid., 191.

151. Darwin used footnotes in the *Botanic Garden*, but his footnotes were not summaries of the stanzas so much as a glossary of technical terms.

152. Ibid., 189–90.

153. Ibid., 189.

154. For more on the chemical revolution in the *Medical Repository*, see Edelstein, "The Chemical Revolution in America."

155. Quoted in Levin, "Venel, Lavoisier," 304. Also see Levin for a careful analysis of what Lavoisier might have meant by "une révolution en physique et en chimie" in 1773. Marcellin Berthelot is credited with coining the more succinct phrase in his book titled *La Révolution Chimique: Lavoisier* (Paris, 1890). For examples of the vibrant history and historiography of the chemical revolution over the past century, see James Bryant Conant's second case in *Harvard Case Histories in Experimental Science*; Kuhn, *Structure of Scientific Revolutions*, esp. chap. 6; Chang, "Hidden History of Phlogiston"; and Eddy, Mauskopf, and Newman, "An Introduction to Chemical Knowledge in the Early Modern World."

156. Priestley, *Experiments and Observations* (1775), 2:vii–viii, 1:vi. Furthermore, Priestley argued, "The *system of nature* is superior to any *political system* upon earth" (1:xxvi, original emphasis).

157. On July 14, 1791, Priestley and his group were gathered to celebrate the anniversary of the fall of the Bastille when British citizens attacked in what would be known as the Birmingham or "Priestley Riots." The government at least tacitly supported the rioters, having no desire to see Priestley's Dissenters succeed in their campaign for rights. The mob burned Priestley's house, destroyed his laboratory, and forced him into hiding.

158. See Graham, "Revolutionary in Exile."

159. For some of the debate over Lavoisier's work in relation to French politics, see Levin, "Venel, Lavoisier" and Perrin, "Revolution or Reform."

160. Mitchill, "The Doctrine of Septon," 191.

161. Ibid.

162. Ibid.

163. Ibid., 192.

164. Ibid.

165. Ibid.

166. Ibid., 190.

167. Ibid.

168. Ibid., 191.

169. As Jean-Pierre Poirier writes, when the king attempted to escape and was brought back to Paris in 1791, "Republican posters inspired by Thomas Paine and Condorcet appeared on the walls of the city. Other posters, dictated by La Fayette, replied. The debate over the deposition of the king sparked a quarrel between the partisans of an Orléanist regency and the various republican tendencies. Lavoisier seemed to be undecided . . . [James Hall reported:] 'M. Lavoisier, who is generally very steady, varied back and forwards several times. This appears to me to arise from the fact that they are now for the first time agitating in their minds the comparison between a republic and a monarchy'" (*Lavoisier*, 286). For a complementary discussion of Mitchill's chemistry and politics in relation to yellow fever, see Apel, *Feverish Bodies*, 83–87.

170. In 1797, Mitchill printed his reaction to the volume he had been given in the *Medical Repository* 1, no. 2: 265–67. Priestley also gifted Rush a copy of "Considerations on the Doctrine of Phlogiston," which is currently held with many of his other books at the Library Company of Philadelphia.

171. Priestley, *Considerations*, vi. Perhaps out of consideration for the dead, Priestley calls out Kirwin instead of Lavoisier.

172. Ibid., vii.

173. Edelstein, "The Chemical Revolution in America," 155.

174. "Your opposition to the new doctrine," Mitchill wrote, "has been serviceable to the cause of science. It has prevented too easy and sudden an acquiescence in the novel system of the antiphlogistians, whose difficulties and paradoxes have been admitted by many . . . [but] if they were capable of bringing about a coalition of parties, I might say to you. . . . 'For, Dick, if we could reconcile / Old Aristotle with Gassendus, / How many would admire our toil!'" (*Medical Repository* 1, no. 4 [1798]: 519–20). The Mitchill-Priestley debate occurred in the pages of the *Medical Repository* and is treated more extensively by Edgar Fahs Smith in *Samuel Latham Mitchill*, especially 11–14, and Edelstein, "The Chemical Revolution in America."

175. Priestley was less conciliatory than Mitchill, though he appreciated Mitchill's efforts. Priestley replied to Mitchill's attempts to smooth over the differences between his system and that of the antiphlogistonists: "Dear Sir, Thank you for your ingenious, and well intended, attempt to promote a peace between the present belligerent powers in chemistry; but I much fear your labour will be in vain. In my opinion there can be no compromise of the two systems" (*Medical Repository* 1, no. 4 [1798]: 521). In contrast, he framed his conflict with his European opposition in antagonistic political terms. Priestley wrote caustically that the antiphlogistonist Maclean had not sent a copy of his work to Priestley, as he supposed "the laws of war require," nor had Maclean treated him "with the civility to which I think I am entitled as a veteran in the science. Had he been the victorious Buonaparte, I am old Wurmser, and should have been treated with respect, though vanquished" (*Medical Repository* 1, no. 4 [1798]: 521–22). "But this Mantua has not surrendered yet," Priestley affirmed before closing his letter by assuring Mitchill of his deep respect and his enthusiasm to continue the conversation (*Medical Repository* 1, no. 4 [1798]: 522).

176. "Priestley's Sentiments."

177. While Mitchill supported Priestley by praising his work and downplaying their differences, Priestley supported Mitchill, incorporating Mitchill's work into his own by casting

septon as a theory of physiological decay to complement the investigations Priestley had made into chemical decay.

178. Brown, "Miscellaneous Articles."

179. Mitchill, "The Doctrine of Septon," 189, 185. The full title of the poem is "The Doctrine of Septon. *Attempted after the Manner of Dr. Darwin.*" Mitchill sent the poem to Beddoes on September 15, 1797. In sending his poem to Beddoes, Mitchill sought the support of another literarily inclined physician whose understanding of health diverged from Rush's. In the poem, Mitchill locates health in oxygen rather than in the blood vessels and connects oxygen to "*the principle of* exciteability" (190, original emphasis). "Exciteability" was the central term in British physician John Brown's theory of health, and Beddoes was Brown's principal champion.

180. Ibid., 192.

181. Ibid., 193. Mitchill uses lines from Horace's poem "The Art of Poetry" to chastise himself. This story has a wonderful literature-and-medicine coda: Thomas Beddoes introduced his assistant Humphrey Davy to septon through Mitchill's work (Davy, *Researches*, 453). Although Davy discovered the gas through Mitchill, he was not worried about septon's corrosive nature and conducted his own tests, which he claimed "certainly would never have been made if the hypothesis of Dr. Mitchill had the least influence on my mind" (quoted in Altman, *Who Goes First*, 56). Experimenting first on himself, Davy inhaled the nitrous oxide (septon) and found it to be both pleasant and pain relieving. Afterward, he and Beddoes invited their friends the poets Robert Southey and Samuel Taylor Coleridge to try the gas, both of whom recorded their experience of its sensations for Davy's 1800 book *Researches*. It is, of course, tempting to connect Southey and Coleridge's participation in these medical experiments back to their imaginative poetry, but what is certain is that Davy's and Coleridge's ideas about their scientific and artistic imaginations influenced one another. See Smith, *Fact and Feeling*, 77–91 for a terrific discussion of Davy and Coleridge.

182. Rush, *Kelroy*, 15–16.

183. Ibid., 16. See 139–41 for an example of his medical incompetence.

184. The notable exception is Dunlevy's injured servant—whose "battered body," Dana Nelson points out, serves as romantic plot device—who falls ill when the plot needs him to be and recovers in time for Dunlevy to realize "he had been drawn [to Mrs. Hammond's house] in part by compassion for Sancho, but more by his admiration of the beautiful Emily" (introduction to ibid., xx, 145).

185. Two key scenes strikingly illustrate Rebecca Rush's recentering of female sympathy toward the ends of health. The first is the fire that destroys the Hammonds' house. Kelroy saves both mother and daughter, but Mrs. Hammond lies "in a state of alternate delirium, and insensibility, which soon made her life despaired of" (*Kelroy*, 122). No doctor attends her, but Emily, "for some time severely indisposed" herself, cares for her mother "and from the moment her strength permitted, she was constantly in her chamber, where she waited in sorrowful expectation of receiving her last sigh" (122). Helen Cathcart also exhibits "active kindness"; "Mrs. Cathcart, who had really a compassionate heart, did everything in her power to relieve and console the afflicted Emily" (123–24). In addition to being "extremely attentive both to her and her mother," Mrs. Cathcart eventually discovers what Dr. Blake in his care for the servant cannot: the cause of the condition. A network of women's sympathetic alliances girds the ailing woman's body, keeping her from "the confines of the grave" (ibid.). Emily's death scene also refigures sympathetic affiliation. After Mrs. Hammond's death Emily learns her mother lied about Kelroy, which prompts a "death-like swoon . . . succeeded by a fever which

reduced her to the borders of the grave" (189). Emily calls Helen—not a doctor—to her death-bed. Helen cares for her, receiving Emily's request to clear her reputation. Helen cannot save Emily, but, sympathizing with Emily, she does what she can to heal the social disorders caused by Mrs. Hammond's lies.

186. See Chapter 4 for a discussion of the rise of this discourse of medical difference.

187. Holmes, *Border Lines*, 252; Virchow, *Cellular Pathology*, vii. Virchow continues that this doctrine is "in opposition to the one-sided humoral and neuristical (solidistic) tendencies which have been transmitted from the mythical days of antiquity to our own times, and at the same time to contrast with the equally one-sided interpretations of a grossly mechanical and chemical bias—the more delicate mechanism and chemistry of the cell" (vii–viii). No wonder Holmes admired the work of Virchow.

188. Holmes, "Report," 287.

189. Ibid., 288.

190. Holmes, *Border Lines*, 236–37.

191. Ibid.

192. Ibid., 237.

193. Ibid., 252.

194. Ibid., 236.

CHAPTER 2

1. Powell, *Bring Out Your Dead*, ix.

2. See, e.g., the second number of the first volume of the *Medical Repository*, which lists yellow fever in 1797 attacking Bristol and Providence (Rhode Island), Philadelphia, Baltimore, Norfolk (Virginia), and possibly Charleston. Furthermore, other manifestations of fall fevers appeared in Sheffield (Massachusetts), New Milford (Connecticut), and Hanover (New Hampshire). That was only the domestic "Medical News" (see p. 253). The volume also discussed fevers in Jamaica, Granada, Newburyport, Boston, New York, Philadelphia, and Martinique. Much has been written on the 1793 yellow fever epidemic. For primary sources, see Carey's *Short Account* and Rush's *An Account of the Bilious Remitting Yellow Fever*, and for useful secondary sources, see Apel, *Feverish Bodies*; Arner, "Making Yellow Fever American"; Finger, *Contagious City*; Gould, "Race, Commerce"; Pernick, "Politics, Parties, and Pestilence"; and Taylor, "'We live in the midst of death.'"

3. The cause of yellow fever would not be discovered until 1901.

4. In referring to "contagionists," I depend more on the contemporary use of the term rather than on the more conflicted historical use of "contagion" suggested by the chapter's epigraph.

5. See, e.g., Pernick, "Politics, Parties, and Pestilence."

6. Historian Martin Pernick explains of the medico-political context that "more than one-third of the most prominent national and local political leaders in Philadelphia took a public position on the cause of the epidemic . . . [and t]he party leaders, moreover, moved rapidly to exploit the many political implications they discovered in the medical controversy" ("Politics, Parties, and Pestilence," 566–68). Of the volume of ink spilled during the crisis, critic Bryan Waterman quips, "As a concrete body of early American writing, [the work on yellow fever] is so large that it should perhaps be considered a second set of constitutional debates, this one concerned not with the previous decade's U.S. Constitution but with comprehending the con-

stitutions of America's soils and climates, as well as the impact of the fever on its manners and populations" (*Republic of Intellect*, 193).

7. Freneau, "Pestilence," 230, emphasis added.

8. Freneau had little patience for doctors' disputes and ineffectual treatment. In his poem "The Crows and the Carrion: A Medical Story," he writes, "Each [doctor] looks at each with vengeful eyes. . . . One talks of cure by CALOMEL; / But his wise brother Sydrophel, / Swears, 'tis the readiest way to hell. / While one the lancet recommends, / Another for a blister sense, / And each his every cure defends" (ibid., 9).

9. According to the *OED*, the use of "communicable" in relation to disease dates at least to the seventeenth century.

10. See this chapter's epigraph for the complete definitions.

11. "Extracts of a letter."

12. See a longer discussion in the introduction.

13. Rush, *An Account*, 23.

14. Ibid.

15. Ibid., 31–32.

16. Ibid., 22.

17. Carey, *A Short Account* (January 16, 1794), 18.

18. "New Port, New York."

19. Ibid.

20. Ibid.

21. "Philadelphia; Melancholy."

22. Ibid., emphasis added.

23. For other accounts of the Carey, Jones, and Allen history, see especially Gould, "Race, Commerce" and Stern, *Plight of Feeling*, esp. 219–22, 231–33.

24. Carey, *A Short Account* (January 16, 1794), 86–87.

25. Carey, *A Short Account* (November 23, 1793), v.

26. Ibid., vi.

27. Rush, *An Account*, iii.

28. Carey, *A Short Account* (November 23, 1793), vii–viii.

29. Carey, *A Short Account* (January 16, 1794), viii.

30. Ibid.

31. Ibid., 27.

32. Ibid., 32.

33. Ibid., 89.

34. Ibid., 74.

35. Jones and Allen, *A Narrative*, 3.

36. Ibid., 4.

37. Ibid.

38. Ibid., 10–11.

39. Ibid., 11.

40. Ibid., 19.

41. Ibid.

42. Ibid.

43. Ibid.

44. Both of these poems have tight rhyme schemes; they are instructive but also highly ordered forms of rhetoric.

45. For an analysis of private correspondence during the yellow fever epidemic, see Miller, "The Wages of Blackness."

46. Rush, *An Account*, 17.

47. Ibid., 147.

48. Ibid., 152.

49. For example, in 1796, Smith wrote to Rush that he had "not the least doubt of the justice of your [climatist] doctrine, which considers all Fevers, of this kind, as varying only in *degree*" (*The Diary*, 214).

50. Ibid., 215.

51. Also see Philip Gould's analysis of this important contradiction in "Race, Commerce" for a discussion of the economic implications of Rush's coffee hypothesis, especially pp. 164–65.

52. Smith, *The Diary*, 215.

53. Rush, *Medical Inquiries and Observations*, 2:111.

54. Smith, *The Diary* (manuscript held at Cushing/Whitney Medical Historical Library, Yale University), 3:109. Note: Cronin's edition of Smith's diary is incomplete. Where "*The Diary*" is followed by a volume number, it refers to the Yale manuscript edition.

55. Ibid.

56. Although tar was made locally, it was primarily used to seal the vessels of Atlantic trade.

57. Smith respectfully disagreed with Rush on other features of the fever as well—most specifically on the appearance of the blood drawn in the fever. In the enumeration that closes his September 9 letter to Rush, he details five objections to Rush's theories, the longest of which describes "the appearances exhibited by the blood" (Smith, *The Diary*, 218). Contrary to Rush's beliefs, the blood did not resemble "hyper-oxygenation," looked different from pneumonia and consumption, rarely contained "Scarlet sediment," and only once appeared as "greenish black, coagulated Blood" (ibid.). In his concerns about the appearance of drawn blood Smith extends his critiques of expelled blood to further distinguish his ideas from Rush's. However, Smith deferred to Rush until he could undertake more research himself: "I pretend not to decide on this subject. The blood has been very imperfectly examined; it is a most interesting object of curiosity . . . Dr. Mitchill & myself purpose to institute a series of experiments on the Blood, at some future time. Perhaps we may be able to gain some knowlege [*sic*] in this almost unexplored field" (ibid.). He was unable to conduct these experiments before his early death.

58. Smith, Miller, and Mitchill, "Circular Address," viii.

59. "Article II," *Medical Repository*, 1, no. 1 (1797):136.

60. Smith, Miller, and Mitchill, "Circular Address," viii–ix.

61. *Medical Repository* 1, no. 1 (1797): 125; *Medical Repository* 1, no. 1 (1797): 129, 1, no. 2 (1797): 269; *Medical Repository* 1, no. 1 (1797): 132; *Medical Repository* 1, no. 3 (1798): 306; *Medical Repository* 1, no. 3 (1798): 369; *Medical Repository* 1, no. 3 (1798): 336, 337; *Medical Repository* 1, no. 3 (1798): 372.

62. *Medical Repository* 5 (New York, 1802), title page.

63. Smith, Miller, and Mitchill, "Circular Address," vii.

64. Ibid. The *Medical Repository* might have imagined itself built only on facts, but as Lorraine Daston and Peter Galison have shown, doctors and scientists still understood the kinds of facts privileged by Smith, Miller, and Mitchill to be constructed in epistemologically weighty minds (see Daston and Galison, *Objectivity*).

65. Here, too, we can see an early version of the rationalism/empiricism debate that would consume many physicians of the period, though, as the chapter indicates, Smith was still very much a rationalist.

66. Darwin, *Zoonomia* (1818), 1:v. Darwin dates this preface January 1, 1796. While there were earlier editions and it is clear that the Friendly Club avidly read Darwin, Samuel Latham Mitchill would produce an edition of his own in 1818.

67. See the introduction, for example, for his discussion of the effect of the male imagination on a baby during conception.

68. See, e.g., Bechtold, "A Revolutionary Soundscape."

69. Even Mitchill, "The Doctrine of Septon," as Bryan Waterman observes, "links such decomposing matter with the figure of corrupted communication" (*Republic of Intellect*, 211). For more on "The Doctrine of Septon," see the previous chapter.

70. Smith, *The Diary*, 60. Also see Kaplan's discussion in *Men of Letters*, 87.

71. In this belief we can hear the echoes of *Zoonomia* and the Friendly Club. In Samuel Latham Mitchill's 1802 preface to *Zoonomia*, he represents Darwin's own fear of circulating medical stories. Darwin, he explains, hoping "to avoid the contagion of opinion . . . had read no medical book for five whole years" (*Zoonomia* [1803], xxv).

72. For the centrality of collections of letters to the production of Atlantic medicine since the Renaissance, see Siraisi, *Communities of Learned Experience*.

73. Seth, "Textually Transmitted Diseases," 133.

74. Dunlap, *Memoirs*, 44.

75. Quoted in Waterman, *Republic of Intellect*, 206.

76. Smith, *The Diary*, 458.

77. Cahill, *Liberty of the Imagination*, 171.

78. Brown, *Edgar Huntly*, 3.

79. Ibid., 3–4.

80. Smith's tragic death was full of irony: Smith caught an imported disease as he firmly decried importationism, and died nursing a physiocrat back to health, one who also believed strongly in the effect of local conditions on corporeal and political health. For more on Scandella, including his prominence in the 1790s United States, see Juliani, *Building Little Italy*, 14–16. Contemporary readers of Smith's diary also note the irony, as Waterman does, that Smith records "the relentless buzzing and biting of mosquitoes" that carried yellow fever (*Republic of Intellect*, 3).

81. Brown, *Arthur Mervyn*, 130. The first sentence of this passage is particularly interesting: grammatically and syntactically, it is unclear whether Mervyn laments the pleasure of others' pain or whether the sublime nature of serious illness perverts "consternation" and "pity" with a "tincture of the pleasing." In either case, the sentence emphasizes the pleasure of illness narratives.

82. From Sydney J. Krause and S. W. Reid's appended "Historical Essay," in Brown, *Arthur Mervyn*, 449.

83. Ibid., 130.

84. For another reading of these two responses, see Roberts, "Gothic Enlightenment." While her broader idea of alternate forms of the social contract proposed by *Arthur Mervyn* is compelling, I respectfully disagree with her analysis of the novel's trajectory and with her reading of disease and contagion in the novel as largely mobilized by Brown for metaphorical ends. As an example of the divergences in our approaches, Roberts reads this second scenario

of individuals falling ill upon hearing rumors of the fever as a "fail[ure] to distinguish fact from fiction . . . in Brown's view, [this] amounts to contracting the disease" (314). Furthermore, Roberts reads Mervyn's mockery of the victims as "adaptable" in the face of a "paradigm shift" (315).

85. See, e.g., "The Man at Home" (1798) and *Ormond* (1799).

86. Sontag, *Illness as Metaphor*, 3.

87. Charles Brockden Brown to James Brown, July 26, 1799, quoted in Dunlap, *Memoirs*, 205.

88. Brown published the first nine chapters between June and August 1798. Smith died in September. The first full volume of the novel was published on its own in the spring of 1799 and the second volume appeared in the fall of 1800. See Philip Barnard and Stephen Shapiro's introduction to their edition of *Arthur Mervyn*, ix. All subsequent page numbers are from the Kent State reprint.

89. For other readings on the relationship between narrative and contagious disease, see especially Wald, *Contagious* and Silva, *Miraculous Plagues*.

90. I also mean inoculation in its more contemporary, prophylactic sense, though in the eighteenth century it also referred more broadly to the transmission of diseases.

91. Rush, *An Account*, 31–32.

92. Gaudet, "Fear," 23.

93. "Inoculate," *Oxford English Dictionary*, http://www.oed.com.ezproxy.bpl.org/view /Entry/96368?redirectedFrom=inoculate#eid.

94. Ibid.

95. Ibid.

96. Gaudet, "Fear," 23.

97. Darwin, *A Plan*, 45. See Gaudet, "Fear," 63.

98. Here Rousseau is using "inoculation" in its broader sense to mean the transmission of love and disease.

99. Seth, "Textually Transmitted Diseases," 136–37.

100. Ibid., 127. For more on inoculation in French literature and medicine, see ibid. It seems, here, that Rétif de La Bretonne is playing with two discourses: one in which illness is morally instructive, and one in which inoculation provided a metaphor for inculcating moral values. Literalizing the analogy of inoculation, the story troubles these moralistic formulations when the "cynical lover['s]" actions unnecessarily endanger his paramour (quoted in ibid., 127).

101. See Gaudet's argument in "Fear," chap. 2, for a longer discussion of Darwin, Murray, and "inoculation logic."

102. Quoted in Dunlap, *Memoirs*, 87.

103. Ibid., 45.

104. Brown, *Arthur Mervyn*, 3.

105. Hale, "The Profits," 61; Justus, "Arthur Mervyn," 304. Also see Michael Warner's praise of righteous Mervyn in his chapter on the novel in *Letters of the Republic*.

106. Brancaccio, "Studied Ambiguities," 22; Berthoff, introduction, xvii; Russo, "The Chameleon," title page.

107. Goddu, *Gothic America*, 40.

108. Davidson, *The Revolution and the Word*, 303.

109. Like Smith, Brown saw circulation as the key mechanism of medical and political health. The term has long been central to *Arthur Mervyn* criticism. From Tompkins, "The Importance of Merely Circulating" to more recent scholarship, critics have detailed the novel's

medical, economic, discursive, and political networks of exchange (Tompkins, *Sensational Designs*, chap. 3). Nevertheless, critics are split on the salubriousness of circulation in the novel. As with Rush and Smith, Brown recognized that circulation was the key to both life and disease. Scholars who privilege the corrosive potential of flow trace the dangers that circulating goods, bodies, and information pose to the nation as they course through Philadelphia's twisted, clotted, ill-tended arteries. Following a contagionist model, for example, Andy Doolen sees "the novel enact[ing] a crisis of national identity in which engagement with and dependence on West Indian markets inflicts a deadly pestilence on citizens living in Philadelphia" (*Fugitive Empire*, 77). Similarly, Sean Goudie writes that the movement of West Indian currency destabilizes national order: "Brown transforms the Hamiltonian empire for commerce into a chronotopic zone of instability wherein West Indian and Anglo-American cultures and commodities circulate in ways that resist US attempts to sustain hierarchical distinctions between them" (*Creole America*, 174). Teresa Goddu has traced the novel's "diseased discourse," which Louis Kirk McAuley argues moves "virus-like" through republican print culture (Goddu, *Gothic America*, 31; McAuley, "'Periodic Visitations,'" 308). For other recent work on circulation and contagion in *Arthur Mervyn*, see Teresa Goddu, "Diseased Discourse" in *Gothic America*; McAuley, "'Periodic Visitations'"; Doolen, *Fugitive Empire*; Goudie, *Creole America*; and Roberts, "Gothic Enlightenment." For the seminal work on the politics of Brown's fiction, see Christophersen, *The Apparition in the Glass*, and for more recent discussion, see Otter, *Philadelphia Stories*, esp. 58–69.

110. Brown, *Arthur Mervyn*, 159.

111. Ibid., 144.

112. Ibid.

113. Ibid., 5.

114. Ibid.

115. Edward Stevens was a physician who fought with Rush over the theory and treatment of yellow fever. His belief in its contagiousness came from his experience with the disease in St. Croix. For more on Stevens and his disagreements with Rush, see Stevens's letter in Rush, *An Account*, 216–23.

116. Sian Roberts has made similar observations about Mervyn's movement offering a model of contagion. Nevertheless, in her reading this pattern serves as a broader metaphor for a reworking of the social contract rather than more directly as an experiment with medical theory. See, especially, her section titled "The Contagion Model" in "Gothic Enlightenment," 313–18.

117. Goddu, *Gothic America*, 43.

118. Brown, *Arthur Mervyn*, 143, 181, 355, 379.

119. Cristobal Silva has remarked similarly of the movement of the con man Craig in *Ormond*, "If Craig's actions mimic a form of secret contagion, it is no accident that the Dudley family's tribulations begin with his crime and reach their climax during the yellow fever epidemic" ("Monstrous Plots," 247). Silva also astutely observes of *Ormond* that "the novel therefore enacts the tensions that it describes while trying to use those enactments to anchor its formal and epistemological structure" (248).

120. Waterman, *Republic of Intellect*, 220. For this different take on communication in *Arthur Mervyn*, see Waterman, "Arthur Mervyn's Medical Repository" and *Republic of Intellect*. While Waterman's argument begins aligned with this one, observing that Brown's novel "could serve as a prophylactic, particularly if it conjures up terror in order to habituate or perhaps even to inoculate a reader to fear's unhealthy side effects," he nonetheless argues that the

novel stabilizes these fears through Mervyn's developing medical and narrative authority (*Republic of Intellect*, 191, 214–30). Waterman argues that the novel works to distribute healthy medical information through the republic, despite recognizing its "portrait of communicative chaos" ("Arthur Mervyn's Medical Repository," 233). Taking Brown's preface at its word, others have argued that *Arthur Mervyn* and Brown's other novels "[share] with the medical writings of other Friendly Club members . . . attempts at bodily, narrative, and audience control. The ideas 'afloat' in the community, which Brown noted in his preface, were as dangerous as the floating miasmata that generated the pest" (Waterman, *Republic of Intellect*, 230).

121. Nearing the end, Mervyn feverishly exclaims, "Move on, my quill! wait not for my guidance. Reanimated with thy master's spirit, all-airy light! An hey day rapture!" (Brown, *Arthur Mervyn*, 413). Waterman reads Mervyn's love at the end of the novel as disease (*Republic of Intellect*, 232).

122. For a similar reading, see Wisecup, "Communicating Disease," 254–68.

123. For the metaphor of contagion in *Arthur Mervyn*, see Doolen, "Imperial Geographies and *Arthur Mervyn*," in *Fugitive Empire* and Goudie, "Charles Brockden Brown's West Indian Specie(s)," in *Creole America*.

124. Silva, "Monstrous Plots," 250–51.

125. Brown, *Arthur Mervyn*, 135, original emphasis.

126. Ibid., 165.

127. Much of this work is on pathography, a genre Anne Hunsaker Hawkins defines as "a form of autobiography or biography that describes personal experiences of illness, treatment, and sometimes death. 'What it is like to have cancer' or 'how I survived my heart attack' or 'what it means to have AIDS'" (*Reconstructing Illness*, 1). Pathographies are a particular postwar twentieth-/twenty-first-century form. Nevertheless, illness narratives date back much further. The evolution of the illness narrative into the specific form of pathography is beyond the scope of this argument, but others have argued illness memoir recuperates the personal experience of the sick in the face of professional medicine's exclusionary position. For arguments along these lines, see Frank, *The Wounded Storyteller*.

128. Hawkins, *Reconstructing Illness*, 2.

129. Ibid.

130. Ibid.

131. Ibid., 3.

132. I am conscious of my use of anachronism here. Cristobal Silva has convincingly argued that anachronism "provides for a fruitful analysis . . . precisely because it defamiliarizes narrative histories that segregate [distinct discursive modes] into their modern disciplines, and it transforms our relation to the materials of literary history" (*Miraculous Plagues*, 12).

133. No instance of this narrative instability is more revealing than the story of Clavering. Early in the novel, Arthur Mervyn describes his attachment to the young man who arrives sick on his family's doorstep, sketches a portrait of himself, and dies. In those three days, Mervyn describes the deep attachment both he and his mother developed for their dying, possibly deceitful guest. Clavering tells Mervyn that "some mistress who had proved faithless" drove him insane, but "his speeches seemed . . . like the rantings of an actor, to be rehearsed by rote, or for the sake of exercise" (29–30). Clavering quickly catches "the fever" (it is unclear which since it predates the 1793 epidemic) and dies. Nevertheless, Clavering—whose physical description and storyline echo Mervyn's and whose name comes from the Latin root for key—seems to offer some possibility for unlocking the secret to all of the confusion, lies, and misrepresentations offered by the novel. After all, it is Clavering's self-portrait that Mervyn bundles at the

center of his worldly possessions when he enters the city and Clavering's house (and possibly even clothes) that Mervyn comes to inhabit. Mrs. Wentworth, the only remaining representative of Clavering's family, is the one who encourages Mervyn to record the testimony that composes the novel. When Mervyn loses his bundle with Clavering's image at its core, the narrative suggests that were Mervyn able to repossess the picture of his double and were the reader able to decipher Clavering's fate (Did Mervyn see him die? Is he in Europe? Is the testimony of the South Carolina planter true?), all—we might hope—circulating narrative elements could be comfortably resolved. Exceeding any plausible explanation offered by the novel, Clavering's uncanny resemblance to Mervyn haunts the narrative. If we could only learn more about Clavering, we might better know Mervyn. But the novel resists. Though Mervyn locates the lost image, it is never returned to him. And though Mervyn has ostensibly (accidentally?) entered the city as a body double for Clavering, we are never sure what happened to the original. Unlike disease stories in which narrative sutures earlier events to a post-trauma life story, narrative and identity in *Arthur Mervyn* remain fractured.

134. Dawes, "Fictional Feeling," 438.

135. Brown, *Ormond*, 55.

136. Dawes, "Fictional Feeling," 439.

137. Ibid.

138. Ibid.

139. See, e.g., Brown, "Walstein's School of History: From the German of Krants of Gotha [first part]," "Walstein's School of History: From the German of Krants of Gotha [second and last part]," and "The Difference Between History and Romance."

140. Again, "Walstein's School of History" is a good source for Brown's thoughts about why fiction was better than fact for motivating moral action.

141. The quotations in this paragraph are from a March 11, 1800 letter in the Margaret Bayard Smith Papers, Box 10, Reel 6–7 at the Library of Congress. I am grateful to Bryan Waterman for suggesting this evidence to me. For more on this letter and the Brown-Bayard exchange, see Waterman, *Republic of Intellect*, 289n137.

142. Compiling information from a number of doctors, Smith offers some initial observations on what degree of viral exposure is necessary and what conditions are the best predictors of patient outcomes. Smith draws no conclusions but muses, "It seems highly interesting to determine how far [inoculation's] influence extends; and whether any, and what, effect is to be attributed to the greater or lesser quantity of variolous matter, introduced into the system, by inoculation," then invites others to weigh in on the subject ("Inoculation"). The yellow fever vaccine was not invented until the twentieth century.

143. The inoculation trope repeatedly emerges in critical discussions of Brown's novels, though it is put to a variety of uses. This critical phenomenon is notable since no yellow fever vaccine existed in the eighteenth century. In Goudie's chapter on *Arthur Mervyn*, for example, he treats inoculation as a metaphor of West Indian political, social, and economic contagion, arguing Mervyn's role "can only be performed by an agent hardened through exposure. As the practice of inoculation suggests, Mervyn can contain the potential contagion signified by the West Indies only after being exposed to the pervasive presence of West Indian figures circulating through the American urban landscape" ("On the Origin of American Specie[s]" in *Revising Charles Brockden Brown*, 69).

144. Dunlap, *The Life*, 57.

145. See the introduction of Herzig's *Suffering for Science* for more on Ffirth, Reed, and the history of yellow fever self-experimentation.

146. Ffirth, *Inaugural Dissertation*, 46.

147. Ibid., 54–56.

148. Ibid., 56.

149. Ibid., 60.

150. Reizenstein had only been in the United States a few years when he wrote *The Mysteries of New Orleans*, but already he was engaged in scientific, medical, and literary work. He served in the medical service for Louisiana during the Civil War, wrote amateur entomology, and combined the two in his radical novel about New Orleans (Rowan, introduction to Reizenstein, *Mysteries*, xxiii–xxv).

151. Ibid., 417.

152. For an analysis of the political import of yellow fever in *Clotel*, see Wisecup, "'The Progress of the Heat Within.'" As the next chapter will illustrate, abolitionists also connected the cholera pandemic to Atlantic slavery.

153. See Bryant, Holmes, and Barrett's scientific analysis of the origins of yellow fever in "Out of Africa."

154. Reizenstein exemplifies this difficulty through an expedition, through which "an invisible hand led the captain astray and took him a hundred miles away from the home of the *Mantis religiosa*. The captain later reported to Washington that he'd found the source of the Red River, but the fact that he had not discovered the mysterious plant proved that he had made a great, if excusable, error," an error also made by Alexander von Humboldt and a "Lieutent Pike" (*Mysteries*, 413).

155. See Reed et al., "The Etiology of Yellow Fever."

156. See Pernick, "Contagion and Culture."

157. Quoted in ibid., 860. For an excellent history of contagion and culture across centuries, see Pernick, "Contagion and Culture."

CHAPTER 3

1. Poe, "The Sphinx," 15.

2. For a classic treatment of cholera in the nineteenth century, see Rosenberg, *The Cholera Years*.

3. Whooley, *Knowledge*, 60.

4. See Whooley, *Knowledge*; Starr, *Social Transformation*; Breslaw, *Lotions, Potions*; etc.

5. For example, Starr, *The Social Transformation* cites the title page of Gunn, *Domestic Medicine* as a direct assault on physician authority because it claims to offer medical information "in plain language, free of doctor's terms" (34). Nevertheless, Gunn later praises physicians like John Kearsley Mitchell, "whose names have so much weight," for their efforts to spread useful medical knowledge around the country; for Gunn they are "some of the greatest medical men in the United States" (*Gunn's Domestic Medicine*, 140). Gunn cites Benjamin Rush twenty-six times. See *Gunn's Domestic Medicine* (1835).

6. Poe, "The Sphinx," 15.

7. Ibid.

8. Ibid., 16.

9. For other approaches to the problem of perception in "The Sphinx" see Marks, "The Art of Corrective Vision" and Schenkel, "Disease and Vision."

10. For more on the "epistemic contests" created by the cholera pandemic, see Whooley, *Knowledge*.

11. Brigham, *A Treatise*, 256; Lynch, "Cholera in Paris," 268.

12. For more on image making in the early republic, see Barnhill, "Transformations in Pictorial Printing." The rise of medical cartography owed much to the advent of lithography, a revolutionary technology that had arrived in the United States just fourteen years earlier (Barnhill, "Transformations," 433). While earlier maps were pricey affairs, made slowly, intended for upper-class clients, and cut on metal plates that wore out, lithography transferred drawings directly to the page and in far greater numbers. Lithography was cheaper and faster—and it could produce thousands more images. According to Barnhill, this process "transformed the business of making and selling prints" because they "were easy to produce in abundance. In the 1820s and 1830s, they were being sold directly to consumers for pennies instead of dollars" (434–35).

13. For another take on maps and fear during the pandemics, see Sarah Schuetze, "Mapping a Demon Malady," which appeared after the completion of this manuscript.

14. For this prehistory in New England, see Silva, *Miraculous Plagues*.

15. For more work on this early history of medical cartography, see Barrett, "Finke's Map"; Jarcho, "Yellow Fever, Cholera, and the Beginnings of Medical Cartography"; Koch, "Knowing Its Place"; and Stevenson, "Putting Disease on the Map."

16. This date is based on a March 14, 1832, review of the book in the *Boston Medical and Surgical Journal*. The 1831 title of the map suggests it may have been commissioned sometime before, but the recorded incidents of cholera continue through March 1832.

17. Tacitus, "Communication," n.p.

18. Ibid.

19. Scouttenten, *Medical and Topographical History*, v–vi.

20. "Death of Dr. A. Sidney Doane."

21. Scouttenten, *Medical and Topographical History*, vi.

22. "Cholera in America."

23. Ibid.

24. See Rosenberg, *The Cholera Years*, 75.

25. Quoted in ibid., 74.

26. Caruthers, *The Kentuckian*, 2:23, 6, 28.

27. Tanner, *Geographical and Statistical Account*, iii.

28. Ibid., iv, original emphasis.

29. For more on Brigham and Tanner's maps, see Susan Schulten's terrific book *Mapping the Nation*.

30. Since the hand-drawn lines in the two volumes depict the same content, I have assumed that they were completed at the same time as the "red lines" Doane mentions.

31. The copies at the Huntington Library and the U.S. National Library of Medicine end in Edenton, North Carolina, while the copy at Princeton University ends in Norfolk, Virginia. This appears to be a hand-drawn error, but it could also reveal individuals continuing to trace the course of the disease, though that is less likely given the generally sloppy tracing of cholera's trajectory and the otherwise similar content of the maps.

32. "The Cholera."

33. Mitchell, *Five Essays*, 110, 107.

34. Ibid., 107.

35. The relationship of mapping to the imagination is more complicated than this failure suggests. Many have rightly connected medical mapmaking to a rising interest in empirical methods like statistical thinking, but, as Averill's novel suggests, the new geography was also, necessarily, deeply imaginative (see Koch, *Disease Maps* and Schulten, *Mapping the Nation*, especially). Representing the world from above, geographic writers needed to extrapolate from particulars and occupy perspectives that could not be directly perceived. The inspiration for American geographical thinking in the nineteenth century came from Alexander von Humboldt. In her 1814 translation of Humboldt's work on the Americas Helen Maria Williams wrote that he had "his peculiar manner of contemplating nature in all her overwhelming greatness. The appropriate character of his writings is the faculty he possesses of raising the mind to general ideas without neglecting individual facts; and while he appears only to address himself to our reason, he has the secret of awakening the imagination and being understood by the heart" (Humboldt, *Personal Narrative*, 1:ix). Of this quality Laura Dassow Walls eloquently argues, "The Humboldtian imagination could link individual facts with mind-stretching generalizations and in the same gesture, material reality with poetry and feeling. Head and heart were always present; imagination mediated between them, making science into poetry that was true" (*Passage to the Cosmos*, 43).

36. Fear, one New York physician argued, could enact "a more specific operation upon the human body, than any other passion; it spasmodically contracts the mouths of thousands of our perspiring or exhaling vessels, flings the acrid perspirable matter upon the insides of our digestive organs, which it stimulates, and causes by abstracting much of the watery part of our blood, a looseness and congestion in our bowels, the very proximate cause of the Epidemic Cholera" (Seeger, *A Lecture*, 25).

37. Here my argument departs from that of Emily Waples, who reads "The Fall of the House of Usher" as an example of Poe's "miasmatic imagination" ("'Invisible Agents'"). Also see Walker, "Legitimate Sources," for the connection of Usher to miasma theory.

38. The history in this chapter revises the claims of mycological historian Geoffery Clough Ainsworth, who dates the beginning of medical mycology "precisely" to a moment a few years later, sometime during 1842–44, out of which the fungal theory of cholera grew in the late 1840s (*History*, 8). That moment, Ainsworth writes, was when "David Gruby in Paris published a series of six short, but outstanding, papers in which he showed, very convincingly, that four types of ringworm and also thrush were mycotic in origin" (8). "The mycotic origin of ringworm," Ainsworth explains, "provided inspiration for the claim that fungi were also responsible for other diseases, particularly Asiatic cholera, a pandemic of which began in 1846 and spread to Europe" (40).

39. See Frank and Magistrale, *Poe Encyclopedia*, 125. Scholars have long identified Poe's avid interest in medicine. Margaret Alterton, for example, describes "Poe's familiarity with medical journals. He speaks of the 'high authority and merit' of the '*Chirurgical Journal of Leipsic*.' He speaks, too, with more than ordinary interest of the *London Lancet* . . . [and] welcomes its republication in America, for it gives, he says, facts that concern not only the physician, but those concerning human vitality" (*Origins*, 18), and I. M. Walker writes, "It is known that Poe was a keen student of current scientific opinion including medicine, and it is extremely unlikely that he could have written such convincing realism and accuracy about madness and crime, had he not been familiar with the opinions of 'medical philosophers' then in vogue" ("Legitimate Sources," 588).

40. In addition to scholarship on miasma, there is a long history of scholarship on health-related aspects of the story such as hypochondria (Butler, "Usher's Hypochondriasis"), por-

phyria (Leland and Kim "Poe-phyria"), phrenology (Hungerford, "Poe and Phrenology"), nervous fever (Sloane, "Usher's Nervous Fever"), and vampirism (Bailey, "What Happens"; Kendall, "The Vampire Motif").

41. Poe, "Murders," 167.

42. Wimsatt, "Poe and the Chess Automaton," 138. Mitchell's son Silas Weir Mitchell was also captivated by the automaton and wrote a mock eulogy for the Turk, "The Last of a Veteran Chess Player," after it burned in an 1854 fire.

43. For another story about these rising mechanistic models, see Poe, "The Man That Was Used Up" (1839).

44. Poe, "Usher," 145.

45. Ibid.

46. Ibid.

47. Hoffman, *Poe Poe*, 296; Bailey, "What Happens," 452.

48. Mitchell, *Five Essays*, 50–51.

49. Poe, "Usher," 146.

50. Ibid.

51. Ibid.

52. Ibid.

53. Ibid., 149.

54. Ibid.

55. Mitchell, *Five Essays*, 41. Scientists had known about the existence of cells since the seventeenth century when Robert Hooke first discovered them, but new breakthroughs in microscopy allowed two German scientists, Theodor Schwann and Jacob Schleiden, to propose a revolutionary theory in the late 1830s: that the cell was the basic unit of life. In would take until 1866 for Ernst Haeckel to propose a third kingdom that was neither plant nor animal. For a useful summary of the history of cell theory, see Wolpert, "Evolution of Cell Theory."

56. Poe, "Usher," 146. See, e.g., Bailey, "What Happens," 451–52 and Spitzer, "A Reinterpretation," 357.

57. Poe, "Usher," 149.

58. *Tales of the Grotesque and Arabesque* was published in between, but *Graham's* announced its appearance just four months after the magazine publication of "Usher." Wiley and Putnam's *Tales* would have been a step up for the author, since Wiley and Putnam was a transatlantic publishing house. It is this later version that has been widely reproduced.

59. Poe, *Tales*, 74.

60. Poe, "Usher," 149.

61. Mitchell was also closely connected to other figures in this book. In addition to being the father of Silas Weir Mitchell, he was Nathaniel Chapman's mentee. Mitchell was so taken with Chapman, who will appear more extensively in the next chapter, that he named another of his sons Nathaniel Chapman Mitchell.

62. Lippard, *Quaker City*, 158.

63. Poe, *Complete Works*, 11:241–42.

64. Chivers, *Life of Poe*, 43–44; Lloyd, *Murder*, 117.

65. For more on the daguerreotype of Poe and a figure who is likely Mitchell taken at the Academy of Natural Sciences, see McFarland and Bennett, "The Image of Edgar Allan Poe." Mitchell and Poe had a close relationship, but Mitchell was just one of Poe's physician-poet friends. Thomas Chivers, Joseph Snodgrass, and Pliny Earle were among the other physician-poets who played prominent roles in Poe's life and whose poetry Poe published and praised.

Chivers would, most notably, offer Poe a home in Georgia and later accused Poe of plagiarizing his poetry, and Snodgrass was the old friend Poe sought out during the days before his death in Baltimore.

66. Reprints appear in Mitchell, *Five Essays*. Mitchell also edited an American edition of Faraday, *Chemical Manipulation* in 1831.

67. Mitchell, *Five Essays*, 291, 304.

68. Ibid., 324–25, emphasis added.

69. "Cryptogamous."

70. Mitchell, *Five Essays*, 47.

71. Ibid., 37, original emphasis.

72. Ibid., 51, original emphasis.

73. Ibid., original emphasis.

74. Ibid., 36, 57, 48, 56, 38–39.

75. Ibid., 60–62.

76. Ibid., 39–40.

77. Ibid.

78. Ibid.

79. Ibid., 24.

80. Poe, "Usher," 145.

81. Mitchell, *Five Essays*, 35.

82. For examples of "tribe" language, see ibid., 29, 50, 56, 75, 105.

83. Ibid., 47.

84. See, e.g., Cowdell, *A Disquisition on the Pestilential Cholera* and Budd, *Malignant Cholera*.

85. Poe to Maria Clemm, July 7, 1849: "I have been *so* ill—have had the cholera, or spasms quite as bad, and can now hardly hold the pen. The very instant you get this, *come* to me. The joy of seeing you will almost compensate for our sorrows. We can but die together."

86. Graves, "Thompson the Confederate," 182.

87. Ibid. Thompson would later publish a fictionalized version of this story as "The Advent of the Cholera."

88. Rosenberg, *The Cholera Years*, 47–53.

89. Ibid., 121–25.

90. Ibid., 126. For more on religious responses to cholera, see especially chaps. 2, 3, and 7.

91. For more on this chronology, see Hank Trent's notes in his edition of Williams, *Narrative*, 68–69.

92. Ibid., 27.

93. Douglass, *My Bondage*, 129.

94. Quoted in Stowe, *Life*, 120.

95. Quoted in ibid., 124.

96. Perhaps Stowe originally conceived her theory that cholera was divine retribution for slavery because the first cholera epidemic of 1831–32 coincided with Nat Turner's 1831 revolt and the 1831 slave rebellion in Jamaica.

97. Stowe, *Life*, 128.

98. Stowe, *Dred*, 2:91.

99. Ibid., 2:91.

100. Ibid., 2:113.

101. Ibid.

102. Ibid., 2:114.

103. Ibid., 2:90.

104. For example, the first case the doctor encounters "'presented itself in an entirely different aspect from what he had expected. The remedies,' he said, 'did not work as he anticipated; the case was a peculiar one.' Alas! before the three months were over, poor doctor, you found many peculiar cases!" (ibid., 2:115).

105. Ibid., 2:111–12.

106. Ibid., 2:274. Schoolman rightly notes the "uncanny" nature of the Dismal Swamp (*Abolitionist Geographies*, 171). Murison likewise observes that Stowe "overturn[s . . .] medical classification in her description of the swamp" (*The Politics of Anxiety*, 133).

107. Stowe, *Dred*, 2:274.

108. Ibid., 2:6.

109. Ibid.

110. Schoolman, *Abolitionist Geographies*, 171.

111. Stowe, *Dred*, 2:275.

112. *Thirteenth Annual Report*, 193.

113. Levine, introduction to Stowe, *Dred*, xv.

114. For prominent scholarship situating *Blake* as a response to *Uncle Tom's Cabin*, see Gilroy, *Black Atlantic*, 27; for a book that argues for *Blake* as a response to *Dred*, see Levine, *Martin Delany*, 177. As Levine notes, part of this argument in *The Black Atlantic* is based on a misattribution: "Gilroy incorrectly states that *Blake* 'took its epigraph from Harriet Beecher Stowe's *Uncle Tom's Cabin*'" (*Martin Delany*, 292).

115. Williams, "Delany, Martin R.," 373.

116. Quoted in Levine, *Martin Delany*, 25.

117. Delany, *Condition*, 143–44. As Delany clarifies, Wells was trained at Washington Medical College but never graduated, perhaps over a dispute with the faculty.

118. For more on *Blake* in terms of Delany's science, see Britt Rusert's wonderful article "Delany's Comet."

119. Delany, *Blake*, 313. All subsequent page references refer to Floyd J. Miller's edition of *Blake*.

120. Delany, after all, writes in response to the political effects of *Uncle Tom's Cabin*. Cathy Davidson has argued for a longer genealogy of the novel's political engagement: "The early American novel carved out its literary territory in the here and now of the contemporary American social and political scene and commented upon and criticized that scene, but left the solution of these problems up to the individual reader—the indeterminacy of the solution as basic to the form of incisiveness of its critique" (*The Revolution and the Word*, 303).

121. "The writer of said work, as will be seen, is also the author of a new theory of the Attraction of Planets, Cohesion, &c. and is at the head of a scientific corps of colored gentlemen." *Anglo-African Magazine* 1.1 (1859): 17–21.

122. This advertisement appeared on the wrapper of at least every volume of the 1859 monthly (collection held at the American Antiquarian Society).

123. Delany, *Blake*, 41.

124. Ibid., emphasis added.

125. Rosenberg, *The Cholera Years*, 1.

126. Jeffrey Amherst wrote to Henry Bouquet on July 16, 1763, "You will do well to inoculate the Indians by means of blankets, as well as to try every other method that can serve

to extirpate this execrable race," to which Bouquet wrote he would "try to inoculate the bastards with some blankets that may fall into their hands, and take care not to get the disease myself. As it is a pity to expose good men against them, I wish we could make use of the Spanish methods, to hunt them with English dogs" (quoted in Anderson, *Crucible of War*, 809). (Here Amherst uses the term "inoculate" in its alternative eighteenth-century sense, meaning to transmit disease.)

127. Delany, *Blake*, 83.

128. Ibid., 114.

129. Ibid., 115.

130. Rosenberg, *The Cholera Years*, 101.

CHAPTER 4

By 1848, the Greek for sympathy as "with suffering" was dropped from the definition, as I discuss in the following chapter.

1. The key to Morton's image was printed on the back of the page.

2. See, e.g., Caldwell, "The Strange Death of the Animated Cadaver," in which she describes the fundamental changes in nineteenth-century medical illustration from "the 'before' of the animated cadaver" to "the 'after' of the faceless corpse" (343). Daston and Galison (*Objectivity*) have identified this as a shift toward objectivity in the latter half of the nineteenth century. As the orangutan illustrates, these perspectives also existed simultaneously.

3. See Bird's humanistic illustration of a different orangutan in Harlan, "Description of a New Species of Orang," in *Medical and Physical Researches*, 9–18. The essay was likely composed in 1831.

4. See, e.g., the human figures by Andreas Vesalius (1514–1564), often considered the father of modern anatomy, in *Bruxellensis suorum de Humani corporis fabrica librorum Epitome*. For a discussion of Vesalius's nudes in the context of the relationship between anatomy and sexual difference, see Londa Schiebinger, "Skeletons in the Closet."

5. Harlan understood that he could never have ethically performed his study on a human hermaphrodite, and thus the Borneo orangutan avoided the "great difficulties," as he called them, such a subject "might have occasioned . . . in a case of legal medicine" (*Medical and Physical Researches*, 24).

6. Ibid., xiv.

7. The *Lancet*'s image includes only the orangutan's torso, which nonetheless draws more attention to the animal's human-looking face.

8. For this history of sex, see Schiebinger, *Nature's Body* and Laqueur, *Making Sex*. Laqueur explains that while earlier ideas about the sexes "arrayed [them] according to their degree of metaphysical perfection, their vital heat along an axis whose telos was male," this view "gave way by the late eighteenth century to a new model of radical dimorphism, of biological divergence. An anatomy and physiology of incommensurability replaced a metaphysics of hierarchy in the representation of women in relation to man" (*Making Sex*, 5–6). For a complicating view of this account, see Stolberg, "A Woman Down to Her Bones."

9. Harlan, *Medical and Physical Researches*, 13. See Poe, "Murders."

10. In another essay Harlan quoted an anthropomorphizing letter he had received about another orangutan: "She was of a very gentle disposition, only monkeys displeased her. . . . She always walked in the upright attitude, and could even run very fast: when walking on a table,

or among china-ware, she was very careful not to break any thing; when climbing she used only her hands; her knees resembled those of man. . . . When sick she whined like a child, and was fond of being nursed. . . . She was commonly melancholy and pensive. When answering the call of nature on board of ship, she would hold on to a rope and evacuate into the sea" (*Medical and Physical Researches*, 10–11). Bird drew the illustrations.

11. For more on Richard Harlan and his relationship to Morton, see Fabian, *Skull Collectors*, esp. 19–21.

12. For foundational scholarship that informs this chapter's broad summaries of the period, see Pessen, *Jacksonian America*; Remini, *The Life of Andrew Jackson*; Schlesinger, *The Age of Jackson*, and Wilentz, *Chants Democratic*. For more recent scholarship on the period, see, for example, Howe, *What Hath God Wrought*; Reynolds, *Waking Giant*; and Wilentz, *The Rise of American Democracy*.

13. For this French influence on American medicine see Warner, *Against the Spirit of the System*.

14. For cards to Chapman's lectures in the University of Pennsylvania Bird Collection (Box 26, Folder 334) and lecture notes in the Miscellaneous Manuscripts collection (Box 2, Folder 13).

15. Richman, *Brightest Ornament*, 1. For a full biographical treatment, see ibid., especially pp. 55–63 for a more complete discussion of the Rush-Chapman controversy.

16. Ibid., 5.

17. Richerand, *Elements of Physiology*, 580, 594. From the textbook *Elements of Physiology* by Anthelme Richerand and edited by Chapman.

18. See Dunglison, *Medical Lexicon* (1839).

19. Cullen developed solidism in eighteenth-century Edinburgh. In Cullen's version of solidism, the solid parts of the body were responsible for life and health with nerves responsible for communication between organs.

20. Richerand, *Elements of Physiology*, 40.

21. Rush, *Letters*, 2:1061.

22. Chapman, *Discourses*, 1:42–43.

23. Chapman, *Chapman's Lectures*, 100.

24. Chapman, *Discourses*, 1:45.

25. Ibid., 1:46. Chapman could be even more direct. Distilling the difference between his theory and Rush's, Chapman paves the way for his own American physiology: "My theory of the operation of medicines is of modern date, and alleges, that they all act by exciting a local impression which is extended through the medium of sympathy. By many, however, it is still believed, that certain articles, at least, enter the circulation and produce their effects in this way. This latter hypothesis is evidently a relict of humoral pathology. By the believers of that sect, it was held, that disease consists in a deprivation of the blood, 'from a too great tenuity or viscidity, by an excess of acid or alkaline acrimony, by morbific matter entering from without, or generated within'" (ibid., 1:42). The attack is barely veiled: "Many," by whom he means Rush and his followers, "still believed, that certain articles, at least, enter the circulation, and produce their effects this way." Unwilling to concede any ground, Chapman criticizes the veracity, originality, and timeliness of Rush's medical philosophy. Rush's unitary theory is only a "left over of 'humoral pathology'" that even his mentors in Edinburgh had left behind. Chapman's attack is notably unfair, but it is useful in understanding his reimagining of American medicine. Aligning Rush with early eighteenth-century Dutch medicine, Chapman denies the Americanness of his mentor's thinking and severs the intellectual link between Rush and

Cullen. By doing this, Chapman could claim his own role as Cullen's descendant even as he moves beyond Cullen's solidism to craft his own medical vision.

26. Ibid., 1:51.

27. Chapman note in Richerand, *Elements of Physiology*, 40.

28. Chapman's interest in the stomach likely stemmed from its therapeutic value: the stomach could receive medicines and transmit their effects sympathetically to the body's diseased organs. The stomach was a more central nexus of stimuli than the brain: "No viscus or organ, not even the brain itself, can be compared to it, in this respect, or which occupies so important a station in the animal economy" (Chapman, *Elements*, 80). In addition to the argument offered above, see Nathaniel Chapman's editor's note in Murray, *System of Materia Medica*, 98–99.

29. From John E. Espy's notes of Chapman, *Elements*, 76.

30. At the time he edited the text, Chapman believed he would shortly be hired to take Rush's place as professor of the Institutes of Medicine at the University of Pennsylvania (Richerand, *Elements of Physiology*, iii). "Nor is my primary object entirely defeated," he wrote, after learning he had not gotten the post. "As I must necessarily introduce into my lectures on Materia Medica a variety of speculations relative to the laws of the animal economy, the work will still be exceedingly useful to my class" (ibid.). Bird, who graduated in 1826, took Chapman's classes and likely read this text, since Chapman had his 1813 edition reprinted in Philadelphia four times in the eight years before Bird graduated (1818, 1821, 1823, 1825).

31. Richerand, *Elements of Physiology*, 35.

32. Ibid., 35–36.

33. Chapman, *Discourses*, 1:51.

34. Chapman, *Elements*, 1:80.

35. Ibid., 1:73.

36. Ibid., 1:79–80.

37. Ibid., 1:82.

38. Ibid., 1:84.

39. Ibid.

40. Ibid.

41. See discussion of sympathy in Chapter 1.

42. Horner, "Observations," 291.

43. Ibid.

44. Bird, *Difficulties*, 16.

45. Richerand, *Elements of Physiology*, 63.

46. Park, Daston, and Galison, "Bacon," 288.

47. Horner, "Observations," 297.

48. Ibid., 286.

49. Issues of particularity and bioethics merged in an 1830 debate in the *New-York Medical Journal*. Physician S. W. Avery looked to clear himself from what he viewed as accusations that he had inappropriately used vivisection. His reviewer had written, "We object to this application of the results of experiments made on the digestive organs of dogs, or other animals, for the purpose of proving the human powers of the human stomach. It is *brutalizing it—reducing it to the filthy disposition of 'returning to its vomit.' More practical and satisfactory means of observation and experience, are abundant*" (Graves, "Communication," 510, original emphasis). From this Avery understood that the journal critiqued him for improperly applying information gained from physical experiments on dogs to principles of the gastric medicine.

An appalled Avery retorted, "Does the reviewer imagine from my words . . . that I have subjected animals to vivisection, for the purpose of studying their digestion? If so, his zeal 'in the performance of a duty' *he owes to his 'readers and the profession,'* has led him into a *trifling error*" (Graves, "Communication," 510, original emphasis). Looking to clear himself from accusations of animal cruelty, Avery denies vivisecting. But the debate here extends beyond the morality of such experimentation to its epistemological value of drawing analogies between animal and human stomachs, citing other, more appropriate "means of observation and experience." For more on this history of animal rights activism, see Guither, *Animal Rights*.

50. Mandeville, *Fable*, 101.

51. Chapman, *Selected Speeches*, 14.

52. Chapman's journal makes strong claims for an original U.S. medicine. In the prospectus he argues, "Candidly examined, our history will show, that whatever course the energies of our people have been directed, there we are eminently distinguished. . . . It may be safely said, that *in no country is medicine, strictly defined, better understood, or more successfully practised than in the United States.* European physicians do surpass us, in classical education, and in variety, depth and extent of erudition. But in acuteness of penetration, and promptness of remedial resource,—in that species of tact, without which genius is cold, and knowledge inert,—the power whereby the means are accurately adapted to the end, and which in the treatment of disease confers vigour and efficiency, we are perhaps unrivalled" (Chapman, *Philadelphia Journal*, xi, emphasis added). Beginning with innate American "genius," Chapman highlights the link between knowledge and practice in the United States. He admits that Europeans may have read more but Americans' exceptional ability, their "acuteness of penetration, and promptness of remedial resource" offer citizens "perhaps unrivalled" care. Chapman is quick to assign this medical greatness to the combination of American resourcefulness and self-reliance in the absence of European medical institutions and their unfettered learning. Taking a dig at what he perceives to be a stifling, unproductive European medical climate, Chapman argues American doctors are "neither perverted by prejudice, nor enfeebled by any undue reverence for authority." The "medical mind of the country" during times of crisis is "every where open to the reception of new impressions" (ibid., x). In this, Chapman almost echoes Rush's claims about the promise of American medicine lying in an original relationship to the land.

53. Chapman, *Selected Speeches*, 17. In the late eighteenth century, Chapman wrote for the literary journal *Port Folio*. In 1808, his medical career not yet made, Chapman took time out of his physician life to edit five volumes he called *Selected Speeches, Forensick and Parliamentary*, a project he declared would foster "the rising genius of the country" (*Selected Speeches*, 14).

54. Chapman, *Discourses*, 39.

55. Ibid., 38, 39.

56. See, e.g., Chapman, *Lectures*, 6–8.

57. Ibid., 8.

58. Bird, "Notes on Pulmonary Consumption," 1–2. Bird's medical thesis was completed in 1826 and passed in 1827. It is held in the University of Pennsylvania's Collection of Medical Theses on Pulmonary Consumption.

59. Ibid., 2.

60. Ibid.

61. Ibid., 23.

62. Ibid., 34.

63. See nineteenth-century translation by F. Howes in Horace, *The Epodes*, 6.

64. Bird, "Notes on Pulmonary Consumption," 3–4.

65. Ibid., title page.

66. The skull work in *Crania Americana* has been long credited with instantiating a quantified brand of scientific racism that would breed eugenics. For a terrific recent account of Morton's work in *Crania Americana*, see Fabian, *Skull Collectors*, especially chap. 3.

67. Bird to Morton, March 1833 in Kislak Miscellaneous Manuscripts collection, Box 2, Folder 13.

68. Bird, *Life*, 30.

69. Over the course of his life, Bird developed more definitive ideas about Native American difference. The 1837 edition of *Nick of the Woods* delivered a fairly damning portrayal of Native Americans but still with some contrition. In the 1837 preface, Bird wrote that he owed "perhaps, some apology for the hues we have thrown around the Indian portraits in our picture" whereas by 1853, Bird was more confident that he had portrayed "real Indians," each of whom "in his natural barbaric state . . . is a barbarian—and it is not possible he could be anything else" ([1837], 1:vi, [1853] iv–v). Bird flirted with polygenesis in the 1853 edition. On one hand, Bird teased his offended readers by declaring, "The Indian is doubtless a gentleman; but he is a gentleman who wears a very dirty shirt" (iv). On the other hand, he "differed from his critical friends, and from many philanthropists, in believing the Indian to be capable . . . of civilization" (iv).

70. See Traister, "Robert Montgomery Bird."

71. Ann Fabian notes that the naming of Morton's volume displayed his explicit nationalism (*Skull Collectors*, 85).

72. Morton, "Morton's Crania Americana," 404.

73. This map also owed a clear debt to Alexander von Humboldt, who had immensely influenced U.S. geographical thinking (see, e.g., Schulten, *Mapping the Nation*, 85).

74. Morton, *Crania Americana*, 95.

75. Ibid.

76. Ibid., 292.

77. Ibid., 262.

78. Ibid.

79. Ibid., i.

80. Fabian, *Skull Collectors*, 85.

81. Ibid., 88.

82. See Daston and Galison, *Objectivity* for this progression.

83. Morton, *Crania Americana*, 2.

84. For Morton's relationship to polygenism, see Fabian, *Skull Collectors*, chap. 3.

85. In Matthew Rebhorn's essay on *Sheppard Lee*, he calls this an ontological problem.

86. Christopher Looby brilliantly introduces the strangeness of *Sheppard Lee* in his 2008 edition.

87. The reading of sympathy I offer in this chapter owes much to Justine Murison's analysis in her terrific book *The Politics of Anxiety*. Nevertheless, this chapter takes a different approach, reading the novel's exploration of sympathy in terms of Chapman's particular, more-than-nervous medical vision and by approaching *Sheppard Lee* as a medical experiment with dominant notions of health.

88. Bird, *Sheppard Lee*, 86, 373.

89. Ibid., 392.

90. Ibid., 407, 406, 408.

91. Ibid., 407.

92. Ibid., 408.

93. The notes read thus: "When he finds and reenters his own body, and with that steps out of the case, the spectators are all horror-struck; but recovering courage, as he decamps, they start after, headed by the abhorred doctor. He gets into a ship (being in Europe,) reaches America," Kislak Bird Collection, Box 11, Folder 259.

94. James Lilley offers a complementary but alternative reading of Feuerteufel's medicine in *Common Things*, 104–5.

95. Bird, *Sheppard Lee*, 7.

96. Ibid.

97. Ibid., 37, 413.

98. Bird, *Difficulties*, 9.

99. Looby, introduction to Bird, *Sheppard Lee*, xxvii–xxix.

100. Sellers aptly characterizes this shift from agrarian ideal to speculative fantasy as revolutionary. Sellers argues that opening global markets during the Jacksonian era fomented unprecedented cultural, social, economic, and political change, "ignit[ing] a generation of conflict" between "the capitalist market" and "history's most conservative force, the land" (*Market Revolution*, 4). The market revolution drove "Americans into unparalleled mobilization, both spiritual and political," partly because of market allure and partly because agricultural dependence became more tenuous (ibid.). *Sheppard Lee* plays out this mobilization quite literally as Lee's agricultural failure and hunt for Kidd's treasure (the spoils of global exchange) spur new relationships between Americans and their bodies.

101. Bird in Kislak Bird Collection, Box 11, Folder 258.

102. Or, as James Lilley has recently argued, "within the economy of the novel, both persons and property participate in a Gothic regime of convertibility, their once-stable values now opened up to the whims of modern exchange" (*Common Things*, 112).

103. Bird, *Sheppard Lee*, 247. This lack of reflection prompts a long meditation on the nature of pain (253).

104. This view emerges repeatedly. Tom's corpse is reanimated by electricity to behave as it had in life; Lee asserts that Skinner body's controls his thoughts and actions; and Lee appropriates the speech, thoughts, and movements of his corpses. See Rush, *MIODM*.

105. In Lee's first incarnation, Higginson's mind takes over almost immediately, though remnants of Lee's spirit repeatedly reemerge. "There was a great search made for my—that is, Sheppard Lee's—body," Lee-as-Higginson haltingly narrates, "the general belief being that I—that is, John H. Higginson—had cast [Lee] into the swamp" (Bird, *Sheppard Lee*, 63). The oddness of a fused consciousness surfaces later, too, when Longstraw's Quaker "verily"s infect Lee's prose, but the effect is comical and nonthreatening.

106. Bird's ambivalence about sympathy as the "consent of parts"—like his ambivalence about medicine—is striking in Lee's later occupations, particularly Longstraw and Megrim. Longstraw is repeatedly punished for his sympathetic misjudgment—particularly for errors in empathy. Wrongly feeling for criminals and enslaved people, Longstraw is mocked, beaten, scratched, shoved, scolded, scalded, whitewashed, kicked, gored, and on his way to being killed again (ibid., 284–85). Similarly, Megrim's sympathies are madness. Imagining himself a dog, coffeepot, cannon, and clock, Megrim collapses his interests with those of animals and inanimate objects. Megrim needs to be physically beaten out of inappropriate sympathy. See

Murison, *The Politics of Anxiety*, for more on these sympathetic mistakes, especially her reading of hypochondria as an error in sympathy.

107. Bird, *Sheppard Lee*, 210.

108. Ibid., 141.

109. Ibid., 339.

110. Ibid., 341.

111. Ibid.

112. Murison, *The Politics of Anxiety*, 38.

113. E.g., Skinner's greed corrupts his sons, who celebrate his death and are driven to madness and suicide upon his reanimation.

114. Morton, *Crania Americana*, 5–7.

115. Ibid., 260.

116. Ibid., i.

117. Ibid.

118. Ibid., 268–69.

119. He notes, for example, "a singular harmony between the mental character of the Indian, and his cranial developments as explained by Phrenology" (ibid., i).

120. Ibid., 276.

121. See Buikstra's Introduction to *Crania Americana*.

122. Bird, *Sheppard Lee*, 277.

123. Morton, *Crania Americana*, 7.

124. Bird, *Sheppard Lee*, 21.

125. Ibid.

126. Ibid., 20.

127. Ibid., 424.

128. Cf. Dunglison, *Medical Lexicon* (1839), 588. This root had long been central to medical definitions (see Quincy, *American Medical Lexicon* [1811]).

129. See Henry S. Patterson's "Memoir of Samuel George Morton" in Nott and Gliddon, *Types of Mankind*, xxiv–xxv.

130. Translation in Spencer, "Samuel George Morton's," 331.

131. Bird, *Sheppard Lee*, 47.

132. Ibid.

133. Ibid., 77.

134. Ibid., 96, 101.

135. Ibid., 199.

136. Ibid., 332.

137. Quoted in Pernick, *Calculus*, 32. See esp. 42–58.

138. Bird in Bird Collection, Box 11, Folder 259. The soldier likely suffers from scrofula, "the King's Evil."

139. Bird, *Sheppard Lee*, 101.

140. Ibid., 424–25.

141. Ibid., 425. *Sheppard Lee* went to press in the wake of the terrifying 1830s cholera pandemic, the Indian Removal Act, and the congressional ban on slavery discussion. The health and unity of U.S. bodies remained anything but certain. Lee returns to an easier, antiquated model of health in which one body could stand in for all others—a Jeffersonian retreat from a Jacksonian world—but the conclusion is medically and politically dangerous. For more, see Lilley, *Common Things*, esp. 103–8.

142. For a classic definition of the picaresque, see Thrall and Hibbard, *A Handbook*, 351–53.

143. For more on the features of the "picaresque mode," see Wick, "The Nature of Picaresque Narrative," esp. 244–45.

144. For another terrific take on the problem of sympathy and medical work in fiction, see Thrailkill, "Statistical Pity," in *Affecting Fictions*, especially 56–63, in which she argues Oliver Wendell Holmes used a novel to criticize his contemporary Charles Meig for writing medical narratives that "allowed the physician's need for sympathy to eclipse that of the patient" (63). For examples of medical humanists using "fellow feeling" to define empathy, see Peloquin, "Art" and Bourke, "Pain, Sympathy and the Medical Encounter."

145. Quoted in Foust, *The Life*, 120.

146. Ibid.

147. I am grateful to Chris Looby for suggesting this metaphor for the relationship.

148. The notes in this paragraph were found in the Bird Collection at the University of Pennsylvania, Box 11, Folders 255 and 256 (*Peter Pilgrim*) and 259 (*Sheppard Lee*). The title of the book Lee is to write is "Peter Pepper" rather than "Peter Pilgrim." Bird was fond of experimenting with similar sounding names before settling on one. Bird accounts for Lee's new career by explaining, "His design [is] to make a trade, in consequence of the great encouragement given to American Literature—Ironical—" (Folder 259).

149. Morton, "Morton's Crania Americana," 404.

150. For example, see the image Bird drew of an orangutan for Harlan's essay on the new species in *Medical and Physical Researches*, n.p. Harlan positioned it next to an unattributed drawing, presumably of its skull, which likely came from his skull collection.

151. For more about these images, see the Penn Library Exhibition on Bird, especially case 12: https://www.library.upenn.edu/exhibits/rbm/bird/case12.html.

152. Bird, *Peter Pilgrim*, 2:47.

153. Ibid., 2:49.

154. Ibid.

155. Ibid., 2:49–50.

156. Ibid., 2:78, emphasis added.

157. Ibid., 2:64.

158. Ibid.

159. Morton, *Crania Americana*, 234.

160. Bird, *Peter Pilgrim*, 2:136.

161. Morton, *Crania Americana*, 246.

162. Bird, *Peter Pilgrim*, 2:136.

163. Ibid., 2:137–38, original emphasis.

164. Ibid., 2:137.

165. Ibid., 2:140.

166. Ibid., 1:42.

167. Ibid.

168. Ibid., 1:45.

169. Ibid., 1:44.

170. Ibid., 1:45.

171. The pre-Adamites had a millennia-long history that was deeply entangled in the question of human difference. Early suggestions of nonbiblical groups of humans were often dismissed as the stuff of fables and myth, but early European encounters with Native Americans

provided more empirical evidence for pre-Adamitic theories. In the seventeenth century theologian Isaac La Peyrère (1596–1676) claimed biblical evidence for pre-Adamites, an assertion that attracted charges of heresy. Nevertheless, the nineteenth-century rise of polygenesis popularized pre-Adamitic theories once more, especially among defenders of slavery who were interested in seeing a world full of bodies that were incommensurably distinct. By the mid-nineteenth century, these theories, as well as those of monogenesis and polygenesis, were becoming increasingly more scientific. Morton played an important, if initially ambivalent, role. As with orangutans, the possibility of pre-Adamitic peoples provided an important limit case for developing ideas about human speciation. *Peter Pilgrim* thus appears to be invested explicitly in the polygenic thinking with which Morton was grappling. For a more complete history of the idea of pre-Adamites, especially in the nineteenth century, see Popkin, "Pre-Adamism in 19th Century American Thought"; Sayre, "The Mound Builders"; and Livingstone, *Adam's Ancestors*, esp. chap. 5.

172. Bird, *Peter Pilgrim*, 1:45.

173. Ibid., 1:46.

174. Ibid., 1:51.

175. Ibid., 1:48.

176. Ibid., 1:49.

177. Ibid., 1:50.

178. Ibid., 1:52.

179. Ibid.

180. Ibid., 1:57.

181. Ibid., 1:62.

182. Ibid., 1:63.

183. Bird to Morton, April 20, 1841 in Morton Collection, American Philosophical Society (APS) Series I: Correspondence.

184. Ibid.

185. Unless otherwise noted, these letters are located in the Morton Collection, APS, Series I: Correspondence.

186. Bird to Morton, April 24, 1842.

187. Ibid.

188. Bird to Morton, May 19, 1842; Bird, "To Doctor," March 14, 1843 in Miscellaneous Manuscripts (Kislak Center).

189. Ibid.; undated letter to "My dear Doctor" from "New Castle, Saturday Morning" in Miscellaneous Manuscripts (Kislak Center).

190. Morton taught anatomy and physiology and Bird taught materia medica and pharmacy. The medical school was dismantled partly because of financial difficulty and partly because of personal feuds. Bird did not end up returning to Pennsylvania Medical College but stipulated that if he were to return, he would do so only on the condition that Benjamin Rush's son William Rush did not. For more on ill-fated history of the college, see Abraham, *Extinct Medical Schools*, chap. 1 and Wilbank, *Statement*.

CHAPTER 5

1. For Warren's account of the experiment, see *Etherization*, 4–7. For scholarly accounts, see Moscoso, *Pain*, 111–13 and Pernick, *Calculus*, 3–4. This story of anesthesia's "discovery" is

highly contested, and the development of anesthesia has a much longer history. While late eighteenth-century experiments with nitrous oxide by Joseph Priestley and Humphrey Davy suggested that nitrous oxide "appears capable of destroying physical pain" and might "be used with advantage during surgical operations," these suggestions lay fallow for some decades (quoted in Dunster, *History*, 5). (See endnote 181 in Chapter 1 for a lengthier discussion of Davy, Coleridge, and nitrous oxide.) Instead, nitrous oxide ("laughing gas") and ether were used principally for entertainment; in the first decades of the nineteenth century, Americans used them for party games, the most famous of which were known as "ether frolics." In 1842 Georgia physician Crawford Long began experimenting with ether for surgery, but his procedures were largely unknown. In 1844, Hartford dentist Horace Wells witnessed a man named Samuel Cooley seriously injure himself without pain while intoxicated on nitrous oxide and saw his opportunity. He and prominent physician and professor Charles T. Jackson (1805–1880) introduced Morton to ether and its potential uses for dentistry. Wells's own presentation of ether's pain-relieving properties at Massachusetts General Hospital in 1845 was unsuccessful, but Morton took a chance in the same amphitheater just one year later. Crucial to William Morton's claim of discovery was that he demonstrated it successfully in medical—rather than dental—surgery, that the former dean and professor at Harvard Medical School John Collins Warren performed the surgery, and that the experiment was legitimized in the halls of Massachusetts General Hospital. Meanwhile, Ralph Waldo Emerson adamantly insisted on his brother-in-law Jackson's claim to the discovery of anesthesia. Jackson had likely not been allowed to perform the Massachusetts General demonstration because he and Bigelow hated each other, so Bigelow had supported Morton's work. For the history of anesthesia, see Halttunen, *Murder*, 64–65; Dunster, *History*; Bruhm, "Aesthetics and Anesthetics"; and Pernick, *Calculus*.

2. Quoted in the *Railway Surgeon*, 415.

3. Ibid.

4. Scarry, *Body in Pain*, 29.

5. Quoted in Morton, *Tentamen Inaugurale*, 2. Morton attributes the quotation to "a recent writer." For my translation of this text I am indebted to Brendan Cook.

6. Dunglison, *Medical Lexicon* (1839), 441. This definition remains the same throughout the period.

7. For the relationship between anesthesia and aesthetics, see Bruhm, "Aesthetics and Anesthetics" and Davis's brief discussion in relation to race in *Bodily and Narrative Forms*, 156–60.

8. From Chapman's edition of Richerand, *Elements of Physiology*, 41.

9. Ibid. Perhaps more troublingly, Richerand then asks, "Those who have exhausted every kind of enjoyment, and who have had no pleasures ungratified, are led to suicide from a weariness of life; who can live, when all power of feeling is gone?" (ibid.).

10. Quoted in Van Dijkhuizen and Enenkel, *The Sense of Suffering*.

11. Quincy, *Lexicon* (1736), 345.

12. Ibid.

13. Burke, *Philosophical Enquiry*, 248, 44.

14. Dunglison, *Medical Lexicon* (1848), 545.

15. Morton, *Tentamen Inaugurale*, 21–27.

16. All of these virtues and drawbacks of pain can be found in Morton, *Tentamen Inaugurale*.

17. Dewees, *An Essay*, 61.

18. Rush, *Medical Inquiries and Observations*, 2:29.

19. Morton, *Tentamen Inaugurale*, 28, 31.

20. Ibid., 37.

21. Ibid.; the list appears on pages 6–7.

22. From Chapman's edition of Richerand, *Elements of Physiology*, 42–43.

23. Pope, *Essay on Man*, 10.

24. Morton, *Tentamen Inaugurale*, 4.

25. Ibid., 33.

26. Ibid.

27. Smith, *Theory*, 3.

28. Ibid., 8.

29. See the previous chapter.

30. Van Dijkhuizen and Enenkel, *The Sense of Suffering*, 5. Also see Bruhm, "Aesthetics and Anesthetics"; Wall, *Pain*; and Morris, *The Culture of Pain* for more on this problem.

31. See Van Dijkhuizen and Enenkel, introduction to *The Sense of Suffering*.

32. Dunglison, *Human Physiology*, 1:230.

33. Morton, *Tentamen Inaugurale*, 35.

34. Ibid.

35. Halttunen, "Humanitarianism," 304.

36. See Pernick, *Calculus*, esp. 8.

37. See Cahill, *Liberty of the Imagination*.

38. Peabody, "The Word 'Aesthetic,'" 1. This section on Peabody and the aesthetic is indebted to Paul Gilmore's discussion in *Aesthetic Materialism*, especially his introduction. It is worth noting that Henry David Thoreau's "Resistance to Civil Government" appeared in the same issue.

39. This overview of the aesthetic is indebted to the work of both Edward Cahill in *Liberty of the Imagination* and Paul Gilmore in *Aesthetic Materialism*.

40. See Morris's more general use of this term in *The Culture of Pain*, which treats pain in history and culture more generally.

41. For more on the "man of feeling," see, especially, Chapman and Hendler, *Sentimental Men* and Hendler, *Public Sentiments*.

42. While "hyperaesthesia" was coined earlier, according to Google ngrams, it was barely used until the mid-1840s. In 1886, New York novelist Mary Cruger wrote a novel called *Hyperaesthesia* that explored the condition.

43. Again, Halttunen, "Humanitarianism" and Pernick, *Calculus* are great resources for thinking about this proliferation, as are Abruzzo, *Polemical Pain* and Clark, "'The Sacred Rights of the Weak.'" Of the uses of pain in antislavery writing, for example, Abruzzo writes, "Early nineteenth-century debates over slavery lacked the rhetorical clarity that characterized the sharp antagonism of the 1830s" (119). It was not until the late 1830s, she argues, that "proslavery and antislavery activists had committed themselves to proving slavery's humaneness or cruelty. . . . Humaneness gained moral power precisely because humaneness seemed so clear; it demanded an end to the deliberate infliction of unnecessary pain" (159). Clark furthers that "only by understanding the changing cultural and religious conceptions of the nature of pain, the value of suffering, and the duty of compassion" that arose in the 1840s and 1850s "can we understand how, by the later nineteenth century, legal standards came to incorporate (albeit imperfectly) the idea that to be free of physical coercion and deliberately inflicted pain was an essential human right" (463).

44. Thompson, *Venus*, 298.

45. Melville, *Moby-Dick*, 355.

46. For more on the absence of corporeal particularity in U.S. literature before 1815, see Altschuler, "'Ain't One Limb Enough?'" For more on aesthetics and American Romanticism, see Gilmore, *Aesthetic Materialism*.

47. Depicting pain thus was a strategy used earlier in slave narratives than in fiction. Given how central pain was to slavery and popular discourse that depicted black bodies as less susceptible to pain and therefore less human, it is unsurprising that the move toward depicting pain would arise earlier in antislavery texts. Representing black bodies in pain was a powerful argument for the humanity of the enslaved. In 1810, for example, Boyrereau Brinch (1742–1827) describes a whipping scene in his memoir in horrible, painful detail: striking a girl repeatedly, a slave driver "again turned the butt of his whip and struck her on the other temple, which leveled her with the ground; she seemed frantic, and instantly rose upon her feet, the driver with a terrible grin and countenance, that bespoke his brutality, struck her with a drawing blow over the left shoulder, which came round under her right arm, near the pit of her stomach, and cut a hole through, out of which the blood gushed every breath . . . the blood gushing from her wounds every breath, [she] then fell down and expired" (Brace, *Blind African*, 38).

48. Brown, *Narrative*, 15.

49. Ibid., 15–16.

50. Douglass, *Narrative*, 5–6.

51. Ibid., 6.

52. Philip Gould writes, "The overall technique of the scene cannot help but recall the famous opening of Adam Smith's highly influential treatise *The Theory of Moral Sentiments*" ("Early Black Atlantic Writing," 110).

53. For the ways in which the discovery of anesthesia complicated representations of pain in slave narratives, see Gomaa, "Writing to 'Virtuous' and 'Gentle' Readers." Gomaa writes, "By making sympathy 'spectorial,' Karen Halttunen argues, nineteenth-century reform literature confirmed the 'social distance' between 'the virtuous spectator and the (imaginary) suffering victim' (309). Jacobs and Wilson challenge this presumed social distance in their writing by being simultaneously the sufferer and the spectator" (380).

54. Dunglison, *Human Physiology*, 1:235.

55. Ibid.

56. For an excellent examination of this in the late nineteenth century, see Davis, "'The Ache of the Actual,'" which explores pain and aesthetics as a context for the realist novel.

57. Rush, *MIODM*, 246.

58. Ibid., 247.

59. Reiss, "Bardolatry in Bedlam," 769.

60. Morton quotes the following passage to explain the situation-dependent experience of pain: "How light and portable my pain seems now, / When that which me bends—makes the king bow!" (*Tentamen Inaugurale*, 29).

61. Nott and Gliddon, *Types*, xxiv.

62. Ibid., xxiv–xxv.

63. See Pernick, *Calculus*.

64. Ibid.

65. Warren, *Etherization*, 1.

66. Warren himself had unsuccessfully tried a number of other painkillers for surgery including alcohol, opium, "other narcotics," mesmerism, and neurologism (ibid., 1, 31).

67. See Channing, *Etherization*, 135–58.

68. Morton, *Tentamen Inaugurale*, 28.

69. Quoted, e.g., in Channing, *Etherization*, 142.

70. Channing had been trained at the University of Pennsylvania medical school and in England and Scotland before he took up the post at Harvard, which he held from 1815 to 1854.

71. Channing, *Etherization*, dedication.

72. Ibid., 7–8.

73. Ibid., 8.

74. Channing's work was deeply empirical, a comprehensive compilation not only of the cases he himself had attended but also of the history of opinion and correspondence on the issue between prominent physicians. This heavily empirical work decried the work of medical philosophy and the imagination on its title page, quoting an "old play": "Give me the facts, said my Lord Judge: your reasonings are the mere guess-work of the imagination" (ibid., title page). Perhaps the obvious complication of quoting an imaginative work to authoritatively decry the use of the imagination was lost on Channing, as it was on the reviewer at *Little's Living Age* who quoted Channing's epigraph on the "guess-work of the imagination," before turning to another poem to praise ether (ibid., 8).

75. Ibid., 135.

76. Ibid., 138.

77. Ibid., 138–39.

78. Quoted at Cervetti, *S. Weir Mitchell*, 50–51.

79. Ibid.

80. For more on this exchange, see ibid.

81. Van Buren, "Anaesthesia," 49.

82. Ibid.

83. Ibid., 84.

84. Mott, "Remarks," 9.

85. "Perry Davis' Vegetable Pain Killer."

86. For example, see the definitions in Dunglison, *Medical Lexicon* (1848), 819, and Dunglison, *Medical Lexicon* (1860), 888–89. The sense of sympathy deriving from "suffering" can also be found in earlier texts. Quincy's *Lexicon Physico-Medicum* (1736) finds sympathy's roots in "to suffer with" (438), and *The American Medical Lexicon* (1811) locates them in the Greek for "to suffer together" (n.p.).

87. See Holmes, *Poems*.

88. Maier, *First Editions*, 109.

89. For more on Holmes's biography and more excellent recent work on Holmes, see Gibian, *Oliver Wendell Holmes*; Weinstein, *The Imaginative Prose of Oliver Wendell Holmes*; and Dowling, *Oliver Wendell Holmes in Paris*.

90. From a reprint of "The Mechanism of Vital Actions," in Holmes, *Currents and Counter-Currents*, 327.

91. Ibid., 328.

92. Ibid., 327.

93. Holmes was revising his 1857 essay for republication as he serialized *Elsie Venner*, and the novel bears the imprint of this thinking. An advertisement for the "nearly ready" *Currents and Counter-Currents* appears in the first edition of *Elsie Venner*. For a different take on Holmes's relationship to medical knowledge in *Elsie Venner*, see Davis, *Bodily and Narrative Forms*, chap. 1.

94. Holmes, *Over the Teacups*, 251.

95. Holmes, *The Professor's Story*, 88. In his 1861 preface, Holmes writes that the first installment appeared in December 1859, but it appears he was mistaken.

96. Holmes, *The Professor's Story*, 88–89.

97. Ibid., 91.

98. This character was well loved enough that a professor at Johns Hopkins would write in 1880, "In this new university we consider 'the Professor at the Breakfast Table' as one of the permanent members of the academic staff, and though we do not hear his voice or see his smile we feel his power and enjoy his wit" (letter in "The Holmes Breakfast," 22).

99. Holmes, *Elsie Venner*, 1:ix.

100. Ibid., 1:ix–x.

101. Ibid., 2:305.

102. See Oberndorf, *The Psychiatric Novels*.

103. For statistics, contagion, and childbed fever, see Thrailkill, "Killing Them Softly." Holmes's analysis of the novel's statistical work in relation to the novel's attention to individual particularity is an especially compelling reading of the medical work of the novel.

104. Elsie's venom-tainted blood resembles Dick Venner's half-Spanish blood.

105. See, e.g., Joan Burbick's lengthy discussion, "Allegories of Nervous Fever," in *Healing the Republic*, 241–64. As a critique of homeopathy, we need look no further than the preface to an 1861 collection of essays, in which Holmes footnotes a statement decrying "the old barbarous notion that sick people should feed on poisons" with the same term—*Crotalus*—he repeatedly uses to describe the snakes that poisoned Elsie Venner: "*Lachesis*, arrow-poison, obtained from a serpent (Pulte). *Crotalus horridus*, rattlesnake's venom (Neidhard). The less dangerous *Pediculus capitis* is the favorite remedy of Dr. Mure, the English 'Apostle of Homeopathy.' These are examples of the retrograde current setting toward barbarism" (Holmes, *Currents*, viii).

106. Dunglison, *Human Physiology* (1856), 1:236. Holmes began his study of medicine just after the publication of this volume.

107. See Harlan, *Medical and Physical Researches*, 459–90, esp. 503.

108. Cervetti, *S. Weir Mitchell*, 157.

109. Quoted in Earnest, *S. Weir Mitchell*, 37.

110. Ibid. Mitchell later published a book of Rush's historical notes.

111. Holmes, *Elsie Venner*, 1:73, 1:104–5, 1:131. Jane Thrailkill makes a slightly different point about our inability to feel with Elsie: "Elsie's near inability to use language places her outside the realm of human sympathy" (*Affecting Fictions*, 78).

112. Holmes, *Elsie Venner*, 1:100.

113. Dunglison, *Medical Lexicon* (1860), 57.

114. Holmes, *Elsie Venner*, 1:131–32.

115. Ibid., 1:132.

116. Ibid., 2:229.

117. Ibid., 2:229–30. Many have commented on the problematic racial politics of the novel. The relationship between Sophy and Elsie supports race-science arguments that claimed African Americans possessed less feeling than white Americans. See Burbick, *Healing the Republic*, esp. 241–64.

118. Holmes, *Elsie Venner*, 2:234.

119. Ibid.

120. For a terrific reading of Elsie's particularity in relation to her separation from language, see Thrailkill's section on "pathological particularity" in *Affecting Fictions*, especially 74–79.

121. Holmes, *Elsie Venner*, 2:230.

122. Ibid.

123. The first part of Holmes's analogy probably refers to the hardier nineteenth-century technology of steel engraving (as opposed to copper), since the "words" are worn down by "innumerable contacts."

124. Holmes, *Elsie Venner*, 2:256.

125. Ibid., 2:272.

126. Ibid., 2:202–3.

127. Ibid., 2:203.

128. Upholding the importance of imagination, the novel elsewhere highlights the instability of observation. The physician-narrator relates a story in which his own observation was distorted in the process of reporting. Meeting a friend everyone supposed to be dead, he returns home to hear "the story had gone before that he was among the lost, and I alone could contradict it to his weeping friends and relatives. I did contradict it; but alas! I began soon to doubt myself, penetrated by the contagion of their solicitude; my recollection began to question itself; the order of events became dislocated; and when I heard that he had reached home in safety, the relief was almost as great to me as to those who had expected to see their brother's face no more" (*Elsie Venner*, 2:204–5).

129. Holmes stages this exactly in dialogue between Dr. Kittredge (the physician) and Reverend Dr. Honeywood in the middle of the novel.

130. Holmes, *The Writings*, 5:ix.

131. For example, see Gibian's note that "Edmund Wilson, in a series of letters on Holmes, gives the Doctor's 'medicated novels' an important role in the birth of the psychological novel as a genre" (*Oliver Wendell Holmes*, 369).

132. Holmes, *The Poet*, 25–26.

133. Holmes, *Writings*, 6:xiv.

134. Holmes, *Border Lines*, 236.

135. Quoted in Earnest, *S. Weir Mitchell*, 37.

136. Ibid.

137. Mitchell, "Medical Department," 17.

138. Cervetti, *S. Weir Mitchell*, 69.

139. Mitchell, "Medical Department," 16.

140. Ibid.

141. Ibid.

142. Rosenberg, *Care of Strangers*, 98.

143. For more on early American hospitals, see Rosenberg, *Care of Strangers*. There was an enormous difference between the two, of course: the hospital, despite its attendant ills (uncleanliness, poor care, etc.), being far preferable to the almshouse. Nevertheless, as Rosenberg makes clear, "It was not until after midcentury that such prejudices [against the hospital] were overcome . . . and even highly contagious cases were often removed from boarding houses only by force" (26). Hospitals were an attractive place to practice for Philadelphia's most eminent physicians because they offered opportunities for learning and a variety of sick bodies, but they were not places Americans wanted to seek care (60).

144. Ibid., 98.

145. See, for example, Mitchell's 1877 essay "The Relation of Pain to Weather." In that essay, Mitchell footnotes the first sentence with a quotation from Dr. Edward Jenner's "lively lines" to explain prevailing beliefs about the relationship of weather to pain: "Hark how the

chairs and tables crack, / Old Betty's bones are on the rack" (305). Of course, his more famous work on the nerves also offers an extended exploration of particular pains.

146. Mitchell, "Medical Department," 16.

147. Mitchell, Morehouse, and Keen, *Gunshot Wounds*, 19. Also see discussion in Cervetti, *S. Weir Mitchell*, 76.

148. Ibid., 101.

149. Ibid., 101–2.

150. Mitchell, *Injuries of the Nerves*, 272.

151. Mitchell, Morehouse, and Keen, *Gunshot Wounds*, 148–51.

152. Ibid., 152.

153. There is a robust scholarship on the relationship between case histories and literature. For example, see Caldwell, *Literature and Medicine*; Kennedy, *Revising the Clinic*; and Tougaw, *Strange Cases*.

154. "The Case of George Dedlow" is the first piece in a journal issue that also contains articles explaining Darwinian theory, the "Physical History of the Valley of the Amazons," and a description of "Indian Medicine" in addition to poetry and fiction. The journal's unsorted table of contents invites readers to judge the nature of "George Dedlow" for themselves.

155. Mitchell, "George Dedlow," 1.

156. Mitchell, *Autobiography*, ix.

157. Ibid.

158. Ibid.

159. Ibid., 3.

160. Ibid.

161. Ibid.

162. Ibid.

163. Ibid.

164. Ibid.

165. Ibid.

166. Ibid.

167. Ibid., 3–4.

168. Ibid., 4.

169. Ibid., 5.

170. Ibid.

171. He experiences the first instance of pain when they situate him to amputate his legs.

172. Mitchell, "George Dedlow," 5, 6.

173. Ibid., 6.

174. Ibid.

175. Ibid.

176. Ibid.

177. Ibid., 7.

178. Ibid.

179. Ibid.

180. Ibid.

181. Ibid., 8.

182. Ibid.

183. Ibid.

184. Ibid., 11.

185. Ibid., 8.

186. Ibid., 11. Mitchell did not believe in spiritualism.

187. Mitchell, *Autobiography*, ix–x.

188. It's worth noting that both *Lippincott's* and the *Atlantic* describe themselves as journals of literature and science.

189. Mitchell, "Phantom Limbs," 563.

190. Ibid., 564.

191. Ibid.

192. Ibid., 565.

193. Ibid., 565–66.

194. Mitchell, *Autobiography*, x.

195. Quoted in Cervetti, *S. Weir Mitchell*, 78.

CONCLUSION

1. Emerson, *Letters*, 10.

2. Ibid.

3. Historian Michael Bliss writes about Osler's frequent use of and belief in humanistic inquiry: "In his early forties, the early Hopkins years, Osler broadens his reading, thinking, and oratorical reach. . . . Having stopped doing postmortems of people, he turns to the postmortem literary discipline, history, as a way of understanding. His command of good literature increases. His style becomes more self-consciously literary. . . . He indulges in his lifelong penchant for quotation, simile, and metaphor" (*William Osler*, 196). Also see Osler's lecture "John Keats, the Apothecary Poet."

4. Macfie, *Romance*, vi.

5. Starr, *The Social Transformation*, 116–23.

6. Ibid., 117.

7. See Duffy, "The Flexner Report."

8. Henry S. Pritchett, introduction to Flexner, *Medical Education in the United States*, x.

9. See chap. 2 of Flexner, *Medical Education in the United States*, "The Proper Basis of Medical Education." For an overview of Flexner and the report, see Duffy, "The Flexner Report."

10. Osler, *Science and Immortality*, 78. Also see Cervetti, *S. Weir Mitchell*, 167.

11. Herter, "Imagination and Idealism," 429.

12. Flexner, *Medical Education in the United States*, 56–57.

13. All quotations are derived from William Dalby, "An Address to Students," 632.

14. Holmes, *Mortal Antipathy*, 97.

15. Ibid., 167.

16. Burr, "The S. Weir Mitchell Oration," 17.

17. Gilman, "Why I Wrote 'The Yellow Wallpaper?' "

18. Ibid.

19. Ibid.

20. See, e.g., Thrailkill, "Doctoring 'The Yellow Wallpaper' " and Cutter, "The Writer as Doctor."

21. Scholars have long understood that a vibrant exchange between psychology and literature flourished in the late nineteenth and early twentieth centuries. The field of psychology,

as we now know it, was only just beginning. Prominent fin-de-siècle figures Weir Mitchell, William James, and Sigmund Freud all theorized psychology and psychotherapy in literary terms. The intersection between psychology and literature comes as no surprise to today's scholar, well acquainted with the debts literary theory owes to psychoanalysis and the narratological features of psychotherapy, but this collaboration reads quite differently when imagined as the narrowing, rather than the broadening, of cross-disciplinary exchange. For the intersection between psychology and literature in this period, see, e.g., Ryan, *The Vanishing Subject*; Frankland, *Freud's Literary Culture*; and Kennedy, "Modernist Autobiography."

22. Burr, "William Osler," 626.

23. Ibid.

24. For more on Flexner's later thinking, see his 1925 text; Pellegrino, "The Reconciliation of Technology and Humanism"; and Bonner, *Iconoclast*. Bonner writes that "as early as 1913 [Flexner] had warned that the typical medical school closed 'down upon the enterprising student . . . with an exhausting and depressing uniformity.' In 1921, he had told Harvey Cushing that the imposition of rigid standards by accrediting groups was making the medical curriculum 'a monstrosity'" (188). Here we might differentiate between Abraham Flexner, the man whose ideas about education continued to develop, and "Flexner" the author of the report that authorized wholesale changes to the medical curriculum sought by interested parties looking to make American medicine more exclusively scientific. Here Flexner's widespread influence resembles Bruno Latour's account of Louis Pasteur's vast uptake, which was more about the usefulness of his ideas to powerful groups and institutions in France than the pure scientific value of his ideas; see Latour, *The Pasteurization of France*.

25. Flexner, *Medical Education: A Comparative Study*, 18. "Uniformity will not come about and is not in itself desirable," he continues, advocating "an enlightened spirit, seeking stimulus and suggestion wherever they are to be found. It is upon the latter that progress largely depends" (18).

26. Ibid., 141.

27. Ibid.

28. David Doukas, Laurence McCullough, and Stephen Wear work to recuperate Flexner as a medical humanist in "Reforming Medical Education in Ethics and Humanities by Finding Common Ground with Abraham Flexner." Nevertheless, they admit, he "did not explicitly incorporate this position into his 1910 report" (318). Far from being inexplicit about the role of the humanities in medical education, he made no space for it at all in the 1910 report that changed the next hundred years of medical education. And, while he would later come to regret his stance in the Flexner Report, it was too late.

29. The medical humanities began in the 1960s but really took off in the twenty-first century.

30. The more recently coined term "health humanities" is more productive and capacious; it decenters medicine from ways of knowing and working with human health. Nevertheless, I use the term "medical humanities" here to name the narrower—yet vastly more popular—programs nationwide and to emphasize the necessary work of bringing a robust vision of the humanities into medicine as well as into other health professions. For excellent examples of work in the health humanities, see Jones, Wear and Friedman, *Health Humanities Reader* (2014).

31. This summary is intended as an overview of the field rather than a critique of individual programs. See Wachtler, Lundin, and Troein, "Humanities for Medical Students?" for an analysis of the problems that result from curricula driven by the interests of medical schools that remains relevant. The goals of undergraduate medical and health humanities programs are,

furthermore, largely aimed pragmatically at stemming the tide of dropping enrollments in the humanities. It is not coincidental that in 2008, when many humanities programs saw tenure lines pulled and programs shuttered, the medical humanities began to grow exponentially where they had been growing arithmetically. For the statistics on this growth, see Berry, Lamb, and Jones, *Health Humanities*, 4–5.

32. Krisberg, "Humanities Programs." See endnote 92 in the introduction for information on more expansively conceived programs and field-structuring work.

33. Wachtler, Lundin, and Troein, "Humanities for Medical Students?"

34. Ibid.

35. This problem is closely related to ever more common arguments about the uselessness of the humanities. Arguments against the humanities suggest, on one hand, that they are too obscure and ungrounded and, on the other hand, that the elements of the humanities integral to and deeply involved in the workings of everyday life are common sense—practices, easily learned and taught by all empathetic and thoughtful people. This is largely true even when humanists are hired to teach medical humanities in medical schools; their marginal and often precarious positions significantly limit the work they can do.

36. "Instructions for Authors."

37. Ibid.

38. See Dolev, Friedlaender, and Braverman, "Use of Fine Art."

39. Charon, *Narrative Medicine*, 10.

40. Charon uses the term "narrative competence" to mean "the ability to acknowledge, absorb, interpret, and act on the stories and plights of others. Medicine practiced with narrative competence, called *narrative medicine*, is proposed as a model for humane and effective medical practice" by "adopting methods such as close reading of literature and reflective writing" (Charon, "Narrative Medicine," 1897).

41. Metzl, "Structural Competency," 216. Other scholars also argue that narrative is a necessarily salubrious form that heals patients by returning their agency and humanity. See, e.g., Thrailkill, "Statistical Pity," in *Affecting Fictions*, 54–83.

42. For this thinking about the language of competencies, I am indebted to a series of conversations I had with Michelle Lampl as we worked to build a Health and Humanities program at Emory University. There are strategic benefits to including empathy in this list (including fit with existing programs) but also significant drawbacks, as I have already suggested.

43. Even for those—like medical historians David Jones, Jeremy Greene, Jacalyn Duffin, and John Harley Warner—who worry about the "tyranny of competencies" in medical education, competencies are helpful for articulating the value of history for medical education to "define precisely the contributions that history offers to medical history and practice, frame these, as needed, in the language of competencies, and engage with the ongoing reforms of medical education" (Jones et al., "Making the Case," 642, 652). For a discussion of the "tyranny of competencies" in current medical education, see ibid., 642 and Kumagai, "From Competencies to Human Interests." Jones et al. nevertheless use the language of competencies to distinguish medical history from the medical and health humanities, arguing that the history of medicine should really be a part of medical training, whereas they view the medical and health humanities contributing only to "medical professionalism" ("Making the Case," 623).

44. For an overview of competency-based medical education, see Frank et al., "Competency-Based Medical Education." This work began in 2002. For more, see "ACGME Core Competencies."

45. While most agree that knowledge and skill are at the core of competency, definitions vary greatly (Fernandez et al., "Varying Conceptions," 357). Competency also contains "intangible" components "related to the individual's personal characteristics, attitudes and values" that are "comparatively difficult to observe and assess," at least from the perspective of the medical establishment (360).

46. Medical humanists have already suggested that the humanities contribute to ACGME's competencies; see Doukas, McCullough, and Wear, "Perspective: Medical Education in Medical Ethics and Humanities as the Foundation for Developing Medical Professionalism." Doukas, McCullough, and Wear suggest that the humanities can help with competency of professionalism, which unwittingly replicates the medical humanities' general practice of confusing the humanities with human interest.

47. For more on existing methods for using art history to train medical students, see Boudreau, Cassell, and Fuks, "Preparing Medical Students" and Bardes, Gillers, and Herman, "Learning to Look."

48. For important examples of this work, see Daston and Lunbeck, *Histories of Scientific Observation* and Daston and Galison, *Objectivity*.

49. For important examples of this work, see Garland-Thomson, *Staring* and Siebers, *Disability Aesthetics*.

50. See Kristeller, "'Creativity' and 'Tradition'" and Cummings, "On Creativity." Only in the mid-twentieth century, intellectual historian Paul Oskar Kristeller demonstrates, did "any person who is original in his field and who produces something novel [gain] a right to be called creative" ("Creativity," 108). Kristeller connects creativity's emergence to changing ideas of what it means to create. An ngram of *creativity* and *imagination* from 1940 to 2008, however, reveal their uses to be inversely proportional. In the late twentieth century, creativity came to describe a portion of acts that were once understood as imaginative.

51. Whereas later definitions stress the unreal nature of imagination, earlier definitions of "imagination," such as those in Webster's 1913 dictionary, emphasize the faculty's basis in observation and perception.

52. E.g., see the *Lancet*'s 2006 essay collection titled "Medicine and Creativity."

53. A few people are currently thinking about how to cultivate creativity in medicine; see Liou et al., "Playing" and Baruch, "Doctors as Makers."

54. Campo, "Medical Humanities," 1010.

55. See Shapin and Shaffer, *Leviathan and the Air-Pump*, especially 3–21, for the history of the experiment.

BIBLIOGRAPHY

ARCHIVES CONSULTED

Albert and Shirley Small Special Collections Library, University of Virginia
American Antiquarian Society
American Philosophical Society
College of Physicians of Philadelphia
Cushing/Whitney Medical Historical Library, Yale University
Historical Society of Pennsylvania
Kislak Center for Special Collections, Rare Books, and Manuscripts, University of Pennsyl-
    vania
Library Company of Philadelphia
Library of Congress
New York Academy of Medicine Library

PUBLISHED SOURCES

Aberbach, Alan David. *In Search of an American Identity: Samuel Latham Mitchill, Jeffersonian Nationalist.* New York: P. Lang, 1988.
Abraham, Harold J. *Extinct Medical Schools of Nineteenth-Century Philadelphia.* Philadelphia: University of Pennsylvania Press, 1966.
Abruzzo, Margaret. *Polemical Pain: Slavery, Cruelty, and the Rise of Humanitarianism.* Baltimore: Johns Hopkins University Press, 2011.
"ACGME Core Competencies." *Educational Commission for Foreign Medical Graduates.* http://www.ecfmg.org/echo/acgme-core-competencies.html. Accessed 5 September 2016.
Adams, John. *The Works of John Adams.* 10 vols. Ed. Charles Francis Adams. Boston: Little, Brown, 1850.
"The Advent of the Cholera: A Tale of the Arabesque." *Southern Literary Messenger* 22 (January 1856): 63–67.
Ainsworth, Geoffery Clough. *Introduction to the History of Medical and Veterinary Mycology.* Cambridge: Cambridge University Press, 1986.
Alterton, Margaret. *Origins of Poe's Critical Theory.* New York: Russell and Russell, 1925.
Altman, Lawrence. *Who Goes First: The Story of Self-Experimentation in Medicine.* New York: Random House, 1986.
Altschuler, Eric Lewin. "Informed Consent in an Edgar Allen [*sic*] Poe Tale." *Lancet* 362 (November 2003): 1504.

————. "Prescient Description of Frontal Lobe Syndrome in an Edgar Allan Poe Tale." *Lancet* 363 (2004): 902.

Altschuler, Sari. "'Ain't One Limb Enough?': Historicizing Disability in the American Novel." *American Literature* 86, no. 2 (June 2014): 245–74.

————. "From Blood Vessels to Global Networks of Exchange: The Physiology of Benjamin Rush's Early Republic." *Journal of the Early Republic* 32, no. 2 (Summer 2012): 207–31.

The American Museum of Literature, Science, and the Arts. Baltimore: Brooks and Snodgrass, 1838–39.

Anglo-African Magazine. New York: T. Hamilton, 1859–60.

Apel, Thomas. *Feverish Bodies, Enlightened Minds: Science and the Yellow Fever Controversy in the Early American Republic*. Stanford, CA: Stanford University Press, 2016.

————. "The Thucydidean Moment: History, Science, and the Yellow-Fever Controversy, 1793–1805." *Journal of the Early Republic* 34, no. 3 (2014): 315–47.

Arner, Katherine. "Making Yellow Fever American: The Early American Republic, the British Empire and the Geopolitics of Disease in the Atlantic World." *Atlantic Studies* 7, no. 4 (2010): 447–71.

Averill, Charles E. *The Cholera-Fiend, or, The Plague Spreaders of New York, A Mysterious Tale of the Pestilence in 1849*. Boston: George H. Williams, 1850.

Bailey, Edward. "Lines composed on the prevailing malignant cholera." Lansingburgh, NY, 1832. Broadside held at the American Antiquarian Society, Worcester, MA.

Bailey, J. O. "What Happens in 'The Fall of the House of Usher'?" *American Literature* 35, no. 4 (January 1964): 445–66.

Bailyn, Bernard. *The Ideological Origins of the American Revolution*. Cambridge, MA: Harvard University Press, 1967.

Baker, Jennifer. *Securing the Commonwealth: Debt, Speculation, and Writing in the Making of Early America*. Baltimore: Johns Hopkins University Press, 2005.

Bardes, Charles L., Debra Gillers, and Amy E. Herman. "Learning to Look: Developing Clinical Observational Skills at an Art Museum." *Medical Education* 35, no. 12 (2001): 1157–61.

Barker-Benfield, G. J. *The Culture of Sensibility: Sex and Society in Eighteenth-Century Britain*. Chicago: University of Chicago Press, 1992.

Barlow, Frank. "The King's Evil." *English Historical Review* 95, no. 374 (January 1980): 3–27.

Barnard, Philip, Mark L. Kamrath, and Stephen Shapiro, eds. *Revising Charles Brockden Brown: Culture, Politics, and Sexuality in the Early Republic*. Knoxville: University of Tennessee Press, 2004.

Barnes, Barry, and Steven Shapin, eds. *Natural Order: Historical Studies of Scientific Culture*. Beverly Hills, CA: Sage, 1979.

Barnes, Elizabeth. *States of Sympathy: Seduction and Democracy in the American Novel*. New York: Columbia University Press, 1997.

Barnhill, Georgia. "Transformations in Pictorial Printing." In *An Extensive Republic: Print, Culture, and Society in the New Nation, 1790–1840*, eds. Robert Gross and Mary Kelley, 422–40, Vol. 2 of *A History of the Book in America*, 5 vols., Chapel Hill: University of North Carolina Press, 2010.

Barrett, Frank A. "Finke's 1792 Map of Human Diseases: The First World Disease Map?" *Social Science & Medicine* 50, no. 7 (2000): 915–21.

Barton, David. *Benjamin Rush: Signer of the Declaration of Independence*. Aledo, TX: Wallbuilders, 1999.

Baruch, Jay M. "Doctors as Makers." *Academic Medicine* 92, no. 1 (2017): 40–44.

Baucom, Ian. *Spectres of the Atlantic: Finance, Capital, Slavery, and the Philosophy of History.* Durham, NC: Duke University Press, 2005.

Beaumont, William. *Experiments and Observations on the Gastric Juice, and the Physiology of Digestion.* Plattsburgh, NY, 1833.

Bechtold, Rebeccah. "A Revolutionary Soundscape: Musical Reform and the Science of Sound in Early America, 1760–1840." *Journal of the Early Republic* 35, no. 3 (2015): 419–50.

Beer, Gillian. *Darwin's Plots: Evolutionary Narrative in Darwin, George Eliot and Nineteenth-Century Fiction.* London: Routledge and Paul, 1983.

Benatar, Solomon. "Imperialism, Research Ethics, and Global Health." *Journal of Medical Ethics* 24 (1998): 221–22.

Bennet, Charles E. "A Poetical Correspondence Among Elihu Hubbard Smith, Joseph Bringhurst, Jr., and Charles Brockden Brown in 'The Gazette of the United States.'" *Early American Literature* 12, no. 3 (Winter 1977/1978): 277–85.

Berlant, Lauren. "Poor Eliza." *American Literature* 70, no. 3 (September 1998): 635–68.

Berry, Sarah L., Erin Gentry Lamb, and Therese Jones. *Health Humanities Baccalaureate Programs in the United States.* Hiram, OH: Center for Literature and Medicine, Hiram College, 2016.

Berthoff, Warner. Introduction to *Arthur Mervyn.* 1799–1800, vii–xxi. Repr., New York: Holt, Rinehart, and Winston, 1962.

Bewell, Alan. "Erasmus Darwin's Cosmopolitan Nature." *ELH* 76, no. 1 (Spring 2009): 19–48.

Bird, Mary Mayer. *Life of Robert Montgomery Bird.* Ed. Seymour Thompson. Philadelphia: University of Pennsylvania Library, 1945.

Bird, Robert Montgomery. *The Difficulties of Medical Science: An Inaugural Lecture.* Philadelphia, 1841.

———. "The Mammoth Cave of Kentucky." *American Monthly Magazine* (May and June 1837): 417–38, 525–46.

———. *Nick of the Woods: Or, the Jibbenainosay; A Tale of Kentucky.* 2 vols. Philadelphia: Carey, Lea, and Blanchard, 1837.

———. *Peter Pilgrim; Or, A Rambler's Recollections.* 2 vols. Lea & Blanchard, 1838.

———. *Sheppard Lee: Written by Himself.* 1836. Repr., ed. Christopher Looby. New York: New York Review of Books, 2008.

———. *Valedictory Address Delivered Before the Graduates of Pennsylvania Medical College; Session of 1842–3.* Philadelphia, 1843.

Bliss, Michael. *William Osler: A Life in Medicine.* New York: Oxford University Press, 1999.

Bonner, Thomas Neville. *Iconoclast: Abraham Flexner and a Life in Learning.* Baltimore: Johns Hopkins University Press, 2002.

Bono, James J. "Perception, Living Matter, Cognitive Systems, Immune Networks: A Whiteheadian Future for Science Studies." *Configurations* 13 (2005): 135–81.

Boudreau, J. Donald, Eric J. Cassell, and Abraham Fuks. "Preparing Medical Students to Become Skilled at Clinical Observation." *Medical Teacher* 30, no. 9–10 (2008): 857–62.

Boudreau, Kristin. Review of *Rehabilitating Bodies: Health, History, and the American Civil War* by Lisa A. Long and *Mark Twain and Medicine* by K. Patrick Ober. *American Literature* 76, no. 4 (2004): 889–91.

Bourke, Joanna. "Pain, Sympathy and the Medical Encounter Between the Mid-Eighteenth and the Mid-Twentieth Centuries." *Historical Research* 85, no. 229 (2012): 430–52.

Brace, Jeffrey. *The Blind African Slave: Memoirs of Boyrereau Brinch, Nicknamed Jeffrey Brace.* 1810. Repr., Madison: University of Wisconsin Press, 2005.

Brake, Mark. *Alien Life Imagined: Communicating the Science and Culture of Astrobiology.* Cambridge: Cambridge University Press, 2012.

Brancaccio, Patrick. "Studied Ambiguities: *Arthur Mervyn* and the Problem of the Unreliable Narrator." *American Literature* 42, no. 1 (1970): 18–27.

Breslaw, Elaine G. *Lotions, Potions, Pills, and Magic: Health Care in Early America.* New York: New York University Press, 2012.

Brigham, Amariah. *A Treatise on Epidemic Cholera; Including an Historical Account of Its Origin and Progress to the Present Period.* Hartford, CT: H. and F. J. Huntington, 1832.

Brodsky, Alyn. *Benjamin Rush: Patriot and Physician.* New York: Truman Talley Books, 2004.

Brody, Howard. "Defining the Medical Humanities: Three Conceptions and Three Narratives." *Journal of Medical Humanities* 32, no. 1 (2011): 1–7.

Brown, Charles Brockden. *Arthur Mervyn, or, Memoirs of the Year 1793.* 1799–1800. Repr., Kent, OH: Kent State University Press, 1980.

———. *Arthur Mervyn, or, Memoirs of the Year 1793.* 1799–1800. Repr., Indianapolis: Hackett, 2008.

———. *Collected Writings of Charles Brockden Brown: Letters and Early Epistolary Writings.* Vol. 1. Ed. Philip Barnard, Elizabeth Hewitt, and Mark Kammrath. Lewisburg, PA: Bucknell University Press, 2013.

———. "The Difference Between History and Romance." *Monthly Magazine* 2, no. 4 (April 1800): 251–53.

———. *Edgar Huntly, or, Memoirs of a Sleep-walker, with Related Texts.* 1799. Repr., ed. Philip Barnard and Stephen Shapiro. New York: Hackett, 2006.

———. "Miscellaneous Articles of Literary and Philosophical Intelligence." *Monthly Magazine, and American Review* 2, no. 2 (February 1800): 155.

———. *Ormond, or, The Secret Witness.* Ed. Stephen Shapiro and Philip Bernard. Indianapolis: Hackett, 2009.

———. "Walstein's School of History: From the German of Krants of Gotha [first part]." *Monthly Magazine* 1, no. 5 (August 1799): 335–38.

———. "Walstein's School of History: From the German of Krants of Gotha [second and last part]." *Monthly Magazine* 1, no. 6 (September–December 1799): 407–11.

Brown, William Wells. *Narrative of William W. Brown, A Fugitive Slave.* Boston, 1847.

Bruhm, Steven. "Aesthetics and Anesthetics at the Revolution." *Studies in Romanticism* 32, no. 3 (Fall 1993): 399–424.

Bryant, Juliet E., Edward C. Holmes, and Alan D. T. Barrett. "Out of Africa: A Molecular Perspective on the Introduction of Yellow Fever Virus into the Americas." *PLoS Pathogens* 3, no. 5 (2007). http://journals.plos.org/plospathogens/article?id=10.1371/journal.ppat.0030075. Accessed 6 September 2016.

Budd, William. *Malignant Cholera: Its Mode of Propagation and Its Prevention.* London: Churchill, 1849.

Buel, Richard, Jr. *America on the Brink: How the Political Struggle over the War of 1812 Almost Destroyed the Young Republic.* New York: Palgrave Macmillan, 2005.

Buikstra, J. E. Introduction to *Crania Americana.* 1839, i–xxxvi. Repr., Davenport, Iowa: Gustav's Library, 2009.

Burbick, Joan. *Healing the Republic: The Language of Health and the Culture of Nationalism in Nineteenth Century America.* Cambridge: Cambridge University Press, 1994.

Burgan, Michael. *Robert Hooke: Natural Philosopher and Scientific Explorer*. Minneapolis: Compass Point Books, 2008.

Burke, Edmund. *A Philosophical Enquiry into the Origin of our Ideas of the Sublime and Beautiful*. London, 1759.

Burr, Anna Robeson. *Weir Mitchell: His Life and Letters*. New York: Duffield and Company, 1930.

Burr, Charles Chauncey. "Immoral Writers." *Quaker City Weekly*, January 13, 1849, 1.

Burr, Charles Walts. "Sir William Osler as a Man of Letters." *Journal of the American Medical Sciences* (1920): 625–30.

———. "The S. Weir Mitchell Oration: S. Weir Mitchell, Physician, Man of Science, Man of Letters, Man of Affairs." Philadelphia: College of Physicians of Philadelphia, 1920.

Butler, David W. "Usher's Hypochondriasis: Mental Alienation and Romantic Idealism in Poe's Gothic Tales." *American Literature* 48, no. 1 (1976): 1–12.

Butler, Judith. *Bodies That Matter: On the Discursive Limits of Sex*. New York: Routledge, 1993.

Cahill, Edward. *Liberty of the Imagination: Aesthetic Theory, Literary Form, and Politics in the Early United States*. Philadelphia: University of Pennsylvania Press, 2012.

Caldwell, Janis McLarren. *Literature and Medicine in Nineteenth-Century Britain: From Mary Shelley to George Eliot*. Cambridge: Cambridge University Press, 2004.

———. "The Strange Death of the Animated Cadaver: Changing Conventions in Nineteenth-Century British Anatomical Illustration." *Literature and Medicine* 25, no. 2 (Fall 2006): 325–57.

Campo, Rafael. *The Healing Art: A Doctor's Black Bag of Poetry*. New York: W. W. Norton, 2003.

———. "'The Medical Humanities,' for Lack of a Better Term." *JAMA* 294, no. 9 (2005): 1009–1011.

Caplan, Arthur L. "No Method, Thus Madness?" *Hastings Center Report* 36, no. 2 (2006): 12–13.

Carey, Mathew. *A Short Account of the Malignant Fever, Lately Prevalent in Philadelphia: with the Proceedings That Took Place on the Subject in Different Parts of the United States*. 4 editions. Philadelphia: Mathew Carey, 14, 23, 30 November 1793; 16 January 1794.

Carper, Barbara. "Fundamental Patterns of Knowing in Nursing." *Advances in Nursing Science* 1, no. 1 (1978): 13–24.

Caruthers, William Arthur. *The Kentuckian in New-York, or, The Adventures of Three Southerners*. 2 vols. New York: Harper and Brothers, 1834.

Cash, Philip. "Pride, Prejudice, and Politics." In *Blacks at Harvard: A Documentary History of African-American Experience at Harvard and Radcliffe*, ed. Werner Sollors, Caldwell Titcomb, and Thomas A. Underwood, 18–31. New York: New York University Press, 1993.

Castiglia, Christopher. *Interior States: Institutional Consciousness and the Inner Life of Democracy in the Antebellum United States*. Durham, NC: Duke University Press, 2008.

Castronovo, Russ. *Necro Citizenship: Death, Eroticism, and the Public Sphere*. Durham, NC: Duke University Press, 2001.

Catalogue of the Medical Graduates of the University of Pennsylvania. Philadelphia, 1839.

Cervetti, Nancy. *S. Weir Mitchell, 1829–1914: Philadelphia's Literary Physician*. University Park: Pennsylvania State University Press, 2012.

Chambers, Jan. "President's Message." *National Fibromyalgia & Chronic Pain Association*. http://www.fmcpaware.org/about-nfmcpa/presidents-message.html. Accessed 26 June 2013.

Chang, Hasok. "The Hidden History of Phlogiston." *HYLE–International Journal for Philosophy of Chemistry* 16, no. 2 (2010): 47–79.

Channing, Walter. "Essay on American Literature and Language." *North American Review* 1 (Boston, 1815): 307–14.

———. *A Treatise on Etherization in Childbirth: Illustrated by Five Hundred and Eighty-one Cases*. Boston: William D. Ticknor and Company, 1848.

Chapman, Mary, and Glenn Hendler, eds. *Sentimental Men: Masculinity and the Politics of Affect in American Culture*. Berkeley: University of California Press, 1999.

Chapman, Nathaniel. *A Compendium of Lectures on the Theory and Practice of Medicine, delivered by Professor Chapman, in the University of Pennsylvania*. Transcribed by N. D. Benedict. Philadelphia: Lea and Blanchard, 1846.

———. *Discourses on the Elements of Therapeutics and Materia Medica*. Vol. 1. Philadelphia: James Webster, 1817.

———. *Elements of Therapeutics and Materia Medica*. Vol. 1. Philadelphia: Carey and Lea, 1823.

———, ed. *Philadelphia Journal of Medical and Physical Sciences*. Vol. 1. Philadelphia: M. Carey and Sons, 1820.

———, ed. *Selected Speeches, Forensick and Parliamentary*. Philadelphia: Hopkins and Earle, 1807.

Charon, Rita. "Narrative Medicine: A Model for Empathy, Reflection, Profession, and Trust." *JAMA* 286, no. 15 (2001): 1897–1902.

———. *Narrative Medicine: Honoring the Stories of Illness*. Oxford: Oxford University Press, 2006.

Charvat, William. *The Profession of Authorship in America, 1800–1870*. 1968. Repr., New York: Columbia University Press, 1992.

Chivers, Thomas Holley. *Chivers' Life of Poe*. Ed. Richard Beale Davis. New York: E. P. Dutton & Co., 1952.

"Cholera." *Charleston Courier*, November 24, 1832, 2.

"The Cholera." *Hampshire Gazette* (Northampton, MA), June 6, 1832, 3.

"Cholera in America." *American Traveller* (*Boston Traveler*), June 19, 1832, 2.

Christophersen, Bill. *The Apparition in the Glass: Charles Brockden Brown's American Gothic*. Athens: University of Georgia Press, 1993.

Clark, Elizabeth B. "'The Sacred Rights of the Weak': Pain, Sympathy, and the Culture of Individual Rights in Antebellum America." *Journal of American History* 82, no. 2 (1995): 463–93.

Coakley, Sarah. Introduction to *Pain and Its Transformations: The Interface of Biology and Culture*, ed. Coakley and Kay Kaufman Shelemay, 1–16. Cambridge, MA: Harvard University Press, 2007.

Cohen, I. Bernard. *Revolution in Science*. Cambridge, MA: Harvard University Press, 1985.

Conant, James Bryant. *Harvard Case Histories in Experimental Science*. Ed. Leonard K. Nash. Cambridge, MA: Harvard University Press, 1957.

Cornish, William, Robert Cowley, James Deaver, and Remus Harvey. "Memorial of the Free People of Colour." *African Repository and Colonial Journal* 2, no. 10 (December 1826): 293–98.

Cowdell, Charles. *A Disquisition on the Pestilential Cholera*. London, 1849.

Coxe, John Redman. *From the Proceedings of the Trustees of the University of Pennsylvania, Vacating the Chair of Materia Medica and Pharmacy*. Philadelphia, 1835.

———. *An Inquiry into the Claims of Doctor William Harvey to the Discovery of the Circulation of the Blood; with a More Equitable Retrospect of that Event.* Philadelphia: C. Sherman & Co., 1834.

Crain, Caleb. *American Sympathy: Men, Friendship, and Literature in the New Nation.* New Haven, CT: Yale University Press, 2001.

Crary, Jonathan. *Techniques of the Observer: On Vision and Modernity in the Nineteenth Century.* Cambridge, MA: MIT Press, 1990.

Crookshank, F. G. "The Importance of a Theory of Signs and a Critique of Language in the Study of Medicine." In C. K. Ogden and I. A. Richards, *The Meaning of Meaning*, 337–55. 1923. Repr., San Diego: Harcourt Brace Jovanovich, 1989.

Crouch, Robert, and John Arras. "AZT Trials and Tribulations." *Hastings Center Report* 28, no. 6 (1998): 26–34.

"Cryptogamous." *Oxford English Dictionary.* http://www.oed.com.ezproxy.gc.cuny.edu/view /Entry/276486?redirectedFrom=cryptogamous#eid. Accessed 12 June 2011.

Csengei, Ildiko. *Sympathy, Sensibility, and the Literature of Feeling in the Eighteenth Century.* New York: Palgrave, 2012.

Cullen, William. *An Account of the Life, Lectures, and Writings of William Cullen.* Ed. John Thomson. Edinburgh: Blackwood, 1859.

———. *The Works of William Cullen, M.D.* Ed. John Thomson. Vol 2. Edinburgh: Blackwood, 1827.

Cummings, Alex Sayf. "On Creativity, Knowledge, and Epistocracy." https://www.academia.edu/29240150/On_Creativity_Knowledge_and_Epistocracy. Accessed 15 October 2016.

Cutter, Martha J. "The Writer as Doctor: New Models of Medical Discourse in Charlotte Perkins Gilman's Later Fiction." *Literature and Medicine* 20, no. 2 (Fall 2001): 151–82.

Dalby William. "An address on the pleasures of medicine and surgery." *Lancet* 144 (1894): 837–40.

Darwin, Erasmus. *The Botanic Garden.* 1789. Repr., London, 1790.

———. *The Botanic Garden.* Ed. Elihu Hubbard Smith. 1789. Repr., New York, 1798.

———. *A Plan for the Conduct of Female Education, in Boarding Schools, Private Families, and Public Seminaries.* Philadelphia, 1798.

———. *Zoonomia, or, The Laws of Organic Life.* 2 vols. London, 1794.

———. *Zoonomia, or, The Laws of Organic Life.* Part 2. Vol. 1. Ed. Charles Caldwell. Philadelphia: T. Dobson, 1797.

———. *Zoonomia, or, The Laws of Organic Life.* 2 vols. Boston: D. Carlisle, 1803.

———. *Zoonomia, or, The Laws of Organic Life.* 2 vols. Philadelphia: Edward Earle, 1818.

Daston, Lorraine. "Fear and Loathing of the Imagination in Science." *Daedalus* 127, no. 1 (Winter 1998): 73–95.

Daston, Lorraine, and Peter Galison. *Objectivity.* New York: Zone, 2010.

Daston, Lorraine, and Elizabeth Lunbeck. *Histories of Scientific Observation.* Chicago: University of Chicago Press, 2011.

Davidson, Cathy N. *The Revolution and the Word: The Rise of the Novel in America.* 1986. Repr., New York: Oxford University Press, 2004.

Davis, Curtis Carroll. *The Chronicler of the Cavaliers: A Life of the Virginia Novelist Dr. William A. Caruthers.* Richmond, VA: Dietz Press, 1953.

Davis, Cynthia J. "'The Ache of the Actual': Pain and the Aesthetics of US Literary Realism." *American Literature* 87, no. 3 (2015): 547–74.

———. *Bodily and Narrative Forms: The Influence of Medicine on American Literature, 1845–1915.* Palo Alto, CA: Stanford University Press, 2000.

Davis, Nathan S. *History of the American Medical Association up to January 1855.* Philadelphia: Lippincott, Grambo, and Co., 1855.

Davy, Humphrey. *Researches, Chemical and Philosophical, Chiefly Concerning Nitrous Oxide, or, Dephlogisticated Nitrous Air, and Its Respiration.* London, 1800.

Dawes, James. "Fictional Feeling: Philosophy, Cognitive Science, and the American Gothic." *American Literature* 76, no. 3 (September 2004): 437–66.

"Death of Dr. A. Sidney Doane." *New York Times*, January 28, 1852, 1.

"Death of Samuel George Morton, M.D." *Medical Examiner, and Record of Medical Science* 7 (June 1851): 382–85.

Delany, Martin Robison. *Blake, or, The Huts of America.* Ed. Floyd J. Miller. 1859, 1861–62. Repr., Boston: Beacon Press, 1970.

———. *The Condition, Elevation, Emigration, and Destiny of the Colored People of the United States.* Philadelphia, 1852.

———. *Martin R. Delany: A Documentary Reader.* Ed. Robert S. Levine. Chapel Hill: University of North Carolina Press, 2003.

Delbourgo, James, and Nicholas Dew, eds. *Science and Empire in the Atlantic World.* New York: Routledge, 2008.

D'Elia, Donald. "Dr. Benjamin Rush and the Negro." *Journal of the History of Ideas* 30 (1969): 413–22.

Dewees, William P. *An Essay on the Means of Lessening Pain, and Facilitating Certain Cases of Difficult Parturition.* 2nd ed. Philadelphia: Thomas Dobson and Son, 1819.

"Doctor Mitchell on Malarious and Epidemic Fevers." *Edinburgh Medical and Surgical Journal: Exhibiting a Concise View of the Latest and Most Important Discoveries in Medicine, Surgery, and Pharmacy* 73 (1850): 473–81.

Dolev, Jacqueline C., Linda Krohner Friedlaender, and Irwin M. Braverman. "Use of Fine Art to Enhance Visual Diagnostic Skills." *JAMA* 286, no. 9 (2001): 1020–21.

Donegan, Kathleen. "The Bonds of Immunity." *William and Mary Quarterly* 70, no. 4 (October 2013): 813–16.

———. "Response to Cristobal Silva." *William and Mary Quarterly* 70, no. 4 (October 2013): 839–40.

Doolen, Andy. *Fugitive Empire: Locating Early American Imperialism.* Minneapolis: University of Minnesota Press, 2005.

Douglass, Frederick. *My Bondage and My Freedom.* New York: Miller, Orton & Mulligan, 1855.

———. *Narrative of the Life of Frederick Douglass, an American Slave.* Dublin: Webb and Chapman, 1845.

Doukas, David J., Laurence B. McCullough, and Stephen Wear. "Perspective: Medical Education in Medical Ethics and Humanities as the Foundation for Developing Medical Professionalism." *Academic Medicine* 87, no. 3 (2012): 334–41.

———. "Reforming Medical Education in Ethics and Humanities by Finding Common Ground with Abraham Flexner." *Academic Medicine* 85, no. 2 (2010): 318–23.

Dowling, William C. *Oliver Wendell Holmes in Paris: Medicine, Theology, and the Autocrat of the Breakfast Table.* Hanover, NH: University Press of New England, 2006.

Downie, Robin. "Science and the Imagination in the Age of Reason." *Journal of Medical Ethics* 27 (2001): 58–63.

Duffy, Thomas P. "The Flexner Report—100 Years Later." *Yale Journal of Biology and Medicine* 84, no. 3 (2011): 269–76.

Dunglison, Robley. *Human Physiology*. 2 vols. Philadelphia: Carey and Lea, 1832.

———. *Human Physiology*. 2 vols. Philadelphia: Blanchard and Lea, 1856.

———. *Medical Lexicon: A New Dictionary*. 2nd ed. Philadelphia: Lea and Blanchard, 1839.

———. *Medical Lexicon: A Dictionary of Medical Science*. 7th ed. Philadelphia: Lea and Blanchard, 1848.

———. *Medical Lexicon: A Dictionary of Medical Science*. Philadelphia: Blanchard and Lea, 1860.

———. *The Medical Student, or, Aids to the Study of Medicine*. Philadelphia: Carey, Lea and Blanchard, 1837.

Dunglison, Robley, and John Green. *A New Dictionary of Medical Science and Literature*. Boston: Charles Bowen, 1833.

Dunlap, William. *The Life of Charles Brockden Brown*. 2 vols. Philadelphia: James P. Parke, 1815.

———. *Memoirs of Charles Brockden Brown: The American Novelist, With Selections from His Original Letters and Miscellaneous Writings*. London: Henry Colburn and Co., 1822.

Dunster, Edward Swift. *A History of Anaesthesia*. Ann Arbor, MI: Fiske and Douglas, 1875.

Earnest, Ernest. *S. Weir Mitchell: Novelist and Physician*. Philadelphia: University of Pennsylvania Press, 1950.

Eddy, Matthew Daniel, Seymour H. Mauskopf, and William R. Newman. "An Introduction to Chemical Knowledge in the Early Modern World." *Osiris* 29, no. 1 (2014): 1–15.

Edelstein, Sidney M. "The Chemical Revolution in America from the Pages of the 'Medical Repository.'" *Chymia* (1959): 155–79.

Emerson, Ralph Waldo. *Letters and Social Aims*. Boston: Osgood and Company, 1876.

Emery, Clark. "Scientific Theory in Erasmus Darwin's 'The Botanic Garden' (1789–91)." *Isis* 33, no. 3 (September 1941): 315–25.

"Empathy." *Oxford English Dictionary*. http://www.oed.com.ezproxy.bpl.org/view/Entry/61284 ?redirectedFrom=empathy#eid. Accessed 15 July 2014.

Eve, Joseph. "Professional Qualifications and Character." *Southern Medical and Surgical Journal* 1, no. 12 (May 1837): 705–11.

Ewell, Thomas. *Plain Discourses on the Laws or Properties of Matter*. New York: Brisban & Brannan, 1806.

"Extracts of a letter from a gentleman in Philadelphia, to the Printers of this Paper, dated September 23rd." *The Daily Advertiser* (New York) 2 October 1793, 2.

Fabian, Ann. *The Skull Collectors: Race, Science, and America's Unburied Dead*. Chicago: University of Chicago Press, 2010.

Faraday, Michael. *Chemical Manipulation: Being Instructions to Students in Chemistry, on the Methods of Performing Experiments of Demonstration or of Research, with Accuracy and Success*. Ed. John Kearsley Mitchell. Philadelphia: Carey and Lea, 1831.

Farnham, John H. "Extract of a Letter from John H. Farnham, Esq., a Member of the American Antiquarian Society, describing the Mammoth Cave, in Kentucky." *Archaeologia Americana: Transactions and Collections* 1 (1820): 355–61.

Fernandez, Nicolas, Valerie Dory, Louis-Georges Ste-Marie, Monique Chaput, Bernard Charlin, and Andree Boucher. "Varying Conceptions of Competence: An Analysis of How

Health Sciences Educators Define Competence." *Medical Education* 46, no. 4 (2012): 357–65.

Ffirth, Stubbins. *An Inaugural Dissertation on Malignant Fever: With an Attempt to Prove Its Non-contagious Nature, From Reason, Observation, and Experiment*. Philadelphia, 1804.

"Fiction Anticipates Science." *New York Times*, May 7, 1895, 4.

Fiedler, Leslie. *Love and Death in the American Novel*. New York: Criterion, 1960.

Finger, Simon. *The Contagious City: the Politics of Public Health in Early Philadelphia*. Ithaca, NY: Cornell University Press, 2012.

Fleck, Ludwik. *Genesis and Development of a Scientific Fact*. Ed. Thaddeus J. Trenn and Robert K. Merton. Trans. Frederick Bradley. 1935. Repr., Chicago: University of Chicago Press, 1981.

———. "Some Specific Features of the Medical Way of Thinking [1927]." In *Cognition and Fact: Materials on Ludwik Fleck*, ed. Robert S. Cohen and Thomas Schnelle, 39–46. Dordrecht, Holland: D. Reidel, 1986.

Flexner, Abraham. *Medical Education: A Comparative Study*. New York: Macmillan, 1925.

———. *Medical Education in the United States and Canada: A Report to the Carnegie Foundation for the Advancement of Teaching*. 1910. Repr., New York: Carnegie Foundation, 1972.

Forget, Evelyn. "Evocations of Sympathy: Sympathetic Imagery in Eighteenth-Century Social Theory and Physiology." *History of Political Economy* 35, no. 1 (2003): 282–308.

Foucault, Michel. *The Birth of the Clinic: An Archaeology of Medical Perception*. Trans. A. M. Sheridan Smith. New York: Vintage, 1994.

———. *The Order of Things: An Archaeology of the Human Sciences*. 1966. Repr., New York: Vintage, 1994.

Foust, Clement Edgar. *The Life and Dramatic Works of Robert Montgomery Bird*. New York: Lenox Hill, 1919.

Frank, Arthur. *The Wounded Storyteller: Body, Illness, and Ethics*. Chicago: University of Chicago Press, 1995.

Frank, Frederick S., and Tony Magistrale. *The Poe Encyclopedia*. Westport, CT: Greenwood, 1997.

Frank, Jason. *Constituent Moments: Enacting the People in Postrevolutionary America*. Durham, NC: Duke University Press, 2009.

———. "Sympathy and Separation: Benjamin Rush and the Contagious Public." *Modern Intellectual History* 6, no. 1 (2009): 27–57.

Frank, Jason R., Linda S. Snell, Olle Ten Cate, Eric S. Holmboe, Carol Carraccio, Susan R. Swing, Peter Harris, et al. "Competency-Based Medical Education: Theory to Practice." *Medical Teacher* 32, no. 8 (2010): 638–45.

Frankland, Graham. *Freud's Literary Culture*. Cambridge: Cambridge University Press, 2000.

Freneau, Philip. "The Crows and the Carrion: A Medical Story." In *Poems Written and Published During the American Revolutionary War*, 2:8–10. Philadelphia, 1809.

———. "Pestilence." In *Poems Written and Published During the American Revolutionary War*, 2:230–31. Philadelphia, 1809.

Freud, Sigmund. *The Standard Edition of the Complete Psychological Works of Sigmund Freud: Pre-psycho-analytic Publications and Unpublished Drafts*. Trans. James Strachey. London: Hogarth Press, 1966.

Friedberg, Fred. "Chronic Fatigue Syndrome, Fibromyalgia, and Related Illnesses: A Clinical Model of Assessment and Intervention." *Journal of Clinical Psychology* 66, no. 6 (2010): 641–65.

Furst, Lilian, ed. *Medical Progress and Social Reality: A Reader in Nineteenth-Century Medicine*. Albany: State University of New York Press, 2000.

Garden, Rebecca Elizabeth. "The Problem of Empathy: Medicine and the Humanities." *New Literary History* 38, no. 3 (2007): 551–67.

Garland-Thomson, Rosemarie. *Staring: How We Look*. Oxford: Oxford University Press, 2009.

Gaudet, Katherine Sarah. "Fear of Fiction: Reading and Resisting the Novel in Early America." PhD diss., University of Chicago, 2011.

"Georgia. By His Excellency Edward Telfair, Governor and Commander in Chief in and over the state aforesaid, A Proclamation." *Georgia Gazette* 561 (October 24, 1793): 3.

Gibian, Peter. *Oliver Wendell Holmes and the Culture of Conversation*. Cambridge: Cambridge University Press, 2001.

Gill, William Fearing. *The Life of Poe*. New York: C. T. Dillingham, 1877.

Gilman, Charlotte Perkins. "Why I Wrote 'The Yellow Wallpaper?'" *Forerunner* 4 (October 1913): 271.

Gilmore, John. *The Poetics of Empire: A Study of James Grainger's* The Sugar Cane *(1764)*. London: Athlone Press, 2000.

Gilmore, Paul. *Aesthetic Materialism: Electricity and American Romanticism*. Stanford, CA: Stanford University Press, 2009.

Gilroy, Paul. *The Black Atlantic: Modernity and Double Consciousness*. Cambridge, MA: Harvard University Press, 1993.

Goddu, Teresa A. *Gothic America: Narrative, History, and Nation*. New York: Columbia University Press, 1997.

Gomaa, Sally. "Writing to 'Virtuous' and 'Gentle' Readers: The Problem of Pain in Harriet Jacobs's Incidents and Harriet Wilson's Sketches." *African American Review* 43, no. 2 (2009): 371–81.

Goodman, Kevis. *Georgic Modernity and British Romanticism: Poetry and the Mediation of History*. Cambridge: Cambridge University Press, 2004.

Goudie, Sean X. *Creole America: The West Indies and the Formation of Literature and Culture in the New Republic*. Philadelphia: University of Pennsylvania Press, 2006.

Gould, Philip. *Barbaric Traffic: Commerce and Antislavery in the 18th Century Atlantic World*. Cambridge, MA: Harvard University Press, 2003.

———. "Early Black Atlantic Writing and the Cultures of the Enlightenment." In *Beyond Douglass: New Perspectives on Early African-American Literature*, ed. Michael Drexler and Ed White, 107–22. Lewisburg, PA: Bucknell University Press, 2008.

———. "Race, Commerce, and the Literature of Yellow Fever in Early National Philadelphia." *Early American Literature* 35, no. 2 (2000): 157–86.

Gould, Stephen Jay. *The Mismeasure of Man*. New York: W. W. Norton, 1981.

Graham, Jenny. "Revolutionary in Exile: The Emigration of Joseph Priestley to America, 1794–1804." *American Philosophical Society* 85, no. 2 (1995): i–xii, 1–213.

Graves, Charles Marshall. "Thompson the Confederate." *Lamp* 29, no. 3 (October 1904): 181–90.

Graves, John. "Communication." *New-York Medical Journal* 1 (1830): 503–16.

Griffith, Devin S. "The Institutions of Analogy in Erasmus Darwin's Poetics." *Studies in English Literature, 1500–1900* 51, no. 3 (Summer 2011): 645–65.

Gross, Robert A., and Mary Kelley, eds. *A History of the Book in America*. Vol. 2, *An Extensive Republic: Print, Culture, and Society in the New Nation, 1790–1840*. Chapel Hill: University of North Carolina Press, 2010.

Guither, Harold. *Animal Rights: History and Scope of a Radical Social Movement.* Carbondale: Southern Illinois University Press, 1998.

Gunn, John C. *Gunn's Domestic Medicine, or, Poor Man's Friend, in the Hours of Affliction, Pain, and Sickness.* 4th ed. Springfield, OH: John M. Gallagher, 1835.

Haber, Samuel. *The Quest for Authority and Honor in the American Professions, 1750–1900.* Chicago: University of Chicago Press, 1991.

Hale, Dorothy. "The Profits of Altruism: Caleb Williams and Arthur Mervyn." *Eighteenth-Century Studies* 22, no. 1 (1988): 47–69.

Hall, William Whitty. "Dr. Edward Jenner." *The Bizarre. Notes and Queries, A Monthly Magazine of History, Folk-Lore, Mathematics, Mysticism, Art, Science, Etc.* Vol. 5, 175–76. Manchester, NH: S. C. & L. M. Gould, 1888.

———. *Hall's Health Tracts.* New York, 1868.

Halttunen, Karen. "Humanitarianism and the Pornography of Pain in Anglo-American Culture." *American Historical Review* 100, no. 2 (April 1995): 303–34.

———. *Murder Most Foul: The Killer and the American Gothic Imagination.* Cambridge, MA: Harvard University Press, 1998.

Harken, Alden H. "Oxygen, Politics and the American Revolution (with a note on the bicentennial of phlogiston)." *Annals of Surgery* 184, no. 5 (1976): 645.

Harlan, Richard. *Medical and Physical Researches, or, Original memoirs in medicine, surgery, physiology, geology, zoology, and comparative anatomy.* Philadelphia, 1835.

Harvey, William. *Exercitatio Anatomica de Motu Cordis et Sanguinis in Animalibus.* Trans. C. D. Leake. 1628. Repr., Springfield, IL: Thomas, 1930.

Hawke, David Freeman. *Benjamin Rush: Revolutionary Gadfly.* Indianapolis: Bobbs-Merrill, 1971.

Hawkins, Anne Hunsaker. *Reconstructing Illness: Studies in Pathography.* 1993. Repr., West Lafayette, IN: Purdue University Press, 1999.

Hedges, William L. "Benjamin Rush, Charles Brockden Brown, and the American Plague Year." *Early American Literature* 7, no. 3 (Winter 1973): 295–311.

Heibert, Erwin N., Aaron J. Ihde, and Robert E. Schofield. *Joseph Priestley: Scientist, Theologian, and Metaphysician.* Lewisburg, PA: Bucknell University Press, 1980.

Hendler, Glenn. *Public Sentiments: Structures of Feeling in Nineteenth-Century American Literature.* Chapel Hill: University of North Carolina Press, 2001.

Herminghouse, Patricia. "The German Secrets of New Orleans." *German Studies Review* 27, no. 1 (February 2004): 1–16.

Herndl, Diane Price. *Invalid Women: Figuring Feminine Illness in American Fiction and Culture, 1840–1940.* Chapel Hill: University of North Carolina Press, 1993.

Herter, Christian A. "Imagination and Idealism in the Medical Sciences." *JAMA* 54, no. 6 (1910): 423–30.

Herzig, Rebecca. *Suffering for Science: Reason and Sacrifice in Modern America.* New Brunswick, NJ: Rutgers University Press, 2005.

Hoffman, Daniel. *Poe Poe Poe Poe Poe Poe Poe.* Baton Rouge: Louisiana State University Press, 1972.

Holloway, Karla. *Private Bodies, Public Texts: Race, Gender, and a Cultural Bioethics.* Durham, NC: Duke University Press, 2011.

Holmes, Oliver Wendell. *Border Lines of Knowledge in Some Provinces of Medical Science.* Boston: Ticknor and Fields, 1862.

———. *Currents and Counter-Currents in Medical Science with Other Addresses and Essays.* Boston: Ticknor and Fields, 1861.

———. *Elsie Venner.* Vol. 2. Boston: Ticknor and Fields, 1861.

———. "Experiments in Medicine." *Boston Medical and Surgical Journal* 30, no. 10 (April 1844): 201–3.

———. *The Guardian Angel.* In *The Writings of Oliver Wendell Holmes.* Vol. 6. Cambridge, MA: Riverside Press, 1891.

———. *A Mortal Antipathy: First Opening of the New Portfolio.* London: Sampson Low, Marston, Searle and Rivington, 1885.

———. *Over the Teacups.* Boston: Houghton Mifflin, 1891.

———. *Poems.* Boston, 1836.

———. *The Poet at the Breakfast-table.* Boston: James R. Osgood and Company, 1872.

———. "The Professor's Story." *Atlantic Monthly* 5 (January 1860): 88–99.

———. "Report of the Committee on Medical Literature." In *The Transactions of the American Medical Association,* 1:249–88. Philadelphia, 1848.

———. *The Writings of Oliver Wendell Holmes.* Vol. 6. Cambridge, MA: Riverside Press, 1891.

Holmes, Oliver Wendell, and John Torrey Morse. *Medical Essays, 1842–1882.* Boston: Houghton Mifflin, 1883.

"The Holmes Breakfast." *Atlantic Monthly Supplement* 45 (January 1880): 1–24.

Hooker, Claire, and Estelle Noonan. "Medical Humanities as Expressive of Western Culture." *Medical Humanities* 37, no. 2 (2011): 79–84.

Hope, James. *A Treatise on the Diseases of the Heart and the Great Vessels and on the Affections which may be Mistaken for Them.* London: William Kidd, 1832.

Horace. *The Epodes and Secular Odes of Horace.* Trans. F. Howe. Norwich: Charles Muskett, 1841.

Horne, Philip. *Henry James: A Life in Letters.* New York: Penguin, 1999.

Horner, William E. "Observations and Experiments on Certain Parts of the Nervous System." *Philadelphia Journal of Medical and Physical Sciences* 1 (1820): 285–99.

Howe, Daniel Walker. *What Hath God Wrought.* Oxford: Oxford University Press, 2007.

Humboldt, Alexander von. *Personal Narrative of Travels to the Equinoctial Regions of the New Continent, During the Years 1799–1804.* Trans., Helen Maria Williams. 7 vols. London, 1814.

Hume, David. *A Treatise of Human Nature.* 1739. Repr., New York: Oxford University Press, 2007.

Hungerford, Edward. "Poe and Phrenology." *American Literature* 2, no. 3 (1930): 209–31.

Huston, R. M. "Death of Nathaniel Chapman, M.D." *Medical Examiner and Record of Medical Science* 9 (1858): 532–35.

"Instructions for Authors." *JAMA Network.* http://jamanetwork.com/journals/jama/pages /instructions-for-authors#SecArticleTypeViewpoint. Accessed 16 October 2016.

James, William. *The Principles of Psychology.* 1890. Repr., New York: Henry Holt, 1910.

Jarcho, Saul. "Yellow Fever, Cholera, and the Beginnings of Medical Cartography." *Journal of the History of Medicine and Allied Sciences* 25, no. 2 (1970): 131–42.

Jones, Absalom, and Richard Allen. *A Narrative of the Proceedings of the Black People During the Late Calamity in Philadelphia in the Year 1793: And Refutation of Some Censures, Thrown upon them in some late Publication.* Philadelphia, 1794.

Jones, David S., Jeremy A. Greene, Jacalyn Duffin, and John Harley Warner. "Making the Case for History in Medical Education." *Journal of the History of Medicine and Allied Sciences* 70, no. 4 (2014): 623–52.

Jones, Therese, Delese Wear, and Lester D. Friedman, eds. *Health Humanities Reader*. New Brunswick, NJ: Rutgers University Press, 2014.

Juliani, Richard N. *Building Little Italy: Philadelphia's Italians Before Mass Migration*. University Park, PA: The Pennsylvania State University Press, 2005.

Jurecic, Ann. "Empathy and the Critic." *College English* 74, no. 1 (September 2011): 10–27.

Justus, James H. "Arthur Mervyn, American." *American Literature* 42, no. 3 (1970): 304–24.

Kames, Henry Home. Lord. *Elements of Criticism*. Boston: Samuel Etheridge, 1796 [1762].

———. *Essays on the Principles of Morality and Natural Religion*. Edinburgh, 1751.

Kaplan, Catherine O'Donnell. "Elihu Hubbard Smith's 'The Institutions of the Republic of Utopia.'" *Early American Literature* 35, no. 3 (2000): 294–336.

———. *Men of Letters in the Early Republic: Cultivating Forums of Citizenship*. Chapel Hill: University of North Carolina Press, 2008.

Kaufman, Martin. "The American Anti-Vaccinationists and their Arguments." *Bulletin of the History of Medicine* 41, no. 5 (1967): 463–78.

Kendall, Lyle H. "The Vampire Motif in 'The Fall of the House of Usher.'" College English 24, no. 6 (March 1963): 450–53.

Kennedy, Meegan. "Modernist Autobiography, Hysterical Narrative, and the Unnavigable River: The Case of Freud and HD." *Literature and Medicine* 30, no. 2 (2012): 241–75.

———. *Revising the Clinic: Vision and Representation in Victorian Medical Narrative and the Novel*. Columbus: Ohio State University Press, 2010.

Kerridge, I. "Altruism or Reckless Curiosity? A Brief History of Self Experimentation in Medicine." *Internal Medicine Journal* 33, no. 4 (2003): 203–7.

Kilman, John Collins. "Robert Montgomery Bird: Physician and Man of Letters." PhD diss., University of Delaware, 1978.

Kirby, William, and William Spence. *An Introduction to Entomology, or, Elements of the Natural History of Insects*. Philadelphia: Lea and Blanchard, 1846.

Kirmayer, Laurence J. "Toward a Medicine of the Imagination." *New Literary History* 37, no. 3 (Summer 2006): 583–605.

Klebs, Arnold C. "The Historic Evolution of Variolation." *Johns Hopkins Hospital Bulletin* 265, no. 1 (1913): 69–83.

Kleinman, Arthur. *The Illness Narratives: Suffering, Healing, and the Human Condition*. New York: Basic Books, 1988.

Knott, Sarah. *Sensibility and the American Revolution*. Durham, NC: Duke University Press, 2009.

Koch, Tom. *Disease Maps: Epidemics on the Ground*. Chicago: University of Chicago Press, 2011.

———. "Knowing Its Place: Mapping as Medical Investigation." *Lancet* 379, no. 9819 (2012): 887–88.

Kodish, E., J. D. Lantos, and M. Siegler. "The Ethics of Randomization." *CA: A Cancer Journal for Clinicians* 41, no. 3 (May/June 1991): 180–86.

Krisberg, Kim. "Humanities Programs Help Medical Students See Life Through a Patient's Eyes." *AAMC Reporter*. May 2014. https://www.aamc.org/newsroom/reporter/may2014/380438/humanities.html. Accessed 21 July 2014.

Kristeller, Paul Oskar. "'Creativity' and 'Tradition'." *Journal of the History of Ideas* (1983): 105–13.

Kuhn, Thomas. *The Structure of Scientific Revolutions.* 1962. Repr., Chicago: University of Chicago Press, 1996.

Kumagai, Arno K. "From Competencies to Human Interests: Ways of Knowing and Understanding in Medical Education." *Academic Medicine* 89, no. 7 (2014): 978–83.

Laqueur, Thomas. *Making Sex: Body and Gender from the Greeks to Freud.* Cambridge, MA: Harvard University Press, 1992.

Lather, Patti. "Against Empathy, Voice, and Authenticity." In *Voice in Qualitative Inquiry: Challenging Conventional, Interpretive, and Critical Conceptions in Qualitative Research.* New York: Routledge, 2009.

Latour, Bruno. *The Pasteurization of France.* Trans. Alan Sheridan and John Law. 1988. Repr., Cambridge, MA: Harvard University Press, 1993.

———. *Reassembling the Social: An Introduction to Actor-Network Theory.* Oxford: Oxford University Press, 2005.

———. *We Have Never Been Modern.* Cambridge, MA: Harvard University Press, 1993.

Leavitt, Gerald M. *The Turk, Chess Automaton.* Jefferson, NC: McFarland, 2006.

Levin, A. "Venel, Lavoisier, Fourcroy, Cabanis and the Idea of Scientific Revolution: The French Political Context and the General Patterns of Conceptualization of Scientific Change." *History of Science* 22, no. 3 (1984): 303–20.

Levine, George. *One Culture: Essays in Science and Literature.* Madison: University of Wisconsin Press, 1987.

Levine, Robert. "Clinical Trials and Physicians as Double Agents." *Yale Journal of Biology and Medicine* 65 (1992): 65–74.

Levine, Robert S. *Martin Delany, Frederick Douglass, and the Politics of Representative Identity.* Chapel Hill: University of North Carolina Press, 1997.

Lilley, James D. *Common Things: Romance and the Aesthetics of Belonging in Atlantic Modernity.* New York: Fordham, 2013.

Lindman, Janet Moore, and Michele Lise Tarter, eds. *A Centre of Wonders: The Body in Early America.* Ithaca, NY: Cornell University Press, 2001.

Liou, Kevin T., Daniel S. Jamorabo, Richard H. Dollase, Luba Dumenco, Fred J. Schiffman, and Jay M. Baruch. "Playing in the 'Gutter': Cultivating Creativity in Medical Education and Practice." *Academic Medicine* 91, no. 3 (2016): 322–27.

Lippard, George. *The Quaker City, or, The Monks of Monk Hall.* Philadelphia: T. B. Peterson and Brothers, 1845.

Livingstone, David N. *Adam's Ancestors: Race, Religion, and the Politics of Human Origins.* Baltimore: Johns Hopkins University Press, 2008.

Lloyd, J. A. T. *The Murder of Edgar Allan Poe.* London: Stanley Paul & Co., 1928.

Long, Thomas. "Legible Signs: Science and Medicine in Early American Culture." *American Literary History.* 2014. http://alh.oxfordjournals.org/content/early/2014/06/03/alh.aju024. Accessed 5 March 2015.

Loughran, Trish. *The Republic in Print: Print Culture in the Age of US Nation Building, 1770–1870.* New York: Columbia University Press, 2009.

Lucian of Samosata. *Lucian of Samosata.* Trans. William Tooke. London: Longman, Hurst, Rees, Orme, and Brown, 1820.

Lynch, Jordan R. "Cholera in Paris." *Lancet,* May 26, 1832, 268–70.

Macfie, Ronald Campbell. *The Romance of Medicine.* London: Cassell and Company, 1907.

MacIntyre, Alisdair. "Epistemological Crises, Dramatic Narrative and the Philosophy of Science." *Monist* 60, no. 4 (October 1977): 453–72.

Madden, Etta. "'To Make a Figure': Benjamin Rush's Rhetorical Self-Construction and Scientific Authorship." *Early American Literature* 41, no. 2 (2006): 241–72.

Maier, Frank. *First Editions of American Authors: The Library of Frank Maier of New York*. New York: Anderson Auction Company, 1909.

Mandeville, Bernard. *The Fable of the Bees, or, Private Vices, Public Benefits*. London, 1795.

Manningham, Richard. *An Exact Diary of what was Observ'd During a Close Attendance Upon Mary Toft: The Pretended Rabbet-breeder of Godalming in Surrey . . . Together with an Account of Her Confession of the Fraud*. London, 1726.

Marks, William S. "The Art of Corrective Vision in Poe's 'The Sphinx.'" *Pacific Coast Philology* 22, no. 1/2 (1987): 46–51.

Marshall, David. *The Surprising Effects of Sympathy: Marivaux, Diderot, Rousseau, and Mary Shelley*. Chicago: University of Chicago Press, 1988.

Matthiessen, F. O. "Poe." *Sewanee Review* 54, no. 2 (1946): 175–205.

McAuley, Louis Kirk. "'Periodic Visitations': Yellow Fever as Yellow Journalism in Charles Brockden Brown's *Arthur Mervyn*." *Eighteenth Century Fiction* 19, no. 3 (Spring 2007): 307 40.

McCullough, Laurence B. "Hume's Influence on John Gregory and the History of Medical Ethics." *Journal of Medicine and Philosophy* 24, no. 4 (1999): 376–95.

McFarland, Benjamin J., and Thomas Peter Bennett. "The Image of Edgar Allan Poe: A Daguerreotype Linked to the Academy of Natural Sciences of Philadelphia." *Proceedings of the Academy of Natural Sciences* 147 (1997): 1–32.

McKechnie, Claire Charlotte. "Anxieties of Communication: The Limits of Narrative in the Medical Humanities." *Medical Humanities* 40, no. 1 (June 2014): 1–6.

"Medical Humanities." http://medhum.med.nyu.edu/. Accessed 25 October 2011.

Medical Repository. Vols. 1–5. Ed. Edward Miller, Samuel Latham Mitchill, and Elihu Hubbard Smith. New York: T. J. Swords, 1797–1802.

Melville, Herman. *Moby-Dick, or, The Whale*. 1851. New York: Norton, 2001.

Metzl, Jonathan M. "Structural Competency." *American Quarterly* 64, no. 2 (June 2012): 213–18.

Miller, Alexa Rose. "Arts Practica." http://www.artspractica.com/about/. Accessed 12 May 2016.

Miller, Floyd John. *The Search for Black Nationality: Black Emigration and Colonization, 1787–1863*. Champaign: University of Illinois Press, 1975.

Miller, Jacquelyn C. "The Wages of Blackness: African American Workers and the Meanings of Race during Philadelphia's 1793 Yellow Fever Epidemic." *The Pennsylvania Magazine of History and Biography* 129, no. 2 (2005): 163–94.

Millner, Michael. *Fever Reading: Affect and Reading Badly in the Early American Public Sphere*. Durham: University of New Hampshire Press, 2012.

Mitchell, John Kearsley. *Five Essays*. Ed. S. Weir Mitchell. Philadelphia: J. B. Lippincott, 1859.

———. *Indecision: A Tale of the Far West*. Philadelphia: E. L. Carey and A. Hart, 1838.

Mitchell, Silas Weir. *The Autobiography of a Quack and the Case of George Dedlow*. New York: Century, 1900.

———. "The Automaton Chess Player." *Chess World: A Magazine Devoted to the Cultivation of the Game of Chess* 3 (1868): 1–4.

———. "The Case of George Dedlow." *Atlantic Monthly* 18, no. 105 (July 1866): 1–11.

———. *Doctor and Patient*. Philadelphia: J. B. Lippincott, 1888.

———. *Fat and Blood: An Essay on the Treatment of Certain Forms of Neurasthenia and Hysteria.* 1877. Repr., Philadelphia: J. B. Lippincott, 1898.

———. "Historical Notes of Dr. Benjamin Rush, 1777." *Pennsylvania Magazine of History and Biography* 27, no. 2 (1903): 129–50.

———. *Injuries of the Nerves and Their Consequences.* Philadelphia: J. B. Lippincott, 1872.

———. "The Last of a Veteran Chess Player." *Chess World: A Magazine Devoted to the Cultivation of the Game of Chess* 1 (February 1857): 3–4.

———. "The Medical Department in the Civil War." Philadelphia, 1914.

———. "Phantom Limbs." *Lippincott's Magazine of Popular Literature and Science* 8 (1871): 563–69.

———. "The Relation of Pain to Weather, being a study of the natural history of a case of Traumatic Neuralgia." *American Journal of the Medical Sciences* 73 (April 1877): 305–29.

Mitchell, Silas Weir, George R. Morehouse, and William W. Keen. *Gunshot Wounds and Other Injuries of Nerves.* Philadelphia: J. B. Lippincott, 1864.

Mitchill, Samuel Latham. "An Address, &c. After a continued struggle of many centuries against the absurd systems of ancient physicians." New York, 1796.

———. "The Doctrine of Septon." *Medical Repository* 1, no. 2 (1797): 189–92

———. "Outlines of Medical Geography." *Medical Repository* 2, no. 1 (1799): 39–47.

Morris, David B. *The Culture of Pain.* Berkeley: University of California Press, 1991.

Morton, Samuel George. *Crania Aegyptiaca, or, Observations on Egyptian Ethnography.* Philadelphia: John Penington, 1844.

———. *Crania Americana, or, A Comparative View of the Skulls of Various Aboriginal Nations of North and South America.* Philadelphia: John Penington, 1839.

———. *Illustrations of Pulmonary Consumption.* Philadelphia: Key & Biddle, 1834.

———. "Morton's Crania Americana." *American Medical Intelligencer* 1 (1838): 403–5.

———. *Synopsis of the Organic Remains of the Cretaceous Group of the United States.* Philadelphia: Key & Biddle, 1834.

———. *Tentamen inaugurale de corporis dolore.* Edinburgh, 1823.

Moscoso, Javier. *Pain: A Cultural History.* London: Palgrave Macmillan, 2012.

Mott, Valentine. "Remarks on the Importance of Anaesthesia from Chloroform in Surgical Operations." *New-York Journal of Medicine* (July 1851): 9–21.

Much Ado About Nothing, or, A Plain Refutation of All that has been Written or Said Concerning the Rabbit-Woman of Godalming. London, 1727.

Murison, Justine S. "Hypochondria and Racial Interiority in Robert Montgomery Bird's *Sheppard Lee.*" *Arizona Quarterly* 64, no. 1 (Spring 2008): 1–25.

———. *The Politics of Anxiety in Nineteenth-Century American Literature.* New York: Cambridge University Press, 2011.

Murray, John. *System of Materia Medica and Pharmacy.* Philadelphia: Thomas Dobson, 1815.

Nelson, Dana. *National Manhood: Capitalist Citizenship and the Imagined Fraternity of White Men.* Durham, NC: Duke University Press, 1998.

"New Port, New York." *Thomas's Massachusetts Spy, or, The Worcester Gazette* 22, no. 1068 (September 19, 1793): 3.

Nott, J. C., and George R. Gliddon. *Types of Mankind, or, Ethnological Researches, Based upon the Ancient Monuments, Paintings, Sculptures, and Crania of Races.* Philadelphia: Lippincott, Grambo & Co., 1854.

Oberndorf, Clarence P. *The Psychiatric Novels of Oliver Wendell Holmes.* New York: Columbia University Press, 1943.

Osborn, Matthew Warner. "Diseased Imaginations: Constructing Delirium Tremens in Philadelphia, 1813–1832." *Social History of Medicine* 19, no. 2 (2006): 191–208.

Osler, William. "John Keats, The Apothecary Poet." Baltimore: Friedenwald Company, 1896.

———. *Science and Immortality*. London: Archibald Constable & Co., 1906.

Otter, Samuel. *Philadelphia Stories: America's Literature of Race and Freedom.* New York: Oxford University Press, 2010.

Paine, Thomas. *Rights of Man, Common Sense, and Other Political Writings.* Ed. Mark Philp.
New York: Oxford, 1998.

Park, Katherine, Lorraine J. Daston, and Peter L. Galison. "Bacon, Galileo, and Descartes on
Imagination and Analogy." *Isis* 75, no. 2 (June 1984): 287–89.

Park, Roswell. *An Epitome of the History of Medicine: Based upon a Course of Lectures.* Philadelphia: F. A. Davis, 1898.

Peabody, Elizabeth. "The Word 'Aesthetic.'" In *Aesthetic Papers,* ed. Elizabeth Peabody. Boston: Peabody, 1849.

Pellegrino, Edmund D. "The Reconciliation of Technology and Humanism: A Flexnerian Task
75 Years Later." In *Flexner: 75 Years Later: A Current Commentary on Medical Education,*
ed. Charles Vevier. Lanham, MD: University Press of America, 1987.

Peloquin, Suzanne M. "Art: An Occupation with Promise for Developing Empathy." *American Journal of Occupational Therapy* 50, no. 8 (1996): 655–61.

Pernick, Martin. *A Calculus of Suffering: Pain, Anesthesia, and the Utilitarian Professionalism
in Nineteenth-Century American Medicine.* New York: Columbia University Press,
1979.

———. "Contagion and Culture." *American Literary History* 14, no. 4 (2002): 858–65.

———. "Politics, Parties, and Pestilence: Epidemic Yellow Fever in Philadelphia and the Rise
of the First Party System." *William and Mary Quarterly* 29, no. 4 (October 1972): 559–86.

Perrin, Carleton E. "Revolution or Reform: The Chemical Revolution and Eighteenth Century
Concepts of Scientific Change." *History of Science* 25, no. 4 (1987): 395–423.

"Perry Davis' Vegetable Pain Killer . . . Entered . . . in the Year 1860 . . . Perry Davis & Son,
Providence, R.I." [Cincinnati], 1860. Held at the American Antiquarian Society, Worcester, MA.

Pessen, Edward. *Jacksonian America: Society, Personality, and Politics.* 1969. Repr., Homewood,
IL: Dorsey Press, 1978.

"Philadelphia; Melancholy; Digging; Indiscriminately." *Greenfield Gazette* (Greenfield, MA),
October 17, 1793, 3.

Pocock, J. G. A. *The Machiavellian Moment: Florentine Political Thought and the Atlantic Political Tradition.* Princeton: Princeton University Press, 1975.

Poe, Edgar Allan. *Complete Works.* New York: Modern Library, 1938.

———. "The Fall of the House of Usher." *Burton's Gentleman's Magazine and American
Monthly Review* 5 (September 1839): 145–52.

———. Letter to Maria Clemm. July 7, 1849. "The Letters of Edgar Allan Poe." LTR-323.
Edgar Allan Poe Society of Baltimore. http://www.eapoe.org/works/letters/p4907070
.htm. Accessed 26 June 2015.

———. "Maelzel's Chess Player." *Southern Literary Messenger* 2 (April 1836): 318–26.

———. "The Murders in the Rue Morgue." *Graham's Magazine* 18 (April 1841): 167–79.

———. "The Sphinx." *Arthur's Magazine of Elegant Literature and Art* 5, no. 1 (January 1846):
15–16.

———. *Tales by Edgar A. Poe.* New York: Wiley and Putnam, 1845.

Poirier, Jean-Pierre. *Lavoisier: Chemist, Biologist, Economist*. Trans. Rebecca Balinski. 1993. Philadelphia: University of Pennsylvania Press, 1998.

Poirer, Suzanne. "The Physician and Authority: Portraits by Four Physician-Writers." *Literature and Medicine* 2 (1983): 21–40.

Pope, Alexander. *An Essay on Man and Other Poems*. London: John Sharpe, 1829.

Popkin, Richard H. "Pre-Adamism in 19th Century American Thought: 'Speculative Biology' and Racism." *Philosophia* 8, no. 2 (1978): 205–39.

Porter, Roy. "The Rise of Physical Examination." In *Medicine and the Five Senses*, ed. William F. Bynum and Roy Porter, 179–98. Cambridge: Cambridge University Press, 1993.

Powell, J. M. *Bring Out Your Dead: The Great Plague of Yellow Fever in Philadelphia in 1783*. 1949. Repr., Philadelphia: University of Pennsylvania Press, 1993.

Priestley, Joseph. *Considerations on the Doctrine of Phlogiston, and the Decomposition of Water*. Philadelphia, 1796.

———. *Experiments and Observations on Different Kinds of Air*. Vol. 1. 1773. Repr., Birmingham, 1790.

———. *Experiments and Observations on Different Kinds of Air*. Vol. 2. London, 1775.

"Priestley's Sentiments on the Doctrine of Septon." *Medical Repository* 3, no. 3 (1800): 307.

"The Program in Narrative Medicine." http://www.narrativemedicine.org. Accessed 25 October 2011.

Quincy, John. *The American Medical Lexicon: On the Plan of Quincy's Lexicon*. New York: T. and J. Swords, 1811.

———. *Quincy's Lexicon-Medicum. A New Medical Dictionary*. Ed. Robert Hooper. Philadelphia: Benjamin Warner, M. Carey & Son, and Edward Parker, 1817.

———. *Lexicon Physico-Medicum Improved, or, A Dictionary of Terms Employed in Medicine*. New York, 1802.

———. *Lexicon Physico-Medicum, or, A New Medicinal Dictionary*. London, 1736.

Quinn, Arthur Hobson. *Edgar Allan Poe: A Critical Biography*. Baltimore: Johns Hopkins University Press, 1998.

Ragland, Evan R. "Experimenting with Chemical Bodies: Science, Medicine, and Philosophy in the Long History of Reinier De Graaf's Experiments on Digestion, from Hervey and Descartes to Claude Bernard." PhD diss., Indiana University, 2012.

The Railway Surgeon. Vol 1. The Railway Age and Northwestern Railroader, 1895.

Ramsay, David. *An Eulogium upon Benjamin Rush, M.D.* Philadelphia: Bradford and Inskeep, 1813.

Rebhorn, Matthew. "Ontological Drift: Medical Discourse and Racial Embodiment in Robert Montgomery Bird's Sheppard Lee." *ESQ: A Journal of the American Renaissance* 61, no. 2 (2015): 262–96.

Redman, John. *An Account of the Yellow Fever as It Prevailed in Philadelphia in the Autumn of 1762*. Philadelphia, 1865.

Reed, Walter, James Carroll, Aristides Agramonte, and Jesse W. Lazear. "The Etiology of Yellow Fever: A Preliminary Note." *Public Health Papers and Reports* 26 (1900): 37–53.

Rees, John T. "Remarks on the Medical Theories of Brown, Cullen, Darwin, & Rush." Medical Thesis, University of Pennsylvania, 1805.

Reese, David Meredith. *Plain and Practical Treatise on the Epidemic Cholera, as it Prevailed in the City of New York in the Summer of 1832*. New York, 1833.

Reiss, Benjamin. "Bardolatry in Bedlam: Shakespeare, Psychiatry, and Cultural Authority in Nineteenth-Century America." *ELH* 72, no. 4 (2005): 769–97.

————. *Theaters of Madness: Insane Asylums and Nineteenth-Century American Culture.* Chicago: University of Chicago Press, 2008.

Reizenstein, Ludwig Von. *The Mysteries of New Orleans.* Trans. and ed. Steven Rowan. 1844–45. Baltimore: Johns Hopkins University Press, 2002.

Remini, Robert V. *The Life of Andrew Jackson.* 1981. Repr., New York: Harper Collins, 2001.

Reverby, Susan, and David Rosner. "Beyond the 'Great Doctors.' " In *Health Care in America: Essays in Social History,* ed. Susan Reverby and David Rosner, 3–16. Philadelphia: Temple University Press, 1979.

Reynolds, David S. *Beneath the American Renaissance: The Subversive Imagination in the Age of Emerson and Melville.* New York: Knopf, 1988.

————. *Waking Giant: America in the Age of Jackson.* New York: Harper Perennial, 2008.

Richerand, Anthelme. *Elements of Physiology.* Trans. G. J. M. De Lys. Ed. Nathaniel Chapman. Philadelphia: Thomas Dobson, 1813.

Richman, Irwin. *The Brightest Ornament: The Biography of Nathaniel Chapman, M.D.* Bellefonte, PA: Pennsylvania Heritage, 1967.

Rickman, Leland S., and Choong R. Kim. "Poe-phyria: Madness, and The Fall of the House of Usher." *JAMA* 261, no. 6 (1989): 863–64.

Roberts, Sian Silyn. "Gothic Enlightenment: Contagion and Community in Charles Brockden Brown's *Arthur Mervyn.*" *Early American Literature* 44, no. 2 (Summer 2009): 307–32.

Rodgers, Daniel T. "Republicanism: The Career of a Concept." *Journal of American History* 79, no. 1 (1992): 11–38.

Roediger, David R. *The Wages of Whiteness: Race and the Making of the American Working Class.* New York: Verso, 1991.

Rosenberg, Charles. *The Care of Strangers: The Rise of America's Hospital System.* Baltimore: Johns Hopkins University Press, 1995.

————. *The Cholera Years: The United States in 1832, 1849, and 1866.* 1962. Repr., Chicago: University of Chicago Press, 1987.

————, ed. *Explaining Epidemics and Other Studies in the History of Medicine.* New York: Cambridge University Press, 1992.

Rosenbloom, Julia M., and Robert B. Schonberger. "Toward an Understanding of the Equality of Pain: Crawford Long and the Development of Anesthesia in Antebellum Georgia." *Journal of Anesthesia History* 1, no. 1 (January 2015): 14–17.

Rosenfeld, Sophia. "Benjamin Rush's Common Sense." *Early American Studies* 15, no. 2 (2017): 252–73.

————. *Common Sense: A Political History.* Cambridge, MA: Harvard University Press, 2011.

Rosner, Lisa. "Thistle on the Delaware: Edinburgh Medical Education and Philadelphia Practice, 1800–1825." *Social History of Medicine* 5, no. 1 (1992): 19–42.

Rothstein, William. *American Physicians in the 19th Century.* Baltimore: Johns Hopkins University Press, 1974.

Rousseau, Jean-Jacques. *Miscellaneous Works of Mr. J. J. Rousseau.* Vol. 1. London, 1767.

————. "La nouvelle Héloïse: Ou lettres de deux amans, habitans d'une petite ville au pied des Alpes/recueillies et publiées par J.-J. Rousseau." Paris: Duchesne, 1764.

Rusert, Britt. "Delany's Comet: Fugitive Science and the Speculative Imaginary of Emancipation." *American Quarterly* 65, no. 4 (December 2013): 799–829.

Rush, Benjamin. *An Account of the Bilious Remitting Yellow Fever, as it Appeared in the City of Philadelphia, in the Year 1793.* Philadelphia, 1794.

————. *The Autobiography of Benjamin Rush: His Travels through Life together with his Commonplace Book for 1789–1813*. Ed. George W. Corner. Philadelphia: American Philosophical Society, 1948.

————. *A Course of Lectures on the Theory and Practice of Medicine. By Benjamin Rush M.D. Professor on Theory & Practice of Medicine in the College of Philadelphia &c. &c. Read in the College from November 1st 1790 to February 1st 1791*. Cushing/Whitney Medical Historical Library, Yale University.

————. *Essays: Literary, Moral, and Philosophical*. 1806. Repr., ed. Michael Meranze. Philadelphia: Union College Press, 1988.

————. *Lectures on the Mind*. Ed. Eric T. Carlson, Jeffrey L. Wollock, and Patricia S. Noel. 1809. Repr., Philadelphia: American Philosophical Society, 1981.

————. *Letters of Benjamin Rush*. Ed. L. H. Butterfield. 2 vols. Princeton: Princeton University Press, 1951.

————. *Medical Inquiries and Observations*. 4 vols. Philadelphia: J. Conrad and Co., 1805.

————. *Medical Inquiries and Observations Containing an Account of the Yellow Fever, as it Appeared in Philadelphia in 1797, and Observations upon the Nature and Cure of the Gout, and Hydrophobia*. Philadelphia: Thomas Dobson, 1798.

————. *Medical Inquiries and Observations Upon the Diseases of the Mind*. Philadelphia: Kimber and Richardson, 1812.

————. "Observations Intended to Favour a Supposition That the Black Color (As It Is Called) of Negroes Is Derived from Leprosy." *Transactions of the American Philosophical Society* 4 (1799): 289–97.

————. *The Selected Writings of Benjamin Rush*. Ed. Dagobert D. Runes. New York: Philosophical Library, 1947.

————. *Sixteen Introductory Lectures to Courses Upon the Institutes and Practice of Medicine, with a Syllabus of the Latter: To which are added, two lectures upon the pleasures of the senses and the mind, with an inquiry into their proximate cause: Delivered in the University of Pennsylvania*. Philadelphia: Bradford and Innskeep, 1811.

————. "The Subject of an American Navy Continued." *Pennsylvania Gazette* (Philadelphia), July 31, 1782.

————. *Travels Through Life or Sundry Incidents in the Life of Dr. Benjamin Rush*. Lanoraie, PA, 1905.

Rush, Rebecca. *Kelroy*. 1812. Repr., New York: Oxford, 1993.

Russo, James. "The Chameleon of Convenient Vice: A Study of the Narrative of *Arthur Mervyn*." *Studies in the Novel* 11, no. 4 (Winter 1979): 381–405.

Rutkow, Ira. *Seeking the Cure: A History of Medicine in America*. New York: Simon and Schuster, 2010.

Ryan, Judith. *The Vanishing Subject: Early Psychology and Literary Modernism*. Chicago: University of Chicago Press, 1991.

Sappol, Michael. *A Traffic of Dead Bodies: Anatomy and Embodied Social Identity in Nineteenth-Century America*. Princeton, NJ: Princeton University Press, 2002.

Sayre, Gordon M. "The Mound Builders and the Imagination of American Antiquity in Jefferson, Bartram, and Chateaubriand." *Early American Literature* 33, no. 3 (1998): 225–49.

Scarry, Elaine. *The Body in Pain: The Making and Unmaking of the World*. New York: Oxford University Press, 1985.

Schenkel, Elmar. "Disease and Vision: Perspectives on Poe's 'The Sphinx.'" *Studies in American Fiction* 13, no. 1 (1985): 97–102.

Schiebinger, Londa. "Human Experimentation in the Eighteenth Century: Natural Boundaries and Valid Testing." In *The Moral Authority of Nature*, ed. Lorraine Daston and Fer-
nando Vidal, 384–408. Chicago: University of Chicago Press, 2004.

———. *Nature's Body: Gender in the Making of Modern Science*. New Brunswick, NJ: Rutgers
University Press, 1993.

———. "Skeletons in the Closet: The First Illustrations of the Female Skeleton in Eighteenth-
Century Anatomy." *Representations* 14 (Spring 1986): 42–82.

Schiller, J. "Physiology's Struggle for Independence in the First Half of the Nineteenth Century."
History of Science 7 (1968): 64–89.

Schlesinger, Arthur Meier, Jr. *The Age of Jackson*. Boston: Little, Brown, 1945.

Schneck, J. M. "Edgar Allan Poe's 'William Wilson' and Capgras Syndrome." *Journal of Clinical Psychiatry* 51 (1990): 387–88.

Schoolman, Martha. *Abolitionist Geographies*. Minneapolis: University of Minnesota Press,
2014.

Schuetze, Sarah. "Mapping a Demon Malady: Cholera Maps and Affect in 1832." *Commonplace* 17, no. 1 (2017). http://common-place.org/book/mapping-a-demon-malady-cholera
-maps-and-affect-in-1832/. Accessed 6 May 2017.

Schulten, Susan. *Mapping the Nation: History and Cartography in Nineteenth-Century America*.
Chicago: University of Chicago Press, 2013.

Scoutetten, Henri. *A Medical and Topographical History of the Cholera Morbus*. Trans. A. Sidney Doane. Boston: Carter and Hendee, 1832.

Seeger, C. L. *A Lecture on the Epidemic Cholera*. Boston, 1832.

Sellers, Charles. *The Market Revolution: Jacksonian America, 1815–1846*. Oxford: Oxford University Press, 1991.

Seth, Catriona. "Textually Transmitted Diseases: Smallpox Inoculation in French Literary and
Medical Works." *Studies on Voltaire and the Eighteenth Century* 4 (2013): 125–38.

Shapin, Steven, and Simon Schaffer. *Leviathan and the Air-Pump: Hobbes, Boyle, and the Experimental Life*. Princeton, NY: Princeton University Press, 2011.

Shapiro, Johanna, Jack Coulehan, Delese Wear, and Martha Montello. "Medical Humanities
and Their Discontents: Definitions, Critiques, and Implications." *Academic Medicine* 84,
no. 2 (2009): 192–98.

Shapiro, Johanna, and Lloyd Rucker. "Can Poetry Make Better Doctors? Teaching the
Humanities and Arts to Medical Students and Residents at the University of California, Irvine, College of Medicine." *Academic Medicine* 78, no. 10 (2003): 953–57.

Sherman, Rachel, and John Hickner. "Academic Physicians Use Placebos in Clinical Practice
and Believe in the Mind-Body Connection." *Journal of General Internal Medicine* 23, no. 1
(January 2008): 7–10.

Shorter, Edward. *From Paralysis to Fatigue: A History of Psychosomatic Illness in the Modern Era*.
New York: Simon and Schuster, 1992.

Shyrock, Richard. *The Development of Modern Medicine*. New York: Knopf, 1947.

Siebers, Tobin. *Disability Aesthetics*. Ann Arbor: University of Michigan Press, 2010.

Silva, Cristobal. "Epidemiology as Method: Literary Criticism in the Age of HIV/AIDS." *William and Mary Quarterly* 70, no. 4 (October 2013): 832–38.

———. *Miraculous Plagues: An Epidemiology of Early New England Narrative*. New York:
Oxford University Press, 2011.

———. "Monstrous Plots: An Epidemiology of American Narrative." PhD diss., New York
University, 2003.

Silverman, Gillian. *Bodies and Books: Reading and the Fantasy of Communion in Nineteenth-Century America*. Philadelphia: University of Pennsylvania Press, 2012.

Siraisi, Nancy. *Communities of Learned Experience: Epistolary Medicine in the Renaissance*. Baltimore: Johns Hopkins University Press, 2013.

Slaughter, Philip. *The Virginian History of African Colonization*. Richmond, VA: Macfarlane and Fergusson, 1855.

Sloane, David E. E. "Usher's Nervous Fever: The Meaning of Medicine in Poe's 'The Fall of the House of Usher.'" In *Poe and His Times: The Artist and His Milieu*, ed. Benjamin Franklin Fisher, 146–53. Baltimore: The Edgar Allan Poe Society, 1990.

Smith, Adam. *Theory of Moral Sentiments*. 1759. Repr., London: George Bell and Sons, 1875.

Smith, Edgar Fahs. *Samuel Latham Mitchill—A Father in American Chemistry*. New York: Columbia University Press, 1922.

Smith, Elihu Hubbard, ed. *American Poems, Selected and Original*. Vol. 1. Litchfield, CT, 1793.

———. *The Diary of Elihu Hubbard Smith (1771–1798)*. Ed. James E. Cronin. Philadelphia: American Philosophical Society, 1973.

———. "Inoculation." *Medical Repository* 1, no. 1 (1797): 96.

———. "Introduction." *Medical Repository* 1, no. 1 (1797): 1–2.

———. "The Plague of Athens." *Medical Repository* 1, no. 1 (1797): 3–29.

Smith, Elihu Hubbard, Edward Miller, and Samuel Latham Mitchill. "Circular Address." 1796. Repr., *Medical Repository* 1, no. 1 (1797): viii–xii.

Smith, James McCune. *The Works of James McCune Smith: Black Intellectual and Abolitionist*. Ed. John Stauffer. New York: Oxford, 2006.

Smith, Jonathan. *Fact and Feeling: Baconian Science and the Nineteenth-Century Literary Imagination*. Madison: University of Wisconsin Press, 1994.

Smith, Kirk L. "Medicine in the Humanities: Recovering a Tradition." *JAMA* 274, no. 21 (December 1995): 1738.

Sneader, Walter. *Drug Discovery: A History*. Chichester: Wiley, 2005.

Snow, C. P. *The Two Cultures*. 1959. Cambridge: Cambridge University Press, 1998.

Snow, John. *Cholera and the Water Supply in the South Districts of London in 1854*. London: T. Richards, 1856.

———. *On the Mode of Communication of Cholera*. London: John Churchill, 1849.

Sontag, Susan. *Illness as Metaphor and AIDS and Its Metaphors*. 1978. Repr., New York: Picador, 2001.

"South-Carolina Convention, Nov. 21." *Charleston Courier*, November 24, 1832, 2.

Spencer, Frank. "Samuel George Morton's Doctoral Thesis on Bodily Pain: The Probable Source of Morton's Polygenism." *Transactions and Studies of the College of Physicians of Philadelphia* 5, no. 4 (December 1983): 321–38.

Spitzer, Leo. "A Reinterpretation of 'The Fall of the House of Usher.'" *Comparative Literature* 4, no. 4 (Fall 1952): 351–63.

St. André, Nathaniel. *A Short Narrative of an Extraordinary Delivery of Rabbets: Perform'd by Mr. John Howard, Surgeon at Guilford*. London, 1727.

Starr, Paul. *The Social Transformation of American Medicine*. New York: Basic Books, 1982.

Staughton, William. *An Eulogium in Memory of the Late Dr. Benjamin Rush*. Philadelphia, 1813.

Stedman, Arthur, and Ellen Mackay Hutchinson. *A Library of American Literature from the Earliest Settlement to the Present Time*. Vol. 4. New York: Charles L. Webster & Company, 1888.

Steinke, Hubert. *Irritating Experiments: Haller's Concept and the European Controversy on Irritability and Sensibility, 1750–90*. Amsterdam: Brill, 2005.

Stern, Julia. *The Plight of Feeling: Sympathy and Dissent in the Early American Novel*. Chicago: University of Chicago Press, 1997.

Sterne, Laurence. *The Works of Laurence Sterne*. Vol. 1. London, 1783.

Stevenson, Lloyd G. "Putting Disease on the Map: The Early Use of Spot Maps in the Study of Yellow Fever." *Journal of the History of Medicine and Allied Sciences* 20, no. 3 (1965): 226–61.

Stolberg, Michael. "A Woman Down to Her Bones: The Anatomy of Sexual Difference in the Sixteenth and Early Seventeenth Centuries." *Isis* 94, no. 2 (June 2003): 274–99.

Stowe, Harriet Beecher. *Dred: A Tale of the Great Dismal Swamp*. 2 vols. Boston: Phillips, Sampson, and Company, 1856.

———. *Dred: A Tale of the Dismal Swamp*. Ed. Robert S. Levine. 1856. Repr., Chapel Hill: University of North Carolina Press, 2000.

———. *Life of Harriet Beecher Stowe: Compiled from Her Letters and Journals*. Ed. Charles Edward Stowe. London: S. Low, Marston, Searle and Rivington, 1889.

———. *Uncle Tom's Cabin: Or, Life among the Lowly*. Boston: John P. Jewett and Company, 1852.

Strickland, Stuart. "The Ideology of Self-Knowledge and the Practice of Self-Experimentation." *Eighteenth-Century Studies* 31, no. 4 (1998): 453–71.

Sweet, James H. *Domingos Álvares, African Healing, and the Intellectual History of the Atlantic World*. Chapel Hill: University of North Carolina Press, 2011.

Tacitus. "Communication." *Daily National Intelligencer* (Washington, DC), January 2, 1832.

Tanner, Henry Schenck. *The American Traveller, or, Guide Through the United States, Containing Grief Notices of the Several States, Cities, Principal Towns, Canals and Rail Roads, &c.* Philadelphia, 1834.

———. *A Geographical and Statistical Account of the Epidemic Cholera: From Its Commencement in India to Its Entrance into the United States*. Philadelphia, 1832.

Taylor, Sean P. " 'We live in the midst of death': Yellow Fever, Moral Economy and Public Health in Philadelphia, 1793–1805." PhD diss., Northern Illinois University, 2001.

Tenney, S. Marsh. "The Father of American Physiology." *Physiology* 9 (1994): 43–44.

Terrell, Colleen. " 'Republican Machines': Franklin, Rush, and the Manufacture of Civic Virtue in the Early Republic." *Early American Studies* 1, no. 2 (Fall 2003): 100–132.

The Thirteenth Annual Report of the American and Foreign Anti-Slavery Society. New York: American Anti-Slavery Society, 1853.

Thompson, George. *Venus in Boston and Other Tales of Nineteenth-Century City Life*. Eds. David S. Reynolds, and Kimberly R. Gladman. Amherst: University of Massachusetts Press, 2002.

Thomson, John. *An Account of the Life, Lectures, and Writings of William Cullen*. Edinburgh: Blackwood, 1859.

Thrailkill, Jane. *Affecting Fictions: Mind, Body, and Emotions in American Literary Realism*. Cambridge, MA: Harvard University Press, 2007.

———. "Doctoring 'The Yellow Wallpaper.'" *ELH* 69, no. 2 (Summer 2002): 525–66.

———. "Killing Them Softly: Childbed Fever and the Novel." *American Literature* 71, no. 4 (1999): 679–707.

Thrall, William Flint, and Addison Hibbard. *A Handbook to Literature*. New York: Odyssey, 1960.

"To the citizens of Massachusetts: the cholera. This dreadful malady, which has raged to such deplorable extent in Asia and in Europe, having crossed the Atlantic, and commenced its destructive rage in Canada, has induced the municipal authorities of many cities and towns to prosecute measures for preventing, as much as possible, its spread in the United States." Boston, 1832. Held at the American Antiquarian Society, Worcester, MA.

Tompkins, Jane. *Sensational Designs: The Cultural Work of American Fiction, 1790–1860.* New York: Oxford University Press, 1985.

Tougaw, Jason. *Strange Cases: The Medical Case History and the British Novel.* New York: CRC Press, 2006.

Traister, Daniel. "Robert Montgomery Bird: Writer and Artist." *Penn Library Exhibitions.* https://www.library.upenn.edu/exhibits/rbm/bird/index.html. Accessed 15 July 2015.

Valenčius, Conevery Bolton. *The Health of the Country: How American Settlers Understood Themselves and Their Land.* New York: Basic Books, 2003.

Valenza, Robin. *Literature, Language, and the Rise of the Intellectual Disciplines in Britain, 1680–1820.* New York: Cambridge University Press, 2009.

Van Buren, Peter. "Anaesthesia." *Documents of the Assembly of the State of New-York Eighty-first Session—1858.* Vol. 3, No. 51-85. Albany, 1858. 49–84.

Van Dijkhuizen, Jan Frans, and Karl AE Enenkel, eds. *The Sense of Suffering: Constructions of Physical Pain in Early Modern Culture.* Leiden: Brill, 2009.

Van Sant, Ann Jessie. *Eighteenth-Century Sensibility and the Novel: The Senses in Social Context.* Cambridge: Cambridge University Press, 1993.

Veatch, Robert. *Disrupted Dialogue: Medical Ethics and the Collapse of Humanist-Physician Communication (1770–1980).* Oxford: Oxford University Press, 2005.

Vickers, Neil. "Coleridge, Thomas Beddoes and Brunonian Medicine." *European Romantic Review* 8, no. 1 (1997): 47–94.

Virchow, Rudolf. *Cellular Pathology, As Based Upon Physiological and Pathological Histology.* Trans. Frank Chance. London: John Churchill, 1860.

Vogel, Morris J., and Charles E. Rosenberg. *Therapeutic Revolution: Essays in the Social History of Medicine.* Philadelphia: University of Pennsylvania Press, 1979.

Wachtler, Caroline, Susanne Lundin, and Margareta Troein. "Humanities for Medical Students? A Qualitative Study of a Medical Humanities Curriculum in a Medical School Program." *BMC Medical Education* 6, no. 1 (2006). https://bmcmededuc.biomedcentral.com/articles/10.1186/1472-6920-6-16. Accessed 2 September 2016.

Walker, I. M. "The 'Legitimate Sources' of Terror in 'The Fall of the House of Usher'." *The Modern Language Review* (1966): 585–92.

Wald, Priscilla. "American Studies and the Politics of Life." *American Quarterly* 64, no. 2 (2012): 185–204.

———. *Contagious: Cultures, Carriers, and the Outbreak Narrative.* Durham, NC: Duke University Press, 2007.

Wall, Patrick David. *Pain: The Science of Suffering.* New York: Columbia University Press, 2000.

Walls, Laura Dassow. *Emerson's Life in Science: The Culture of Truth.* Ithaca, NY: Cornell University Press, 2003.

———. *The Passage to the Cosmos: Alexander Von Humboldt and the Shaping of America.* Chicago: University of Chicago Press, 2009.

———. *Seeing New Worlds: Henry David Thoreau and Nineteenth-Century Natural Science.* Madison: University of Wisconsin Press, 1995.

Waples, Emily. "'Invisible Agents': The American Gothic and the Miasmatic Imagination." *Gothic Studies* 17, no. 1 (2015): 13–27.

Warner, John Harley. *Against the Spirit of the System: The French Impulse in Nineteenth-Century American Medicine*. Baltimore: Johns Hopkins University Press, 2003.

———. "The History of Science and the Sciences of Medicine." *Osiris* 10 (1995): 164–93.

———. *The Therapeutic Perspective: Medical Practice, Knowledge, and Identity in America, 1820–1885*. Princeton, NJ: Princeton University Press, 1997.

Warner, John Harley, and Janet A. Tighe. *Major Problems in the History of American Medicine and Public Health*. Boston: Houghton Mifflin, 2001.

Warner, Michael. *Letters of the Republic: Publication and the Public Sphere in Eighteenth Century America*. Cambridge, MA: Harvard University Press, 1992.

Warren, John Collins. *Etherization: With Surgical Remarks*. Boston: Ticknor and Company, 1848.

Washington, Harriet A. *Medical Apartheid: Medical Experiments on Black Americans from Colonial Times to the Present*. New York: Doubleday, 2006.

Waterman, Bryan. "Arthur Mervyn's Medical Repository and the Early Republic's Knowledge Industries." *American Literary History* 15, no. 2 (2003): 213–47.

———. *Republic of Intellect: The Friendly Club of New York City and the Making of American Literature*. Baltimore: Johns Hopkins University Press, 2007.

Webster, James, Caleb B. Matthews, and Isaac Remington. *The Medical Recorder: Of Original Papers and Intelligence in Medicine and Surgery*. Vol. 12. Philadelphia: James Webster, 1827.

Webster, Noah. *American Dictionary of the English Language: Exhibiting the Origin, Orthography, Pronunciation, and Definitions of Words*. 2 vols. New York: S. Converse, 1828.

Weekly Anglo-African 1, no. 2 (August 10, 1861).

Weimerskirch, Philip J. "Benjamin Rush and John Minson Galt, II: Pioneers of Bibliotherapy in America." *Bulletin of the Medical Library Association* 53, no. 4 (1965): 510–26.

Weinstein, Michael A. *The Imaginative Prose of Oliver Wendell Holmes*. Columbia: University of Missouri Press, 2006.

Weithman, Paul. "Political Republicanism and Perfectionist Republicanism." *Review of Politics* 66, no. 2 (2004): 285–312.

Wetmore, Alex. *Men of Feeling in Eighteenth-Century Literature*. New York: Palgrave, 2013.

Whalen, Terrance. *Edgar Allan Poe and the Masses*. Princeton, NJ: Princeton University Press, 1999.

Whooley, Owen. *Knowledge in the Time of Cholera: The Struggle over American Medicine in Nineteenth-Century America*. Chicago: University of Chicago Press, 2013.

Whytt, Robert. *The Works of Robert Whytt*. Edinburgh, 1768.

Wick, Ulrich. "The Nature of Picaresque Narrative: A Modal Approach." *PMLA* 89, no. 2 (March 1974): 240–49.

Wilbank, John. *Statement: A Statement of the Facts Connected with the Late Re-organization of the Faculty of the Medical Department of Pennsylvania College: Together with a Documentary History of Said Department, from its Origin to the Present Time*. Philadelphia, 1856.

Wilcox, Reynold Webb. "The Field of Internal Medicine." In *Transactions of the American Congress on Internal Medicine: First Scientific Session*, New York City, December 28–29. New York, 1917.

Wilentz, Sean. *Chants Democratic: New York City and the Rise of the American Working Class, 1788–1850*. New York: Oxford University Press, 1984.

———. *The Rise of American Democracy: Jefferson to Lincoln*. New York: W. W. Norton, 2005.

Will, Thomas E. "Liberalism, Republicanism, and Philadelphia's Black Elite in the Early Republic: The Social Thought of Absalom Jones and Richard Allen." *Pennsylvania History* 69, no. 4 (Autumn 2002): 558–76.

Williams, Hettie V. "Delany, Martin R." *Encyclopedia of African American History*. Ed. Leslie M. Alexander and Walter C. Rucker Jr., 372–74. Santa Barbara, CA: ABC-CLIO, 2010.

Williams, James, John Greenleaf Whittier, and Maxwell Whiteman. *Narrative of James Williams an American slave who was for several years a driver on a cotton plantation in Alabama*. New York: American Anti-Slavery Society, 1838.

Williams, Wade. "Religion, Science, and Rhetoric in Revolutionary America: The Case of Dr. Benjamin Rush." *Rhetoric Society Quarterly* 30, no. 3 (Summer 2000): 55–72.

Wimsatt, W. K. "Poe and the Chess Automaton." *American Literature* 11, no. 2 (May 1939): 138–51.

Wisecup, Kelly. "Communicating Disease: Medical Knowledge and Literary Forms in Colonial British America." PhD diss., University of Maryland. Ann Arbor: ProQuest/UMI, 2009.

———. *Medical Encounters: Knowledge and Identity in Early American Literatures*. Amherst: University of Massachusetts Press, 2013.

———. "'The Progress of the Heat Within': The West Indies, Yellow Fever, and Citizenship in William Wells Brown's Clotel." *Southern Literary Journal* 41, no. 1 (2008): 1–19.

Wolpert, L. "Evolution of Cell Theory." *Philosophical Transactions: Biological Sciences* 349 (1995): 227–33.

Wood, Gordon S. *The Creation of the American Republic, 1776–1787*. New York: W. W. Norton, 1969.

———. *The Radicalism of the American Revolution*. New York: Vintage, 1992.

Woods, Angela. "The Limits of Narrative: Provocations for the Medical Humanities." *Medical Humanities* 37, no. 2 (2011): 73–78.

Worboys, Michael. "Practice and the Science of Medicine in the Nineteenth Century." *Isis* 102, no. 1 (2011): 109–15.

Yeo, Richard. *Encyclopaedic Visions: Scientific Dictionaries and Enlightenment Culture*. Cambridge: Cambridge University Press, 2001.

Young, Joseph. "Correspondence." *Medical Repository* 5, no. 3 (1802): 358–70.

INDEX

Page numbers in italics refer to illustrations.

theories and, 143; Richerand on, 128, 129;
Rush on, 28–31, 49, 215n53, 218n121; Adam
Smith on, 142–43, 164–65, 169, 215n50;
Elihu Hubbard Smith on, 38, 65, 218n121

Tanner, Henry Schneck, 93–94, *94*, 97,
98, 137
Taylor, Zachary, 110
temperance movement, 150, 167–69
Tennyson, Alfred Lord, 194
Thompson, George, 168
Thompson, John R., 109
Thomsonian herbalism, 86
Thoreau, Henry David, 248n38
Thrailkill, Jane, 19
thrush, 234n38
Toft, Mary, 10
Traister, Daniel, 135
Trenn, Thaddeus, 210n78
Troein, Margareta, 198
Tronchin, Théodore, 70
truth-to-nature approach, 138, 220n140
tuberculosis, 84, 134–35, 194
Turner, Nat, 110, 119, 236n96
typhoid fever, 84, 85
typhus, 84, 85

University of Pennsylvania, 21, 126, 130,
250n70; Institutes of Medicine at,
209n69, 240n30; medical curriculum at,
7, 128
urinary tract infections, 164
utopian fiction, 36–39, 67, 79, 218n117,
218n121

Valenčius, Conevery Bolton, 221n147
vampirism, 235n40
Van Buren, Peter, 173
Van Dijkhuizen, Jans Frans, 165
Vesalius, Andreas, 238n4
Vesey, Denmark, 119
Vibrio cholerae, 120
Virchow, Rudolf, 49, 224n187
Virgil, 7

vital materialism, 101, 214n33
vivisection, 12–13, 210n76; Avery on,
240n49; Dunglison on, 170; Horner and,
130–32; movement against, 162, 167, 169,
170; Rush and, 25. *See also* anatomy
Voltaire, 25

Wachtler, Caroline, 198
Wald, Priscilla, 19
Walker, I. M., 234n39
Walls, Laura Dassow, 234n35
War of 1812, 48
Warner, John Harley, 256n43
Warren, John Collins, 160, 171, 247n1,
249n66
Warren, Joseph, 62–63, 65
Waterman, Bryan, 19, 224n6, 229n120
Webster, Noah, 15, 51, 220n140
Wells, Horace, 247n1
Wells, Lewis G., 117
Whiskey Rebellion, 45
Whitman, Walt, 207n24
Whittier, John Greenleaf, 207n24
Whytt, Robert, 10, 215n50
Williams, Helen Maria, 234n35
Williams, James, 110, 111
Williams, William Carlos, 197
women's health, 10, 48–49, 124, 195–96,
223n185, 238n8; childbirth and, 161,
163, 172
Wood, Gordon, 213n16

xenophobia, 108, 109

yellow fever, 16, 17, 51–84; race and, 58–60;
as epistemic crisis, 52, 53, 56, 61, 81–82;
etiology of, 52, 60–61, 83–84; legacies of,
81–84; in New Orleans, 82; in New York
City, 61, 218n117; Rush on, 54, 57–61;
Elihu Hubbard Smith on, 60, 61, 66,
218n117, 226n57; symptoms of, 55, 61
Young, Joseph, 4

Zola, Émile, 175

ACKNOWLEDGMENTS

Writing a book can be a solitary process, but I've been lucky that mine has been wonderfully social. As with the world of the doctors and writers whose stories populate these pages, my own work has been buoyed, creatively expanded, and vastly improved by a world of smart, imaginative, supportive, and generous people. I am deeply grateful to them for helping me think better and more capaciously about the medical imagination, especially as its history took me between and across disciplines.

I owe this project's intellectual origins to friends and mentors I met while living in New York including Martin Burke, Sarah Chinn, Justin Rogers-Cooper, Duncan Faherty, Bill Kelly, Steve Kruger, Brooks Hefner, Bridget McGovern, Neil Meyer, Emily Moore, and Maura Spiegel. Jesse Schwartz and Zach Samalin in particular have been talking me through this book from the very beginning, and I continue to depend on their warmth, wit, and wisdom as ballasts during the twists and turns of academic life. I owe a great deal to David Reynolds, who nurtured this project from its earliest stages and has been a wonderful supporter for many years. In those years I was also very fortunate to meet Rachel Adams, who has, ever since, been a fantastic interlocutor, a wonderful friend, and a model of how to be a woman in the profession.

This book owes a tremendous debt to two long-term fellowships that gave me the space and freedom to really develop the project. At the McNeil Center I learned not only how to be a better literary critic but how to be a better colleague and interdisciplinary scholar. The retraining that took place that year encouraged me to write for an audience beyond literary studies. I am deeply grateful to Dan Richter for his friendship and support, then and now, and for the unparalleled community he so artfully makes possible. It would be difficult to overstate how much the friends I made that year have meant to me—especially Mitch Fraas, Cassie Good, Glenda Goodman, Rachel Herrmann, Nenette Luarca-Shoaf, Mark Mattes, Dael Norwood, Jess Roney, Aaron

Tobiason, and Nic Wood. Seth Perry, in particular, helped me work through many of the ideas and also kept me going, often weekly with wonderful camraderie, humor, and support, no matter where in the country we found ourselves. The thirteen months I spent at the American Antiquarian Society (AAS) likewise allowed me to expand the book out of Philadelphia into a story about U.S. medical knowledge in the Atlantic world. For that, I cannot thank Paul Erickson enough: I owe him not only for the fellowship but also for his friendship and for so many conversations at crucial moments in the book's development. I am also tremendously grateful to Lauren Hewes, Tom Knoles, Ashley Cataldo, and the rest of the AAS staff for their day in and day out assistance with my research while I was there. The AAS is a busy place, terrific for exposing its fellows to new ideas. I'm grateful to the many fellow travelers at the AAS and at other archives from whom I have learned over the years—especially Zara Anishanslin, Jennifer Brady, Hunt Howell, Chris Lukasik, Sarah Salter, Lindsay DiCuirci, Margaret Abruzzo, Philippa Koch, Nicholas Guyatt, Greta LaFleur, Justine Murison, Britt Rusert, and especially David Weimer—and to the wonderful long-term residents at the AAS, Brigitte Fielder, Jon Senchyne, Maria Bollettino, Simon Newman, and Marina Moskowitz, for helping make it an incredible year. Tom Augst and Mary Kelley went above and beyond during the nine months we overlapped, serving not only as mentors and confidants but as friends who made life in Worcester sparkle with their kindness, wit, and brilliant intellects. I'm especially grateful to Mary not only for her intelligence and generosity but also for her continuing friendship; she, too, models the kind of woman and scholar I strive to be.

At the University of South Florida, Emory, and Northeastern, I have been likewise very lucky to find wonderful communities who have left their marks on these pages. At USF, my departmental colleagues Carl Herndl, John Lennon, Jay Zysk, Meredith Johnson, and especially Diane Price Herndl helped me through the early stages of this book. Outside the department, Julia Irwin, Steve Prince, Darcie Fontaine, Aaron Walker, Scott Ferguson, Amy Rust, and Brian Connolly sustained my personal and intellectual lives in Florida. I'm grateful to them for the fantastic conversations, for the fun, and for adopting me as an honorary historian. The Emory English department was a wonderful place to develop this book. I'm very grateful to Paul Kelleher, Erwin Rosinberg, Walter Kaladjian, Michael Elliott, Deepika Bahri, Kate Nickerson, Laura Otis, and especially Ross Knecht, who has been a great friend and helped me talk through some of the final twists of the argument. Beyond the department, Dawn Peterson, Javier Garcia, Kylie Smith, Nihad Farooq, Todd Michney,

Danny LaChance, Meredith Schweig, Falguni Sheth, and especially Lauren Klein and Greg Zinman helped make Atlanta a stimulating and warm intellectual home. Above all, Ben Reiss and Rosemarie Garland Thomson have been tremendous colleagues and friends. I am deeply grateful to them for their kindness, advice, guidance, and generosity; their intellectual examples and advice have left a deep mark on the pages that follow, and they, too, are exemplary models for me of how to work and be in the profession. I am also immensely grateful to Michelle Lampl, my director and collaborator at the Center for the Study of Human Health, to whom I owe so much and from whom I learned a great deal about how to work in health *and* the humanities. I am likewise very grateful to Elizabeth Maddock Dillon, Theo Davis, Marina Leslie, Erika Boeckeler, Laura Green, Lori Lefkovitz, and the rest of the Northeastern English department for welcoming me and providing the time, space, and good cheer I needed to finish this manuscript. I am also sincerely thankful for the many students over the years—especially Stephanie Phillips, Lindsey Grubbs, and Stephanie Larson—whose energy, passion, and intellectual curiosity continue to fuel and sustain my own.

I was fortunate enough to workshop drafts of this manuscript twice. Kathleen Brown and Ann Fabian provided incredibly helpful comments on behalf of the Society for the Historians of the Early American Republic prize committee; they gave me the push I needed to expand the project dramatically and terrific strategies for adopting a new writing style better suited to a multi-disciplinary audience. The AAS convened a second manuscript workshop as a part of the Hench fellowship, where I was lucky enough to be able to invite three scholars whose work I greatly admire. I am deeply grateful to Cristobal Silva, Priscilla Wald, and Laura Dassow Walls for making the trip to Worcester to read my first new draft of the manuscript, for asking difficult and important questions, for offering their sincere support, and for pushing me to write the best book I could. Paul Erickson was kind enough to record those conversations for me, and I listened to them a number of times on my commute to and from Worcester until I could hear their voices as I was writing.

I also need to thank a group of wonderful friends who supported me at a further remove over the last seven years and who have left their mark on these pages. Thanks to Lisa Koulish and Matthias Holdhoff for their love, good cheer, and medical perspectives; to Gustavo Carrera for being a great friend and fantastic interlocutor for the last fifteen years; to Sarah Jay and Ian Huntington for good food, excellent company, and thoughtful conversations about the practical difficulties in medicine; to Mavis Biss, whose love sustained me and whose thoughts about the ethical imagination have surely influenced some of the thinking within; and to Kate Fama, with whom I've been fortunate enough to share both laughter and tears about the struggles of academic life every step of the way.

Finally, I owe my greatest debts to my family: Donna Katzin Altschuler, Alan Altschuler, Daniel Altschuler, and Chris Parsons. My interest in the difficulty of knowing the human body began with years of guessing my father's blood sugar. This book now seems the logical product of a daughter whose father has always loved telling the story of his body and whose mother wakes up every morning before work to write poetry. While not academics themselves, they've spent countless hours helping me talk through some of the ideas within these pages and supported me the whole time. My brother, Daniel, has also been a wonderful source of strength and reason during these years, knowing both how to be supportive and when to make sure I didn't take myself too seriously. My husband, Chris Parsons, has logged countless hours as well in recent years, and he knows exactly how much of this book I owe to his love, support, companionship, and stimulating intellectual exchange. The conversations we've had over the past five years have fundamentally structured the arguments within. It has been incredible to find you, love. Thank you so much for everything.

A portion of Chapter 1 appeared in the *Journal of the Early Republic* in the summer of 2012 as "From Blood Vessels to Global Networks of Exchange: The Physiology of Benjamin Rush's Early Republic," and material from the Introduction and Chapter 4 appeared in *American Literary History* in the spring of 2016 under the title "From Empathy to Epistemology: Robert Montgomery Bird and the Future of the Medical Humanities." I am thankful to both journals for permission to use that material in this book. In addition, I am grateful to the McNeil Center for Early American Studies and the American Antiquarian Society for long-term funding and to the Library Company of Philadelphia (especially Jim Green and Connie King), the American Antiquarian Society, and the University of Virginia's Albert and Shirley Small Special Collections Library for short-term funding that made portions of the archival research in this book possible. I would also like to thank the Society for the Historians of the Early American Republic, who believed in this project from its very early stages. Not only did their prize embolden me to write this book with a broader audience in mind, but the early advanced contract also gave me the space and encouragement to develop a new writing style, which better fit the book's material.

It's hard to know how to thank my editor, Bob Lockhart, who had confidence in this project before I could see what it might be myself. It's been a better editorial relationship than I had any right to expect, and I'm deeply grateful to him for knowing how much to support and how much to push at each step. Finally, I would like to thank the editorial staff at Penn Press—particularly Lily Palladino and the two anonymous reviewers of the manuscript whose thoughtful, rigorous, and generous reports made this a substantially better book and whose kind words invigorated me through the final months of revision.

CPSIA information can be obtained
at www.ICGtesting.com
Printed in the USA
JSHW052021231221
21447JS00001B/1

9 780812 225204